Montana

Montana

Patrick "Paddy" Straub

with photographs by BigSkyFishing.com

The Countryman Press ✳ Woodstock, Vermont

F I R S T   E D I T I O N

ISBN 978-0-88150-743-0

Cover photo © Micah May
All interior photos by www.BigSkyFishing.com unless otherwise noted
Book design by Bodenweber Design
Page composition by PerfecType, Nashville, TN
Maps by Mapping Specialists Ltd., Madison, WI © 2008 The Countryman Press

Published by The Countryman Press, P.O. Box 748, Woodstock, Vermont 05091

Distributed by W. W. Norton & Company, Inc., 500 Fifth Avenue, New York,
NY 10110

Printed in the United States of America

10 9 8 7 6 5 4 3 2 1

To all the great people of Montana.

EXPLORE WITH US!

Welcome to *Montana: An Explorer's Guide.* This book contains a broad selection of the many unique, wild, and exciting highlights of the great state of Montana. These were selected on the basis of merit and personal experience, not paid advertising. The book's organization is based on a successful series format, but the following will help get you started on your way.

WHAT'S WHERE

This is a broad-reaching introduction to many of Montana's basic attractions. There is important information in this section that is worth reading before you dig further into the book or venture out on your own.

ORGANIZATION

This guidebook is organized around Montana's six tourism regions. In the 1990s the state decided to create these regions based on geography, historical significance, outdoor recreation, and cultural identities. Each chapter is named for one of these tourism regions. For example, northwestern Montana's tourism region is Glacier Country. We did this so that the details in this guidebook will flow seamlessly with the information provided to travelers from the state tourism bureau. In fact, each region featured in the book has its own tourism bureau. Go to www.visitmt.com for more information; it's one of the best resources available.

The format of the listings is consistent from chapter to chapter, which will help you plan your adventures in various regions. There is a selection of area attractions (*To See, To Do,* and *Wilder Places*), followed by suggestions about where to lay your head at night (*Lodging*) and where to eat (*Dining Out* and *Eating Out*), and finally a selection of annual events in each region that should not be missed (*Special Events*).

LODGING

Lodging establishments were selected entirely on merit and personal experience—no one paid to be included in this book. So you are getting selections that have literally been handpicked by the author. Please keep in mind that things change. Always be sure to inquire about any business's policy on children, pets, smoking, credit cards, parking, etc. And be aware that rates may change on a yearly basis, and may not reflect the 2008 rates listed in this book. Additionally, Montana has state and local room taxes that may change annually and from town to town.

WHERE TO EAT

Montanans are always surprising each other and travelers with their diverse tastes, and we've made a genuine effort to list a wide variety of options in each region. Sometimes that was easy, sometimes it was hard. With the rural nature of much of Montana, it is often hard to find a broad spectrum of options, but we did our best. You will also notice that the restaurant listings are broken down into two categories: *Dining Out* and *Eating Out.* Although subjective in nature, the former applies to places that are generally more expensive and more refined. Think of a place where most entrees are priced $12–$15 and up. *Eating Out* is for establishments with less expensive options, although the food is often just as good.

When considering where to dine, it is highly suggested that you contact a restaurant before making plans. The hours of many places vary by season, as do the activity patterns of locals and travelers. For example, it is often easy to get a meal after 9 P.M. in the months of June and July because the days are so long, but in winter getting a meal after 8:30 P.M. can sometimes be a real adventure.

KEY TO SYMBOLS

- **Special value.** This icon denotes an establishment of exceptional value for a reasonable price.
- **Child friendly.** This icon denotes establishments and attractions that kids will enjoy.
- **Handicapped access.** This icon denotes lodgings, restaurants, and attractions that are partially or completely handicapped accessible. While we have tried to make this as accurate as possible, please inquire locally before venturing out.
- **Author's pick.** This icon denotes anything the author feels is a must-see, must-eat, must-stay, etc. In other words, visit these places.

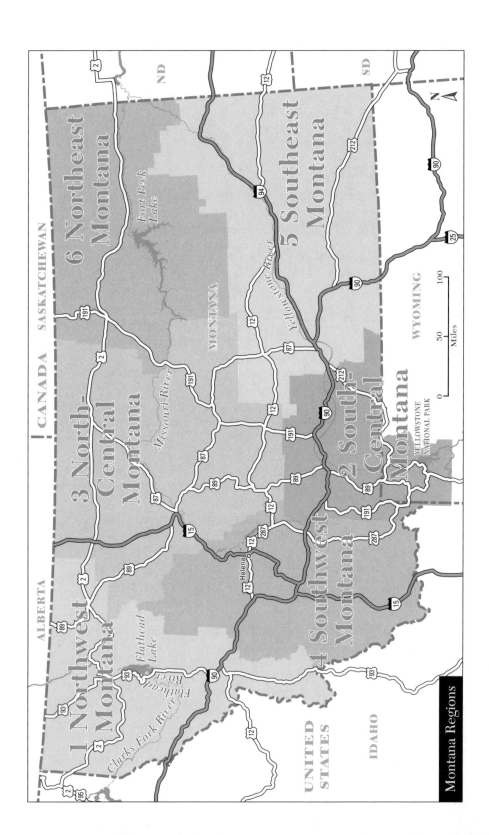

Montana Regions

CONTENTS

11 ACKNOWLEDGMENTS

13 INTRODUCTION

21 WHAT'S WHERE IN MONTANA

37 1 Northwest Montana: Glacier Country and Glacier National Park

121 2 South-Central Montana: Yellowstone Country

179 3 North-Central Montana: Russell Country

223 4 Southwest Montana: Gold West Country

275 5 Southeast Montana: Custer Country

307 6 Northeast Montana: Missouri River Country

333 INDEX

ACKNOWLEDGMENTS

This book would not have been possible without all of the great and interesting people, places, and animals of Montana—past and present. Thank you all for creating a state with so many fascinating qualities.

Special thanks are also reserved for all of the great folks at Countryman Press: Kim Grant and Kermit Hummel were very helpful while developing the project; Jennifer Thompson was a blessing while writing and her encouragement was priceless; and Darren Brown made the manuscript even better.

Thanks to Jim Hug at www.BigSkyFishing.com for the photos used in the book. Anyone who wants more information should check out his Web site, which is a great resource.

Thanks to my parents, Del and Carolyn, for making sure we spent considerable time exploring Montana when I was younger. And to faithful dogs Madison and Ellie, for providing much needed breaks and walks on Mount Helena.

And, finally, a special thanks to my amazing wife, Brandy Moses, whose inspiration and spirit fill my life with happiness—I look forward to seeing you every day of my life.

INTRODUCTION

Montana is big—big in geography, big in history, big in culture and people, all under that beautiful Big Sky. As David James Duncan, a writer who calls Montana home, once said, "Even in Montana, how I long for Montana." What a great way to say just how special this state really is.

Here is a guidebook that is as unique as Montana, and one that is meant for explorers—those people who enjoy intriguing places, inspiring landscapes, and unique people, and who have a taste for excitement but know how to temper it every now and then. Montana has a varied past—both naturally and culturally. From dinosaur fossils to Native American history and culture to modern adventures and recreational opportunities, this state will continually surprise you.

The Treasure State is just that—a bottomless chest containing many of the American West's best features, including Yellowstone and Glacier National Parks, the charm of small towns like Philipsburg, and the rich history of pioneers and Native Americans. This guide will showcase some of Montana's finest, most intriguing, and most awe-inspiring places, events, activities, and attractions. But keep in mind that Montana is a big place with a wide array of diversions. It would take more than a lifetime to experience them all.

After the dinosaurs, a few ice ages, thousands of earthquakes, and who knows what else, human history in Montana began nearly 10,000 years ago. Evidence suggests that humans inhabited most of present-day Montana, living off the abundant game in the foothills of the mountains and on the High Plains. Few of these humans resided in the mountains; rather, they lived in the large valleys where flora and fauna were easily accessible. Eventually many Native American tribes called these lands home. This is only a partial list of the many tribes that may have passed through and/or resided in Montana at one time or another. As you will learn, many of these tribes still call Montana home today. These include the Assiniboine, Arapaho, Arikara, Bannock, Blackfeet, Cheyenne, Crow, Gros Ventre, Kalispel, Kiowa, Kootenai, Nez Perce, Sioux, Pend d'Oreille, and Salish.

Most everyone knows that Lewis & Clark and their men traveled through Montana beginning in 1805. From their first camp near Bainville on April 27, 1805, to when they floated downstream in August of the following year, the Corps of Discovery spent more time in Montana than in any other state. Soon after Lewis & Clark spread the word about the wildlife in what would become

Montana, trappers, traders, and prospectors slowly trickled in—changing things forever. Toward the middle of the 1800s, gold and silver mining brought even more pioneers and prospectors.

Throughout the 19th century, conflicts between pioneers and Native Americans escalated as Native Americans clung to their way of life while homesteaders and pioneers fought to carve out a new existence in a remote and wild landscape. The Native Americans had to deal with a new system of government, the introduction of new diseases, and many other factors, including the dishonorable destruction of the massive herds of buffalo—which wiped out their primary source of sustenance. Many of the bloodiest and most terrible battles between Native Americans and the new settlers occurred in Montana.

By the end of the 19th century, most tribes in Montana were forced onto reservations, and their lives would never be the same.

In 1889 Montana achieved statehood. At that time, sheep and cattle ranching were a large part of the state's economy (as they still are today), but, as technology improved and more willing laborers moved into the state, mining became more prominent. By the turn of the century, the Anaconda Copper Company, founded by the copper baron Marcus Daly, was one of the wealthiest companies in the world. In fact, Butte, Montana, was once referred to as the "richest hill on earth," and in Helena there were more millionaires per capita than in any other city in the world.

As the 20th century unfolded, mining and agriculture played key roles in the state's economic development, but a few other industries gained strength as well.

THE BITTERROOT RIVER IN WESTERN MONTANA

AN OLD RAILROAD SNOWPLOW ONCE USED TO CLEAR THE TRACKS

Toward the end of that century mining slowly declined, yet it remains a large part of the economy here.

Today agriculture (timber harvest, ranching, and farming) and tourism make up a good chunk of the economy; however, as technology changes, Montana is slowly becoming a destination for high-tech engineering and software companies and is also gaining a national reputation for pioneering new energy technologies like wind power, solar energy, and biodiesels.

Tourism gains more momentum here every year. In fact, the state annually reevaluates its statewide tourism programs to continually help visitors (and the residents that depend on tourism) enhance their experience in Montana. Remember, while in Montana you are not only experiencing a fantastic state, you are becoming a part of its history and its future.

The state's geography is also varied. From the rolling grasslands and High Plains in the east to the rugged mountain ranges and dense forests in the west, Montana has many personalities. And this book covers all of them. The state is home to nearly 30 million acres of national lands, including one national park and part of another, more than 8 million acres of land managed by the Bureau of Land Management, and state-owned lands that include more than 40 state parks.

Because our state is so big—the nation's fourth largest—it is helpful to understand a few of Montana's quirks. Here are some tidbits of advice that will go a long way toward making your explorations in Montana easier and more comfortable. This comes from a lifelong resident who has traveled nearly every road, looked under nearly every rock and behind most trees, and waded in nearly every stream.

The average altitude in Montana is 3,400 feet above sea level. For your first few days here, take it easy if you are not in good physical condition. I'm sure you've heard it all before: allow a few days to adjust to the altitude, drink lots of water (if you are in Butte on St. Patrick's Day that might be tough), wear sunscreen when outdoors, take a hat and sunglasses, dress in layers, and be sure to stop every now and then to take in the view. Whatever the season, it is best to be prepared for sudden changes in weather. Our temperatures can change as much as 50 degrees or more in a single day—in fact, on one winter day it was 50 degrees, but by the next day the high was minus 14. And that type of temperature swing can occur at any time of year. A few summers back we topped out at 105 degrees on a Thursday, yet only reached 60 degrees that Friday. The bottom line: plan your day with fun in mind, but just be prepared for anything.

When venturing out by car, get precise directions or take a *Montana Atlas & Gazetteer.* Some of our best attractions are off the beaten path, so be prepared to write down exact directions. Do not use mileage as your guide; inquire locally about how long it may take. Get it in minutes and hours. If traveling in any months other than July or August, get the local road report. In Yellowstone and Glacier National Parks check road closures before planning a drive—you certainly would not want to plan to drive the Going-to-the-Sun Road on your only day in Glacier, only to find out that it won't be open to travel for another month. Most locals tend to drive fast on interstates and other primary highways. Drive with extreme caution until you get a feel for it. You can see forever, but there are lots of critters out and about and deer cannot distinguish a tourist's rental car from a resident's pickup truck.

In rural areas, taking the time to make small talk goes a very long way in making oneself welcome. It is always common courtesy in Montana to ask a stranger how they are doing, especially on a quiet road or at a gas station or small-town watering hole. Most Montanans love to share their knowledge *and* countryside with folks that show an interest. In any restaurant or business, "asking to see the

BIG SKY COUNTRY HAS MANY HIGH-QUALITY SKI RESORTS

manager" or "wanting to talk with the boss" will usually result in poor service or no service at all.

In the end, what matters is to be personable and friendly and to ask strangers, "How are you doing today?" You will be amazed at what this little gesture will do for your visit.

The more popular tourist meccas include the Flathead Valley and the Bozeman/Livingston/West Yellowstone area. These places have many services that cater to visitors. The places in between or beyond these areas are featured in this book right along with some of the more well-known spots. Many of the places off the beaten path have been able to keep their charm over the past 15 years or so, despite substantial population growth throughout Montana.

While exploring, keep in mind that people live and work in these rural areas. A gate is opened or closed for a reason, so leave it the way you find it. Those steel things that you drive over to get onto the interstate are cattle guards. In the summer be sure to take in a local rodeo. Bring a camera. Slow down and enjoy yourself. While driving in Montana, especially on the lesser-used highways, you might see a truck stopped for no reason—just admiring the magnificent Big Sky.

Please use this book as your guide to explore what I think is the most wonderful place in the world. After your first visit you will long for another and then another and another. Soon, like many other visitors, you may find yourself wanting to call Montana home. Perhaps one day you just might be lucky enough to say that you live in Big Sky Country. For now, enjoy your travels.

A HODGEPODGE OF FUN MONTANA FACTS

Size
Total area: 145,338 square miles; fourth largest in area.
Population: 44th in population (944,632, 2006 estimate); population density a little over six people per square mile.
Inland surface water: 1,658 square miles.
Total acres: 94,109,440.
Greatest distance from east to west: 550 miles.
Greatest distance from north to south: 320 miles in western Montana and 280 miles in eastern Montana.

Geographic Center
In Fergus County, about 11 miles west of Lewistown.

Number of Counties
56

Highest and Lowest Points
12,799 feet above sea level at Granite Peak near Red Lodge; 1,820 feet above sea level where the Kootenai River enters Idaho.

Motto
Oro y Plata

State Fish
Westslope cutthroat trout

State Fossil
Duckbilled dinosaur (*Maiasaura peeblesorum*)

State Animal
Grizzly bear

Brief Pronunciation Guide (to help you avoid any goofy looks from the locals)
The town of **Havre** is pronounced HAV-er.
Missoula is pronounced Mizz-OO-luh.
The county of **Pondera** is pronounced pon-dur-AY.
Meagher County is pronounced without the G. Just say MAHR.
The town of **Wibaux** should be pronounced WEE-bow.
The state capital is pronounced HELL-un-hu, not any other way.
Choteau, both the town and the county, is pronounced SHO-toe or SHO-doe.
Glasgow is pronounced GLASS-go.

Cities and Their Days of Sunny Weather in a Year
Miles City, 99.6 days
Billings, 89.4 days
Glasgow, 86.3 days
Havre, 84.2 days
Helena, 82.1 days
Great Falls, 79.7 days
Missoula, 74.7 days
Kalispell, 70.9 days

Mountain Ranges
There are between 25 and 30 mountains with peaks higher than 12,000 feet.
There are 25 distinct mountain ranges.

River Drainages
The three major drainages in North America have river roots in Montana. West of the Continental Divide, waters flow into the Pacific via the Columbia. East of the Divide, waters flow into the Atlantic via the Missouri/Mississippi. And waters from the northeast corner of Glacier National Park flow through the Hudson Bay drainage.

Sports Teams
Montana may be the only state with the following sports mascots—we are not sure, but we feel pretty confident: **Bats** at Belfry; **Penguins** at Whitewater; **Refiners** at Sunburst; **Savages** at Hot Springs; **Sugar Beeters** at Chinook.

Roads
Interstates: 1,200 miles
Primary highways: 5,450 miles
Secondary roads: 4,760 miles (includes about 1,700 miles unpaved)

Ferries
Three ferries cross the Missouri River: **Carter's Ferry,** 14 miles west of Fort Benton and 20 miles north of Great Falls off US 87, then a 5-mile drive on a gravel road; **Virgelle Ferry,** 30 miles northeast of Fort Benton off US 87, then

8 miles on a gravel road; and **McClelland Ferry,** 50 miles north of Lewistown on a gravel road.

Downhill Skiing

There are 15 downhill ski resorts.

Snowmobiling

There are over 4,000 miles of groomed snowmobile trails.

Movies

Over 50 movies have been filmed, at least in part, in Montana.

Fishing

A few state records: brown trout—29 lbs., 1966, Wade Lake; lake trout—42.5", 42.69 lbs., 2004, Flathead Lake; largemouth bass—22", 8.29 lbs., 1999, Many Lakes; rainbow trout—38.62", 33.1 lbs., 1997, Kootenai River; walleye—35", 17.75 lbs., 2007, Tiber Reservoir.

WHAT'S WHERE IN MONTANA

AGRICULTURE In Montana's pioneer days, ranching and farming were paramount in creating the state's identity. Over a hundred years later, agricultural roots still run very deep and are a mainstay of the state's economy. With revenues of more than $2 billion annually, it is clear agriculture in Montana is as much a way of life as summer and winter tourism. Our ag industry relies on cattle (both beef and dairy), sheep, pigs, wheat, honey, cherries, barley, beets, chickens, and many others. Montana is second in the nation for agricultural lands, with nearly 60 million acres of farmland. But despite this large amount of land, farmers and ranchers make up only a small fraction of the state's overall population.

AIRPORTS Flying to Montana used to be an adventure, and air travel typically requires a stop in a hub city like Salt Lake City or Denver. However, some airlines are adding seasonal nonstops from Chicago and Atlanta to Bozeman and Missoula, but schedules are always changing. Montana has several airports. They are listed here in order of the number of flights served daily and the number of airlines that serve each location. Once on the ground, each of these airports has excellent assistance with ground transportation and rental cars. **Billings Logan International Airport** (BIL): www.flybillings.com; 406-238-3420; Alaska/Horizon, Big Sky Airlines, Delta/Delta Connection, Frontier, Northwest, United. **Missoula International Airport** (MSO): www.flymissoula.com; 406-728-4381; Alaska/Horizon, Big Sky Airlines, Delta/Delta Connection, Northwest, United. **Bozeman/Gallatin Field** (BZN) in the Gallatin Valley near Bozeman: www.gallatinfield.com; 406-388-8321; Alaska/Horizon, Big Sky Airlines, Delta/Delta Connection, Northwest, United. **Kalispell/Glacier Park International Airport** (FCA) in the Flathead Valley near Kalispell: www.iflyglacier.com; 406-257-5994; Alaska/Horizon, Big Sky Airlines, Delta/Delta Connection, Northwest, United, U.S. Airways. **Great Falls International Airport** (GTF): www.gtfairport.com; 406-727-3404; Alaska/Horizon, Big Sky Airlines, Delta/Delta Connection, Northwest, United. **Helena Regional Airport** (HLN): www.helenairport.com; 406-442-2821; Alaska/Horizon, Big Sky Airlines, Delta/Delta Connection, Northwest, United. **Butte/Bert**

Mooney Airport (BTM): www.butteairport.com; 406-494-3771; Alaska/Horizon, Big Sky Airlines, Delta/Delta Connection.

AMTRAK AMTRAK (www.amtrak .com; 1-800-872-7245) operates the only commercial train to the state. It runs east-west along the northern border of Montana, similar to the route of US 2. This is AMTRAK's old Empire Builder Line, which travels from Chicago to Seattle. Towns in Montana serviced by this historic line are Wolf Point, Glasgow, Malta, Havre, Shelby, Cut Bank, East Glacier, Essex, West Glacier, Whitefish, and Libby.

ANTIQUES If you are a lover of antiques and old-time craftsmanship, Montana has plenty to keep you busy. Most small towns in Montana have one or two antique stores, and there are always some treasures from a bygone era. A good resource for deal-ers in Montana is **Antiques USA** (www.antiques-usa.com). You can also find an up-to-date list of antique shows across the state at **Montana's Travel and Tourism Web site** (www .visitmt.com).

AREA CODE In Montana we like to keep most things simple, for now we only have one area code—**406.**

ANIMALS Montana is home to a plethora of wildlife, although some animals stick to themselves. Mountain lions, for example, inhabit much of Montana but encounters are rare. Mule deer, on the other hand, are prevalent in most areas of the state and can often be found grazing road-side. Bears, both grizzlies and black, may be encountered. Although seeing a bear is an exciting experience, we must always remind ourselves that bears are wild animals and innate predators. Keep your distance at all times and observe all guidelines if you

are traveling in bear country. It is always your own responsibility to keep yourself safe from bears and other predators while enjoying Montana's outdoor recreation.

AUTOMOBILES By car, Montana is best accessed and enjoyed via Interstates 90, 94, and 15. Interstate 15 runs north-south, while I-90 is the main east-west interstate. Interstate 94 ventures into Montana from North Dakota and meets up with, and then becomes, I-90 a few miles east of Billings. US 2 is the main east-west route in northern Montana, connecting the lush forests of northwestern Montana with the High Plains of the northeastern portion of the state. Keep in mind that Montana covers over 550 miles east to west and nearly 300 miles north to south, so the durations listed below are very general in scope. **From Seattle,** it is a straight shot on I-90 and will take about a full day's drive to most destinations in Montana. **From Portland,** meet up with I-90 near Ritzville, Washington; from there it is about a three-hour drive to the border of Idaho and Montana. **From Salt Lake City,** it is straight shot on I-15. An easy day's drive will get you to the junction of I-15 and I-90 west of Butte. **From Denver,** travel I-25 north from Denver; it merges with I-90 near Buffalo, Wyoming. From Denver to Montana is another solid day's drive. **From Minneapolis,** travel I-94 west from the Twin Cities. It is an easy one-day drive to the state border, but a long one-day drive to most parts of Montana. And plan for two days if you are heading to any destination in western Montana. **From Calgary,** head south on Canada Highway 2 to Lethbridge, where it merges with

Highway 4. Continue to the Montana border, where Highway 4 becomes I-15. It is an easy day's drive to the northern border of Montana from Calgary.

BIKING Montana offers some of the most exhilarating and varied cycling opportunities in the western United States Experienced riders will find challenging day and overnight rides. Casual and less experienced riders will find trails and roads free of leg-busting climbs and traffic, but rides that still offer varying terrain, great vistas, and wildlife. For a complete listing of cycling opportunities, rentals, directions, and maps, visit www.visit mt.com/tripplanner/thingstodo/biking.htm. For a listing of 38 specific cycling trips, visit www.visitmt.com/virtualvisitor/biking. Montana is also home to many local bike shops, which can offer even more information.

BIRD WATCHING Nearly four hundred species of birds can be seen while in Montana—of course not all at once, but it is possible to see as many as 175 bald eagles congregating near the Kootenai River in northwestern Montana. What about the largest population of trumpeter swans in the Lower 48? Yep, near Red Rocks Lake National Wildlife Refuge. Montana is also home to a variety of other species, from the western meadowlark to sage grouse and whooping cranes. In fact, near the Rocky Mountain Front there is a place where more golden eagles have been seen in one day than in anyplace else in the country. For a complete list of birding opportunities, visit www.visitmt.com/tripplanner/thingstodo/bird.htm. For more information, visit Montana Audubon at www.mtaudubon.org.

They have a list of birding hotspots, events, and much more.

BUREAU OF LAND MANAGEMENT LANDS (BLM) With several million acres of land under its jurisdiction, the **Bureau of Land Management** (406-896-5000; www.mt.blm.gov) is worth mentioning. It oversees campgrounds, river and fishing access sites, wild horses, and large parcels of public lands. The BLM is also responsible for nearly 50 million subsurface acres of mineral estates in Montana and North and South Dakota.

BOATING With 2,000 miles of shoreline in Montana, 11 major reservoirs, and countless lakes and rivers, floating enthusiasts will have a hard, yet enjoyable, time deciding where to go. For information on boating on any of the reservoirs (all are managed by the U.S. Bureau of Reclamation), call the **Montana Area Office of the Bureau of Reclamation** (406-247-7298; www.usbr.gov/gp/mtao/). You can also visit www.visitmt.com/trip planner/wheretogo/lakes.htm for more specific information on a given area of the state or a specific body of water.

BUS SERVICE Two bus lines serve Montana, providing service to and within the state: **Greyhound** (1-800-229-9424; www.greyhound.com) and **Rimrock Trailways** (1-800-442-3682; www.rimrocktrailways.com). All of the major towns have local bus lines as well. For more information, contact the friendly folks at Travel Montana (www.visitmt.gov).

BYWAYS Most drives in Montana are scenic, but several have actually been designated as such. Any detailed Montana highway map will list all of the designated scenic byways, but here is a brief sampling: **Beartooth Scenic Byway** (Red Lodge to Cooke City in southeastern Montana); the **Pioneer Mountains Scenic Byway** (Wise River to Grasshopper Creek in southwestern Montana); **Kings Hill Scenic Byway** (White Sulphur Springs to Belt in north-central Montana). For more information on these drives and a detailed list of others, visit www.visitmt.com/tripplanner/wheretogo/drive.htm.

COFFEE Coffee lovers, or addicts, need not worry about finding a great latte or cup of coffee in Montana. Not only are there coffee kiosks on most corners, even in the small towns, but Montana is home to many first-class coffee roasters. A few are listed here, but it is best to explore on your own for your favorite roaster and your favorite blend: **Montana Coffee Traders** (1-800-345-5282; www.coffeetraders.com) in Whitefish; **Morning Light Coffee Roasters** (406-453-8443; www.morninglight.com) in Great Falls and Helena; **City Brew** (1-866-880-2489; www.citybrew.com) in Billings, Whitefish, Bozeman, Kalispell, Missoula, Red Lodge, and Laurel.

CAMPGROUNDS The camping experience in Montana runs the entire spectrum. The campgrounds listed in the *To Do–Camping* listings in this guidebook are sites that lie on public lands. It is the focus of this book to present campgrounds that are little more outdoorsy and adventurous than camping in major towns or private campgrounds—after all, this *is* an Explorer's Guide. Each campground listing includes a season; however, often these campgrounds are open year-round, but the services (running water, pit toilets, flush toilets, etc.) are only open during the season. A fee may be charged year-round despite the lack of services. It is always best to inquire locally before choosing where to pitch your tent or park your RV for the night. A comprehensive and free listing of nearly all of Montana's public campgrounds can be found at www.visitmt.com/trip planner/campandlodge/camp.htm. Once there, click on "Complete Listings." Or order a hard copy from **Travel Montana** (1-800-VISITMT; www.visitmt.com).

CELL PHONES The wireless world has hit Montana, and for many it is a true blessing. Because we are in such a large state, many of us spend considerable time on the road. From ranchers to school teachers to fishing guides, cell phones are part of daily life for most Montanans. Service in cities is nearly always excellent and dropped calls are few and far between. However, once you venture out from a population center you are likely to lose service altogether. Most major providers have service in Montana and the coverage areas are growing every year. When driving, always be on the lookout for other drivers and wildlife.

CITIES Montana is home to well over 900,000 people, many of which live in one of seven incorporated cities. These seven cities have populations of 10,000 or more. The largest in the state is **Billings,** where roughly 100,000 reside. **Helena,** the state capital, is home to about 27,000 people. Keep in mind, however, that near each major city are smaller outlying towns that rely on the cities' local shops and services.

CLIMATE Montana is blessed with a unique climate. We have long and pleasant summers, an autumn that includes Indian summer and cooler weather, a winter with plentiful snowfall and great skiing, and a spring season to relax and enjoy before summer comes. With typical highs in the 70s and 80s, it is clear why most folks visit Montana in the summer. But with our high elevations and relatively consistent snowpack, the winter months also draw skiers, snowmobilers, and winter enthusiasts. If you are looking for a peaceful time with less visitors, spring and fall are great times to visit—and most, if not all, of the services are still open and ready for folks. Plan your day with fun in mind, but just be ready for anything. The warmest temperature recorded in Montana was 117 degrees Fahrenheit in Glendive back in 1893; the lowest was minus 70 degrees Fahrenheit at Rogers Pass in 1954.

COUNTIES Montana has 56 counties. The most populated is Yellowstone County, with nearly 140,000 people; the least populated is Petroleum County, with approximately 500 people. The smallest county in the state is Silver Bow near Butte, and the largest is Beaverhead in southwestern Montana.

DINOSAURS I can promise one thing—that you will not see any live dinosaurs while in Montana. But you may see many fossils in many of the museums and you may even be able to go on a real dinosaur dig. In addition to the museums listed in this book, we have our own **Montana Dinosaur Trail** (www.mtdinotrail .com). The trail is a collaboration of archaeological sites, museums, and

other points of interest. In the summer months it is possible to experience a field dig firsthand.

DUDE RANCHES (GUEST RANCHES) Montana is home to many dude ranches where visitors can get a true feel for what it is like to live and work on a ranch. Whether it is a working cattle ranch or a luxurious, pampering guest ranch with amenities galore—or something in between—Montana has a guest ranch to meet your expectations. With the proper research you will be able to find the right level of comfort balanced with your desired levels of work and play. From posh and cozy to dust-in-your-eyes and mud-on-your-boots, a great resource to start from is the **Montana Dude Ranchers' Association** (www .montanadra.com; 1-888-284-4133). These friendly folks can provide you with a complete and varied listing of the many ranches offering services to guests and visitors. For more informa-

tion within this book, look for Ranch Vacations in the *To Do–Unique Adventures* section in each region. There are several listings for dude and guest ranches offering this type of adventure.

EMERGENCY SERVICES Dial **911** in case of an emergency. More information on local emergency services is provided under Medical Emergencies in each region of this guidebook.

EVENTS Montana hosts events in every season of the year, from arts festivals to evening concert series to summer symphonies to farmer's markets. Listing them all would require a whole other book. The best resource, and it is an excellent one, is the listing at **Travel Montana** (www.visitmt .com/tripplanner/events), which lists events by location, time of year, and type. Even for a lifelong resident of Montana, this listing will turn up some new and intriguing happenings.

FISHING Montana is a world-class destination for anglers. Long famous for trout fishing, the state is slowly gaining a reputation for its walleye and northern pike fishing in a few reservoirs. For more information regarding lakes and reservoirs, see the *To Do–Boating* sections in each chapter. Most rivers in Montana are home to several species of wild trout. Unlike many states, Montana manages its rivers as wild trout fisheries. In order to keep the fisheries in the best condition possible, regulations change annually. A comprehensive online guide is available from **Montana, Fish, Wildlife & Parks** (406-444-2535; www.fwp.state.mt.us/fishing). This guide lists nearly every body of water, types of species, regulations, seasons, and a few other details. If you are planning to hire a guide, start by contacting the friendly folks at the **Fishing Outfitters Association of Montana** (406-763-5436; www .FOAM-Montana.org). Another source for more information is *Montana on the Fly: An Angler's Guide* (Countryman Press). You will also find regional fishing information, guides, and shops under *To Do– Fishing* throughout this guidebook.

GAMBLING A drive down any main drag in the state will expose you to our abundance of casinos. The majority of these are entirely video-based— video poker, keno, and a few others. There are a few casinos on the Indian reservations, and in most towns live poker games are hosted by the various casinos. Inquire locally for more information.

GEOGRAPHY Nearly 550 miles long and 280 miles wide, Montana has 145,552 square miles to explore. It is the fourth largest state in the U.S. The state is easily divided into two geographic regions, with the western third of the state being part of the **Rocky Mountains** and the eastern two-thirds being in the **Great Plains** region. The **Continental Divide** splits the state in the western third. Water on the west side of the Divide runs to the Pacific and water on the east side runs to the Atlantic. Additionally, a small part of Montana lies in the Hudson Bay drainage, thus making Montana the only state in the country whose rivers drain to the Gulf of Mexico, the Pacific Ocean, and Hudson Bay.

GEOLOGY The varied geology of Montana is a wonderland for professional and amateur geologists alike. The eastern portion of the state is filled with wind- and water-eroded formations and glacial till. In the western part of Montana you will discover mountains and valleys carved by glaciers. In Butte, the "richest hill on earth" was once home to the largest copper mine in the world. A great resource for exploring these geologic features is David Alt and Donald Hyndman's *Roadside Geology of Montana* (Mountain Press Publishing Company, 1986).

GOLF COURSES We have more than 70 courses in Montana, some famous, some with great views, all with manicured greens and challenging holes. The most well-known course in Montana is the Jack Nicklaus signature **Old Works Golf Course** (406-563-5989; www.oldworks.org) in Anaconda. This course is a golfer and history buff's dream, as the course is designed around an old mine site using elements of a bygone era. For more information on other courses throughout the state, contact the **Montana State Golf Association** (www.montana.net/msga).

GUIDES AND OUTFITTERS Montana has a long tradition for providing visitors with a great outfitted vacation. Whether you are looking for a big-game hunting outfitter or a fly-fishing outfitter, Montana has a plethora of qualified outfitters at your disposal. The best way to find a fishing outfitter is to check with the **Fishing Outfitters Association of Montana** (406-763-5436; www.FOAM-Montana.org). For hunting outfitters, contact the folks at the **Montana Outfitters and Guides Association** (406-449-3578; www.moga-montana.org). Between these two organizations there are nearly a thousand insured and licensed outfitters working in Montana.

HIGHWAYS Several major highways and interstates traverse Big Sky Country. **I-90** is the main east-west interstate, with **I-94** bisecting the eastern third of the state. **I-15** is the main north-south interstate, but it runs primarily in the west-central portion of the state. **US 93** is a major two-lane highway running north-south in western Montana, while **US 2** is a major two-lane highway running east-west along northern Montana.

HIKING For hikers, Montana is a state with little comparison—nearly every destination has something for you. The easiest way to discover hiking options in a given area is to purchase any of the informative hiking guides to Montana or a specific area of Montana. There are few specific hikes detailed in this book (see *To Do–*

Hiking in each chapter), but for the most part these are short jaunts to special sites or jaunts that are accessible to nearly any age and ability.

HISTORICAL MARKERS AND TRAILS Like many states, Montana has a highway historical maker program. But you may not know that Montana was the first state to utilize roadside historical markers. For a complete listing of all of the markers and their locations, purchase a copy of *Montana's Historical Highway Markers* (Montana Historical Society Press, 1-800-243-9900). Montana also posts roadside markers for the various historical trails that once made their way through Montana. **The Lewis & Clark Trail** is the most obvious and traveled route, but Montana also has the **Bozeman Trail,** the **Nez Perce Trail,** and a few others.

HISTORY Despite its relatively young tenure as a state, Montana has an interesting and diverse history. And Montanans have done extremely well in documenting past events. The **Montana Historical Society** was created even before Montana was a state, in fact, nearly 24 years before statehood was gained. The historical society's museum in Helena is a must-see for visitors. They also publish *Montana: The Magazine of Western History* and several regional history books. For more information, contact them at 406-444-2694 or www.his .state.mt.us. This book also contains many historical facts, figures, and tidbits. You will find recommendations for historical attractions under *To See–Towns; To See–Museums; and To See–Historic Landmarks, Places, and Sites*, among other places.

HOT SPRINGS With Montana's geographic size, it is no surprise that there are a large number of hot springs in the state. Several developed hot springs have spawned resorts around their natural bounty, yet many more undeveloped springs remain. These hot springs offer a great way to relax and unwind after a busy day of exploring. For a complete listing of all the developed hot springs in Montana, visit www.visitmt.com/trip planner/wheretogo/hotsprings.htm.

HUNTING Montana is a big game hunter's dream. **Elk, deer, black bears,** and many other sought-after big game species call Montana home. This is a world-class destination with logistical ease, outfitters, and a long hunting season. Hunters can also chase **mountain goats, bighorn sheep, mountain lion,** and a variety of **upland birds** and **waterfowl.** For more information on hunting, contact **Montana Fish, Wildlife & Parks** (406-444-2535; www.fwp.state.mt.us/hunting). They regulate hunting in Montana, and all hunters should contact them before venturing on a hunting trip.

INDIAN RESERVATIONS Montana boasts a unique Native American culture. On the seven reservations—**Blackfeet, Crow, Flathead, Fort Belknap, Fort Peck, Northern Cheyenne,** and **Rocky Boy's**—visitors will find 11 tribes—**Assiniboine, Blackfeet, Chippewa, Cree, Crow, Gros Ventre, Kootenai, Northern Cheyenne, Pend d'Oreille, Salish,** and **Sioux.** While on these lands, visitors will find numerous attractions and outdoor activities. Annual events on most reservations include pow-wows, rodeos, and historical reenactments. Selected Native American events and attractions are highlighted throughout this book, but for more information visit www.indiannations.visitmt.com.

INTERNET Despite what many folks may think of Montana and its rural nature, we have entered the digital age. Nearly every small town in the state has Internet access and most of the major towns have numerous businesses with wireless access. For folks traveling with laptops or handhelds, staying connected will not be a problem—instead, pulling yourself away from your digital leash may be. Inquire locally or before you make your trip regarding the availability and consistency of access.

LODGING A wide array of lodging is described in this book. Not described, though, are traditional hotels and motels. Instead, the focus is on unique lodging options that are sure to delight and greatly enhance your Montana experience. In each region there are listings for bed & breakfasts, lodges, resorts, and other types of facilities. Most travelers already know what to expect from a traditional hotel or motel. They do exist in Montana, and in a few regions basic hotels and motels are listed, but in those rare cases it is a result of the lack of unique and unusual lodgings. For a complete, up-to-date listing of all lodging in a given area, contact **Montana Travel** (1-800-VISITMT; www.visitmt.com) and ask for the "Montana Travel Planning Kit." The travel kit is a helpful resource for any trip to or within Montana.

MAPS A great resource for travel in Montana is the *Montana Atlas & Gazetteer* (DeLorme Publishing). It is a collection of user-friendly topographic maps for every corner of the state. The maps are very useful for secondary highways and roads, and they are great for finding trailheads, fishing holes, and out-of-the-way places. They even list land ownership so you know if you are on public or private land—but remember to always err on the side of caution. If in doubt, ask first or make an alternate plan.

MICROBREWERIES Montana has nearly 20 licensed and registered microbreweries. For a state with a small population and few large cities, visitors and locals can always find a cold fresh beer. For a complete listing, visit the **Montana State Brewers' Association** (www.montana brewers.org) and you will find the closest beer possible. To only list a few here would be unfair to the others, so I encourage you to visit them all. Stopping at a Montana tap room and sampling some fresh suds is slowly becoming as much a Montana tradition as drifting a dry fly along the currents of your favorite river.

MILEAGE Nearly 550 miles wide and 280 north to south, Montana covers a large area. Mileages listed in this book are always approximate (please report any grave errors to the publisher). It is hard to get lost in Montana *if* you inquire locally and travel with a current map. Another important aspect to traveling in Montana is that most directions and distances are discussed in time rather than distance; e.g., most folks will say it takes "x hours to get from a to b" rather than some-

thing like 200 miles. Much of this is due to changing weather conditions in winter and construction in summer.

MUSIC FESTIVALS Montana is home to many music festivals and concert series. Nearly every town in the state has a music festival or two during the course of the year. For a complete listing of festivals, visit www.visitmt .com/tripplanner/events and select "Music/Concerts" from the drop-down menu.

NATIONAL FORESTS In 1897 President Grover Cleveland created 13 timberland preserves, three of which were in Montana—the **Bitterroot, Flathead,** and **Lewis & Clark National Forests.** Today Montana is home to 10 national forests, totaling more than 18 million acres. These are: **Beaverhead–Deer Lodge** (southwest; 3.3 million acres), **Bitterroot** (southwest; 1.6 million acres), **Custer** (south-central and southeast; 2.5 million acres), **Flathead** (northwest; 3.6 million acres), **Gallatin** (south-central; 1.7 million acres), **Helena** (west-central; 975,000 acres), **Kaniksu** (northwest, 468,500 acres), **Kootenai** (northwest; 2.1 million acres), **Lewis & Clark** (central and north-central; 1.8 million acres), and **Lolo** (west; 2.1 million acres). More detailed information about these forests can be found in the appropriate regional section of the text.

NATIONAL PARKS AND MONUMENTS A little over 1 million acres of timber, rivers, lakes, and spectacular scenery lie within **Glacier National Park** in northwestern Montana. Designated a national park in 1910, this park has long been a draw for visitors and residents. The park's name derives from two large glaciers that 20,000 years ago carved out most of the scenery visitors see today—not from the many small glaciers found there today (which, unfortunately, are disappearing at an alarming rate and may be gone in less than 100 years). Glacier, along with **Waterton Lakes National Park,** is known as **Glacier-Waterton International Peace Park,** the first park of its kind in the world. In addition to the marvels of Glacier, Montana is also home to the main gateways to **Yellowstone National Park,** the world's first national park. Although most of Yellowstone actually lies in Wyoming, many visitors to Yellowstone travel through Montana, so it is important to note that Montana hosts three of the park's five entrances. Montana is also home to the **Little Bighorn Battlefield National Monument, Pompeys Pillar National Monument,** and the **Upper Missouri River Breaks National Monument.**

NATIONAL RECREATION AREAS

Montana is also home to two national recreation areas: **Bighorn Canyon National Recreation Area** (120,000 acres) and **Rattlesnake National Recreation Area** (59,000 acres). More detailed information about these areas can be found in the appropriate regional section.

PADDLING/FLOATING Class V rapids, placid lakes, long overnights—whatever type of paddling or floating experience you desire you will find it in Montana. Not only does Montana have a diversity of waters for floating enthusiasts, these waters are all very accessible. Many of the opportunities described under *To Do–Paddling/Floating* in this book are for novices or folks wanting to dabble in a float or two. There are also a few listings for guide services. But for more serious paddlers and adventurers, those who might want to try some rapids on their own, partake in an overnight, or

reserve a guided expedition, the best place to start is *Paddling Montana* (Falcon Press, 1999).

PUBLIC LANDS Home to nearly 28 million acres of public lands—including two national parks, 8 million acres managed by the **Bureau of Land Management** (BLM), national forests, and state-owned lands and parks—Montana abounds with places to explore. Before venturing out, be sure to confirm that the land you are about to travel on is indeed public or be sure to ask for permission. When in doubt, head elsewhere.

RIVERS Montana boasts two nationally designated **Wild and Scenic Rivers,** the **Flathead** and the **Missouri.** In addition, there are more than a dozen major rivers flowing across the Montana landscape. Add to the rivers the hundreds of small creeks and you do not have to travel far to find flowing water. Many of these rivers provide fine fishing, floating, and paddling opportunities, but they also are in dire need of protection and preservation as a prolonged drought has brought low flows, or zero flows, to many of the smaller waterways. For more information on protecting the rivers and creeks in Montana, contact **Montana River Action** (406-587-9181; www.montanariveraction.org).

ROAD REPORTS There is a common joke in Montana—we are the state of two seasons: winter and road construction. Fortunately, the **Montana Department of Transportation Traveler Information** Web site (www.mdt.state.mt.us/traveinfo) has realtime information on construction, travel advisories, road closures, and other information related to travel in Montana, including live images from roadside Web cams. A 24-hour, toll-free number (1-800-226-7623) is also available for statewide road conditions.

ROCKHOUNDING Known for fossils and gold panning, rockhounds will find plentiful opportunity in Montana. The **BLM Montana/Dakotas** even has a page on its Web site dedicated to rockhounding rules and regulations (www.blm.gov/mt/st/en/info/browse/rockhounding.html). Another good resource is the book *Rockhounding Montana* (Falcon Press, 1996).

RODEOS During the summer and fall months the rodeo circuit hits Big Sky Country. Bucking broncos, bull riders, ropers, and barrel racers swing into action. Most small towns have a local rodeo weekend and the larger towns tend to have a rodeo weekend coupled with a larger county or area fair. It is possible to travel from one corner of Montana to the other and partake in a rodeo each night—a tall order, but for a true rodeo fan it would be a dream come true. For more information and schedules visit the **Northern Rodeo Association** (www.northernrodeo.com). In addition to schedules and listings you will find information about how you could become a rodeo cowboy. You can also find listings at www.visitmt.com/trip planner/events. Once there, select "Rodeos" from the drop-down menu.

RV PARKS If you are an experienced RVer, then you have a good idea of what to expect and where to find information. But if you are new to the state or are perhaps renting an RV for a week or more, Montana has many RV campgrounds and sites. A good place to start is the **Campground Owners Association of Montana** Web site (www.campingmontana .com). It provides an interactive map to the available options throughout the state. RVers can also visit www .visitmt.com and click on "Getting Around" or browse potential camp-sites in the "Campgrounds" section.

SMOKING As of October 2005, Montana has been a smoke-free state. With limited exceptions, the law also prohibits smoking in any indoor area, room, or vehicle that the general public is allowed to enter or that serves as a place of work, including restaurants; stores; public and private office buildings; trains, buses, and other forms of public transportation; health-care facilities; auditoriums, arenas, meeting rooms, and other assembly facilities; family or group day-care homes; buildings that house community colleges; and the state university system. In 2009 all bars and most casinos will become smoke free as well. Most bars currently are smoke free, but some are waiting until the last possible minute.

SNOW SPORTS With nearly five months of winter in most of the state, Montana serves up plenty of winter recreation. Downhill and cross-country skiing, ice skating, snowshoeing, snowmobiling, ice fishing, and dogsledding are among the many ways to enjoy the out-of-doors during our long winters. In addition to the entries under *To Do–Snow Sports* in this book, visit **Winter Montana** of **Travel Montana** (www.wintermt .com) for much more information.

This Web site will also help you plan a trip to Montana in the winter. Be sure to order a hard copy of the **Montana Winter Planning Kit** online or by calling 1-800-847-4868.

SPEED LIMITS AND SEAT BELTS Montana does have day and nighttime speed limits, despite what people might think. On interstates, the speed limit is 75 miles per hour. In a few of the urban areas it is 65 miles per hour. Be sure to watch for the signs. On two-lane highways the daytime speed limit is 70 miles per hour and the nighttime speed limit is 65 miles per hour. One exception is US 93 in western Montana, where the speed limit is 65 miles per hour at all times. Please keep in mind that many of Montana's roads are also used by ranchers and farmers to transport everything from combines to cows; always drive with caution. Seat belts are required at all times by every occupant of a vehicle.

STATE CAPITAL **Helena** is the state capital.

STATE PARKS With 42 state parks, Montana is not without room to play. Most parks have an admission charge for nonresidents. The state parks are administered by **Montana Fish, Wildlife & Parks** (406-444-2535; www.fwp.state.mt.us/parks). Many of these parks are listed in the *To See* and *To Do* sections throughout this book, as the parks provide camping, hiking, fishing, interpretative exhibits, picnicking, and more.

TOURIST RAILROADS Running along the northern portion of the state is **AMTRAK's Empire Builder** (see

AMTRAK in this section). But Montana has several other tourist railroads for rail and history enthusiasts. These are listed under *To Do–Unique Adventures*. For more information, go to www.visitmt.com/tripplanner/thingstodo and click on "Rail Tours," or call 1-800-847-4868.

WEATHER Over the years, forecasts for weather in Montana have slowly become more and more accurate. Most newspapers and online forecasts also are fairly precise. However, the **National Weather Service** (www.nws.noaa.gov) still remains the most accurate and informative. For more information, see *Climate* in this section.

WILDERNESS AREAS Montana has 15 national wilderness areas, providing numerous recreation opportunities in primitive and pristine settings. Wilderness areas are places where no motors of any kind are allowed, not even chainsaws, so it is very important that you know the rules and regulations before venturing into a designated wilderness area. Be sure to practice the principles of **Leave No Trace** (1-800-332-4100; www.lnt.org) and be very aware of limiting your impact while in a designated wilderness area. For a complete list of the wilderness areas in Montana, visit www.wilderness.net. Follow the link for "Explore Wilderness Data."

WILDFLOWERS Any walk in the high country or open plains in Montana will expose you to the state's abundance of wildflowers. There are too many species to list, but any wildflower enthusiast should be sure to have a copy of *Plants of the Rocky Mountains* (Lone Pine, 1998). This book is great for amateurs and more experienced eyes. Its high-quality photographs and detailed descriptions make identifying a species a snap. Another good resource is **Montana Plant Life** (www.montana.plant-life.org). These folks have created an online guide to 250 species, including edible and poisonous plants. You can also purchase a CD with similar information.

WILDLIFE We have a great abundance of wildlife here in Montana. In fact, we claim to have the greatest variety of wildlife in the Lower 48. Some of our well-known inhabitants include **bighorn sheep, mountain goats, mountain lions, grizzly bears, elk, bison, wolves, geese, deer,** and many, many more. Some of our lesser-known inhabitants include **pika, marmot,** and **short-tailed weasel**, among others. Be sure to get a copy of **Travel Montana**'s "Seeing Wildlife Wonders in Montana." You can order one at www.wildlife.visitmt.com. This handy guide includes guidelines for viewing, as well as what, how, and where to watch. **Montana Fish, Wildlife & Parks' Wildlife Division** (406-444-2535; www.fwp.state.mt.us/wildthings) also provides plenty of information on viewing wildlife in Montana.

WILDLIFE REFUGES There are more than 20 wildlife refuges in Montana, 14 of which are national wildlife refuges, and numerous wildlife management areas as well. You will find these refuges and management areas highlighted in this book (usually under *Wilder Places*) with detailed information including directions, seasons, recreation opportunities, and more. Two great sources of information for visiting these refuges are http://refuges.fws.gov/profiles/bystate (click on "MT") and www.visitmt.com/tripplanner/wheretogo/refuge.htm.

WINERIES Known more for vistas and wildlife, Montana has a few wineries producing surprisingly good vino. More detailed information can be found in the *To See–Wineries* sections in this book. The best-known winery in Montana is the **Mission Mountain Winery** (406-849-5524; www.mission mountainwinery.com) on the western shore of Flathead Lake. These folks have been growing grapes and making wine for many years in Montana. Sampling their wines while gazing out over Flathead Lake is a worthwhile experience.

WOMEN'S FIRST Montana was the first state to vote a woman into the U.S. House of Representatives in 1916, when they chose **Jeanette Rankin** to represent the Treasure State.

ZOOS Montana has a few zoos, but most are centers for wildlife rather than what most people think of as a zoo. For a complete listing of zoos, visit www.visitmt.com/tripplanner/thingstodo/zoo.htm. You will also find listings for zoos and wildlife centers under *To See–For Families* in this book.

Northwest Montana: Glacier Country and Glacier National Park

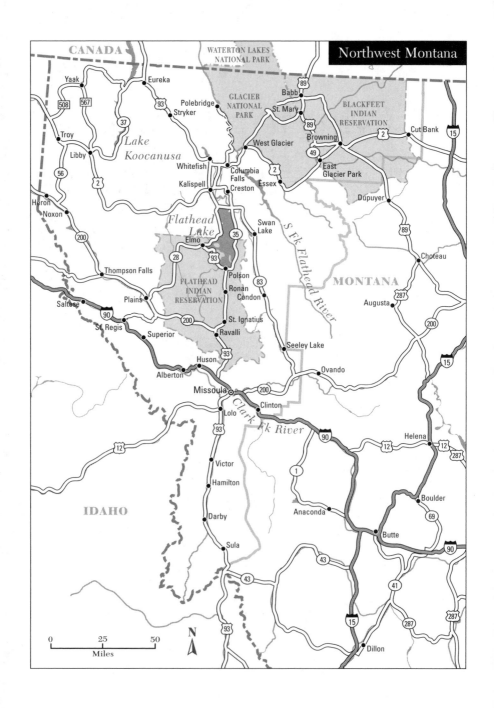

Northwest Montana

NORTHWEST MONTANA:
GLACIER COUNTRY AND GLACIER
NATIONAL PARK

Do not let the name fool you—this region of Montana is more than glaciers. However, most visitors to the region do not leave without experiencing the wonders of Glacier National Park. The park also shares an international border with a similar national park in Canada, Waterton Lakes National Park. The northern border of Glacier National Park and the adjoining area is unique in the world, as the U.S. and Canadian governments have created the Waterton-Glacier International Peace Park. Throughout this chapter, and in any other references in this book, the Peace Park will be simply referred to as Glacier National Park or Glacier (an entire section is dedicated to Glacier National Park at the end of this chapter).

Visitors may think that this region is solely defined by Glacier. But in fact, Glacier is only a small portion of this region—both in size and pursuit. This area of Montana abounds with outdoor recreation opportunities, history, arts, and a host of other leisure activities. And because of Glacier's magnetic pull (for good reason, as it is a beautiful place), many of the region's other draws see far fewer visitors.

To start with, this region bosts some unique history. The state's first permanent white settlement—St. Mary's Mission—was established here in 1841 at the present-day location of Fort Owen Park. Lewis & Clark passed through western Montana, and visitors can trace the path of the Corps of Discovery at Camp Disappointment and Travelers Rest State Park. The Lolo Trail Center, near present-day Stevensville, features exhibits and children's programs. Many towns in this region also feature Lewis & Clark festivals, often held in summer.

But before settlers arrived, this region was home to Montana's first residents, Native Americans. Today, the descendents of these tribes inhabit two of the state's largest Indian reservations: the Blackfeet Indian Reservation is home to the Blackfeet Nation and the Flathead Indian Reservation is home to the Confederated Salish and Kootenai Tribes. Much has changed since these tribes first made their homes in this region, but today they preserve their cultures and traditions despite ever-changing local cultures and politics. Visitors are encouraged to learn more about Montana's Native Americans by experiencing any of the attractions, museums, and exhibits in this region. Of special note are the People's Center and the Museum of the Plains Indian. Other places to add to your list are Council Grove State Park and the National Bison Range.

This region is home to many museums, festivals, and historical sites. The greatest concentrations of museums are in the region's two largest towns, Kalispell and Missoula. The latter is the home of historic Fort Missoula, one of the first forts in Montana.

By Montana standards, Missoula is a big city. The Missoula area boasts a population of nearly 80,000 and is home to the University of Montana. Despite its relative size, Missoula retains its small-town feel. The downtown area is the center of culture and commerce, with the outlying areas harboring the large box stores, chain restaurants, and a more suburban feel. But downtown Missoula is vibrant and active, and visitors can always find something fun and exciting. Most residents are friendly and very proud of their community. In the summer, weekly festivals are common and in winter the downtown is decorated to match the season.

A riverside path follows the Clark Fork River (and the fishing right in town is some of the best in the state) through the downtown area, offering a unique way to explore downtown. For kids, Missoula is home to the Missoula Children's Theatre and a carousel that is open year-round. But one of the best things that Missoula residents love about their "little" hamlet along the Clark Fork River is the plethora of outdoor activities at their doorstep.

Even though Missoula is the largest population center in Glacier Country, Kalispell and the Flathead Valley deserve equal billing. The majority of the Flathead Valley's residents live in one of three towns: Kalispell, Whitefish, or Columbia Falls. All of these towns provide interesting activities, but most visitors use them as jumping-off points for trips to Glacier National Park or other destinations in the area. And there are hundreds of places to explore in this region—adventure is easy to find and takes on many forms.

From a short mountain hike to a multi-day pack trip, Glacier Country provides ample room to roam. With landscapes like the Cabinet Mountains Wilderness, the Bitterroot Mountains, and the Bob Marshall Wilderness, landlubbers will find a lifetime of ground to travel. And river rats, boaters, and paddlers will find white water, reservoirs, and high mountain lakes to explore. Flathead Lake, one of the largest freshwater lakes in the Rocky Mountains, provides boating and fishing. The list of rivers reads like a who's who of nationally known rivers. And the abundance of high-country and backcountry waters provides a lifetime of hikes and paddles.

Anglers also will find a wealth of waters to ply, along with plenty of public access points. In this guide, because there is so much water to explore, I've listed only basic information on the major rivers. This is limited to contact information, general location, access, paddling and floating options, and major fish species present. But a look at a detailed map of Glacier Country will reveal nearly endless boating and fishing opportunities, some remote and some close to towns.

Whether in town or out of town, camping remains a fun way to explore this region, and with a large amount of national forest and state park campgrounds available, visitors will find many camping options. Add in the number of camp-grounds in Glacier National Park and all other places where you can pitch a tent or park an RV and there are so many choices that it would be foolish to try to include them all. Under *To Do–Camping* is a basic list of the national forest campgrounds. They are listed under each national forest and provide enough details (number of campsites, types of campsites, running water, etc.) to help with planning a stay. Be sure to check with a local ranger district or go online, as most campgrounds are only open seasonally. Travel with a good road atlas and do a little prior planning and you will be able to find a place to camp in any season.

If you want to experience a winter wonderland with snow-covered trees, sleigh rides, and exhilarating ski slopes, this region is ideal. Glacier Country is home to more than five downhill ski areas. The well-known Snowbowl (only 15 minutes from downtown Missoula) and Whitefish Mountain Resort (5 miles from Whitefish) ski areas host thousands of visitors each winter. But little-known ski areas like Blacktail Mountain and Lost Trail provide skiers with some solitude and freshly groomed slopes. If downhill skiing is not your thing, there are several cross-country ski areas as well as endless national forest trails. Snowmobile trails crisscross much of the national forest land and enthusiasts are encouraged to check with a local ranger station for trail conditions and availability.

Whether you visit in summer or winter, spring or fall, this region is an out-door enthusiast's dream. With Glacier National Park, Flathead Lake, hundreds and hundreds of miles of rivers and streams, thousands of vertical feet of ski slopes, and national forest trails galore, Glacier Country provides ample reasons to be outside exploring under Montana's Big Sky.

GUIDANCE **Bigfork Area Chamber of Commerce** (406-837-5888; www.big fork.org), 8155 MT 35, P.O. Box 237, Bigfork 59911.

Bitterroot Valley Chamber of Commerce (406-363-2400; www.bvchamber .com), 105 E. Main Street, Hamilton 59840.

Blackfeet Nation/Blackfeet Indian Reservations (406-338-7521; www.black feetnation.com), P.O. Box 850, Browning 59417.

Browning Town Center (406-338-2344; www.browningmontana.com), 124 2nd Avenue N.W., P.O. Box 469, Browning 59417.

Columbia Falls Chamber of Commerce (406-892-2072; www.columbiafalls chamber.com), US 2, 1 mile north of intersection with MT 206, P.O. Box 312, Columbia Falls 59912.

Confederated Salish and Kootenai Tribes (1-888-835-8766 or 406-675-2700; www.cskt.com), 51383 US 93 N., P.O. Box 278, Pablo 59855.

Cut Bank Area Chamber of Commerce (406-873-4041; www.cutbank chamber.com), 725 E. Main Street, P.O. Box 1243, Cut Bank 59427.

Eureka Chamber of Commerce (406-889-4636; www.welcome2eureka.com), P.O. Box 186, Eureka 59917.

Flathead Convention and Visitor Bureau (406-756-9091; www.fcvb.org), 15 Depot Park, Kalispell 59901.

Flathead Indian Reservation. See *Confederated Salish and Kootenai Tribes* above.

Glacier Country Regional Tourism Commission (1-800-338-5072; www .glaciermt.com), 836 Holt Drive, Suite 320, P.O. Box 1035, Bigfork 59911.

Hot Springs Chamber of Commerce (406-741-2662; www.hotsprings.net), 216 Main Street, P.O. Box 580, Hot Springs 59845.

Kalispell Chamber of Commerce (406-758-2800; www.kalispellchamber .com), 15 Depot Park, Kalispell 59901.

Lakeside-Sommers Chamber of Commerce (406-844-3715; www.lakeside chamber.com), P.O. Box 177, Lakeside 59922.

Libby Area Chamber of Commerce (406-293-4167; www.libbychamber.org), 905 W. 9th Street, P.O. Box 704, Libby 59923.

Mineral County Chamber of Commerce (406-822-4891; www.montana rockies.org), 100 2nd Avenue E., P.O. Box 483, Superior 59872.

Missoula Chamber of Commerce (406-543-6623; www.missoulachamber .com), 825 E. Front Street, P.O. Box 7577, Missoula 59807.

Missoula Convention and Visitors Bureau (406-532-3250; www.missoulacvb .org), 1121 E. Broadway, Suite 103, Missoula 59802.

Plains-Paradise Chamber of Commerce (406-826-4700; www.wildhorse plainschamber.com), P.O. Box 1531, Plains 59859.

Polson Chamber of Commerce (406-883-5969; www.polsonchamber.com), #4 2nd Avenue E., P.O. Box 667, Polson 59860.

Ronan Chamber of Commerce-Mission Mountain County Visitor's Center (406-676-8300; www.ronanchamber.com), 207 Main Street, P.O. Box 254, Ronan 59864.

St. Ignatius Chamber Visitor Center (406-745-3900), 333 Mountain View, P.O. Box 566, St. Ignatius 59865.

Seeley Lake Area Chamber of Commerce (406-677-2880; www.seeleylake chamber.com), MT 83 Mile Marker 12.5, P.O. Box 516, Seeley Lake 59868.

Swan Lake Chamber of Commerce (406-886-2080), MT 83, P.O. Box 5199, Swan Lake 59911.

Thompson Falls Chamber of Commerce (406-827-4930; www.thompson fallschamber.com), P.O. Box 493, Thompson Falls 59873.

Troy Chamber of Commerce (406-295-1064; www.troymtchamber.com), P.O. Box 3005, Troy 59935.

Whitefish Chamber of Commerce (1-877-862-3548 or 406-862-3501; www .whitefishchamber.org), 520 E. 2nd Street, Whitefish 59937.

GETTING THERE For additional travel information, see also *Airports, AMTRAK,* and *Bus Service* in "What's Where in Montana."

Interstate 90 cuts right through the middle of this region, running diagonally from southeast to northwest. Missoula is the main town on I-90, and the junction

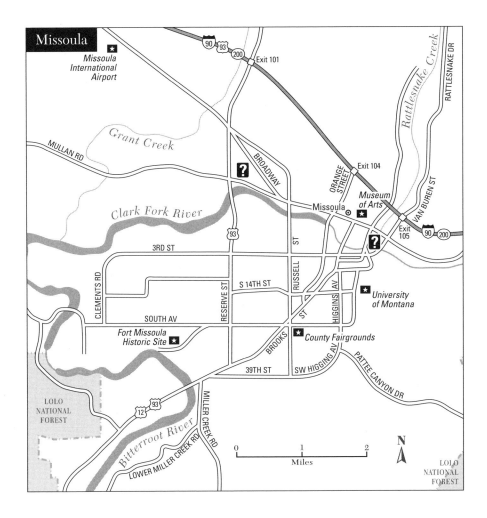

Missoula

Missoula International Airport ★

Grant Creek

MULLAN RD

Clark Fork River

BROADWAY

Exit 101

90 93 200

Rattlesnake Creek

RATTLESNAKE DR

ORANGE STREET

Exit 104

Museum of Arts ★

Missoula ⊙ ■

VAN BUREN ST

Exit 105

90 200

93

3RD ST

CLEMENTS RD

RESERVE ST

S 14TH ST

ST

RUSSELL

HIGGINS AV

University of Montana ★

SOUTH AV

Fort Missoula Historic Site ★

BROOKS

County Fairgrounds ★

SW HIGGINS AV

PATTEE CANYON DR

39TH ST

MILLER CREEK RD

LOLO NATIONAL FOREST

12 93

Bitterroot River

LOWER MILLER CREEK RD

0   1   2
Miles

N

LOLO NATIONAL FOREST

of I-90 and US 93 is nearby. US 93 is the main north-south highway in this region. It connects Hamilton in the south with the Flathead Valley in the north. Whitefish, Kalispell, Somers, Lakeside, Polson, Ronan, St. Ignatius, Missoula, Stevensville, Corvallis, Hamilton, and a few smaller towns all lie along US 93. Running east to west along the northern edge of this region is US 2. Cut Bank, Browning, East Glacier, West Glacier, Columbia Falls, Kalispell, Libby, and Troy all lie along US 2. US 93 and MT 28 bisect the Flathead Indian Reservation. The Blackfeet Indian Reservation is accessed by US 89 and US 2. Heading south from Kalispell, MT 35 is the main route to Bigfork, Swan Lake, and the east shore of Flathead Lake. The Seeley-Swan area and the western boundary of the Bob Marshall Wilderness are accessed by MT 83. West of Plains and northwest of Missoula, MT 200 passes through Thompson Falls and travels the length of the lower Clark Fork River.

MEDICAL EMERGENCIES Keep in mind that this is, for the most part, a rural area. The local sheriff's dispatch or 911 will know the nearest 24-hour emergency facility. The following listings typically offer 24-hour care.

Blackfeet Community Hospital (406-338-6194), Hospital Circle, Browning.

Clark Fork Valley Hospital (1-800-826-3601 or 406-826-4800), 110 Kruger Road, Plains.

Community Medical Center (406-728-4100), 2827 Fort Missoula Road, Missoula.

Kalispell Regional Medical Center (406-752-5111), 310 Sunnyview Lane, Kalispell.

Marcus Daly Memorial Hospital (406-363-2211), 1200 Westwood Drive, Hamilton.

Mineral Community Hospital (406-822-4841), 1208 6th Avenue E., Superior.

Northern Rockies Medical Center (406-873-2251), 802 2nd Street S.E., Cut Bank.

North Valley Hospital (1-888-815-5528 or 406-863-3500), 6575 US 93 S., Whitefish.

St. John's Lutheran Hospital (406-293-0100), 350 Louisiana Avenue, Libby.

St. Joseph Medical Center (406-883-5377), 6 13th Avenue E., Polson.

St. Luke Community Hospital (406-676-4441), 107 6th Avenue S.W., Ronan.

St. Patrick Hospital and Health Sciences Center (406-543-7271), 500 W. Broadway, Missoula.

✴ To See

TOWNS Bigfork. Nestled among the tall pines along the northeast shore of Flathead Lake on MT 35, Bigfork's downtown area is quaint and unique, with **art galleries, antique shops,** and a few **bistros.** The town itself is home to over 15 world-class galleries, the **Bigfork Summer Playhouse,** and other cultural highlights. Located on a sparkling bay where the Swan River meets Flathead Lake, Bigfork offers a nice mix of recreation and culture. The outlying areas offer spectacular views of Flathead Lake and are home to many **hiking trails, boating facilities, golf courses,** and an **orchard** complete with some of the best cherries in the Pacific Northwest. Many lodging options exist in the Bigfork area, making this lakeside hamlet a fine choice as vacation base for summertime activities.

Bitterroot Valley. Home to several small towns, the Bitterroot Valley is a broad valley that runs north to south and is accessed by US 93. To the west lie the jagged peaks of the **Bitterroot Mountains,** where hikers, bikers, and anglers will find lots of adventure. The **Bitterroot River** runs the entire length of the valley (see also *To Do–Fishing* and *To Do–Paddling/Floating*). Hamilton, Corvallis, Stevensville, and Victor all provide full services and are great bases for excitement and culture in "the Bitterroot."

Browning. On the eastern slope of the Rocky Mountain Front and Glacier National Park, Browning is one of the more ruggedly scenic towns in Montana. Sitting at the junction of US 2 and US 89, Browning serves as the unofficial eastern gateway to Glacier National Park. It is also the administrative center for the Blackfeet Indian Reservation, which covers 1.5 million acres. The **Museum of the Plains Indian** is located in Browning and certainly worth a visit, especially during its **North American Indian Days** (see *Special Events*). The area around Browning, most of which lies within Glacier or the Blackfeet Reservation, includes nearly 200 miles of rivers and streams and entrances to Glacier National Park, and the town itself is a good jumping-off point for longer trips into Glacier Country.

Hot Springs lies southwest of Flathead Lake via a short jaunt off MT 28. The area was named "big medicine" by many Pacific Northwest tribes. Across the globe, hot springs enthusiasts boast of the healing powers of natural mineral springs. This town, located on the Flathead Indian Reservation, is home to hot springs that have been compared to Germany's famous Baden-Baden springs. The springs around Hot Springs can be accessed by a few privately owned businesses, and there is a small public facility on the edge of town. However, be sure to check locally for the seasonal maintenance schedule. (For contact information, see *Guidance;* see also **Symes Hot Springs Hotel** under *To Do–Hot Springs*).

Libby lies at the junction of US 2 and MT 37 in the extreme northwest corner of Montana. Within minutes of Libby, one can be lost in the splendor of the **Kootenai National Forest** (see *Wilder Places–Forests*), leave all motors and traces of humankind behind with a hike in the **Cabinet Mountains Wilderness,** or wrestle with large trout in the **Kootenai River.** The surrounding area is also home to a swinging bridge across the Kootenai River, the majestic Kootenai River Falls, and the 90-mile-long **Lake Koocanusa.** Libby also hosts the Libby Logger Days and Black Powder Days, two uniquely western arts and history festivals.

Pablo, south of Polson on US 93, is the administrative center of the 1.3-million-acre **Flathead Indian Reservation.** Home to the Confederated Salish and Kootenai Tribes, this reservation is the second largest in Montana. The reservation includes a good chunk of the **Flathead Lake** shoreline, as well as the **National Bison Range.** Visitors can also learn about the culture and history of the Salish and Kootenai tribes with visits to the **People's Center** (see *Museums*) or the **Flathead Indian Museum and Trading Post** (406-745-2951), located south of town in St. Ignatius.

Polson is a thriving lakeside town on the southern end of Flathead Lake, at the junction of US 93 and MT 35. Polson literally lies between the lake and the mountains, making it an ideal place for exploring. Home to many shops, accommodations, and great places to dine, Polson has been discovered, yet still retains a small-town and uncrowded feel. At the **Polson-Flathead Historical Museum** (406-883-3049; 708 Main Street) and the **Miracle of American Museum, Inc.,** (406-883-6804; 58176 US 93) visitors can learn about the area's culture and history. Of special mention are the links at the **Polson Country Club,** as it is the only course in the area located on the shores of Flathead Lake. The views from nearly every tee box will make it hard to concentrate on your swing.

Seeley Lake sits in a narrow valley along MT 83. Anyone traveling between Glacier National Park and central or southern portions of Montana should plan a trip through Seeley Lake and the Seeley-Swan area (see also *Scenic Drives*). Laced with lakes and surrounded by national forest and wilderness areas, the area around Seeley Lake is home to boundless recreational opportunities. In summer, hiking, fishing, floating, swimming, golf, and horseback riding are all possible, along with whatever else you can dream up. In winter there are groomed cross-country ski trails, groomed snowmobile trails, and even a nationally recognized sled-dog race.

MUSEUMS **Conrad Mansion Museum** (406-755-2166; www.conradmansion .com). Unchanged since Spokane architect Kirtland Cutter designed and built the home in 1895, this mansion is an outstanding testament to the luxurious living of a bygone era in the Pacific Northwest. Ownership remained in the Conrad family for nearly a hundred years. Today visitors can tour it Tuesday–Sunday, May 15 to October 15. During the Christmas season, tours are available November 25–December 22.

Ⴑ **Glacier County Historical Museum** (406-873-4904; www.glaciercountymt .org/museum), 107 Old Kevin Highway, Cut Bank. Open Memorial Day–Labor Day, Tuesday through Saturday, 10 A.M.–5 P.M. This quaint museum tells the story of the surrounding area, including the Lewis & Clark Expedition, the

THE NATIONAL BISON RANGE BELOW THE MISSION MOUNTAINS

Blackfeet Indians, homesteading, the founding of Cut Bank, and the interesting history of Glacier National Park. There's also a unique exhibit of artist John Clark. On-site are some historic structures such as an old schoolhouse, oil derrick and workers' house, and caboose. On selected weekends families with kids might enjoy the living history performances.

 Historical Museum at Fort Missoula (406-728-3476; www.fortmissoula museum.org), Building 322 at Fort Missoula, Missoula. Open Memorial Day– Labor Day, Monday through Saturday, 10 A.M.–5 P.M. and Sunday, noon–5 P.M.; open Labor Day through Memorial Day, Tuesday–Sunday, noon–5 P.M.; $3 adults, $2 seniors, $1 students, and $10 maximum per family. The museum was established in 1975 to collect, preserve, and interpret the history of Missoula County and western Montana. The exhibits are designed for the education, recreation, and cultural enrichment of visitors and area residents. The museum is located within historic Fort Missoula and has 13 historic structures and is accredited by the American Association of Museums.

 Hockaday Museum of Art (406-755-5268; www.hockadaymuseum.org), 302 Second Avenue East, Kalispell. Housed in a turn-of-the-century Carnegie Library, this fine arts museum is a must for art enthusiasts in the Flathead area. Their permanent collection is substantial, but it is the rotating exhibits of local art and culture that are worth seeing—from Glacier National Park to local artists. The Hockaday also organizes the summer Arts in the Park series, an art and music festival the fourth weekend of July.

 Missoula Art Museum (406-728-0447; www.artmissoula.org), downtown Missoula. Open Tuesday through Friday, 10 A.M.–5 P.M. and Saturday, 10 A.M.–3 P.M.; free. With education at the core of its mission, MAM offers tours and classes for all ages and collaborates with local art, literary, and music communities to develop lectures and workshops. MAM also offers classes through the Summer Art School. Programs like gallery tours, artist lectures, and panel discussions are designed for every exhibit. MAM manages the Missoula County Art Collection, as well as its own collection, which is distinguished by the Contemporary American Indian Art Collection and works from regional and local artists, including: Dale Chihuly, Jacob Lawrence, Jaune Quick-to-See Smith, Susan Stewart and E. S. Paxson. MAM's recent acquisitions include works by Terry Melton, Preston Singletary (Tlingit), Branson Stevenson, and Gail Tremblay (Onondaga Micmac). The museum has published dozens of artist catalogues throughout the years, which are for sale in the Temporary Contemporary museum and online.

 Montana Natural History Center (406-327-0405; www.thenaturecenter .org), Building T-2, Fort Missoula, Missoula. Open Monday–Friday, 9 A.M.– 5 P.M.; free. Dedicated to educating the public about Montana's natural history and the importance of protecting, preserving, and understanding nature, this museum includes a native plant garden, a self-guided nature trail, and natural history exhibits. The museum itself is housed in the historic Post Headquarters Building at Fort Missoula. (See also Historical Museum at Fort Missoula above; Rocky Mountain Museum of Military History below; and Northern Rockies Heritage Center under *Historic Landmarks, Places, and Sites.*)

NORTHWEST MONTANA: GLACIER COUNTRY AND GLACIER NATIONAL PARK

Museum of the Plains Indian (406-338-2230; www.iacb.doi.gov), junction of US 2 and US 89, Browning. Open daily June through September, 9 A.M.–4:45 P.M.; open October through May, Monday–Friday, 10 A.M.–4:30 P.M.; $4 adults, $1 students 6–12, children 5 and under free, $1 per person for groups of 10 or more. The Museum of the Plains Indian is a permanent exhibition gallery, which presents a rich collection of historic arts created by tribal people of the Northern Plains. There are three dioramas, and carved wood panels by Blackfeet sculptor John Clarke are on display. Come and admire the murals by Blackfeet artist Victor Pepion. Founded in 1941, this museum's collection centers on the artwork of regional Native Americans, both past and present. Northern Plains tribes represented include Arapaho, Assiniboine, Blackfeet, Chippewa, Cree, Crow, Flathead, Nez Perce, Northern Cheyenne, Sioux, and Shoshone. This is a great place to visit on your trip to or from Glacier National Park. In addition to the artwork, the craftsmanship and artistry of the riding gear, clothing, tools, weapons, bags, and household goods are also on display and deserve appreciation.

& **Ninepipes Museum of Early Montana** (406-644-3435; www.ninepipes.org), US 93 Charlo. Open daily, Memorial Day through Labor Day, 8 A.M.–6 P.M.; open Labor Day through Memorial Day, Wednesday through Sunday, 11 A.M.–5 P.M.; $4 adults, $3 students, $2 children 6–12, children 5 and under free. Established in 1998 to discover and memorialize the history and culture of the Flathead Indian Reservation and early Montana. Long-term exhibits include weaponry (clubs, bows and arrows, guns), spurs and saddlery, a "grizzly set," a vast collection of Native American beadwork, life-sized dioramas of wild animals and of an Indian camp. An old cabin and wagons and buggies dot the museum grounds. This is a fun place for families and kids. The grounds are also handicapped accessible and include a short nature trail.

& **The People's Center** (406-675-0160; www.peoplescenter.org), US 93 Pablo. Open daily, May through September, 9 A.M.–6 P.M.; open October through April, Monday through Friday, 9 A.M.–5 P.M. In the heart of western Montana's Flathead Indian Reservation is a unique cultural center, built by the region's original creators of fine arts and crafts: the Salish, Kootenai, and Pend d'Oreille. This well-thought-out center is more than a museum; it is a vital, living encounter with Native American culture, as centuries-old wisdom for living harmoniously with the earth is practiced and taught. The center features an exhibit gallery, educational programs, and interpretive tours focusing on Native American heritage, natural history, and cultural interpretation. (See also Native Edventures under *To Do–Unique Adventures.*)

& **Ravalli County Museum** (406-363-3338; www.cybernet1.com/rcmuseum), 205 Bedford Street, Hamilton. Open daily Monday, Thursday, Friday, 10 A.M.–4 P.M.; Saturday, 10–2 P.M.; and Sunday, 1–4 P.M. Built by A. J. Gibson in 1900, the building served as the Ravalli County Courthouse until 1979, when it was saved from the wrecker's ball by a vote of the people. It now houses, arguably, the finest little museum in the Northwest. Permanent collections include a Native American collection, a fly-fishing exhibit, Ricketts Museum commemorating the development of the Rocky Mountain Laboratory, an antique kitchen, miner/trapper room, a veteran's display, Ernst Peterson photo exhibits, extensive archives, Victorian rooms, and a Railway Express Agent Office. There is also a weekly Sunday Series Program at 2 P.M.

Rocky Mountain Museum of Military History (406-549-5346; www.geo cities.com/fortmissoula), Buildings T-310 and T-316 at Fort Missoula, Missoula. Open daily, June 1 through Labor Day, noon–5 P.M.; open Sunday only, Labor Day through Memorial Day, noon–5 P.M., free. This testament to military might promotes the commemoration and study of the U.S. armed services from the Frontier period to the War on Terrorism. The museum strives to impart a greater understanding of the roles played by America's servicemen and service-women through this period of dramatic global change. The U.S. Fourth Infantry Regiment and the Civilian Conservation Corps constructed the museum build-ings (ca. 1936) during the Great Depression and the exhibits are from a wide collection of documents and artifacts ranging from Civil War artillery to Vietnam-era antitank missiles. (See also Historical Museum at Fort Missoula and Montana Natural History Center above and Northern Rockies Heritage Center under *Historic Landmarks, Places, and Sites.*)

&. ☻ **Smokejumper Visitor Center** (406-329-4934; www.smokejumpers.com), 5765 West Broadway, west of Missoula. Open Memorial Day–Labor Day, daily, 8:30 A.M.–5:00 P.M.; in winter please call two days ahead for a reservation; free. Home to the largest active smokejumper base in the nation, the Smokejumper Vis-itor Center is a unique opportunity to learn about this unusual, demanding, and dramatic occupation. A tour of the facility is also available. As you walk through the center you will visit the National Smokejumper Memorial, go inside a replica of a 1930s lookout tower, and tour the smokejumper loft, where the smokejumpers work when they are not fighting fires. Also tour the ready room and load master's room, where the smokejumpers prepare for fire calls. Tours are available at 10 and 11 A.M. and 2, 3, and 4 P.M. daily, and the tour is free of charge.

HISTORIC LANDMARKS, PLACES, AND SITES Twelve miles northeast of Browning, on US 2 at mile marker 233, lies a historical marking highlighting **Camp Disappointment.** The actual site of Lewis & Clark's Camp Disappoint-ment is on private land, so this marker is approximately 4 miles south of the northernmost point of the Corps of Discovery's adventures. On July 23, 1806, the Corps arrived at Camp Disappointment. Here they saw the Marias River flowing out of the Rocky Mountains and their hopes of the river extending to 50 degrees north latitude were dashed—hence, the name Camp Disappointment. In 1925 the Great Northern Railroad erected a commemorative monument on an overlooking hillside. This site is on the National Register of Historic Places. Another significant site, also situated on private land, is the **Meriwether Lewis Two Medicine Fight Site.** This lies 25 miles southeast of Browning, where Lewis & Clark's only violent encounter with Native Americans occurred.

Conrad Mansion Museum. This 13,000-square-foot, 1895 mansion is a National Historic Site. The mansion's Victorian architecture presents a breath-taking exterior, but the interior of Virginia native Charles Conrad's home outdoes the outside. In each of the 26 rooms, original furniture is restored and protected; even toys and clothing are preserved.

Council Grove State Park (406-542-5500; http://fwp.mt.gov/lands/site_280907
.aspx), west of Missoula on Mullan Road (turn at the junction of Mullan Road
and US 93). Open year-round for day use only; free. On this site in 1885 Isaac
Stevens negotiated the 1855 Hellgate Treaty, creating the Flathead Indian
Reservation. Stevens, along with the Salish, Kootenai, and Pend d'Oreille Indians, established the 1.3-million-acre reservation. Today visitors can picnic, hike,
and view local wildlife in the park's 87 acres.

& **Daly Mansion** (406-363-6004; www.dalymansion.org), 251 Eastside Highway
(MT 269), Hamilton. Open for tours daily from mid-April through October 15,
10 A.M.–5 P.M.; open by appointment in the off-season; $8 adults, $7 seniors, $5
children 6–12, children 5 and under free. An astounding home set among hum-
ble homes in a breathtaking Montana valley. The summer home of copper baron
and millionaire Marcus Daly, his wife Margaret, and their four children has
evolved from a two-story farmhouse into a 24,000-square-foot mansion with 25
bedrooms and 15 bathrooms in the heart of the Bitterroot Valley. The home was
named Riverside for its proximity to the Bitterroot River, and it served to entertain guests. Foreign plants, a swimming pool, and a playhouse were all added to
Riverside after the Dalys' arrival. Today the mansion still entertains guests from
all around the country, whether it is tours, weddings, or just relaxing on the covered deck and playing checkers. Riverside remains an amazing, historic getaway
for all ages.

& **Darby Historical Visitor Center** (406-821-3913), 712 N. Main Street,
Darby. Built in the late 1930s as the Bitterroot National Forest's first ranger station, this center has housed a wide array of organizations. Most notably, from
1965 to 1990 it was the home of the Bitterroot National Forest fire crew. Today
it is dedicated to educating and entertaining visitors and also serves as an interpretive center for the **Bitterroot National Forest.**

Fort Owen State Park (406-542-5500; http://fwp.mt.gov/lands/site_280846
.aspx), US 93, 25 miles south of Missoula to Stevensville, then 0.5 mile east on
MT 269. Open year-round, but for day use only; free. Fort Owen's adobe and log
remains mark the site of the first permanent white settlement in Montana.
Major John Owen established the fort as a regional trade center in 1850 and
period furnishings and artifacts are displayed in the restored rooms of the east
barracks. In 30 minutes you can browse through a small museum housed in preserved and partially reconstructed structures. This site is listed on the National
Register of Historic Places.

Missoula County Courthouse (406-721-5700; www.co.missoula.mt.us), 200
West Broadway, Missoula. Open Monday through Friday, 8 A.M.–5 P.M.; free.
Constructed from 1908 to 1910, this massive building covers an entire city block.
Listed on the National Register of Historic Places, its historical significance is
nearly outdone by the building's south foyer, which contains eight murals painted
from 1912 to 1914 by western artist Edgar S. Paxson.

Northern Rockies Heritage Center (406-728-3662; www.nhrc.org), located in
Building 30 at Fort Missoula, Missoula. Open year-round; free. Dedicated to
protecting and preserving 13 of Fort Missoula's historic buildings, this organiza-

tion allows visitors the opportunity to view a historic water tower, parade grounds, and other structures. All of the structures contained within are listed on the National Register of Historic Places. (See also Historical Museum at Fort Missoula, Montana Natural History Center, and Rocky Mountain Museum of Military History under *Museums*.)

& **St. Ignatius Mission** (406-745-2768), just off US 93 in St. Ignatius. Open in summer, 9 A.M.–8 P.M.; open fall through spring, 9 A.M.–5 P.M.; free. In 1854 Catholic missionaries established the mission in the stunningly beautiful Mission Valley—hence, the name of the valley. In the 1890s the church was constructed by Native Americans, under the direction of the Catholic missionaries. Inside the church, Brother Joseph Carignan painted nearly 60 murals on the walls and ceilings. The church and surrounding grounds are a registered National Historic site. Sunday mass is held weekly at 9:15 A.M.

& **St. Mary's Mission** (406-777-5734; www.saintmarysmission.org), 4th Street (three blocks from Main Street), Stevensville. Open for tours April 15 through October 15; $6 adults, $4 students. Friar Pierre DeSmet founded the mission in 1841. Friar Anthony Ravalli was recruited from Italy to help design and build the log chapel that stands today. The interior of the chapel has been restored to the original colors of the 1880s era. Its furnishings are the handiwork of Friar Ravalli, Montana's first medical doctor. The attached study and dining room, as

MISSOULA COUNTY COURTHOUSE

well as Friar Ravalli's house/pharmacy, are completely restored and furnished with items made by him. Listed in the National Register of Historic Places, St. Mary's Mission is a cultural and historical icon of the early days of Montana.

& **Tobacco Valley Historical Village** (406-297-7654), S. Main Street, Eureka. Open Memorial Day through Labor Day, 1 P.M.–5 P.M.; free. When Lake Koocanusa was created in 1971 by Libby Dam, concerned citizens imported three buildings to Eureka that would have been drowned in the new lake. Since that time this historic village has added a plethora of historic buildings. A general store, railroad depot, church, schoolhouse, caboose, hand-hewn log house, cabin, library, and fire tower make up this unique hamlet. Inside all of these historic structures, visitors will find artifacts and memorabilia from a bygone era. Via the village, those looking for more adventure can access hiking/biking trails along the banks of the Tobacco River.

& **Travelers Rest State Park** (406-273-4253; www.travelersrest.org), 8 miles south of Lolo via US 93, then 0.25 mile west on Mormon Creek Road. Open daily June through October, 8 A.M.–8 P.M.; open November through Memorial Day, 8 A.M.–5 P.M.; free. There is one guarantee when visiting this site—that you will be following the exact path Lewis & Clark took upon walking the shores of Mormon Creek. The Corps of Discovery had two camps here, one in 1805 on the journey west and the second camp in 1806 on the journey east. This is one of the few Corps campsites where archaeologists have unearthed physical evidence of their journey. A fire ring and latrine have been discovered. Additionally, this site was also a much-used campsite, trail crossing, and rendezvous for generations of Native Americans. Visitors will find many interpretive signs on the grounds.

FOR FAMILIES ✔ **Big Sky Waterpark** (406-892-2139; www.bigskywp.com), 7211 US 2 E., Columbia Falls. Open Memorial Day through Labor Day, 10 A.M.–6 P.M. or until 8 P.M. in midsummer. Admission $21.95 adults, $16.95 adults over 60 and children under 48 inches tall; twilight and nonrider rates also available. Miniature golf, carousel ride, and waterpark are included in the full-day rate. Situated close to Glacier National Park in Columbia Falls, this is a fun place for kids, and adults, to let out a little vacation energy. This is Montana's largest waterpark and also features bumper cars, a video game arcade, and a few other entertaining games.

& ✔ ✿ **A Carousel for Missoula** (406-549-8382; www.carrousel.com), 101 Carousel Drive, Missoula. Open June–August, 11 A.M.–7 P.M.; open September–May, 11 A.M.–5:30 P.M.; $1.50 adults, $.50 seniors, $.50 children under 19; free for those with disabilities. In 1991 local cabinetmaker Chuck Kaparich agreed to spearhead the making of this hand-carved carousel. After the city council agreed to never dismantle it, volunteers began the long process of building a carousel in Missoula. After 100,000 volunteer hours, the carousel opened in 1995 and since has been an exciting and cherished part of downtown Missoula.

✔ ✿ **Dragon Hollow Play Area** (406-549-8382; www.carrousel.com), 1 Caras Park, Missoula. Open year-round, dawn to dusk; free. Next to a Carousel for

Missoula, Dragon Hollow is one cool playground and it is obvious that a lot of thought went into its planning. Themed with green and yellow dragons, this playground is a maze of obstacle courses, ladders, monkey bars, slides, musical instruments, and even a special area for kids under 5. Even adults will enjoy the surprisingly artistic qualities of the playground.

SCENIC DRIVES **Garnet Backcountry Byway** consists of 12 miles along Garnet Range Road; head northeast on MT 200 east of Missoula for 30 miles until you see the sign on the south side, then follow signs as you head southeast. Closed January 1–March 31. Groomed and open to snowmobile traffic January 1–April 30. The Garnet Byway provides a 12-mile journey through the **Garnet Mountain Range. Garnet Ghost Town** is a major point of interest along the byway. As the byway climbs 2,000 feet into the evergreen forest of the Garnet Mountains, outstanding panoramas of the Blackfoot River Valley, the Swan Range, the Mission Mountains, and the Bob Marshall Wilderness come into view. In winter the road provides access to 31.5 miles of snowmobile and cross-country ski trails in the **Garnet National Winter Recreation Trail System.** In summer the trails can also be used for hiking, biking, and horseback riding. Anglers and campers will also find ample access and opportunities.

Lake Koocanusa Scenic Byway is a 67-mile journey from Libby to Eureka on MT 37. You can also travel on the west side of the lake on Forest Road 228, but this route is a little more bumpy and adventuresome. When Libby Dam was built in 1974, these two roads (one on the east side and one on the west) were also built. The lake itself is 90 miles in length and either road offers great recreational opportunities for boating (four ramps), fishing (both rainbow and bull trout inhabit the lake), wildlife viewing, camping (developed and undeveloped sites; see also **Kootenai National Forest** under *To Do–Camping*), and more. The lake's name was the result of a contest—a woman from nearby Eureka suggested it as it contains three letters each from "Kootenai" (after the Kootenai Indian tribe), "Canada" (which is home to part of the reservoir), and, of course, "USA." (See also Lake Koocanusa Loop under *To Do–Bicycling.*)

Quartz-Loon Scenic Drive (37 miles total). Start in Libby and follow MT 37 for 0.5 mile north to River Road. Go west 4.4 miles to Quartz Creek Road to Pipe Creek Road (MT 567). Proceed south 17 miles back to MT 37. The Kootenai River parallels the route for the first 5 miles, providing a scenic foreground to the Cabinet Mountains. Be sure to take your binoculars and drive at a slow pace. Whitetail deer and ruffed grouse are common along the entire length of this drive. Moose may be seen in the upper Quartz Creek/Loon Lake area and blue heron, loons, and osprey may be seen at Loon Lake. There are numerous beaver dams and lodges, and elk and black bear are occasionally seen. Bighorn sheep may be seen on River Road. The roads on this scenic route are good-quality paved or gravel. Be careful on the many curves as you may encounter logging traffic. This drive also provides access to the **Skyline National Recreation Trail**. And you will pass by **Loon Lake** and the **Turner Mountain Ski Area**.

St. Regis–Paradise National Forest Scenic Byway runs 30 miles east on MT 135 from St. Regis to MT 200 in Paradise. Originally a meandering trail that

LAKE KOOCANUSA IN THE NORTHWEST CORNER OF THE STATE

followed the Clark Fork River between St. Regis and Paradise, this byway lies entirely within the Lolo National Forest. This may be one of the few scenic routes with a motto: the River, the People, the Land. It takes motorists through varying terrain, from spacious, rolling flats to steep canyon walls where it winds through the Coeur d'Alene Mountains. It also serves as a route to the **National Bison Range.** The **Clark Fork River** parallels the road for a good chunk of the drive, providing recreational opportunities along the byway. However, floaters should consult local knowledge and be very aware of their own ability as this stretch provides some thrilling, yet challenging, whitewater.

Seeley-Swan Scenic Drive runs 90 miles along MT 83 from Seeley Lake to Swan Lake. Trees, lakes, trees, lakes, deer, and more lakes make up this journey. In fact, there are hundreds of natural lakes, ranging in size from a few acres to several thousand acres, squeezed into this narrow, heavily forested valley. To the west, the Mission Mountains rise majestically, and to the east the Swan Range walls off this pristine valley, giving travelers here a unique feeling of solitude. This drive also offers abundant opportunity for outdoor recreation from boating to fishing, golf, and horseback riding in summer; and in winter everything from snowmobiling to dogsledding. The Seeley-Swan Valley butts up against the **Bob Marshall Wilderness.** A unique way to see lots of wildlife is to check out the **Clearwater Canoe Trail.** An easy, meandering route, this 4-mile journey takes about one to two hours. The well-marked put-in is 4 miles north of Seeley Lake on MT 83.

Yaak Loop Scenic Tour (90 miles round-trip). Head west on US 2 from Libby, then north on Yaak River Road (MT 508), then south on Pipe Creek Road (MT 567) back to Libby. The ride through the Yaak Valley is spectacular in itself. The area abounds with wildlife and the surrounding mountains offer a beautiful contrast to the low-lying valley bottom. The road follows much of the Yaak River and you can visit **Yaak Falls.** The falls are 7 miles north of US 2 on MT 508 and the turn is well marked. Much of the drive has you in the **Kootenai National Forest** and there are seven Forest Service campgrounds along the way (or slightly off the main route, but easily found with an accurate map). It may be difficult to make the entire loop as it is nearly 100 miles, therefore consider the **Quartz-Loon Scenic Loop,** which covers similar terrain and begins from Libby as well.

WINERIES ○ **Mission Mountain Winery** (406-849-5524; www.missionmoun tainwinery.com) is located at Dayton, on the west shore of Flathead Lake on US 93, 23 miles north of Polson. Open May 1–November 1, 10 A.M.–5 P.M. This is a family-owned winery and the first bonded winery in Montana. The initial vineyard was started 23 years ago and the first vintage was 1984. They currently produce approximately 6,500 cases of wine a year, and their Monster Red blend is a local favorite. A winner of over 50 awards, even some international recognition, this is a great little secret in a beautiful part of Montana.

Painted Rocks Winery (406-349-9463), 9747 West Fork Road, Alta; south of Darby on US 93, then west on MT 473 for about 25 miles to Painted Rocks Lake, and then 5 more miles beyond the lake. Open Tuesday through Saturday, reservations are required so call ahead. Nestled in the scenic Bitterroot Valley, this winery is a great place to sample local wines while enjoying the scenery of the valley and the well-cared-for grounds. This is also a great stop on a trip to **Painted Rocks State Park** or, as the owners of the winery suggest, try a real adventure at **Hot Creek Hot Springs.**

Ten Spoon Vineyard and Winery (406-829-9083; www.tenspoonvineyard .com). Head up Rattlesnake Canyon north of downtown Missoula 3 miles until you find a yellow, barnlike structure in a pasture beside a field of grapevines. Hours are by appointment only. In 2006, their vintage year, they produced 4,500 cases of wine. Oenophiles should plan a visit to this unique place while in Missoula.

Trail Creek Winery (406-677-8992; www.trailcreekwinery.com). In the town of Seeley Lake, head east on Locust Lane and follow the signs to the winery. Open all year, Friday, 6–8 P.M., Saturday, 2–8 P.M., Sunday, 2–6 P.M. This is a small, yet intimate winery where you are certain to get individual attention. Their grapes are from out of the area, but they have a fun tasting room with great appetizers.

NATURAL WONDERS **Flathead Lake** lies along US 93 and MT 35 in the northwest corner of the state. The largest natural freshwater lake west of the Mississippi River, it provides locals and visitors an abundance of recreation and scenic beauty. Its size is enough to marvel at—over 200 square miles of water and 185 miles of shoreline—however, the lake often plays second fiddle to nearby **Glacier National Park.** The lake is home to many species of game fish (species include lake trout, lake whitefish, westslope cutthroat trout, and a few other species). Boaters and water-sports enthusiasts will find a plethora of access points and well-maintained boat ramps. Campers have a wide choice of public and private campgrounds. The southern portion of the lake lies within the **Flat-**

head **Indian Reservation** and anyone using any of the facilities or access points on the reservation must purchase a tribal permit. Montana Fish, Wildlife & Parks (FWP) (406-752-5501; http://fwp.mt.gov) maintains many public access points around the lake, including fishing access sites. The agency also manages six separate locations that make up **Flathead Lake State Park.** A favorite area of the state park is **Big Arm State Park** (406-849-5255; http://fwp.mt.gov/lands/site_280041.aspx), 14 miles north of Polson on US 93. Open year-round for day use, and free for residents and $5 for nonresidents; May 1–September 30 for camping, $15 per night. This location also has a boat launch, a nice beach, and yurt rental (inquire via the Web site or by calling 406-751-4577). It is a popular jumping-off point for trips to **Wild Horse Island State Park.** (Boat access to this day-use-only, primitive park is regulated to protect the 2,000-acre island.) The largest island in Flathead Lake, Wild Horse has been a landmark rich with history since the Salish-Kootenai Indians were reported to have used it to pasture horses to keep them from being stolen by other tribes. (For trips to Wild Horse Island, see Pointer Scenic Cruises under *To Do–Unique Adventures.*) **West Shore State Park** is another nice park and it lies farther north on US 93. **Finley Point State Park, Yellow Bay State Park,** and **Wayfarers State Park** all lie north of Polson on or just off MT 35. Camping is allowed at all of these locations and if you are planning a trip it's best to visit the Montana FWP Web site (http://fwp.mt.gov/lands/searchparks.aspx) for current fees and hours.

Kootenai Falls is accessible 6 miles east of Troy along US 2. These are some of the more stunning falls in the Northwest, and perhaps the country. You can view the falls by stopping at Kootenai Falls County Park. In fact, these are the biggest falls in Montana—at least of any that have not yet been dammed. For the Kootenai tribe, these falls represent the center of the world and a place for peaceful meditation and spiritual communion and guidance. For anyone not interested in peaceful communion, but rather raucous adrenaline inductions, plan for a walk across the river on the swinging bridge. The bridge spans the gorge at a height of 2,100 feet and standing on the bridge with the water rushing below is a heart-pumping experience. From the county park, a short trail leads you down to the falls. Picnic tables, restrooms, and a fishing access site round out the visitor services at the park. Movie buffs will also enjoy the fact that *A River Wild* was filmed here. For mountain bikers, a trail begins across the river, but to get to the trailhead after crossing the bridge requires pushing the bike about 1.5 miles over some shale. However, bikers can also access the trailhead at the terminus of Kootenai River Road.

& **Ross Creek Cedar Grove Scenic Area** lies southeast of Troy on MT 56. Since 1960, this 100-acre tract in the Kootenai National Forest has been set aside for preservation and research, as well as public access and appreciation. There is a large collection of old-growth western red cedars. Along the 0.9-mile interpretative trail, you will view these ancient behemoths close up. Some of these trees measure 8 feet in diameter and over 200 feet in height. On the trail you will also learn about the area's other wildlife. Fishing and picnicking are available as well.

BICYCLING ♿ **Blue Mountain Recreation Area,** US 93 south of Missoula 2 miles, then west on Blue Mountain Road to the parking lot. If you are looking for just a cycling area, then this is not the place. However, if you are looking for a user-friendly and diverse area with lots of trails and lots of options, then this area within 10 minutes of Missoula is for you. A 1.5-mile interpretive trail follows the banks of the Bitterroot River, and branching off from that are plenty of other trails worth exploring. For more information on some specific trails, visit www.fs.fed.us/r1/lolo/recreation-trails/trails-by-name.shtml.

♿ **Clark Fork Riverfront Trail System.** The city of Missoula and Missoula County have created a riverside trail that is accessible from numerous locales. A main access point is Caras Park in downtown Missoula (see a Carousel for Missoula under *To See–For Families*). Most of the trail system is paved, wide, and open to joggers, walkers, bikers, strollers, in-line skaters, and just about anyone looking to spend a nice day out and about. Local anglers will also use this trail to access the river. Picnic tables, benches, and many parks are found along the path.

Clark Fork River Trail. From St. Regis, travel east on the Frontage Road. Just after you cross the Clark Fork River, turn north on Mill Creek Road for 2 miles, turn left onto Forest Road 223 and travel 2.5 miles to the trailhead. Not to be confused with the trail that originates in Missoula, this trail begins at St. Regis and travels 18 miles and is all singletrack. The trail runs through the Lolo National Forest, hugging the east bank of the Clark Fork River. The smooth singletrack is almost entirely rideable; it's a lot of fun as you roll up and down through thick forest and open meadow sections and along the riverbank. Once you're done biking, try soaking your legs at **Quinn's Hot Springs,** located a couple of miles north of the trailhead on MT 135.

Holland Lake Lodge Trail is reached by traveling north from Clearwater Junction (intersection of MT 83 and MT 200) for 14.2 miles. Then turn east on FR 4353 (West Morrell Road), and continue 2 miles to the trailhead. This is a moderate 13.5-mile, one-way, mostly downhill ride near Holland Lake in the Swan River Valley with a variety of trail conditions. The trail ends at Holland Lake, where you can take the road or ride the trails through the campground to a very scenic lunch spot at the Holland Lake Lodge. Consider adding the 4-mile singletrack loop down to and around Clearwater Lake or the 2-mile hike to the falls at Holland Lake. Loops can be made by riding south on MT 83 from Holland Lake and up West Morrell Road to the FR 4370 intersection.

Hornet Peak Look begins just off North Fork Road near the Ford Work Center north of Polebridge. This outstanding 22-mile loop traverses the Salish Range west of Whitefish. This is a ride better suited for experienced bikers. On certain portions of the route you'll whiz through impressive stands of tall timber, with the occasional view of the Flathead Valley and the west side of Glacier National Park. The ride begins and ends at Tally Lake, the deepest lake in Montana. There is a campground and great swimming opportunities at the lake. You can also use the campground as a base camp for further adventures, as there's a wealth of mountain and road bike rides in the area.

HOLLAND LAKE LIES NORTH OF SEELEY LAKE, CLOSE TO THE BOB MARSHALL WILDERNESS

Kreis Pond Mountain Bike Trails are accessible from Kreis Pond Campground. Take Exit 82 off I-90, then continue on MT 10 for 1.4 miles west of Remount Road, then 2.7 miles north to Ninepipe Ranger Station, then north on FR 476, then west on FR 456, then south on FR 2176 to the parking area in the Lolo National Forest. This is a great area for novices and experienced mountain bikers, as there are 35 miles of trails and forest roads. Four loops offer varying degrees of difficulty. Camping is also available near the trailhead. For more information, be sure to pick up a map at the Ninepipe Ranger Station on your way to the biking area.

Lake Koocanusa Loop starts at the junction of MT 37 and Fisher River Road east of Libby, then goes north on MT 37 to the bridge across the lake, then south of FR 228 back to your starting point. This 80-mile loop ride is arguably one of the best road-riding opportunities in Montana. When the government created Libby Dam in 1972, they flooded towns and the Kootenai River Valley and created 90 miles of a road cyclist's dream. For experienced riders this trail will delight, but novice or less fit riders might find it a little frustrating as it is difficult to find a level section on this ride—you will continually find yourself going either up or down and around another bend as the road runs high above the lake shore. The hills and the distance earn this ride an experienced rating. However, novice riders could certainly enjoy an easy out-and-back ride and still experience much of the beauty of the Kootenai National Forest.

Railroad-Daly Loop is a 16-mile mountain bike loop in the Bitterroot National

Forest, which offers numerous additional trails and roads for riding. To access this ride, take US 93 south from Hamilton, then go east on MT 38 (the Skalkaho Highway) for about 13 miles, and then turn southeast and park in the open area. Begin your ride up FR 75 for 2 miles to its junction with FR 711. Follow 711 as it arcs around (be sure to stay on the main road to avoid getting lost or biting off more than you can chew), as it brings you back to MT 38 (now dirt). At this junction, turn left and proceed back to your vehicle. Though the trail presents little in the way of technical challenges, this ride requires better-than-average fitness because of its length and its ups and downs.

Seeley Creek Mountain Bike–Nordic Ski Trails are accessed by MT 83, 0.5 mile north of Seeley Lake, then west on Morrell Creek Road for about 1 mile to the parking area. This is a great collection of short (1-mile) to medium (6-mile) loops in a beautiful area of the Lolo National Forest. These trails are all suitable for the not-so-experienced, but by lengthening the ride experience bikers can find some challenges as well. For experienced riders seeking more adventure, you can link up with nearby Forest Service roads for a more exhilarating and longer ride. In the designated area the trails are well marked, and maps are available at the Seeley Lake Ranger Station 3 miles north of Seeley Lake on MT 83. In winter these trails are also groomed for cross-country skiing.

Whitefish Lake is a favorite road-biking route of many locals. The best route begins at the junction of 2nd Avenue and Baker Street in downtown Whitefish. This 22-mile out-and-back ride features plenty of rolling hills and passes by scenic creeks and ranches while giving outstanding views of Whitefish Lake. To begin the ride on Baker Street, go across the railroad viaduct bridge toward Whitefish Mountain; the road becomes Wisconsin Avenue. Pass by the Whitefish Mountain turnoff; the road becomes East Lakeshore Drive. After passing by Upper Whitefish Road (gravel), it becomes Delray Road. When the pavement runs out, simply turn around and head back to Whitefish, retracing your route. You can add some serious climbing to this route by taking one of several spur roads. The climb up to Whitefish Mountain Resort is a little over 5 miles and gains some 1,800 feet in elevation. A little closer to town and heading east, look for Reservoir Road, which climbs for a little over 2 miles and 800 feet. Once finished, grab a cold, fresh beer at the Great Northern Brewery.

BOATING ✪ **Flathead Lake** is the largest natural freshwater lake west of the Mississippi River. Boating enthusiasts will find ample access to the lake's 200 square miles of water. (For more information, see also *To See–Natural Wonders* and visit http://fwp.mt.gov/fishing/guide/q_Flathead_Lake__1140996479165.aspx.)

Hungry Horse Reservoir is located in the Flathead National Forest south of US 2 between West Glacier and Columbia Falls. Travel West Side Road (FR 895) or East Side Road (FR 38) to the lake. The lake is easily accessed via 10 boat ramps. With 24,000 acres of water, anglers and boaters will have ample room to explore. Home to mainly westslope cutthroat trout, mountain whitefish, and bull trout, Hungry Horse is a place to catch species unique to Montana. Other species are present, but most anglers pursue cutthroat and bull trout. Be sure to check the special regulations before venturing out. The reservoir was created in 1953 with the construction of the dam, and lots of campgrounds and access points were eventually added.

&. **Lake Como Recreation Area** is in the Bitterroot National Forest, accessed via US 93 south of Missoula. Open year-round, but for day use only. There is a nominal use fee of less than $5. The lake was constructed in 1905 to provide irrigation for ranches in the valley, but today it also provides scenic and accessible recreation. The boat launch features 30 vehicle/boat and 7 passenger vehicle parking spots and accessible toilets, but no overnight camping is allowed at the boat launches. Boating begins Father's Day weekend and then drops off by mid-August depending on the water level. Weekend use in July and August typically exceeds capacity, so if you are planning a summer visit be prepared to share the experience. There is also a nice beach with good swimming in a roped-off area, ample fishing (main species are mountain whitefish and westslope cutthroat trout), a horseback riding camp, Woods Cabin (which can be rented nightly or for day use for up to 15 adults for $60), and access to Lake Como National Recreation Loop Trail, an easy 7-mile hike that circles the lake and intersects with other trails.

&. **Painted Rocks State Park** (406-542-5500; http://fwp.mt.gov/lands/site _280864.aspx). Take US 93 for 17 miles south of Hamilton, then continue 23 miles southwest on MT 473. Open year-round for day use and camping; free. This is a remote park mostly surrounded by Idaho, but located in Montana. Located in the scenic Bitterroot Mountains, this 23-acre park offers boating, water sports, and fishing opportunities. Because of its relative distance from a major town, this is a nice place for RVers desiring a little more solitude than what is normally offered at more easily accessible RV campgrounds.

WHITEFISH LAKE, WITH WHITEFISH MOUNTAIN RESORT IN THE BACKGROUND

& **Placid Lake State Park** (406-677-6804; http://fwp.mt.gov/lands/site_280895 .aspx) is accessed by MT 83 three miles south of Seeley Lake, then 3 miles west on Placid Lake Road (it is well marked). Open May 1–November 30; day use is free for residents, $5 for nonresidents; camping $15 until September 30, then $13 after that. There is a nice boat ramp, dock, and 12 boat slips (first come, first served), making this a popular spot for boaters. The waters and the surrounding shoreline are a fun place for swimmers. Fishing for brown trout, kokanee salmon, largemouth bass, mountain whitefish, rainbow trout, westslope cutthroat trout, and yellow perch offers anglers the opportunity for a diverse catch. Camping is allowed in designated sites for up to 14 days.

& **Salmon Lake State Park** (406-677-6804; http://fwp.mt.gov/lands/site _280904.aspx), 5 miles south of Seeley Lake on MT 83. Open for day use May 1 through November 30; free for residents, $5 for nonresidents; camping is $15. Nestled among the tall pines on the shores of Salmon Lake, this state park is a great place to visit. Plan to fish (species present include brown trout, kokanee, mountain whitefish, northern pike, rainbow trout, westslope cutthroat trout, yellow perch), picnic, launch your boat, water-ski, read, review interpretive signs, or let your children get the wiggles out after a long drive in this woodland setting of western larch, ponderosa pine, and Douglas fir. There are also weekly amphitheater events, but be sure to contact the park for scheduling.

& **Whitefish Lake State Park** (406-862-3991; http://fwp.mt.gov/lands/site _280100.aspx), 1 mile west of Whitefish on US 93, then 1 mile north to the park entrance. Open year-round for day use; free for residents, $5 for nonresidents; May 1–September 30 for camping, $15. With nearly 3,000 acres of lake and so close to Whitefish, this is a great place for folks who love water sports—boating, waterskiing, fishing, and swimming. Anglers can target arctic grayling, brook trout, bull trout, coho salmon, westslope cutthroat trout, kokanee salmon, lake trout, northern pike, and rainbow trout. For families or folks wanting to have a nice meal while camping, this state park is a great option because of its proximity to Whitefish.

CAMPING & **Bitterroot National Forest** (www.fs.fed.us/r1/bitterroot) covers most of the land west of US 93 south of Missoula, as well as southeast of Hamilton, and east of US 93. There are four ranger districts and each district manages its campgrounds. **Darby Ranger District** (406-821-3913) manages six developed campgrounds, including two on **Lake Como.** The **Stevensville Ranger District** (406-777-5461) has three developed campgrounds, including **Charles Waters Campground,** 5 miles north of Stevensville, then 2 miles east of Bass Creek Road. This campground features handicapped accessible sites and is open May through early September, with a cost of $9. The **Sula Ranger District** (406-821-3201) has six developed campgrounds, including **Spring Gulch Campground,** 3 miles northwest of Sula on US 93 (handicapped accessible; open May 15 through September 15; $12). The **West Fork Ranger District** (406-821-3269) has eight developed campgrounds, including **Alta Campground,** 4 miles south of Darby on US 93, then 30 miles southwest on MT 473 (open May through November; $7). The forest also has five cabins and two historic lookouts that can be rented nightly for $25 to $50 a night.

&. **Flathead National Forest** covers 2.3 million acres of land west of the Continental Divide. The forest occupies much of the land west of Glacier National Park and south of the Canadian border and stretches nearly 130 miles south to Flathead Lake and the Flathead Indian Reservation. There are five ranger districts and each district manages various campgrounds. **Glacier View Ranger District** (406-387-3800) has four developed campgrounds, including **Big Creek Campground,** 20.5 miles north of Columbia Falls via MT 486 and 2.5 miles south of the Camas Creek entrance to Glacier. Big Creek Campground is handicapped accessible, open Memorial Day through Labor Day, and sites cost $10. **Hungry Horse Ranger District** (406-387-3800) has 12 developed campgrounds, of which the most popular is **Lost Johnny Campground,** approximately 10 miles south of Hungry Horse Reservoir via West Side Road. This is a good campground to use as a base if venturing into Glacier or traveling upstream on the South Fork of the Flathead River. Lost Johnny campsites are handicapped accessible, open mid-May through September, and cost $10. **Spotted Bear Ranger District** (406-758-5376) has three developed campgrounds, including the remote **Spotted Bear Campground** located 55 miles southeast of Martin City on East Side Road. This campground south of Hungry Horse Reservoir is ideal for venturing into the Bob Marshall Wilderness. It is open mid-June through mid-September, handicapped accessible, and sites are available for $10. **Swan Lake Ranger District** (406-837-7500) has four developed campgrounds, including **Swan Lake Campground,** 1 mile northwest of Swan Lake on MT 83. This campground has handicapped access, is open mid-May through September, and sites cost $12. **Tally Lake Ranger District** (406-863-5400) has four developed campgrounds, including **Tally Lake Campground,** 6 miles west of Whitefish on US 93, then 15 miles west on Tally Lake Road (FR 113). Tally Lake is handicapped accessible, open Memorial Day through Labor Day, and costs $12.

&. **Kootenai National Forest** covers nearly 2.2 million acres in the northwest corner of Montana. With five ranger districts, this forest offers plenty of options for campers. **Cabinet Ranger District** (406-827-3533) has six developed campgrounds. Of these, **Bull River Campground** is one of the favorites. Located 4 miles west of Noxon on MT 200, this campground is open April 15 through November 30 and sites are $8. **Fortune Ranger District** (406-882-4451) has five developed campgrounds, with **North Dickey Lake Campground** a local favorite. This campground is 5 miles south of Fortine on US 93 and is open April 15 through November 30; sites are $7. **Libby Ranger District** (406-293-7773) has seven developed campgrounds, including **McGregor Lake Campground,** 53 miles southeast of Libby on US 2, or 32 miles southwest of Kalispell on US 2. This campground is open May 15 through September 10 and sites are $8. **Rexford Ranger District** (406-296-2536) has seven developed campgrounds, most with handicapped access and site fees under $10. Many of the campgrounds can be accessed by traveling the shores of **Lake Koocanusa. Three Rivers Ranger District** (406-295-2536) has 10 developed campgrounds. Anglers, floaters, and paddlers, and wildlife buffs will enjoy **Yaak River Campground**

7 miles west of Troy on US 2. The national forest is also home to **four rental cabins** and **five historic lookout towers** that are all available for nightly rentals for under $30. An easy and efficient way to reserve many of these campsites is through the National Recreation Reservation Service (1-877-444-6777; www.reserveusa.com).

& **Lolo National Forest** covers nearly 2 million acres surrounding the city of Missoula. The forest also abuts other national forests and public lands. Five ranger districts manage the campgrounds. **Missoula Ranger District** (406-329-3750) has nine campgrounds. **Ninemile Ranger District** (406-626-5201) has two developed campgrounds, including **Kries Pond Campground** (Exit 82 off I-90, then MT 10 for 1.4 miles west to Remount Road, then 2.7 miles north to Ninepipe Ranger Station, then north on FR 476, then west on FR 456, then south on FR 2176). This campground is a good one for cyclists and for folks wanting a place a little more off the beaten path. There is handicapped access, it is open April 1 through December 1, and there is no cost. **Plains–Thompson Falls Ranger District** (406-826-3821) has seven developed campgrounds. **Seeley Lake Ranger District** (406-677-2233) has seven developed campgrounds, including a great one for paddlers and boaters—**Seeley Lake Campground** 4 miles northwest of Seeley Lake on FR 77. This campground is well marked, has handicapped access, is open Memorial Day through Labor Day, and sites are $10. **Superior Ranger District** (406-822-4233) has three developed campgrounds, most of which are on or near the Clark Fork River; and the forest also has **five cabins/houses** and **four historic lookout towers** that are available for overnight rentals, with rates ranging from $20 to $100.

FISHING & **The Bitterroot River** (406-542-5500; http://fwp.mt.gov/fishing/guide/q_Bitterroot_River__1141176468612.aspx) meanders for nearly 90 miles south of Missoula in the scenic Bitterroot Valley. US 93 provides much of the access from Conner to Missoula. Beginning where the East and West Forks meet near Conner, the Bitterroot is a free-flowing mountain stream that bends and meanders its way north, where it eventually meets the Clark Fork west of Missoula. Species of fish include brook trout, brown trout, whitefish, rainbow trout, and westslope cutthroat trout. Anglers can float or wade-fish the Bitterroot nearly any day of the year. There are 10 state fishing access sites along the river. Be sure to check locally or with Montana FWP as to which access sites have camping or are day use only. For paddlers, this river is devoid of whitewater; however, it is very important to inquire locally before floating as this river is known for having sweepers (large submerged logs clogging a channel or bank), seasonally changing channels, and high flows.

& **The Blackfoot River** (406-542-5500; http://fwp.mt.gov/fishing/guide/filter query.aspx?q=NAME_blackfoot%20river_1) flows off the west side of the Continental Divide for nearly 130 miles before it joins the Clark Fork River outside Missoula. MT 200 provides most of the access to the Blackfoot. There are 16 access sites along the river and most offer camping or day-use facilities. Anglers will find brook trout, brown trout, bull trout, rainbow trout, whitefish, and westslope cutthroat trout. In the past 20 years this river has experienced a rebirth in the quality of its fishing. Due to poor mining and logging practices, the river suffered until the late 1980s, when conservation and angler groups worked to restore its water quality. Today the Blackfoot provides a special recreation corridor with ample public access. For paddlers and floaters the river contains a few Class II and III rapids and floating the river requires intermediate skills, but most importantly good judgment and some local knowledge before a trip down the river.

&. **The Clark Fork River** (406-542-5500; http://fwp.mt.gov/fishing/guide/q _Clark_Fork_River__1162072481455_9.43000030517578_336.802001953125.asp x) eventually becomes Montana's largest river just before entering Lake Pend Oreille in Idaho. Interstate 90 parallels the river from its source near Butte until St. Regis. Beginning about 30 miles east of Missoula, near the confluence with Rock Creek, the Clark Fork is easily accessible via public access points. There are 16 access points from Turah (15 miles east of Missoula) to St. Regis. At St. Regis the river turns north, leaves I-90, and is paralleled by MT 135, then MT 200 follows it. From St. Regis to where the river dumps into the lake, anglers will find three more access sites. Similar to the Blackfoot, the Clark Fork is a river going through a pleasant improvement in its fishing. Massive damage occurred from poor mining habits at the river's headwaters near Butte and Anaconda. Add in the silt from logging near Missoula, and the Clark Fork had a tough go during most of the 20th century. However the river has recovered well

FISHING IS POPULAR ON THE BITTERROOT RIVER

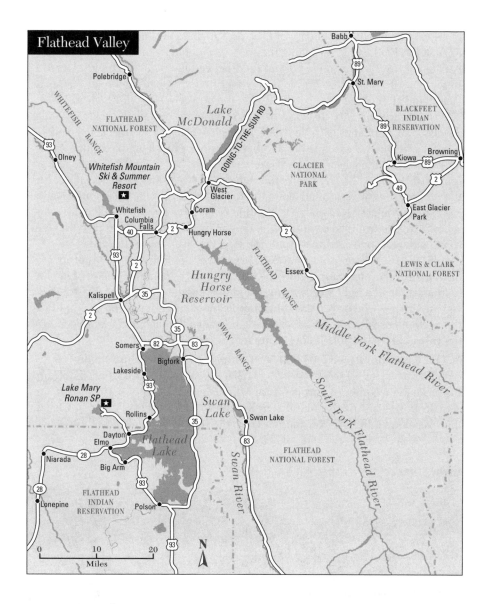

and provides ample recreation for anglers, floaters, and paddlers. It is home to an abundance of game fish, including brook trout, brown trout, northern pike, rainbow trout, smallmouth bass, westslope cutthroat trout, whitefish, and yellow perch. For the most part (not including peak flows during runoff) the river is wide and easy to navigate—except for the area around Alberton Gorge. There are a few Class III and IV rapids between the Alberton and Tarkio accesses and all floaters should be very experienced or go with a professional river outfitter.

&. **The Flathead River** (406-752-5501; http://fwp.mt.gov/fishing/guide/q_Flat head_River__1147748473651.aspx) begins where the North Fork of the

Flathead (the western boundary of Glacier National Park) meets the Middle Fork of the Flathead River (along the southern boundary of Glacier National Park along US 2). The South Fork of the Flathead flows out of Hungry Horse Reservoir. After all of the forks join, the river flows through the broad Flathead Valley, and after about 20 miles flows into the northern edge of Flathead Lake. The river leaves the lake just west of Polson, where it eventually, nearly 80 miles downstream, combines with the Clark Fork near Plains. The river above and below has distinct characteristics and both sections provide ample fishing opportunities. Above the lake access is easier to find, but below Flathead Lake access is more difficult as the river flows through the Flathead Indian Reservation. Five state access sites are scattered along the river, but for specific access information it is best to contact Montana Fish, Wildlife & Parks or inquire locally. The river is home to lake trout, lake whitefish, mountain whitefish, northern pike, rainbow trout, and westslope cutthroat trout. Floating the river above the lake is easy, despite the river's large size. However, because of the lack of accesses proper planning is very important. Below the lake the river is dammed at Kerr Dam (a unique dam and a sight worth seeing), and floating the river is not advised unless you are experienced or you are using a professional outfitter. Keep in mind that this section lies within the Flathead Indian Reservation and it is best to contact the tribal offices in Pablo before planning a float.

&. **The Kootenai River** (406-752-5501; http://fwp.mt.gov/fishing/guide/ q_Kootenai_River__1165027489999_64.2890014648438_161.432998657227.aspx) is tucked in a corner of northwestern Montana near Libby and Troy, but it actually begins in British Columbia in Kootenay National Park. While in Canada, the river flows into Lake Koocanusa. Here the river is harnessed by Libby Dam,

MIDDLE FORK OF THE FLATHEAD RIVER

and there is a great tailwater fishery below the dam. From the dam to where the river enters Idaho, access is via MT 37 or US 2. The river is home to burbot, kokanee salmon, whitefish, rainbow trout, bull trout, and westslope cutthroat trout. Access is easy, as the river is followed by roads for its entire length. Floaters should use this river with extreme caution as flows fluctuate based on releases from the dam, and the Kootenai Falls create quite the hazard for any floater, experienced or not. Aside from the falls, the river harbors several sections of whitewater and it is not recommended that casual floaters float this river. Seek the help of a professional outfitter.

GOLF Despite Montana's broad range of climate, we are blessed with some great places to hit the links. Glacier Country might be one of the better regions for golf due to its relative amount of rainfall and lack of wind compared to the rest of Montana. Few of these courses are closed to public use. One word of advice (and this is true at most courses): in Montana in summer it is best to call several days ahead for weekend tee times. Additionally, because of our long days in summer, many courses offer twilight specials.

Big Mountain Golf Club (406-751-1950; www.golfmt.com), 2 miles north of Kalispell on US 93, Kalispell; 27 holes.

Buffalo Hill Golf Club (406-756-4545; www.golfbuffalohill.com), 1176 North Main Street, Kalispell; 27 holes.

Cabinet View Country Club (406-293-7332), 378 Cabinet View, Libby.

Cedar Creek Golf Course (406-822-4443), 10 Wadsworth Lane, Superior; nine holes.

Cut Bank Golf and Country Club (406-873-2574), 59 Golfcourse Road, Cut Bank; nine holes.

Double Arrow Resort (406-677-2777; www.doublearrowresort.com), 2 miles south of Seeley Lake on MT 83; 18 holes.

Eagle Bend Golf Club (406-837-7300; www.golfmt.com), 279 Eagle Bend Drive, Bigfork; 27 holes.

Glacier View Golf Course (406-888-5471), 640 Riverbend Drive, West Glacier; 18 holes.

Hamilton Golf Club (406-363-4251), 1004 Golf Course Road, Hamilton; 18 holes.

Highlands Golf Club (406-728-7360), 102 Ben Hogan Drive, Missoula; nine holes.

Kings Ranch Golf Course (406-626-4000), 17775 Mullan, off Exit 89 on I-90, Frenchtown; nine holes.

Lake Mary Ronan Wilderness Golf Course (406-849-5459; www.lakemary ronan.com), 1283 Lake Mary Ronan Road, Proctor; nine holes.

Larchmont Municipal Golf Course (406-721-4416), 3200 Fort Missoula Road, Missoula; 18 holes.

Linda Vista Golf Course (406-251-3655), 4915 Lower Miller Creek Road, Missoula; nine holes.

Meadow Creek Golf Course (406-882-4474), 205 1st Street, Fortine; nine holes.

Meadow Lake Golf and Ski Resort (406-892-8700; www.meadowlake.com), 100 St. Andrews Drive, Columbia Falls; 18 holes.

Mission Mountain Country Club (406-676-4653; www.golfmissionmountain .com), 640 Stagecoach Trail, Ronan; 18 holes.

Phantom Links Golf Club (406-532-1000; www.phantomlinks.com), 8500 Mullan Road, Missoula; 18 holes.

Polson Country Club (406-883-8230; www.polsoncountryclub.com), 111 Bayview Drive, Polson; 18 holes.

River's Bend Golf Course (406-827-3438), 46 Golf Course Road, Thompson Falls; nine holes.

Trestle Creek Golf Course (406-649-2680), 1 Trestle Creek Golf Road, St. Regis; nine holes.

University of Montana Golf Course (406-728-8629; www.umt.edu/golf), 515 S. Avenue E., Missoula; nine holes.

Village Greens (406-752-4666; www.montanagolf.com), 500 Palmer Drive, Kalispell; 18 holes.

Whitefish Lake Golf Club (406-862-4000; www.golfwhitefish.com), US 93 N., Whitefish; 36 holes.

Whitetail Golf Course (406-777-3636), 4295 Wildfowl Lane, Stevensville; nine holes.

Wild Horse Plains Golf Course (406-826-5626), 328 MT 200 W., Plains; nine holes.

HIKING **Blodgett Overlook Trail** (Trail #101 in the Bitterroot National Forest) is accessed by heading west out of Hamilton to Blodgett Camp Road (FR 476) and then taking Canyon Creek Road (FR 475) for 3 miles to the trailhead. The Blodgett Overlook Trail begins 100 feet up the Canyon Creek Trail and climbs to the north. The hike is fairly easy, only 3 miles round-trip, and provides an excellent and breathtaking view of Blodgett Canyon and looks into the Selway-Bitterroot Wilderness. It's a wonderful short hike for any age, but be very cautious while hiking, as you are walking along the brink of the canyon. Remember to enjoy the view but also to watch the trail.

Cascade National Recreation Trail (Trail #242 in the Lolo National Forest) is accessed by traveling 8 miles south of Paradise on MT 135 to Cascade Campground. This 1.4-mile round-trip is a great education adventure as there are 25 interpretive signs en route detailing ecological information about the area. On the way, be sure to take time to view Cascade Falls via two scenic overlooks. If you ate a big breakfast and need to work it off, continue on Trail #242 for 6.5 miles to FR 97 and then FR 194 to complete a nice loop hike.

Charles Water Nature Trails are accessed from the parking area for Charles Waters Campground in the Bitterroot National Forest, located 5 miles north of Stevensville on US 93 and then 2 miles east on Bass Creek Road. The trails lie where sagebrush grassland communities intersperse with stands of ponderosa pines. There are a few trails in this area: a 1-mile interpretive trail, the 0.5-mile Charles Water Nature Trail, and a 2.5-mile fire ecology trail. This area provides ample opportunity to see wildlife and experience the ecology of sagebrush grassland meeting up with a soggy creek bottom. While walking, spend some time being silent and listening for how many songbirds you might hear.

Holland Falls National Recreation Trail is accessed by driving 36 miles north on MT 83 from Clearwater Junction. From MT 83, turn right on Holland Lake Road (FR 44) and proceed to the well-marked trailhead. With easy terrain, views of the falls, access to Holland Lake, and vistas of the Swan and Mission Mountains, this 3-mile loop hike is a popular and easy jaunt for most folks. Holland Lake also provides ample opportunity for water sports and fishing (bull trout, kokanee salmon, and rainbow trout), and camping at Holland Lake Campground is available May through September. (See also Flathead National Forest under *Wilder Places* and Holland Lake Lodge under *To Do–Skiing*.)

Kim Williams Nature Area Trail is accessible from the east end of 5th Street (Campus Drive) in Missoula. This is a great trail for a quick nature fix for folks in Missoula. The trail is wide, mostly gravel, and follows an old railroad grade for 2.5 miles on the south side of the Clark Fork River. Meandering through a 134-acre natural area allows the opportunity to view wildlife and the Clark Fork River and enjoy some surprising solitude so close to town. This trail also meets up with the **Clark Fork Riverfront Trail** (see *To Do–Bicycling*). For anyone wanting a serious climb, but with the reward of a view of the entire Missoula Valley, take a huff up the **Mount Sentinel Trail,** which departs from Campus Drive as well. This trail is 2.5 miles straight up, but the climb is worth it.

Leigh Lake Trail (Kootenai National Forest Trail #32) is a 3-mile out-and-back trail. Drive 7 miles south on US 2 from Libby, then west for 3 miles on Bear Creek Road (FR 278); head right on Cherry Creek Road (FR 867) for 4 miles, and then right on Leigh Creek Road (FR 4786) for approximately 2 miles to find the trailhead. Despite its short length, this trail will get the legs burning and the heart pumping. Once at the top, the views of Snowshoe Peak and the Cabinet Wilderness and Leigh Lake are the gain that comes with the pain.

Morrell Falls National Recreation Trail (Lolo National Forest Trail #30) is accessed by taking MT 83 for 0.5 mile north of Seeley Lake and heading east on Morrell Creek Road. Soon this road changes to Cottonwood Lakes Road (FR 477). After 1.1 miles, turn on the left fork, W. Morrell Road (FR 4355), and go roughly 6 miles. Turn right on Pyramid Pass Road (FR 4381). After 0.25 mile, go left on Morrell Falls Road (FR 4364) and travel about a mile to the trailhead. In the Lolo National Forest, this is an easy 5-mile loop trail that takes you to the base of Morrell Falls, one of the more spectacular falls in the area. This is a flat hike (elevation gain is less than 200 feet) among lodgepole pines, firs, spruces, larches, and then eventually to the falls. For diehards, free and undeveloped camping can be had in the picnic area.

HORSEBACK RIDING ✐ **Double Arrow Ranch** (406-677-2777; www.double arrowresort.com), 2 miles south of Seeley Lake on MT 83, Seeley Lake. The folks at the Double Arrow have some of the nicest and calmest horses in the region. They offer trail rides with views of the Mission Mountains, the Bob Marshall, and the Clearwater River. All horseback-riding trips are guided rides, available May through September. It is important to make your reservations for horseback riding in advance. Cost of the ride is $60 per person. Inquire about other horse-related adventures such as an evening cookout, private lessons, horse-drawn sleigh rides in winter, and group lessons. Some of our favorite rides (they are more like adventures) are the day-long trips into the Bob Marshall Wilderness, such as the ride beginning from the Pyramid Pass Trailhead. It climbs to the pass beneath the dramatic, angled face of Pyramid Peak. This is a unique opportunity for those with limited time or money to experience the spectacular scenery of the Swan Range along the Bob Marshall Wilderness Area. At the lakes you can fish for westslope cutthroat trout, hike, or just relax in the rarified alpine air.

High Country Trails (406-755-1283; www.horserentals.com/highcountry .html), 2800 Foy's Lake Road, Kalispell. Day trail rides are their specialty, and their 800-acre ranch located in the Flathead Valley is close to Glacier National Park. They have hourly rides, full-day rides, overnight rides, and custom trips as well. Perhaps try a ride to a high-mountain lake to fish for trout. Rates: half-hour trail ride, $45; two-hour trail ride, $60; half-day ride with lunch, $125; and a half-day ride with steak dinner, $150—now that's Montanan! Be sure to inquire about other options and rates.

Hole in the Wall Ranch (406-683-6500; www.holeinthewallranch.com), Exit 66 off I-90 in Alberton. This ranch has had the same outfitter for nearly 10 years and offers a wide range of riding options, from hour-long rides to full-day rides. The nice thing about Hole in the Wall is that there are lots of options for non-riders as well. Whitewater rafting or kayaking and guided fishing on the Clark Fork River are offered. And there are a few island greens where enthusiasts can test their chips and puts. The ranch also has 12 cabins for rent (ranging from $110–$225 a night; children under 12 are free with parents), a dining room serving lunch and dinner, a hot tub, and paddleboats—all of which come free with a stay at the ranch.

McGinnis Meadows Cattle Ranch & Guest Ranch (406-293-5000; www.mmgranch.com), 60 miles from Kalispell on US 2 and 6 miles from Libby on US 2 (turn south on McGinnis Meadows Road). This is a true working cattle ranch. For visitors looking to "tend some herds" or "break in a bronc," this is the ideal place. Guests will enjoy family-style cookouts, relaxing on the large covered porch, and resting after a hard day of wrangling. Their schedule runs like this: March and April, the cows are calving. Learn from the ground up about starting horses, ride the summer range to learn the country and check fences, and search for shed antlers. May, work with your horse on ranch penning, sorting, cutting, even roping steers (from the ground, of course). June through the end of October, experience moving cattle to new pastures on some spectacular country surrounding the Lost Trail National Wildlife Refuge. This is for more experienced riders; however, there is always ample break-in time for younger or less-experienced riders.

✔ **O'Brien Creek Farm** (406-295-1809), Kootenai National Forest (call the farm for exact directions and meeting place), Troy. A smaller operation in a remote corner of Montana, but for personal service and solitude while on horseback, the folks here will take care of you and your riding desires. Rides by the hour, day, plus evening cookout rides, and breakfast rides. Inquire about rates. An all-day ride takes riders through dense forests and then to a mountaintop with some great views. One of their breakfast rides is a great way to start the day. Overnight adventures are also available, but be sure to contact them well ahead of time.

✔ **Wildlife Adventures, Inc.** (406-642-3262; www.wildlifeadventuresinc.com), 1765 Pleasant View Drive, Victor. This is a full-service guest ranch, with a quaint bed & breakfast as well, that also offers rides by the hour and by the day. Families or individuals will find all the western hospitality and friendly service for which Montana is famous. Relaxing and pressure-relieving activities include horseback rides, fishing, wilderness pack trips, hiking, sightseeing, historic tours, swimming, rafting, rockhounding, wildlife viewing, activities for children, barbecues, and much more. The winter season offers cross-country skiing, snowshoeing, downhill skiing at nearby lifts, wagon ride/dinner, and wildlife viewing. Inquire about rates.

HOT SPRINGS **Alameda's Hot Springs Retreat** (406-741-2283; www.alamedas hotsprings.com), 308 N. Springs St., Hot Springs. Located in downtown Hot Springs, Alameda's Hot Springs Retreat is a quiet, peaceful, relaxing getaway, whether for the day or the week. It is a comfortable, clean, 1930s spa motel

RAFTING THE MIDDLE FORK OF THE FLATHEAD RIVER

located in the town that time forgot—but still has lots of amenities. For the lodging options, units have kitchens, private hot mineral baths, and a large screened porch. Alameda's is a great spot to unwind and slow down. Weekly rates are offered for groups or private parties and if you are in need of something extra for those sore muscles after a day of fishing or hiking, massage therapy is available by appointment. Rooms are $55 to $85 a night.

&. ♂ **Lolo Hot Springs Resort** (406-273-2290; www.lolohotsprings.com), 38500 US 12, Lolo. This is a full-service resort located within an easy drive of Missoula. However, nestled on 125 acres in the middle of the Lolo National Forest, guests feel more in the wilds than one might expect. The pools here are some of the best in the state. They are clean and well maintained, and there are fun things for kids to do (bumper boats, water toys) while Mom and Dad soak away the day's activities. A testament to their amenities: on weekends many locals from Missoula visit. Horseback riding, snowmobiling, a restaurant, bar, and casino are all available on premises. Overnight lodging starts at $55 for a simple cabin and goes up based on cabin size and amenities. Camping is also available for $20 a night, or try a tepee for $25.

Quinn's Hot Springs Resort (406-826-3150; www.quinnshotsprings.com), 190 MT 135, Paradise. Guests here enjoy a clean and chemical-free soak. There are also 18 cabins for guests and 15 rooms in the lodge. They have also added a few riverside suites for anyone interested in fly-fishing or some paddling before or after soaking. The cabins are quite nice and most feature two queen beds, while rooms in the lodge have king-sized beds. The resort also features a gourmet restaurant in the **Harwood House** (try one of the steaks); before or after dinner relax in **Quinn's Tavern.**

Symes Hot Springs Hotel (406-741-2361; www.symeshotsprings.com), 209 Wall Street, Hot Springs. The pools here are fun because they are indoor-outdoor pools connected by a small swimway. Rates start at $55 a night, and the rooms are located in a historic building reminiscent of a bygone era. In 1930 businessman Fred Symes constructed the hotel and much of the nostalgic décor remains today and has been restored. There are 31 guest rooms, some with their own private miner baths. For folks wanting even more indulgence, try a hot-rock therapy, massages, wraps, and more. The **Bathouse Grill** is on premises as well, and the **Daily Grind Espresso Bar** can handle any caffeine fix.

PADDLING/FLOATING Clearwater River Canoe Trail is accessed 4 miles north of Seeley Lake via MT 83, then west 0.5 mile on FR 17597. The turnoff is well marked with a brown-and-white sign. Follow the signs to the put-in. The takeout is 3.5 miles downstream at Seeley Lake Ranger Station. At the take-out, a 1 mile hiking trail will take you back to the put-in. Depending on your speed, the paddle will take up to 1.5 hours. This trail is a designated water trail in the Lolo National Forest. Floating the river allows you to get a close-up view of wildlife, flora, and fauna, and it is a completely different perspective than hiking. One thing to notice is the quiet that overcomes you while paddling compared to walking. Birds you may see will include kingfishers, loons, herons, water ouzels, and more. Beavers and turtles abound, and anglers may expect to catch brook, brown, rainbow, or westslope cutthroat trout. If you do not have a canoe one can be easily rented for a reasonable price at **Seeley Lake Fun Center** (406-677-2287) on MT 83 in downtown Seeley Lake.

✔ **Flathead Lake Raft Company** (406-883-5838; www.flatheadraftco.com), 1501 US 93, Polson. This is the only raft company operating trips on the whitewater of the Flathead River below Kerr Dam. There are several rapids on that stretch, most notably Wild Buffalo Rapids. Half-day trips are $42 for adults, $34 for children, and $36 for seniors. Other trips include kayak trips, leisure floats, kayaking lessons, multi-day trips, or a Native American Interpretive Trip: a paddle or float that includes cultural and historical guidance from a tribal member.

✔ **Pangea Expeditions** (406-239-2392; www.pangea-expeditions.net), 608 Railroad Street, Alberton. The adventuresome folks here focus mainly on the whitewater of Alberton Gorge. They do, on occasion, offer a trip on the Blackfoot River; however, the best concentration of whitewater in the area is on the Clark Fork near the town of Alberton. Call for rates and reservations.

Silver Moon Kayak Company (406-752-3794; www.silvermoonkayaking.com), 1215 N. Somers Road, Kalispell. Silver Moon offers some unique trips in the region. These require little or no experience, but all are done via sea kayak. Their most popular trip is a Flathead River or Flathead Lake summer moonlight paddle. On this trip guests are served hors d'oeuvres and drinks in addition to a moonlight paddle on a gentle section of the Flathead River or calm area of Flathead Lake. They offer kayak instruction and rentals. Inquire for rates.

✔ **10,000 Waves Raft and Kayak Adventures** (406-59-6670; www.10000-waves.com), 1311 E. Broadway, Missoula. This large operation offers whitewater and scenic rafting, inflatable and sit-on-top kayak adventures, kayak instruction, and a whitewater guide school on many of this region's rivers. Their raft trips and kayak lessons range from half-day to five days. They offer day hikes and rentals on rafts, kayaks, and float tubes. Their trips may take you to Alberton Gorge on the Clark Fork River, or down other sections of the Clark Fork or the Blackfoot and Bitterroot Rivers. They work with their guides on teaching the local history and local conservation issues, which the guides then enjoy sharing with guests—making an enjoyable and educational experience for you.

SNOW SPORTS

Ice Fishing
Because of the abundance of lakes in Glacier Country and the length of winter in Montana, ice-fishing opportunities are plentiful. The obvious locale is Flathead Lake (see *To See–Natural Wonders*), with its size and amount of public access points, many of which are open in winter. Other popular lakes to test the ice, and the fishing, are Placid Lake, Salmon Lake, Whitefish Lake, and Lake Como. Holland Lake, Seeley Lake, and Salmon Lake are all popular destinations near Seeley Lake and are accessed by MT 83.

Ice Skating
A little harder to find are developed ice-skating areas. Aside from roughing it on a local pond or lake, the larger towns all have ice rinks and it would be best to

contact the local chambers of commerce for current information. Missoula's **Glacier Ice Rink** (406-728-0316; www.glaciericerink.com), 1101 S. Avenue W. (in the county fairgrounds), and the **Whitefish Ice Rink** (406-863-2477), 725 Wisconsin Avenue (near Whitefish Mountain Resort), are two ice rinks with regular hours and regular maintenance.

Skiing

Glacier Country is home to nearly two-dozen cross-country and downhill ski areas, hundreds of miles of national forest trails, and even more backcountry trails. It would take another entire book to detail all of them. For even more information about local ski areas, especially cross-country areas and trails, please contact any of the businesses listed at the end of this section. They will be able to provide you with maps, trail updates/terrain reports, and more information for your skiing adventure.

Bear Creek Trail is accessed by heading 7 miles south of Libby on US 2, then going west on Bear Creek Road (FR 278). These trails are groomed cross-country ski trails maintained by the Kootenai National Forest and are closed to snowmobiles. There are 5.5 kilometers of trails varying from easy to advanced.

*✍ **Blacktail Mountain** (406-844-0999; www.blacktailmountain.com), 7255 US 93 S., Lakeside. Montana's newest ski area sits on a mountainside with great views of Flathead Lake. They have over 40 kilometers of groomed cross-country ski trails in addition to their lift-accessed downhill terrain. *Lifts:* one triple and two double, a handle tow. *Terrain:* 24 trails—15 percent beginner, 70 percent intermediate, and 15 percent expert; 1,440 feet of vertical. *Average annual snowfall:* more than 250 inches. *Facilities:* base lodge has cafeteria and full-service restaurant and pub. *Ski school:* ski and snowboarding lessons for all ages and levels. *Children:* Their ski groups are named after animals, with Young Fawns ages 4–7, Young Bucks ages 7–13, and Young Blacktails ages 8–15. *Lift tickets:* $34 adults, $28 college students with ID, $24 teens 13–17, $15 children 8–12, $15 seniors over 70, and children under 7 free. For half- and multi-day trips, inquire at the ticket office.

Chief Joseph Cross-Country Ski Trails are accessible at Chief Joseph Pass north of MT 43, about 40 miles south of Hamilton via US 93. The trails are groomed weekly, with eight loop trails that provide a variety of lengths and skill levels. Plowed parking and a toilet and maps are available at the trailhead. There is also a warming hut open December 1–mid-April. These trails are part of the **Bitterroot National Forest.**

Holland Lake Lodge (406-754-2282; www.hollandlakelodge.com) is located 20 miles north of Seeley Lake on MT 83 and it is well marked. In the winter cross-country ski on 25 kilometers of groomed trails. Rentals are available and trails are groomed weekly. This area is for those skiers desiring solitude and beautiful scenery. The lodge has minimal services in winter, but rooms can be had and nearby Seeley Lake has full services and is a very pleasant winter destination.

*✍ **Izaak Walton Inn** (406-888-5700; www.izaakwaltoninn.com) lies across the river from Glacier National Park along US 2 halfway between West Glacier and East Glacier. This Bavarian-style lodge is nestled between Glacier National Park

and the Bob Marshall Wilderness, providing ample opportunity to really get away from the hustle and bustle. Izaak Walton Inn was voted the best cross-country ski resort in the Mountain Region and *Snow Country* magazine named it one of the top 10 cross-country ski resorts in the Rockies. It is listed on the National Register of Historic Places and was constructed in 1939 by the Great Northern Railroad to house winter snow removal crews. Today its 33 kilometers of machine-groomed and tracked trails and extensive backcountry trails cater to all levels of ability. Fifteen kilometers of the trails are rated easiest, 12 are rated more difficult, and 6 kilometers are rated most difficult. Trails are groomed daily and there is a fee to use the trails. Rental equipment is available as well as cross-country ski instruction. The ungroomed trails in and around Glacier National Park provide an opportunity to see mountain goats and majestic mountains and have a true Montana wilderness experience.

✔ **Lost Trail Powder Mountain** (406-821-3211; www.losttrail.com), just off MT 43 and US 93 at the Idaho state border, Conner. Open Thursday through Sunday in season. Located in the **Bitterroot National Forest,** this is a more family-oriented area than some others in the region. This is not a big area, but it's certainly a fun one and an area with little crowds even on the biggest powder day of the year. *Lifts:* 5 doubles, 3 surface tows. *Terrain:* 45 trails—20 percent beginner, 60 percent intermediate, 20 percent expert; 1,800 feet of vertical. *Average annual snowfall:* 300 inches. *Facilities:* base lodge with cafeteria. *Ski school:* skiing and snowboarding lessons for all ages and levels. *Children:* All Mountain Program meets weekly on Saturday or Sunday for 7 weeks. *Rates:* $31 adults, $21 youth 6–12, $4 surface tow only, children 5 and under and seniors 70 and over free; half- and multi-day rates available.

✔ ❀ **Lookout Pass Ski Area** (208-744-1301; www.skilookout.com) is actually on the border of Montana and Idaho along I-90, 30 miles west of St. Regis. It's not a large mountain, but one that receives quite a bit of snow and is easily accessed by I-90. The nice thing about Lookout Pass is that snow comes early, and it snows regularly. And the climate results in snow that tends to be light and fun to ski. There are lodging options in St. Regis or over the hill in Wallace, Idaho. *Lifts:* 2 doubles, 1 rope tow. *Terrain:* 23 trails—25 percent beginner, 50 percent intermediate, 25 percent expert. *Average annual snowfall:* 400 inches. Facilities: a snack bar and deli in the base lodge. *Ski school:* This is the only free ski school in the country, so there is no reason to not get a lesson. *Children:* a few programs, inquire. *Rates:* $23 adult, $20 college students with ID, $17 junior 7–17, senior 62+ $17, rope tow only $8, children 6 and under free.

✔ **Montana Snowbowl Ski Area** (406-549-9777; www.montanasnowbowl.com), take Exit 101 off I-90, then go north on Grant Creek Road, then left on Snowbowl Road; 12 miles northwest of Missoula. For locals in Missoula and visitors, this ski area cannot be beat. Day trips and family vacations are good ideas at this area, overlooking the broad Missoula Valley. There are many options for lodging in nearby Missoula, but the slopeside **Gelandespring Lodge** offers great ski 'n' stay packages. *Lifts:* 2 doubles, 2 handle tows. *Terrain:* 39 trails—20 percent beginner, 40 percent intermediate, 40 percent expert; 2,600 feet of vertical drop. *Average annual snowfall:* 300 inches. *Facilities:* three places on the mountain to

grab food—Double Diamond Café, Grizzly Chalet, and Last Run Inn. *Ski school:* ski and snowboard lessons for all ages and abilities. *Children:* 6-week programs include Polar Bears for ages 4–8, Powder Hounds for ages 6–12, Team Extreme for ages 8–12, Boarderheads for ages 10–16, Shred for ages 10–16. *Rates:* $36 adults, $15 children 6–12, $33 seniors and students; half-day and multi-day rates available.

✦ ✦ **Turner Mountain Ski Area** (406-293-4317; www.skiturner.com), 22 miles north of Libby on Pipe Creek Road. Open Friday through Sunday in season. Small in size, but large in vertical drop and snowfall, Turner Mountain is a nice little secret in a remote corner of Montana—and the locals kind of like to keep it that way. They get plenty of snow, there are lodging options in nearby Libby, and even on most weekends you will feel like you have the mountain to yourself. *Lifts:* one double. *Terrain:* 20 trails—10 percent beginner, 20 percent intermediate, 70 percent expert. *Average annual snowfall:* 250 inches. *Facilities:* snack bar in base lodge. *Ski school:* check for availability. *Rates:* $26 adults, $21 junior, $21 seniors, children 6 and under free; half-day rates available.

✦ **Whitefish Mountain Resort** (406-862-1900; www.skiwhitefish.com), 3840 Whitefish Mountain Road, 8 miles north of Whitefish. This was formerly Big Mountain Ski and Summer Resort (only the name has changed, nothing else). Located in the **Flathead National Forest,** Whitefish Mountain is arguably one of the best mountains in Montana. With more than 3,000 acres, this is one of the largest ski areas in the U.S. and Canada. In addition to the great downhill skiing, terrain park, and full-service mountain village, the resort also is home to 16 kilo-

SNOWBOWL SKI RESORT NEAR MISSOULA

WHITEFISH MOUNTAIN RESORT

meters of cross-country ski trails, a lift-served tubing hill, snowshoeing, sleigh rides, and many other wintertime activities. During summer the mountain is alive with action as mountain bikers can access over 20 miles of trails via the lifts and mountain roads. At the resort and in the town of Whitefish diners and drinkers will find many options to fit any budget. *Lifts:* 1 double, 3 high-speed quads, 5 triples, 4 handle tows. *Terrain:* 93 trails, 4 terrain parks; 2,353 feet of vertical drop. *Average annual snowfall:* 300 inches. *Ski school:* the Snowsports Center offers ski and snowboard lessons for all ages and abilities. *Children:* Kiddie Korner day care for newborns to age 11; variety of group lessons for different ability levels. *Rates:* $54 adults, $45 seniors 65–79 and college students, $40 junior 13–18, $40 children 7–12, free to children 6 and under and to seniors 80 and over, free to Beginner Area and Carpet Lifts. Half- and multi-day rates and packages available.

UNIQUE ADVENTURES This section features a few of the "out of the box" experiences that one can have while in Montana. Most are offered by service providers such as outfitters or professional outdoor schools, some are cruises or the services at a state park, and a few are all-inclusive ranch vacations. However, they all serve up a unique taste (or a collection of everything that may be quintessentially Montana) of a vacation or an adventure in Montana.

Native Ed-Ventures (406-675-0160; www.peoplescenter.org/edventure.htm) is run by the People's Center (see *To See–Museums*) in Pablo. Open most years from May through September, these folks offer a great way to really dive into the culture, history, and present-day life of the people who have lived in this area for thousands of years, and continue to live here today. Native Ed-Ventures provides day programs, customized itineraries, and step-on guides for visitors to the Flathead Indian Reservation. The programs focus on Native American heritage, natural history, and cultural interpretation. Learn the history of the Confederated Salish, Pend d'Oreille, Kootenai tribes, and the Hellgate Treaty of 1855. Tour the tribal government facilities and learn how the treaty impacts the daily lives in present-day affairs. Enjoy a wildlife tour, experience wildlife firsthand, bring your binoculars and cameras. Learn how the Catholic missionaries affected the history of the tribes and continue to affect life today. Meet tribal members and experience the hospitality that makes the tribes unique. Rates are very reasonable, ranging from $40 and up, depending on the tour.

Northwest Connections (406-754-3185; www.northwestconnections.org) is located in the Swan Valley along MT 83, north of Seeley Lake and south of the Flathead Valley. The programs here are for visitors and Montanans looking for a true hands-on vacation—one that is educating, entertaining, and adventuresome. They are a community-based organization specializing in field studies and courses that involve activities that enhance local conservation efforts and your own appreciation for nature and conservation. Options run the entire spectrum from two-day Animal Tracking Clinics to weeklong Backcountry Field Studies deep in the Bob Marshall Wilderness. There are even a few semester- and year-long courses available. The programs and vacations here truly are unique and one-of-a-kind. Contact them for rates, schedules, and more information. The summer courses and adventures book up early so plan ahead.

Cruises to Wild Horse Island State Park are a unique way to experience both Flathead Lake and **Wild Horse Island State Park.** There are several

THE FLATHEAD VALLEY IN WINTER

operators running boat trip and tours to the island. **Pointer Scenic Cruises** (406-837-5617) operates from Bigfork. They offer private cruises to Wild Horse Island, a primitive state park that has bighorn sheep (with full-curl rams), trophy mule deer bucks, eagles, osprey, and a few wild horses. They offer picnics, hikes, and wildlife viewing. Pointer Scenic Cruises also offers twilight and moonlight cruises. Inquire about rates. **Kwa Taq Nuk Marina** (406-883-3636; www.kwa taqnuk.com) is located at the Kwa Taq Nuk Resort in Polson and offers various kinds of boat tours of Flathead Lake. These trips are more of a party-boat atmosphere aboard *The Princess,* which accommodates 48 passengers. Tours run June 15–September 4 and they have a short bay cruise, a Wild Horse Island Cruise, and a twilight cruise. Inquire for rates and reservations.

Dog Sled Adventures (406-881-2275; www.dogsledadventuresmontana.com) is located north of Whitefish in Olney. The tours may be run anywhere near Glacier National Park. If you have not yet traveled by dogsled across a snowy meadow or experienced the thrill of being pulled by working dogs, it is quite a rush and fun for all ages. No experience is required and these folks offer two-hour tours. Inquire for specific rates, operating season (snow-dependent, but usually mid-November through April), and specific directions.

Ranch and Horsemanship Vacations have always been quintessentially Montana, but in recent years the more active ranch vacations (commonly called dude ranch vacations) have been growing in popularity. The ranches listed below all offer guests the opportunity to live and work on a working Montana ranch—if you want to learn, get a little dirty, and live the ranch life, but at the same time have a comfy bed and eat great food, then perhaps an exciting ranch vacation is for you or your family. Many of these ranches can also arrange whitewater rafting trips, guided fishing trips, hikes, and pretty much whatever you would like to do on your vacation. There are several ranches in this region, some of my favorites include **Alta Meadow Ranch** (406-349-2464; www.altameadow.com), Darby; **Bear Creek Guest Ranch** (406-226-4489; www.bearcreekranch.com), East Glacier Park; **Chief Joseph Ranch** (406-821-0894; www.chiefjoseph ranch.com), Darby; **Diamond R Guest Ranch** (406-862-5905; www.diamondr ranch.com), Whitefish; **Double Arrow Resort** (406-677-2777; www.double arrowresort.com), Seeley Lake; **Laughing Water Ranch** (406-882-4680; www .lwranch.com), Fortine; **McGinnis Meadows Cattle & Guest Ranch** (406-293-5000; www.mgmranch.com), Libby; **Pepperbox Ranch** (406-349-2920), Darby; **Rich Ranch** (406-677-2317; www.richranch.com), Seeley Lake; **Triple Divide Ranch** (406-338-5048), Babb near Glacier National Park.

Rocky Mountain Discovery Tours (406-721-4821; www.rmdt.com), 248A N. Higgins Avenue, Missoula. Although headquartered in Missoula (where Capt. Lewis passed through on his return), these folks offer tours for true Lewis & Clark buffs. You can retrace the path the Corps took, immersing yourself in the history and culture of the expedition. You can book a nine-day tour through Montana and Idaho or for the big enchilada you can take the 11-state tour and follow the entire path the expedition traveled from 1804 to 1806—now that is a unique adventure. The packages are all-inclusive (lunch, dinner, lodging, attractions, guides, and speakers), but participants are required to pay transportation from the departure point and home from the endpoint of the journeys. Similar to Lewis & Clark's journey, these trips are unforgettable.

Trailsend Tours (406-387-5763; www.trailsendtours.com), Coram. For those wanting to get intimate with the largest wilderness in the Lower 48, the **Bob Marshall Wilderness,** Trailsend will make it happen. Usually booked in groups (private or a collection of people), your adventure will start with a 45-minute scenic helicopter ride. From there you will be guided on an interpretive hike. If a helicopter ride is not in your cards you can take a scenic and interpretive van ride. Trailsend also offers trail rides, western history and ecological tours, bus tours, hunting and fishing pack trips, and wildlife tours. Inquire about rates.

See also Flathead Lake Raft Company, Silver Moon Kayak Company, and 10,000 Waves Raft and Kayak Adventures under *Paddling/Floating;* and Lodgepole Tipi Village under *Lodging–Other Options.*

✱ Wilder Places

PARKS *See also Glacier National Park at the end of this chapter.*

The listings contained here are only a sampling of the many state, city, and county parks in Glacier Country. For a complete listing of state parks, visit http://fwp.mt.gov/parks/default.html. Here you will find up-to-date fee information, dates and hours of operations, and more.

& **Beavertail Hill State Park** (406-542-5500; http://fwp.mt.gov/lands/site_280871 .aspx). Beavertail Hill State Park is located 26 miles southeast of Missoula on I-90 to Beavertail Hill, Exit 130, then 0.25 mile south on a county road. Just off

LOOKING INTO THE BOB MARSHALL WILDERNESS

I-90 east of Missoula, this small park offers river frontage, tepee rentals, a one-hour walking nature trail through a thick canopy of cottonwoods, and developed campsites and picnic areas. For anglers or casual picnic-goers, this is an easily accessible park.

Finley Point State Park (406-887-2715; http://fwp.mt.gov/lands/site_280032 .aspx) lies 11 miles north of Polson on MT 35, then 4 miles west on a well-marked country road. This park is located in a secluded, mature pine forest near the south end of Flathead Lake. Enjoy one of the 16 campsites here with water and electrical hook-ups, plus a boat pumpout station. This is a great place to swim, camp, or relax and enjoy some quiet on the shores of Flathead Lake.

&. ✍ **Frenchtown Pond State Park** (406-542-5500; http://fwp.mt.gov/lands/site_280880.aspx) is 15 miles west of Missoula on I-90. Take Exit 89, then go 1 mile west on Frenchtown Frontage Road. Plan to bring everyone in the family to this day-use-only park for a whole afternoon of picnicking, swimming, sun-bathing, fishing, sailboarding, kayaking, canoeing, snorkeling, and reading. Non-motorized boating only. This small, spring-fed lake has a maximum depth of about 18 feet and the shores are mostly grass-lined, so swimming and playing along the shoreline are easy and enjoyable.

Lake Mary Ronan State Park (406-849-5082; http://fwp.mt.gov/lands/site _280125.aspx). From US 93 in Dayton, head northwest on MT 352 for 7 miles and you will see the signs. If you are traveling on busy US 93 along the west side of Flathead Lake, this state park offers a great diversion. Just 7 miles west of Flathead Lake, off the beaten path, and shaded by Douglas fir and western larch, this park provides a quiet opportunity to pick huckleberries, hunt mush-rooms, and spot interesting birds. Trails lead into the surrounding area, which abounds in wildflowers and wildlife. You can also fish, swim, and camp.

Thompson Falls State Park (406-752-5501; http://fwp.mt.gov/lands/site _280084.aspx) is 1 mile northwest of Thompson Falls on MT 200. This shaded, quiet campground is located on the Clark Fork River in the rugged and beautiful Cark Fork Valley. This site provides excellent fishing and boating opportunities on the Clark Fork or on Noxon Reservoir. It's also a nice place to walk, bird-watch, or just relax. Kids can fish for trout in the pond, and a riverside trail pro-vides ample river access. A small boat launch is provided, and a full-sized launch for larger boats is available 0.5 mile from the park.

&. **Woodland Park,** at Conrad Drive and Woodland Drive, Kalispell. This is a city park in the heart of Kalispell, but you wouldn't know it on your stroll along the 2 miles of paved paths through stands of pine. You will also see various birds, including Canada geese and kingfishers. In winter the pond is typically frozen and ice skaters glide across the surface. This park was created by the efforts of the citizens of Kalispell. Today it is a great place for a nice little "nature break" while in the town of Kalispell.

FORESTS

National Forests
Bitterroot National Forest (406-363-7100; www.fs.fed.us/r1/bitterroot/) covers

WOODLAND PARK IN KALISPELL

1.6 million acres in southwestern Montana and parts of Idaho. Beginning west and south of Missoula, mostly down the west side of US 93, this national forest is also home to the **Selway-Bitterroot Wilderness, Anaconda-Pintler Wilderness,** and **Frank Church–River of No Return Wilderness.** Boating, hiking, fishing, camping, horseback riding, rockhounding, snow sports, rock climbing, mountain biking, and more are available—in fact, whatever you could dream up there is space to do it in the Bitterroot National Forest. For more information, visit their Web site.

Flathead National Forest (406-758-5204; www.fs.fed.us/r1/flathead/) stretches along the west side of the Continental Divide from the U.S.–Canada border south approximately 120 miles. The 2.3-million-acre Flathead National Forest is home to several ski areas, the **Bob Marshall Wilderness, Great Bear Wilderness,** and **Mission Mountain Wilderness,** the **Jewel Basin Hiking Area,** the Swan Mountain Range, thousands of lakes, hundreds of miles of rivers and streams, and more. The landscape is often rugged and varied as it was built from block fault mountain ranges sculpted by glaciers and is now covered with a rich, thick forest. By providing abundant recreation and a wealth of natural resources, the Flathead is a perfect place to relax and enjoy yourself. Visitors will enjoy a multitude of activities, but be sure to try to pick some huckleberries if they're in season, as no permit is required for up to 10 gallons per adult.

Kootenai National Forest (406-293-6211; www.fs.fed.us/r1/kootenai/) encompasses 2.2 million acres of land in northwestern Montana and into northern Idaho. Accounting for a third of the acreage is the **Cabinet Mountains Wilder-**

ness, a rugged and scenic area. Within this forest is the **Northwest Peaks Scenic Area** (west of Yaak, mostly primitive, and accessed by FR 338), where you can find abundant fishing, hiking, wildlife viewing, and horseback riding. The **Ten Lakes Scenic Area** is home to nearly 100 miles of trails for exploring. This area is accessible via US 93 south of Eureka by taking FR 114 northeast to FR 319. From boating to cross-country skiing, recreational opportunities are plentiful and varied.

Lolo National Forest (406-329-3750; www.fs.fed.us/r1/lolo/) is 2 million acres in size and encompasses most of the land around the Missoula Valley. Similar to other forests in Montana, the diverse ecosystems are home for 17 conifer and 5 hardwood tree species, over 300 bird species, at least 20 fish species, over 60 mammal species, and an estimated 1,500 plant species, including 250 nonnative plant species. Within this forest are record-sized trees, the Montana champion ponderosa pine located in the Fish Creek drainage and a national cochampion western larch near Seeley Lake. For wilderness explorers and visitors looking to get away from the action, **Rattlesnake Recreation Area and Wilderness** provides great recreation less than 15 minutes from downtown Missoula. The **Welcome Creek Wilderness Area** east of Missoula in the Sapphire Mountains is a unique low-elevation wilderness and is a stark contrast to the craggy peaks and rugged terrain most visitors typically associate with wilderness areas. History buffs can visit **Ninemile Historic Remount Depot** (406-626-5201) in Huson. This is a ranger station that has been in place since 1920 and is still a functioning ranger station today. Numerous outdoor activities abound, but two favorites are floating the Clark Fork River and exploring the area around Seeley Lake.

State Forests

State forests are another way to enjoy and recreate in Montana. Of the seven established state forests in Montana, six are in this region—a testament to the climate and geography. State forests in Glacier Country include **Clearwater**

THE JEWEL BASIN HIKING AREA EAST OF KALISPELL

(around Greenough and Seeley Lake), **Coal Creek** (north of Sula), **Swan River** (south of Swan Lake), and **Thompson River** (northeast of Thompson Falls). **The Department of Natural Resources and Conservation** (406-542-4300; www.dnrc.mt.gov) created these state forests to secure timber production and protect crucial watersheds, and many of the lands surrounding these state forests are national forest lands as well. Recreation opportunities abound and most state forests are open year-round.

WILDLIFE REFUGES AND WILDLIFE MANAGEMENT AREAS Many of the public lands in Glacier Country are located in the national forests; however, there are still some interesting lands and areas that are not in a national forest, national park, or state park. Many of these are open year-round but may have specific seasonal closures to protect specific species. It is always best to check regulations before venturing to one of these areas.

♿ **National Bison Range Complex** (406-644-2211; bisonrange.fws.gov/), north of Dixon and northwest of St. Ignatius on MT 212 in Moiese. Open year-round; hours vary seasonally; entrance fees $4 per vehicle, $10 annual Bison Range pass; $10 Golden Age (Senior) Federal Pass; $65 Golden Eagle Annual Federal Pass; $15 annual Federal Migratory Bird Stamp (good at all national wildlife refuges). Most people know the history of the American bison in the West and how the species was nearly wiped out. Although today they are not in danger of becoming extinct, the animals do not roam freely like they once did. The National Bison Range was established in 1908 and is one of the oldest wildlife refuges in the nation. A large portion of the 18,500-acre range consists of native Palouse prairie. Forests, wetlands, and streams are also found here, providing a wide range of habitats for wildlife. Elk, deer, pronghorn, black bear, coyote, and

RIVERFRONT PARK IN MISSOULA

ground squirrels are just some of the mammals that share the area with 350 to 450 bison. More than 200 species of birds also call this area home, including eagles, hawks, meadowlarks, bluebirds, ducks, and geese. There are two major auto routes in the refuge. Only one is suitable for RVs, the 5-mile Prairie Drive–West Loop; the other is a 36-mile loop that gains 2,000 feet in elevation. There are a few short, developed hiking trails, most with interpretive signs, and a few picnic areas. In addition to the National Bison Range, the complex includes four other national wildlife refuges (NWRs): **Lost Trail NWR** (about 40 miles from Kalispell; this has very limited access and use); **Ninepipe NWR** (5 miles south of Ronan on US 93; fishing and wildlife viewing only); **Pablo NWR** (2 miles south of Polson on US 93; fishing and wildlife viewing only); **Swan River NWR** (1 mile south of Swan River on MT 83; wildlife viewing); as well as the **Northwest Montana Wetland Management District,** responsible for managing a number of smaller wetlands.

Skalkaho Wildlife Preserve (406-821-3913; www.fs.fed.us/r1/bitterroot/) lies within the Bitterroot National Forest. This isolated, mountainous 23,000-acre wildlife preserve is a great place to view wildlife as the entire area is closed to hunting. In the spring and summer, look for gray and Steller's jays, dark-eyed juncos, Brewer's sparrows, olive-sided flycatchers, and hairy woodpeckers. Visitors in the fall may see large concentrations of elk and hear bull elk bugle from the high basins in early morning or late evening. Hikers can see mountain goats around Dome Shaped Mountain, near the junction of Trails 313 and 86, which follow the ridge around Skalkaho Basin. Watch for moose along Trail 321 in the Burnt Fork drainage. Mule deer, badgers, coyotes, and black bears are common throughout the preserve. Mountain bicycling is a good way to see wildlife, especially the fall road closure period, October 15–December 1. Trail 313 offers prime opportunities for overnight cross-country ski trips. Since only the first 10 miles of MT 38 are plowed, winter viewing by car depends on snow depth.

OTHER WILD PLACES THAT SUPPORT WILDLIFE ⅙ ✎ ❦ **Rocky Mountain Elk Foundation Wildlife Visitor Center** (406-523-4545; www.rmef.org), 2291 W. Broadway, Missoula. It is hard to miss if you just look for the giant elk statue along W. Broadway west of Missoula. Open year-round, January through May, Monday–Friday, 8 A.M.–5 P.M., and Saturday, 10 A.M.–5 P.M.; June through December, Monday–Friday, 8 A.M.–6 P.M. and Saturday and Sunday, 9 A.M.–6 P.M. They boast about having the newest and largest conservation education facilities in the Northwest—and they are spot on. The Elk Country Visitor Center features hands-on conservation and hunting heritage exhibits for all ages. The center also includes a Lewis & Clark display, an impressive collection of world-record elk mounts, a western wildlife diorama, and a state-of-the-art conservation theater. Shoppers will also enjoy the Elk Country gift shop full of beautiful wildlife art and many hand-crafted and Montana-made creations. The public is welcome and admission is free. Founded in 1984 and headquartered in Missoula, Montana, the Rocky Mountain Elk Foundation is a nonprofit organization dedicated to ensuring the future of elk, other wildlife, and their habitat. The Elk Foundation and its partners have permanently protected or enhanced 5 million acres, a land area nearly twice as large as Yellowstone National Park. Nearly 500,000 acres previously closed to public access are now open for hunting, fishing, and other recreation. The Elk Foundation has more than 150,000 members, a staff of 150, and 11,000 active volunteers.

Wolf Keep Wildlife Sanctuary (406-244-5207; www.wolfkeep.com), via Sunset Hill Road, on the south side of MT 200 just west of MT 83. Open year-round, Thursday–Monday, 10 A.M.–7 P.M. Beginning in 1996 with Carl Bock's purchase of 12 wooded acres, it has evolved into a scenic and secure home for a pack of gray and arctic wolves. For the first six years it was a private nonprofit center, but in 2002 they began allowing public visits to view the pack. Visitors can see the pack and learn about their fascinating social structure and unique individual characteristics, and come away with a better understanding and appreciation for the wolf's special place in our environment.

✳ Lodging

BED & BREAKFASTS

Alberton

Ghost Rails Inn (406-722-4990; www.ghostrailsinn.com), 702 Railroad. The Ghost Rails Inn B&B is located 30 miles west of Missoula, just off I-90 on Alberton's main street. The Ghost Rails Inn (formerly the Montana Hotel) looks like a set from a western movie. This historic railroad hotel has been brought into the 21st century with its 10 appropriately decorated rooms, private baths, cable TV, and free wireless Internet. The whimsical décor and delicious full breakfast, often accompanied by live harp music, make for a memorable lodging experience. This is an ideal place to stay for adventuring in the Alberton area—whitewater rafting, fishing, scenic driving, exploring the Cabinet Mountains. Rates $70–$90.

Bigfork

Bailiwick Farm Bed & Breakfast (406-837-6826; www.ourbailiwick .com) is 3 miles east of Bigfork on MT 209, look for the big yellow house. Webster's dictionary defines bailiwick as "one's special domain."

The innkeepers, Jack and Barbara Bostedt, invite you to see why. Situated on 6 rural acres just 3 miles east of Bigfork, the property has beautiful monarch cottonwood trees and an unobstructed view of the Swan Mountain Range. There are even wild turkeys wandering through the yard and deer raiding the apple trees, and occasionally a glimpse of a black bear. Breakfast at the farm varies with the season. Huckleberry pancakes, French toast, fresh-baked muffins, sweet rolls or biscuits, ham and eggs, fruits, juices—something different every day to get you off to a good start. The Bostedts hope you'll find it's your bailiwick, too. Rates $110 and up.

Beardance Inn and Cabins (406-837-4551; www.beardanceinn.com), 135 Bay Drive. A quaint inn in downtown Bigfork where guests stay in private cabins. Each cabin has at least one double bed, a kitchen, and a private bath. There are no phones or televisions so you have a quiet, undistracted stay. After a day of adventuring the hot tub is a fine place to soak your bones—they even provide complimentary robes. There is a full breakfast and they even have private boat docks for any guests who might be traveling by boat—now wouldn't that be nice. Rates $120 and up.

Columbia Falls

Bad Rock Bed & Breakfast Inn (406-892-2829; www.badrock.com) is south of Columbia Falls on MT 206; look for Bad Rock Drive, then follow the signs. Bad Rock was selected as one of the top 12 inns for the U.S. and Mexico by *Country Inns Bed & Breakfast* magazine and is just 20 minutes from the west entrance to Glacier National Park. The inn rests on 10 rolling acres in a gorgeous farming valley of open fields interspersed with battalions of towering pine trees. Enjoy the spectacular views of the Swan Mountain Range, the quiet countryside, the geese flying overhead, and the coyotes howling at night. They offer three beautiful guest rooms in the house and outside are four rooms in two exquisite square-hewn log buildings with white gas log fireplaces and handmade lodgepole pine furniture. The newest addition is Swan Mountain Cabin, with a king bed upstairs and living space down. The breakfasts are hearty and unique: how about bacon-wrapped polenta or Montana potato pie? These and others are sure to keep you fueled as you explore.

Elmo

Wild Horse Hideaway Bed & Breakfast (406-849-6161; www .wildhorsehideaway.com), 79466 Old US 93. You will be hard-pressed to find a B&B better suited for enjoying Flathead Lake. They have their own beach on Flathead Lake, all rooms have a lake view, and the breakfasts are plentiful. In addition, the groups of pine and cherry trees on the property allow a sense of privacy and a remote feeling. In the evening, pick some Flathead cherries from the on-premise trees and top them on your homemade ice cream while watching the sunset on the lake. Rates $110 and up.

Darby

Tin Cup Lodge B&B (406-821-1620; www.tincuplodge.com), 582 Tin Cup Road. The Tin Cup sits in a beautiful spot in the Bitterroot Valley. Set atop one of the many foothills of the Bitterroot Range, the lodge boasts 80-mile views of the entire valley. All accommodations have custom log furnishings, satellite TV, embroidered robes, private bath, and private entrance. Surrounded on two sides by national forest, you can hike right out of your cabin and onto the trail. A nice aspect of the private cabins here: They have private hot tubs. Outside there is a nice area for evening campfires. The Tin Cup is ideal for folks wanting a quieter stay but a little more luxury than just a cabin in the woods.

Hamilton

Big Sky Bed & Breakfast (406-363-3077; www.bigskybandb.com), drive south on US 93 from Missoula; 2 miles south of Hamilton turn left on Skalkaho Pass Road. Continue 3.75 miles and turn right on South Shoshone Loop (do not take the first South Shoshone Loop road). Keep going another 0.7 mile and take the road to your left up the hill (this is Mariah Lane, which is not marked). It is the first house on the left, 703 Mariah Lane. A newer B&B, this was built with scenery in mind as the two guest rooms (yes, they only have two rooms) have spectacular views of the Sapphire and Bitterroot Mountains. A full breakfast is served each morning along with a homemade dessert in the evenings. Rates $80 and up.

Deer Crossing Bed & Breakfast (406-363-2232; www.deercrossing montana.com) is halfway between Hamilton and Darby. Look for Camas Creek Loop Drive 12 miles south of Hamilton; follow the signs from there. Breakfasts here are had in the sunroom, which offers views of the Sapphire Mountains. There are guest rooms and cabins here. Experience the Charlie Russell Suite, rich in western art and memorabilia, featuring a double Jacuzzi tub; the Big Sky Suite with private balcony and ever-changing views, two gracious guest rooms; the Bunk House Cabin, a restored homestead building with a full bath, charming porch and a hammock strung between two lovely, old crabapple trees; or the new creekside log cabin with full kitchen. Rates $110 and up.

Kalispell

Emerald Sunrise Bed & Breakfast (406-755-4348; www.emeraldsunrise bnb.com), 115 Emerald Cove Road. Located on the shores of Ashley Lake 30 miles west of Kalispell, this is a place for folks who want a retreat away from town. There are two rooms on the property, both are lakeside, with private bath and a private entrance. This is a fun place for anglers or paddlers, as the lake is literally a stone's throw from the rooms. Rates $90 and up.

The Master Suite B&B (406-752-8512; www.mastersuitebedandbreak fast.com), 354 Browns Road in Kalispell. This is a great spot for you and a loved one to get away from it all. With 1,500 square feet of living space on 15 acres, only one couple is booked here per stay—so you've got this all to yourself. The views are incredible, and there is a fantastic sleigh-style queen-size bed, 1.5 bathrooms, and additional amenities. A full breakfast can be had indoors or outside on one of three patios. Afternoon hors d'oeuvres provide a good reason to perhaps enjoy a nap. Rates $195 and up.

Libby

The Huckleberry House (406-293-9720; www.huckleberryhouse), 1004 Main Street, downtown Libby. This is more like a traditional B&B, but it is located in Libby, which is minutes from some of the best recreation in Glacier Country. There are four bedrooms, two of which share a bath. The B&B is within walking distance of downtown Libby, as well as some hiking trails. Breakfasts are hearty and often feature its namesake (the huckleberry) in one way or another. Rates $70 and up.

Missoula

Blue Mountain Bed & Breakfast (406-251-4457; www.bluemountain bb.com), 6980 Deadman Gulch, west of Missoula and 3 miles north of Lolo. The Blue Mountain is situated on 20 acres. The hosts, Brady and Elaine, have created a very relaxing B&B in the heart of some great recreational country. There are only four rooms, which fill up early, but they have three separate buildings on the property, so whether you are a family or a couple, having your own space here is easy. Each room has fantastic views of the Missoula Valley and the surrounding mountains, so you can plan your next adventure while enjoying an evening dessert. Rates $105 and up.

Foxglove Bed & Breakfast (406-543-2927; www.foxglovecottage.net) is located up the Rattlesnake north of Missoula. From I-90, take the Van Buren exit and go north onto Van Buren Avenue. After a bend to the right, the road becomes Rattlesnake Drive. Gilbert Avenue is to your left just before Rattlesnake Drive bends back to the left. Go one block to Lolo. After the stop sign, continue on Gilbert Avenue. Foxglove Cottage is the third house on the left behind a large hedge. This is a charming 100-year-old cottage surrounded by a Victorian garden. There are four distinctively decorated rooms, all with queen-size beds and TV/VCRs. Two rooms share a bath and they can even be combined for a two-bedroom suite. Rates $85 and up.

Goldsmith's Bed & Breakfast (406-728-1585; www.goldsmithsinn.com), 809 E. Front Street, downtown Missoula. Located in a quiet residential area of Missoula, this restored 1911 brick home sits along the banks of the Clark Fork River. With seven rooms, all with private baths, guests are sure to have their own space. But once outside, you can enjoy Missoula's open space. Four of the rooms are suites with private balconies and, weather permitting, breakfast can be had on your private balcony. This is also the closest riverfront B&B to the University of Montana. Rates $90 and up.

Noxon
Bighorn Lodge Bed & Breakfast (406-847-4676; www.bighornlodge montana.com), Bighorn Lane, off MT 53. Almost out of place in what feels like the middle of nowhere, this larger B&B is a gem. With five guest rooms, all with private baths and access to a hot tub, a riverside vacation house, and complete hearty breakfasts set among the carpeted hillsides of western Montana, you may feel like you've found your own personal Eden. Prices include the use of boats and mountain bikes. Dinners can also be added to any stay for an additional fee. Rates $95 and up.

Polson
Hawthorne House (406-883-2723; www.hawthornehouse.com), 303 Third Avenue East, downtown Polson. It is a two-story English Tudor house with seven gables. The quiet shady street just one block from Flathead Lake welcomes the weary traveler. There are four rooms with two shared bath, or two rooms with private baths. Your stay can include a full or continental breakfast with fresh fruit in season. There is a view of Flathead Lake and the beautiful Mission Mountains, a piano in the music room, a cozy living room with TV/VCR, lovely antiques, a plate collection, hat collection, and Indian artifacts. Rates $70 and up.

Somers
Outlook Inn Bed & Breakfast (406-857-2060; www.outlookinnbandb .com), 175 Boon Road. Four guests room provide gorgeous views of Flathead Lake, and each of the rooms has a private bath. The beds themselves are made of hand-peeled logs and offer a great night's sleep. For breakfast try a buffalo sausage and huckleberry pancakes—it might be so much food that you need to lay back down in your nice bed and take a nap while enjoying the view. But you would not want to miss out on exploring Glacier National Park or Flathead Lake or the Bob Marshall Wilderness, all of which are close by. Rates $110 and up.

Stevensville

The Stevensville Hotel (406-777-3087; www.stevensvillehotel.com), 107 E. Third Street, downtown Stevensville. This is a surprisingly fun place to stay while exploring the area around Stevensville. The hotel is located in the former Thornton Hospital, which was built in 1910 and is on the National and Montana Historic Registers. They have seven rooms, and they fill up fast on weekends so book early. The rooms, including two suites, are graced with authentic period furnishings, Supreme Rest queen-size mattresses and luxurious 100-percent cotton linens and custom-tiled baths. Antiques and local art adorn the walls. For those who need it, the hotel has wireless high-speed Internet. In the evenings, sip a cold one or enjoy a homemade dessert on the lovely porch and watch the sun set over the Bitterroot Mountains. Rates $75 and up.

Thompson Falls

Thompson Falls Bed & Breakfast (406-827-0282; www.thompsonfalls bnb.net), 10 Mountain Meadows Lane. Snuggle into the warmth of the handmade quilts that accent the country-style rooms. The spacious and bright Rocky Mountain room offers two queen-size beds and a private bath, as does the Clark Fork River room. The Prospect Creek room has one full and two twin-size beds and a private bath. This room has windows stretching along the full length of the room and then some; it's like sleeping on the porch, but without the chill. Lastly, there is one suite with a king-size bed and private bath, including a jetted tub and large stand-up shower. Rates $90 and up.

Victor

Bear Creek Lodge (406-642-3750; www.bear-creek-lodge.com) is located in a canyon west of Victor. Contact them for exact directions. Bear Creek Lodge (Victor) lies on 150 acres at the mouth of Bear Creek Canyon, next to the Selway-Bitterroot Wilderness. Enjoy understated elegance with massive logs, exquisite decor, superb cuisine, and impeccable service. Eight guest rooms have private baths and entrances. The lodge features fly-fishing and leisure packages for individuals, groups, and family reunions. Hiking, horseback riding, mountain biking, and stream fishing are available right on the property. Rates $275 and up.

Whitefish

Garden Wall Inn Bed & Breakfast (406-862-3440; www.gardenwall.com), 504 Spokane Avenue. The location (right in downtown Whitefish) of this award-winning B&B is only an afterthought once you see the rooms and the detail put into the décor and their antiques. This 1920s home has been fully restored, with five guest rooms, all with period antiques, private baths, and added touches that make a stay special. The three-course breakfast features local ingredients and is good—the owners are also chefs. Rates $110 and up.

Gasthaus Wendlingen Bed & Breakfast (406-862-4886; www.white fishmt.com/gasthaus), 700 Monegan Road. There are many wonderful places to stay in this area, and some fine B&Bs as well, but the Gasthaus Wendlingen deserves special mention, as they have mastered a unique "German-Western" theme. Plus, their location isn't bad at all—8 acres only

2 miles from Whitefish. The breakfasts are very good, with local meats and veggies prepared from family recipes. There are four bedrooms some with private baths and there is a steam room that feels great after a day on the slopes at Whitefish Mountain Resort or after a day spent chasing big cutthroat trout on the fly. Rates $75 and up.

Hidden Moose Lodge Bed & Breakfast (406-862-6516; www.hiddenmooselodge.com), 1735 E. Lakeshore Drive, on the way to Whitefish Mountain Resort. The bedrooms in the appropriately named B&B (it is well hidden from the highway, so watch closely for the sign) are immaculate, with great pillow-top beds, large bathrooms, DVD players, and mini-fridges. Some rooms have Jacuzzi tubs. There is also an outdoor hot tub available for all guests. The main room is a great place for conversation or to plan your next adventure. The breakfasts are tasty and served whenever you would like to eat. Rates $159 and up.

Yaak

River Bend Bed & Breakfast (406-295-5493; www.geocities.com/yaak 59935) is located 11 miles north of Yaak. For those that have been to Yaak—well, 11 miles north of Yaak is pretty remote. This is a great little place, a tad rustic, but if the desire to truly get away from it all strikes you (and to even get away from fluff and pampering), this place is nestled in perhaps the quietest corner of Montana. The breakfasts here are great and there is so much exploring to be done around this B&B that it is certainly worth a visit if you have the time to venture this far off the beaten path. Rates $70 and up.

Browning

Lodgepole Tipi Village (406-338-2787; www.blackfeetculturecamp.com), 2 miles west of Browning on US 2. Situated within sight of the Rocky Mountain Front and the peaks of Glacier National Park, guests can sleep in tipis. Yes, a real tipi. Guests shower in a common shower house with private showers. Meals are served in a common area in the same building housing the showers. This is a unique place and a fun add-on to the already exciting adventures on the Blackfeet Reservation or in Glacier National Park.

Clinton

The Blue Damsel Lodge (406-825-3077; www.bluedamsel.com), 1081 Rock Creek Road, 4 miles from I-90 on the banks of Rock Creek. This used to be a mom and pop B&B, but new ownership has turned it into more of a destination fishing lodge. For folks wanting solitude, it is about 30 minutes west of Missoula. The food is fantastic and rumor has it that they are adding a few more rooms. The lodge is constructed of Montana lodgepoles and has three rooms, two of which share a bath. There are also some cabins on-site. You can choose an assortment of meal plans, as well. Rates $220 and up.

Columbia Falls

See Meadow Lake Golf and Ski Resort under *To Do–Golf.*

Darby

Flying R Guest Cabins (406-821-4631; www.montanaflyingrcabins.com), 4359 West Fork Road, 1.5 miles up West Fork Road, outside of

Darby. The Rogala Family has built a secret little hideaway on the West Fork of the Bitterroot. If you want city lights and fine dining or if your après fishing requires more than enjoying a beautiful sunset, then stay elsewhere. Relax, refresh, and rejuvenate at the Flying R, where the guest cabins sleep up to four people. Trapper Peak, the highest peak in the Selway-Bitterroot Wilderness Area, dominates the view. The cabins feature a complete kitchen, which can be stocked prior to arrival. Sleeping quarters include a queen bed in the loft and a double futon in the living area. Full baths and sunset decks round out these little gems.

Rye Creek Guest Ranch (406-821-3366; www.ryecreeklodge.com), on Rye Creek Road 1.3 miles east of US 93. Choose one of six private, very luxurious log houses, all with stone fireplaces and private outdoor hot tubs, located adjacent to the Bitterroot National Forest. You'll enjoy modern comforts like satellite TV, private phone lines, and fully stocked kitchens. Then step outside into a remote area with Rye Creek nearby and an abundance of recreational opportunities. Keep your eyes open for elk, deer, moose, and other wildlife. Rates $200–$500.

Triple Creek Ranch (406-821-4600; www.triplecreekranch.com), 5551 West Fork Road near Darby. A year-round luxury resort with 19 luxurious cabins nestled under towering ponderosa pines. Features available in cabins range from fireplaces, steam showers, and data ports to hot tubs. Fresh-baked cookies are delivered daily to cabins. In the lodge, share stories of your day while enjoying cocktails and hors d'oeuvres in the lounge. Spend the evening feasting on world-class cuisine in the dining room. Enjoy Executive Chef Jacob Leatherman's Herb and Mustard Crusted Rack of Lamb coated with rosemary, Dijon mustard, and Panko, served with black truffle potato puree and merlot-thyme jus. If you want to be pampered, this is the place.

Hamilton

Bitterroot River Inn and Conference Center (406-375-2525); www.bitterrootriverinn.com),139 Bitterroot Plaza Drive. This is a new and relatively larger hotel in Hamilton and they've done a great job with making it unique. It is large compared to most of the listings in this book, but it is a fine place to stay if you want to be in Hamilton and you want a place that will not break your budget. There are 65 new lodge-style sleeping rooms including suites with garden-size whirlpool tub and fireplace. No pets allowed. The views from every room are fantastic and deluxe continental breakfast will surely keep you going all morning.

Kalispell

Kalispell Grand Hotel (406-755-8100; www.kalispellgrand.com), 100 Main Street. This is a very cool place and the best place to stay in Kalispell if you want a nonchain hotel. They have a deluxe continental breakfast, freshly baked cookies are available, the rooms are large considering the age of the hotel, and the friendly staff aims to please. By staying at the Kalispell Grand you can walk to nearly everything in downtown K-Spell and you are within a half-hour's drive of Glacier National Park and Flathead Lake. The Painted Horse Grille on the premises is a fine place for an evening meal as well. The lobby of the hotel is beautiful and the bar will serve up your favorite drinks, usually stiffer than you might like, but hey, you are on vacation.

Libby

The Evergreen Motel (406-293-4178; www.libbyevergreenmotel.com), 808 Mineral Avenue. The Evergreen Motel is a clean and cozy place minutes from the Kootenai National Forest, Kootenai Falls, and hiking and biking trails. There are microwaves and fridges in every room, pets are welcome, and a few of the rooms have kitchenettes. This place is very nice for the price and the grounds are well manicured. If you want to stay longer than a few nights, inquire about their weekly rates.

Lolo

See Lolo Hot Springs Resort under *To Do–Hot Springs*.

Missoula

The Inn on Broadway (406-532-3300; www.theinnonbroadway.com), 1609 W. Broadway. This basic motel/hotel in downtown Missoula is very convenient to I-90 for quick access to the many outdoor pursuits around town. The owners have completed a massive renovation and this hotel is a great choice for folks who might enjoy downtown Missoula but also want to be able to scoot out of town quickly. The food at the hotel sports bar/restaurant is nothing to write home about, but it is priced right and open late and you will not be disappointed, even at 11 P.M. after hiking or biking all day. They have plenty of rooms, although if you are traveling in the fall and staying on a Saturday night, be sure to make your reservations early because rooms can be hard to find if the University of

Montana football team is playing at home. Rates $90 and up.

The Lodge on Butler Creek (406-542-8307; www.grizzlyhackle.com), 10260 Butler Creek Road; 4 miles north of Broadway on Butler Creek Road, west of Missoula. Just a short drive from the airport and downtown Missoula and secluded in a narrow valley carved by the stream for which it's named, you'll find the Lodge on Butler Creek. This cedar lodge features five bedrooms and picture windows that offer sweeping views of the valley. It was designed with the outdoor enthusiast in mind. Quiet, beautiful, and well appointed, it offers everything you need to relax after a day on the river or hiking in the mountains. It's a lodge that will make you feel right at home. Rates $200 and up.

See also Montana Snowbowl Ski Area under *To Do–Snow Sports*.

Paradise

See Quinn's Hot Springs Resort under *To Do–Hot Springs*.

Polson

Bayview Inn (406-883-3120; www.bayview-inn.com), 914 US 93 E. The Bayview in Polson is a fine place for visitors looking for a reasonably priced option in Polson. This is also a good place to stay if you are planning to explore the west side of the Mission Mountains or the Flathead River below Kerr Dam. Most rooms have views of Flathead Lake. Polson is a fun little town in which to spend some time hanging out in the downtown shops and stores. The Bayview Inn is within walking distance of the marinas, the golf course, and many good places to dine. Rates $80 and up.

Seeley Lake

✪ **The Double Arrow Resort** (406-677-2777; www.doublearrowresort.com), 2 miles south of Seeley Lake on US 2. Situated on several hundred acres near Seeley Lake, the Double Arrow is a great option for folks who want an all-inclusive lodge, but don't want to break the bank. However, don't let the very affordable prices at the Double Arrow fool you—this place is excellent in every aspect. The Double Arrow has a very friendly staff, great food, and is within minutes of hiking, biking, fishing, boating, and more. Whether you stay in one of the guest rooms of the main lodge or any of the log cabins, you'll enjoy a unique blend of European elegance and western hospitality. Standard rooms feature a private bath, charming antiques, and cozy comforters. Deluxe rooms offer more space, choice views, and amenities like kitchenettes, balconies, and fireplaces. Either way, the splendor of Montana is right outside your door. They also have a golf course on the property that is well maintained. Late summer and fall are the best seasons for the Double Arrow. There are lots of options for rooms and cabins, ranging from one- and two-bedroom cabins to four-bedroom houses. Rates $85 and up.

Troy

Linehan Outfitting Company (406-295-4872; www.fishmontana.com), 472 Upper Ford Road. Tim and Joanne, owners of Linehan Outfitting Company, also offer two locations for lodging. Your hosts are exceptionally nice people and will go to extra lengths to ensure you have a great stay. The Linehans have three hand-crafted log cabins in Troy. The homes sit on a mountainside approximately one hour from the Yaak River. Each cabin has a queen bedroom, sleeping loft with two twin beds, one bathroom, a full kitchen, and a gas grill on the porch. And they are well equipped so all you need to bring are groceries and personal items, and plenty of enthusiasm for battling the Kootenai's rambunctious rainbows or trails in the surrounding mountains. They also have a house in Libby available for anglers. The Kootenai Riverhouse, located on the banks of the Kootenai River, is a four-bedroom, two-bath home and is very privately situated on 6.5 acres. Rates $110 and up.

Whitefish

Lakeshore Rentals (406-863-9337; www.lakeshorerentals.us), 1750 E. Lakeshore Drive. Offering quality vacation rentals by the night, week, or month, they have a wide array of houses, condos, cabins, and cottages for you choose from. Some have pools, some are riverfront, some are slopeside. Rates $120 and up.

See also Whitefish Mountain Resort under *To Do–Snow Sports*.

✳ Where to Eat

DINING OUT

Bigfork

♿ **Coyote Roadhouse Restaurant** (406-837-1233; www.coyoteroadhouse.com), 600 and 602 Three Eagle Lane. Open seasonally, reservations required. The name is a little deceiving, as one expects the menu to read like this: Smashed Squirrel Soufflé, Run-down Rabbit Roast, and Plowed Possum Pot-Pie. But that is far from the truth. This place is very good; in fact, it's critically acclaimed as one of the better places in Montana. Their wine list is fabulous, the menu changes quite often, and the food is an exciting blend of Tuscan, Southwestern, Mayan (yes, Mayan), and Cajun influence. Dinners can include veal, seafood, chicken, game, steak, lamb, and more. The salads, baked goods, and desserts are made fresh daily. If you eat so much that you cannot drive home, they also have a few cabins and rooms for rent.

✪ **La Provence** (406-837-2923; www .bigforklaprovence), 408 Bridge Street. If after scaling a mountain talus slope all day or battling the rapids of the Middle Fork of the Flathead you think that there's nothing like some good Provencal food to complete your day, you can find that in Bigfork—and it is worth the extra trip and trouble to find this place. The co-owner is a native of southern France and graduated from the Marie Curie College of Culinary Arts, and his entrees reflect the cuisine of his native region. If you want to keep your day's adventures going, let your taste buds experience a six-course blind-tasting menu. You can also order from the varied menu by choosing from seafood, chicken, game, lamb, beef, and pork. Save room for dessert, for sure. For great food on the go they have a deli on the premises as well, La Petite Provence, offering sandwiches, soups, quiches, salads, and pastries.

Hamilton

Bitterroot Bistro & Catering Company (406-375-2375; www .bitterrootbistro.com), 105 North 2nd Street. If you want gourmet in the valley, this is the place. Dinners are complemented with a wine list that includes some local wines, but also the finest international wines. The menu has a selection of chicken, beef, lamb, fish, and many other options. Be sure to have the Special, at least on your first visit—the food is so good you may return again very soon. Their lunches to go are fantastic and the lunch served at the restaurant is even better. This place is known for its fish and chips. Even though the fish are flown in daily and not from the Bitterroot (which is a good thing because they sell a lot of fish and chips), the Bistro's Fish 'N' Chips are some of the best in the state. They are certainly worth having if you are in the area.

The Spice of Life Café (406-375-2375; www.thespiceinhamilton.com), 163 South 2nd Street. This small place is quite the find in the Bitterroot Valley. Catering to diners who enjoy a little bit of zing and zang to their food, this eatery might be more at home in Manhattan's "Curry Hill" than Montana, but they pull it off with a bang. With a menu covering Indian and Japanese to Cajun and Italian, the Spice of Life features local organic produce when available and Hamilton-grown beef and lamb. They have a great selection of seafood and vegetarian dishes as well, and children also enjoy the menu. This is a fun place to eat with a refreshing menu.

Kalispell

Café Max (406-755-7687; www.cafe maxmontana.com), 121 Main Street. The menu at this downtown Kalispell landmark is always reinventing itself to reflect the seasonal variation in the food of the area; they use the freshest local ingredients. This is one of Kalispell's finer dining establishments, with a smashing wine list and a surprisingly varied seafood selection. The presentation of the food here adds to the taste, but Café Max is a great place to relax and enjoy a nice glass of regional wine in a comfortable environment.

Painted Horse Grille (406-755-8100; www.kalispellgrand.com), 100 Main Street. The Painted Horse Grille is located in the Kalispell Grand Hotel in downtown Kalispell. Chef Keith Matthews creates a menu that reflects local produce and local meats. The menu includes fish, steaks, lamb, and duck, and bison or elk are often featured specials. They offer a friendly, casual upscale atmosphere with full liquor service and a great wine list. Reservations are appreciated, but not a requirement, as most evenings and on the weekend you can walk in and get a table.

Missoula

& **Finn & Porter Missoula** (406-542-4660; www.finnandporter.com), 100 Madison in downtown Missoula. Although this is a national chain, the one in Missoula is continually recommended as one of the best places in town to eat—and it is. The staff is trained to a high level and the service is always enjoyable, paced just right, and the food will never disappoint. Situated at the east end of downtown, you can have a fine-dining experience after a day on the slopes at Snowbowl or mountain biking up the Rattlesnake. Most tables overlook the Clark Fork River, so you can enjoy a drink while watching the fish rise.

& ☻ **Scotty's Table** (406-549-2790), 529 S. Higgins Avenue in downtown Missoula, just south of the Clark Fork River. If country-fried steak and taco nights are not your thing and you want to see Missoula's hip side, Scotty's Table is for you—*but* the food

is worth tasting even if hip and trendy were never your thing. The recipes are fresh, intuitive, and use local ingredients. The servers are well trained and would be at home at a five-star dig in San Francisco or Paris, and the atmosphere is certainly unique to Montana. Dining at Scotty's is a great way to cap a day exploring in Glacier Country, but be prepared to leave full, satisfied, and feeling like you just upped your "coolness" level.

Red Bird (406-549-2906; www.red birdrestaurant.com), 120 West Front Street #105, downtown Missoula. If you've just kayaked solo across Flathead Lake, or seen your first elk in the Bitterroot National Forest, or caught the trophy of your angling life, you can start your celebration with a selection from the Red Bird's great wine list. Located in the historic Florence Hotel, the Red Bird offers some of Montana's finest cuisine. Intimate dining is the norm here and the menu changes often, with daily additions such as fresh seafood and homemade raviolis. Entrees may include bison tenderloin, Rocky Mountain lamb, or wild Alaskan salmon, as well as a few vegetarian options. The chef strives to use local and organic produce.

Paradise

See Quinn's Hot Springs Resort under *To Do–Hot Springs.*

Polson

☻ **Hot Spot Thai** (406-883-4444; www.hotspotthai.com), 1407 US 93. Would you honestly think you could find world-class Thai food in northwest Montana? Neither would most of your fellow readers, but that is the case with this former gas station turned Thai eatery. They have a wide selection of Thai options, as well as a few curries. During the lunch hour, it is not unusual to find doctors and lawyers dining alongside tourists and construction laborers—the food is served relatively fast but it's very good. Throw in their lakeside patio with breathtaking views of the Mission Mountains, Flathead Lake, and the scenic town of Polson, and it is clear why folks traveling from Missoula to Kalispell are only too happy to add an extra hour to their trip just to dine here. Recently, the friendly owners have started a dinner cruise on Flathead Lake.

Lake House Bar, Grill, and Casino (406-887-2115; www.lakehousegrill .com), 4161 E. Shore Route. This is a new addition to the Polson dining scene, and the main appeal here (besides the very good food, of course) is the lakeside dining and outdoor bar with great views of Flathead Lake and the Mission Mountains. They strive to use local produce and meats, which extends to wine from the Mission Mountain Winery (see *To See–Wineries*) just up the road and beer from the Glacier Brewing Company. If you have a few hours to enjoy a drink and watch the sunset, this is a good place to be.

Seeley Lake

♿ **Seasons Restaurant at the Double Arrow Resort** (406-677-2777; www.doublearrowresort.com), 2 miles south of Seeley Lake on MT 83. The food and the view at the Double Arrow dining room are great. The staff here is very friendly and knowledgeable, and you will always get a great meal. The chef uses mostly local meats and strives for local produce. The menu includes chicken, beef, seafood, duck, lamb, and more. In the summer you can dine overlooking a meadow while in the distance the sun sets behind the Mission Mountains, creating quite a backdrop for your evening meal. The bar and dining room are in a log building that has a unique history, and it's certainly worth spending a little time there as well. Be sure to peruse the photographs in the bar as the nostalgia of the log building and the photographs are sure to delight.

Whitefish

419 Wine Bar & Restaurant (406-862-9227), 419 E. 2nd Street. Here you will find one of the area's newest and more chic hangouts, located above the Wasabi Sushi Bar (a very good place in its own right). Relax, you can get sushi upstairs as well. In the wine bar there are nearly three-dozen wines available by the glass. The waitstaff is professional and trained at pairing wines with meals, and they better be because there are over 150 wines available by the bottle. Beyond sushi, other options include seafood, steak, duck, lamb, chicken, and more. This is all set in contemporary fashion, including a fireplace and fantastic views.

Pollo Grille (406-863-9400; www .pollogrill.com), 1705 Wisconsin Avenue. As the name suggests, the specialty here is chicken. But don't be fooled, this is a fine-dining establishment, and you will be pleasantly surprised at the unique and tantalizing ways chicken can be dressed up. Reservations are highly recommended. If you just can't handle the bird, they do offer fine selections of steak, lamb, seafood, and pork. You can choose your sides, and there are even some vegetarian options as well. A children's menu is also available.

Rising Sun Bistro (406-862-1236), 549 Wisconsin Avenue. This one-time house has been converted into a French-style bistro. You have to drive past this fun place on your way to Whitefish Mountain Resort, so why not plan for a relaxing dinner after sliding down the slopes all day? The building previously housed Whitefish Gardens. The owners have embraced the former occupants, and in the spring and summer you can dine in an outdoor garden with great views. They only serve lunch and dinner, but their Sunday brunch is the best in the valley.

Tupelo Grille (406-862-6136; www .tupelogrill.com), 17 Central Avenue. With a name like this, it must be either a shrine to Elvis's birthplace or a restaurant that is strictly Cajun. Thankfully, it's the latter, and the chef here whips up some of the best Cajun, Creole, and southern cuisine in the Pacific Northwest. The menu includes the usual Cajun favorites like crawfish, shrimp, gumbos, jambalayas, grits, and a few others, but they also understand that not everybody loves Cajun all the time so they've added some steak, seafood, and a few other less spicy options. Vegetarians will also have plenty to choose from. A well-thought-out wine list accompanies the enticing menu as well.

See also Whitefish Mountain Resort under *To Do–Snow Sports.*

EATING OUT

Bigfork
& ✈ **Brookies Cookies** (406-837-2447; www.brookiescookies.com), 191 Mill Street. The smell is almost enough to keep you in this place, but the fresh-baked cookies will seal the deal—chocolate chip, snickerdoodle,

peanut butter, ginger, and their house specialty, the Java Jumble. There are also other fresh-baked goods like cinnamon rolls if cookies are not your thing.

Showthyme (406-837-0707; ww.showthyme.com), 548 Electric Avenue. They serve dinner in a very casual environment at this cleverly named restaurant. Try their Chicken Rellen "Montana," which is an original featuring an entire chile stuffed and surrounded with goodies, including cheese, chicken, shrimp sauce, tortilla, and rice—tasty. Other menu items include chicken, veal, lamb, steak, pastas, and more. The wine list leans toward local wines and some internationals, and they also serve cocktails and have a good selection of micros. Children's menus are available. Be sure to bring your appetite and be ready for some creative cuisine.

Columbia Falls
Montana Coffee Traders (406-892-7696), 30 9th Street West. One of several Montana Coffee Traders located throughout the Flathead Valley, the Columbia Falls establishment provides its customers with a unique coffeehouse experience. Located in the old Pines Café & Fish Museum, you can see the giant pine tree in the middle of the café and the fish on the walls. Enjoy a soothing latte or let them satisfy your appetite with a full breakfast and lunch menu. Free wireless Internet. Fun for the whole family, or a nice place just to hang out and read a book by yourself.

Darby
Dotson's Saloon (406-821-0209), 114 Main Street. Dotson's Saloon has been around for over 80 years. It was

erected on the exact site where James Darby, who named the town, lived. The Higgins family bought the saloon from Everett Dotson over 50 years ago and still operate it today. This is a great place for a cold beer and some people watching. The food is good and very reasonably priced, and there is live music and dancing most weekends, along with live poker games.

Hamilton

 ♿ **Nap's Grill** (406-363-0136), 220 North 2nd Street. Nap's Grill has been a local favorite in the Bitterroot Valley since opening in 1993. Known for huge portions of fresh food prepared on an open char-broiler, Nap's has garnered many awards, including "Best Burgers," "Best Steaks," and "Best Salads" in voting by residents of the valley. Also Nap's has been listed in the book "*Where the Locals Eat*," a guide to the best restaurants in America, each year since 1997 for steaks and hamburgers. It's a must-stop when traveling through the beautiful Bitterroot Valley.

A Place to Ponder–Bakery & Café (406-363-0080), 166 South 2nd Street. This cute little bakery has the best pastries and baked goods in town and also makes a great latte. If you are looking for that early morning fix of caffeine and baked goods this is the place. The lunches are all very good, and the menu ranges from pizzas to DIY sandwiches.

Maggie's (406-363-4567), 217 Main Street. Maggie's is a fun blend of various types of cooking. For a nice meal with a good wine list, this place works quite well. Maggie's features French, Mediterranean, and American regional cuisine and offers daily breakfast and lunch concurrently and dinner Thursday through Sunday. Chef/owner

Maggie Sheridan is French and San Francisco–trained and offers true bistro-style dining, with a quaint European ambiance and beautiful mountain views.

Hot Springs
See Symes Hot Springs Hotel under *To Do–Hot Springs*.

Kalispell
Bulldog Pub and Steakhouse (406-752-7522), 208 1st Avenue E. Mostly inhabited by locals, the Bulldog is a nice casual place to go for steaks and burgers. It can be hard to find a steak that is cooked right, but at the Bulldog you don't have to worry about that. They also serve chicken, pastas, and seafood, so the menu will satisfy all tastes and budgets.

Vivienne's Fifth Street Café (406-752-8436), 21 5th Street E. This is mainly a breakfast and lunch place with a comfortable décor that invites you to stay as long as you wish. There are many selections, most with the health-conscious eater in mind. However, the portions are large and the food is very good—with homemade soups, sandwiches, breads, and daily lunch specials. On Wednesdays they even have a proper English tea time.

Libby
Red Dog Saloon & Pizza (406-293-8347), 6788 Pipe Creek Road. This is a classic Montana eatery—peanuts and sawdust on the floor, a great jukebox, and good food. Their specialty is pizza, but they have other items on the menu as well; perhaps try one of their great steaks. When you walk into this place you do not feel like a stranger in a strange land, but rather like one of the locals, which on any given day could be a fishing guide, a logger, a banker, or a carpenter.

Libby Café (406-293-3523), 411 Mineral Avenue. The owners, Gary and Paulette, make dining here a unique experience. The food is very good and the servings are very generous. Bring your appetite or be sure to ask for a box. This is the place for a big breakfast: try the huckleberry pancakes. For lunch or dinner, the country-fried steak is good. And save room for a huckleberry swirl—it may be the best dessert you have while in Montana.

Lolo

See Lolo Hot Springs Resort under *To Do—Hot Springs.*

Missoula

Bernice's Bakery (406-728-1358), 190 South Third Street W. Bernice's is a Missoula institution for baked goods and quality coffee. Known more as a gathering place for Missoula's more "earthy" crowd, the baked goods here are some of the best in the state. Whether you are heading out for a day of excitement or just a stroll around town for some local Missoula color, stop in and try a great latte and an even better pastry.

& ✐ **HuHot Mongolian Grill** (406-829-8888; www.huhot.com), 3521 Brooks Street. I've shied away from mentioning chain restaurants and motels throughout this book, but HuHot in Missoula is just such a fun place to eat, and it has something for everyone. Kids and adults will enjoy creating their own "Mongolian grill dishes" and then watching the chef cook them up on a massive grill. This allows picky eaters (many of which are kids) to literally create their own special meals, complete with an assortment of tasty sauces, oils, and spices. One price gets you in and you

can have as many passes through the goodie and grill line as you want.

Oxford Bar & Café (406-549-0117), 337 North Higgins. This is another Missoula institution. The food is good, not stellar, but the bar is one of the best in Montana, and there are few places in the state better for trading stories and meeting new friends than the Oxford. It is a historic landmark and has been a legend in Missoula for one hundred years. At the Oxford you will share a drink with bankers, loggers, stockbrokers, mill workers, senators, and college students. It has been featured in *Time* and *People* magazines and is worth the hype.

The Old Post (406-721-7399), 103 West Spruce. There are lots of places to dine in Missoula and most are pretty good with quality service and a varied menu. However, every now and then after a long day of trekking or exploring nothing satisfies like a big juicy burger and a cold beer. The thing I like about the Old Post is that the food is good, the beer is cold, and they have a "White Trash Wednesday" where a great burger and a PBR are only $5. Enough said.

Paul's Pancake Parlor (406-728-9071), 2305 Brooks Street. The gruffness of the place will quickly fall by the wayside once you sink your teeth into one of their breakfasts. Breakfast is served all day, but the folks here mix things up with a separate lunch and dinner menu. The food is always served fast and hot and the pancakes are great if you are heading for a big day outdoors in Glacier Country.

Sean Kelly's (406-542-1471), 130 West Pine Street. Sean Kelly's is basic pub food but reasonably priced and always served with a smile. The best part about this place is the people watching on a hot summer day. Enjoy a table outside and go for one of their signature burgers, pizzas, or salads. Talented local and regional bands often perform in the evenings, so if the day's activities didn't provide enough action you can get more at Sean Kelly's.

Tipu's Tiger Indian Cuisine (406-542-0622), 115½ South 4th West. It may seem a tad unusual to find Indian cuisine listed in a guidebook for Montana, but Tipu's is a special place. Not only is it the only Indian restaurant in Montana, but it serves lots of food at a very reasonable price. Many of the locals are also in agreement that a dish of Tipu's curry is a perfect accompaniment to a day spent biking, hiking, fishing, rockhounding, or whatever else floats your boat— especially in the heat of summer when the spicy curries cool down the body. Tipu's makes all its curries in-house and has a following from across Montana and the northern Rocky Mountains.

Polson

&. **Rancho Deluxe Steak House and Rio Café** (406-883-2300), 602 6th Street West. This local joint has been around since the 1930s. Their prime rib is fantastic and served with real horseradish, not the fake blended stuff. They have seafood, pasta, chicken, and a few other options on the menu. The adjacent Rio Café is a southwestern-styled place with a menu that reflects its décor. Both places have a full bar and a casino adjoins the two. The dining room overlooks Flathead Lake and is an enjoyable place to have a meal.

Whitefish

&. **Buffalo Café** (406-862-2833), 514 3rd Street. They will brew fresh coffee in front of you in a French press. After that, a savory breakfast arrives. With huevos rancheros, granola and yogurt, biscuits and gravy, pancakes, breakfast burritos, and more, everyone should find something to enjoy. Lunch has just as many choices, but I really like their quesadillas. A varied kid's menu is also available.

Mambo Italiano (406-863-9600), 234 E. 2nd Street. The Italian food here is almost all made from scratch. The gnocchi is fabulous and sure to refuel your body after a day exploring the hillsides around Whitefish. They also have all the other Italian dishes and they're all great—there is just not enough time, or stomach room, to try them all in one visit. Recently they have added an exciting low-carb menu. Their wine list is thorough and the homemade desserts are worth a try.

Great Northern Bar & Grill (406-862-2816), 27 Central Avenue. This is a happening place in Whitefish with live music most nights and very good beer. The food is casual pub fare, but there's plenty of it. There are a few pool tables and a younger crowd frequents this place. For around $6 you can eat your fill and have plenty of good people watching.

Quickee's (406-862-9866), 28 Lupfer Avenue. Recently voted as having the best sandwiches in Whitefish, Quickee's is perfect for those explorers who want lots of food and fast. The sandwiches pack well and are perfect for throwing in a pack for a day of fishing, biking, hiking, or horseback riding. The name comes from the rumors around town that the restaurant is located in the town's original brothel—you'll have to visit and make your own decision.

✳ Special Events

January: **Annual Ski Fest,** Essex. A worldwide celebration of cross-country skiing, featuring family activities, equipment demonstrations, free ski lessons, discounted ski rentals, and free ski trail passes. Special room rates are available. This is a great way to get acquainted with cross-country skiing. The weekend offers fun for the whole family.

❧ **Winterfest,** Seeley Lake. This action-packed festival takes place the last two weekends of January. It includes Nordic ski races and clinics, free dogsled rides, children's activities, a snow-sculpture contest, and a Christmas tree–fueled bonfire.

February: ❧ **Whitefish Winter Carnival,** Whitefish. For nearly 50 years the whole town and Whitefish Mountain Resort have teamed up for some serious winter fun—ice sculptures, ski races, horse-drawn skiing, snowman contests, and more.

March: **Irish Fair,** Libby. Celebrate Celtic heritage with music, food, dancing, and more.

April: **Black Powder Shoot,** Libby. An exciting marksmen's contest featuring sharpshooting, knife throwing, tomahawk throwing, fire building, and dynamite shooting.

❧ **Montana Storytelling Roundup,** Cut Bank. Storytellers, artists, and entertainers from around the country gather to share tales and talents at the state's only annual storytelling event.

May: ❧ **International Wildlife Film Festival,** Missoula (406-728-9380; www.wildlifefilms.org). This weeklong festival includes showings of award-winning films, the WildWalk Parade, and hands-on educational activities and workshops among other events.

Loon and Fish Festival, Seeley Lake. A Memorial Day festival celebrating local wildlife that includes interpretive talks, kids' activities, an art show, and wildlife viewing.

June: **Montana Mule Days,** Hamilton. Montana's largest mule and donkey show, with over 100 classes featuring driving, riding, cattle, and fun events. Competition comes from up to six different states. Camping is available on grounds, and there are commercial booths and food, along with a covered grandstand and family entertainment. You'll get more than your money's worth at Montana Mule Days.

July: **Annual North American Indian Days,** Blackfeet Indian Reservation. The largest annual event held by the Blackfeet Indians draws tribes from both the U.S. and Canada and includes drumming, dancing contests, arts and crafts, games, and more.

Arts in the Park, Kalispell. A 3-day celebration of the arts sponsored by Hockaday Museum of Art (see *To See–Museums*) that includes an outdoor art show and sale.

Bitterroot Valley Bluegrass Festival, Hamilton. An annual family-friendly event that features not only great music but also workshops for instrument players, arts-and-crafts vendors, and food.

International Choral Festival, Missoula. Hundreds of choir singers from around the world meet in Missoula to share their love of music with concerts that are open to the public.

Lewis & Clark Festival, Cut Bank. An annual community celebration commemorating the explorer's travels through the region, including a children's parade, an all-ages parade, a farmer's market, free concerts, a talent show, an arts-and-crafts fair, and more.

Two Rivers Rendezvous, Libby. An all-ages event re-creating an 1820s–1840s fur traders' camp and rendezvous, with shooting contests, games, and camping.

August: **Cabin Fever Quilters Show,** Superior. This annual quilt show is held by the Cabin Fever Quilters of Mineral County, Montana, in conjunction with the Mineral County Fair. The show exhibits quilts made by local quilters using a wide variety of techniques.

Eureka Montana Quilt Show, Eureka. An annual show with workshops and quilt sales to benefit the Tobacco Valley Historical Village (see *To See–Historical Landmarks, Places, and Sites*).

∂ **Huckleberry Festival,** Trout Creek. A free celebration of huckleberries in the Huckleberry Capital of Montana, with a huckleberry pancake breakfast, arts-and-crafts vendors, fun run/walk, kids' games, a huckleberry dessert–making contest, and more.

September: *∂* **Festival of the Book**, Missoula. A three-day celebration of books, writers, and anything else with the written word. It includes readings, workshops, literary contests, book signings, and more.

Libby Nordicfest, Libby. A yearly celebration of Libby's Scandinavian heritage that includes the International Fjord Horse Show, children's

events, food vendors, a parade, an art show, and more.

October: **Montana Watercolor Watermedia National Exhibition,** Bigfork. Artists from across the nation and Montana enter this highly rated monthlong show. Seventy-five paintings are chosen by a nationally known watermedia artist each year. Cash awards are given as well as merchandise awards totaling over $5,000.

Tamarack Time! Bigfork. Since the tamarack, or western larch, attains greatest size and abundance in western Montana, it is particularly appropriate that the time of spectacular color change be the occasion for the Flathead's autumn celebration.

December: *∂* **Whitefish Christmas Stroll**, Whitefish. Wrap up in your best holiday garb and spirit and get ready to stroll. Visit the stores, ride a horse-drawn wagon, try a roasted chestnut, enjoy enchanting Christmas sounds, and treat yourself to the delicious food and beautiful crafts the street vendors have to offer.

First Night Missoula, Missoula. First Night Missoula is an annual community New Year's Eve celebration of the arts. Hundreds of performing, visual, and literary artists showcase their diverse talents in more than one hundred events throughout Missoula. This spirited, cultural celebration is open to the entire community and is alcohol and drug free. Produced by the Missoula Cultural Council.

WATERTON-GLACIER INTERNATIONAL PEACE PARK

One would be hard-pressed to find an area of the Lower 48, or in all of North America, for that matter, as strikingly beautiful as Glacier National Park and its immediate environs. The park was established in 1910 by an act of Congress, but it took natural forces millions of years to sculpt the park into what it is today—home to 175 named mountains, 200 lakes, 500 streams, and nearly 40 glaciers. Many people assume the park is so named because of the abundance of small glaciers found here; however, it's actually named from the role glaciers and the ice age played in shaping the more than 1 million acres that make up Glacier National Park.

Before Anglos explored this area, the Blackfeet Indians hunted and gathered here seasonally. The Continental Divide literally runs through the middle of the park (from northwest to southeast), and for even the untrained eye, it can almost be traced along the ridgelines of the towering peaks. In fact, there are several places where you can straddle the Divide. Additionally, these mountains have streams that eventually flow into the three major drainages in North America—Hudson Bay (the St. Mary River in the northeast corner of the park), the Gulf of Mexico (all streams on the east side of the Divide), and the Pacific Ocean (all streams on the west side of the Divide). Glacier National Park is home to amazing scenery and outdoor recreation, but it is also home to nearly 350 structures listed on the National Register of Historic Places, some of the best fishing in the region, some exciting whitewater rafting, and almost 800 miles of maintained hiking trails.

In 1932 the governments of Canada and the United States agreed to combine the land that was Glacier National Park (in the U.S.) and the land that was Waterton Lakes National Park (in Canada) into the Waterton-Glacier International Peace Park. This was the first such park of its kind in the world. Waterton Lakes National Park is very similar in topography to Glacier, although not nearly as large. Glacier was designated a World Biosphere Reserve in 1976, and Waterton followed suit in 1979. Later, in 1995, the two parks earned designation as a World Heritage Site.

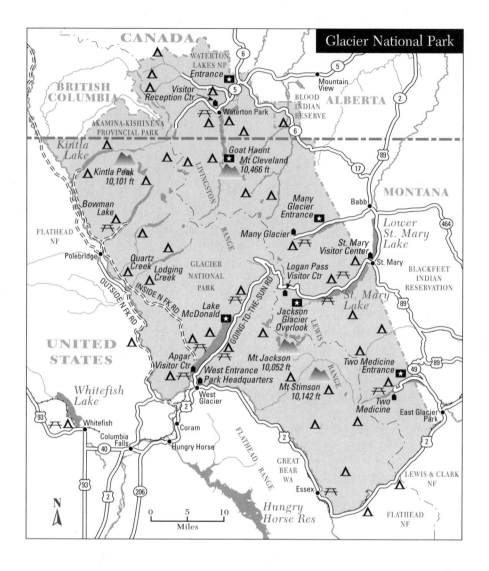

Glacier National Park

Today nearly 2 million people pass through these parks each year. The sights, sounds, and breathtaking beauty of these two parks is always underrated in prose and photographs—the parks really needs to be seen to be truly appreciated.

This guidebook will not attempt to detail every nook and cranny in Glacier, although it's a good start for planning a trip here. There are few listings for Waterton, but the focus of this book is Montana and therefore primarily features Montana listings. If you plan to venture across the border be sure to bring a passport, as new regulations require passports for reentry into the U.S., even for U.S. citizens. For more information on U.S. Customs at the border, visit www .customs.gov, or call 250-887-3413. If you are planning to visit Waterton, please see *Guidance*.

GLACIER NATIONAL PARK'S MOUNTAINS ARE SPECTACULAR FROM ANY ANGLE

If you are planning a backcountry adventure it is strongly suggested that you begin well ahead and contact the Park Service, as they can help with selecting backcountry campsites, bear closures, trail closures, and many other important aspects of backcountry travel. If you are planning to stay at any of the park-operated lodges, keep in mind that many also offer dining; therefore, these listings have been combined and are located in a single section.

GUIDANCE **East Glacier Chamber of Commerce** (406-226-4403; www.east glacierpark.org), P.O. Box 260, East Glacier Park, MT 59434. A small, quaint town serving much of the east side of Glacier. The friendly folks here can help you start planning a trip to the east side of the park.

&. **Glacier National Park** (406-888-7800; www.nps.gov/glac), Park Headquarters, P.O. Box 128, West Glacier, MT 59936. Located at the administrative hub of the park (West Glacier), the headquarters are open all day every day year-round. However, keep in mind that most roads are only open in summer and it is vital to contact the headquarters for current road information—even in summer, snowstorms or landslides still may cause road closures. Entrance rates vary by season, with seven-day, seasonal, or year-round passes. Inquire for specific seasonal rates.

Waterton Lakes National Park of Canada (403-859-2224; www.pc.gc.ca/ waterton), Box 50, Waterton Park, AB, Canada T0K 2M0. Open daily, year-round; entrance fees vary seasonally and by duration of stay.

Waterton Lakes National Park Chamber of Commerce and Visitors Association (403-859-2224; www.watertonchamber.com), Box 55, Waterton Lakes National Park, AB, Canada T0K 2M0.

See also the following listings under *Guidance* at the beginning of this chapter: Bigfork Area Chamber of Commerce, Blackfeet Nation/Blackfeet Indian

Reservations, Browning Town Center, Columbia Falls Chamber of Commerce, Flathead Convention and Visitor Bureau, Glacier Country Regional Tourism Commission, Kalispell Chamber of Commerce, and Whitefish Chamber of Commerce.

GETTING THERE Glacier National Park lies in the northwest corner of Montana, near Flathead Lake. From the south, Glacier can be accessed by US 93 and MT 83, and then via US 2 on the west side of the park. From the east side, US 89 and US 2 meet near Browning, and then US 2 heads west to the southern boundary of the park and US 89 follows the eastern boundary. Near Columbia Falls and along the western border of the park, Outside North Fork Road (MT 486) parallels the boundary. (See also *Airports, AMTRAK,* and *Bus Service* in "What's Where in Montana.")

MEDICAL EMERGENCIES Keep in mind that much of Glacier is very isolated backcountry and any emergencies in the backcountry could be, and often are, life-threatening. It cannot be stressed enough that for any backcountry adventure, go with a licensed professional or contact the Park Service well ahead of your trip. (See also *Medical Emergencies* at the beginning of this chapter.)

✳ To See

VISITOR CENTERS Apgar Visitor Center, 2 miles north of West Glacier on the south side of Lake McDonald. Open daily May 1 through September 30,

THE GOING-TO-THE-SUN ROAD IS ONLY OPEN IN SUMMER—FOR OBVIOUS REASONS

TWO MEDICINE LAKE

9 A.M.–5 P.M.; open 8 A.M.–7 P.M. for extended summer hours from the end of June to just after Labor Day; shorter hours into October and April; weekends only from November to May.

Logan Pass Visitor Information Center, 18 miles west of St. Mary on Going-to-the-Sun Road. Open daily early June through mid-October, 9:30 A.M.–4: 30 P.M.; open 9 A.M.–7 P.M. for extended summer hours from the end of June to just after Labor Day. Closed mid-October to early June.

Many Glacier Ranger Station, west of Babb on US 89 via the Many Glacier entrance. Open from the end of May through mid-September, 8 A.M.–5 P.M.

Park Headquarters Building, located just before the park's entrance at West Glacier. Open weekdays except holidays, 8 A.M.–4:30 P.M.

St. Mary Visitor Center, just west of St. Mary off US 89. Open mid-May through mid-October, 8 A.M.–5 P.M.; open 8 A.M.–9 P.M. for extended summer hours from the end of June to just after Labor Day.

Two Medicine Ranger Station/Camp Store, west of US 49 at Two Medicine Junction. Open mid-May through mid-September, 8 A.M.–4:30 P.M.

HISTORIC LANDMARKS The abundance of historic buildings in this park is always surprising. And thanks to the efforts of many dedicated individuals, past and present, they are restored and protected today. The **Great Northern Railway Buildings National Historic Landmark** makes up a good chunk of the protected buildings. They are grouped in five separate building arrangements:. the **Belton Chalet, Granite Peak Chalet, Many Glacier Hotel, Sperry Chalet,** and **Two Medicine Store.** Most of these lie within or adjacent to the park. Constructed from 1913 to 1915, these buildings have a unique style—one that was used for structures by park concessions during the initial opening of the park. Today, Belton, Granite Peak, and Sperry chalets have been restored and are in good condition, and rooms can be had for very reasonable rates. Many Glacier Hotel has undergone a massive restoration and some say the hotel is back to its former glory—even if the rooms and the floors are not as luxurious as they once were. The views from the hotel are amazing. For more details and contact information, see their individual listings in the *Lodging* section.

SCENIC DRIVES **Chief Mountain International Highway** (MT 17/Alberta Highway 6) is the major route connecting Glacier with Waterton Park in Canada. It is open from mid-May to late September, with hours varying according to season. It is closed for nighttime travel. The entire length of this drive is gorgeous—a good reason to travel it during the day. Views of the front range of the Rocky Mountains are spectacular on this drive, so be sure to plan some extra time for photographs and perhaps a short hike or two off the road.

East Glacier via Browning to Babb, US 2 from East Glacier to Browning, then US 89 to Babb, via St. Mary. Although not a designated scenic drive, this route will provide you with an amazing contrast of forested mountainsides, vast windswept High Plains, gorgeous views of the Rocky Mountain Front, and views of the rugged peaks of Glacier National Park. September is one of my favorite times of the year to make this drive because the aspens and cottonwoods leaves are changing, wildlife abounds, and there is certainly less traffic than in the summer tourist season.

THE FAMOUS GOING-TO-THE-SUN ROAD PROVIDES LIMITLESS VIEWS

Going-to-the-Sun Road is a 52-mile adventure along a narrow, winding paved two-lane road between St. Mary on the east side of the park and West Glacier on the west side. To give you an idea of the splendor and spectacle of this road, it is listed on the National Register of Landmarks. The road took 11 years to build and was completed in 1932. The road itself winds, and winds, and winds, and then winds some more up the sides of mountains. The views truly are too much for words and have to be experienced firsthand to be appreciated. Certain vehicle length and height restrictions are in effect, so be sure to inquire before venturing out, and if you want to leave the driving to somebody else so you can enjoy the views and not worry about staying on the road, look into a guided auto tour (see *To Do–Unique Adventures*).

WILDLIFE Glacier National Park and the surrounding country is home to wolves, grizzly bears, black bears, elk, deer, mountain goats, mountain lions, foxes, coyotes, and more. The birdlife is astounding, and the flora mind-blowing. One of the best ways to see wildlife in this area is to get out of your car and venture at least a mile or two from the road. (As always in the backcountry, take the necessary precautions; the park headquarters can assist you in planning for a backcountry trip.) To spot wildlife with a little effort, simply drive slower and pull off at the many pullouts and take a quick gander. One favorite place to look for mountain goats is **Walton Goat Lick Overlook** along US 2 near Essex. During spring and early summer, groups of mountain goats gather to socialize and eat mineral salts on several cliffs along US 2, providing folks with many viewing opportunities. The best times are sunrise and sunset, as the cliffs become too warm for the mountain goats through the middle of the day.

✳ To Do

BICYCLING **Glacier National Park** restricts cycling to roadways only; however, there is one 2-mile hiking and biking trail from Apgar Visitor Center to West Glacier. The main road in the park is the Going-to-the-Sun Road, and its narrow nature (with busy auto traffic) and extremely steep terrain make it a challenge for cyclists. And portions of the road are actually closed to bike traffic during summer months. It is best to inquire locally about road closures and seasonal cycling opportunities.

BOATING **Glacier National Park** allows boating at Bowman Lake, in the northwestern corner of the park and accessed by Inside North Fork Road; Lake McDonald, located near the west entrance via Going-to-the-Sun Road; St. Mary Lake, located just

A PAIR OF MOUNTAIN GOATS

west of the St. Mary entrance; Swiftcurrent Lake, located near Many Glacier; and Two Medicine Lake, located just west of the Two Medicine entrance. All of these lakes have boat ramps and permit motorized, private boats. Nearly all of the other lakes allow hand-carried and hand-propelled watercraft. However, it is your responsibility to inform yourself about rules, regulations, closures, and fees.

Glacier Park Boat Company (406-257-2426; www.glacierparkboats.com) rents motorboats, canoes, sea kayaks, and rowboats at various locations throughout the park: Apgar, Lake McDonald, Many Glacier, St. Mary Lake, and Two Medicine. It is very important to inquire about rates and reservations—and do so as early as possible because things book up quickly. Last-minute rentals are often available, but if you can plan in advance, all the better. They also provide exciting boat tours and guided hikes.

CAMPING Glacier National Park has 13 developed campgrounds and 66 back-country campsites. Developed campgrounds include **Apgar,** handicapped accessible and open early May through mid-October; **Avalanche,** handicapped accessible and open early June through early September; **Bowman Lake,** open mid-May through mid-September; **Cut Bank,** open late May through late September; **Fish Creek,** handicapped accessible and open June 1 through early September; **Kintla Lake,** open mid-May through mid-September; **Logging**

ST. MARY LAKE

Creek, open July 1 through early September; **Many Glacier,** handicapped accessible and open late May through late September; **Quartz Creek,** open July 1 through early September; **Sprague Creek,** handicapped accessible and open mid-May through mid-September; **St. Mary,** open late May through late September; **Two Medicine,** open late May through mid-September;. The only developed campgrounds that are not first-come, first-served are Fish Creek and St. Mary, which can be reserved by contacting the **National Park Service Reservation System** (1-800-365-CAMP; www.reservations.nps.gov). Backcountry camping requires a permit that can be obtained from any ranger station.

FISHING **Glacier National Park** is home to many lakes, rivers, and streams where anglers can wet a line. Opportunities abound to catch arctic grayling, brook trout, bull trout, cutthroat trout, kokanee salmon, lake trout, mountain whitefish, rainbow trout, and northern pike, among other species. No license or permits are required to fish inside the boundaries of Glacier National Park. However, anglers need to stop at any visitor center or ranger station to obtain a current copy of park fishing regulations. The general fishing season is from the third Saturday in May through November 30, with some exceptions. These exceptions are always listed in current fishing regulations.

GOLF Oddly enough, there are several places to hit the links adjacent to the park. In fact, the courses are quite nice and nearly every golf shot offers an additional chance to enjoy a fabulous view.

Glacier Park Lodge and Golf Resort (406-892-2525; www.glacerparkinc .com), US 2, East Glacier; nine holes.

Glacier View Golf Club (406-888-5471; www.golfmontana.net/glacierview.htm), River Bend Drive, West Glacier; 18 holes.

See also *To Do–Golf* earlier in this chapter.

HIKING There are endless opportunities to hit the trail in and around Glacier. Hundreds of miles of trails provide everything from a quick afternoon jaunt to an overnight, multi-day adventure. Additionally, several service providers offer guided hikes and expeditions. A current list of outfitters and guides who are licensed to operate in Glacier can be obtained at any of the visitor centers or the park headquarters. I have listed a few of my favorite trails below.

Grinnell Glacier is a long day hike, making a 12-mile round-trip. It is worth the work because as you climb along the side of a mountain there are thrilling views of lakes in the valley below. To add even more excitement, take the boat (provided by the Park Service) across Lake Josephine and begin your hike from there.

Hidden Lake Nature Trail is a moderate hike, 3 miles total, from the Logan Pass Visitor Information Center. This is the park's most popular trail, for good reason: As it winds its way through the trees you are then treated to an amazing view of Hidden Lake, almost 800 feet below. My favorite time of year to take this hike is in late spring or early summer, especially after a few days of warm weather, as the wildflowers seem to explode from the hillsides.

THE FAMOUS, ALBEIT SHRINKING, GRINNELL GLACIER

Huckleberry Mountain Nature Trail is ideal for families with kids. It is a 0.6-mile loop trail that begins via Camas Road in the park or via Outside North Fork Road outside the park's west boundary. The trail begins at Camas Creek entrance and is an interpretive hike through a regenerating forest (the area burned in 1967). Kids will enjoy the short duration and the interpretive signs.

Running Eagle Falls Nature Trail is handicapped accessible and is an easy 0.4-mile out-and-back near the Two Medicine entrance. The trail makes a nice stroll along Two Medicine Creek to Running Eagle Falls. The fun part of this hike is that during certain times of the year (mainly after spring runoff) hikers can see two waterfalls on Two Medicine Creek. During runoff the volume of water tumbling down creates one large waterfall.

Sun Point Nature Trail is another easy stroll, but a little longer at 1.4 miles round-trip. It departs west of St. Mary on the Going-to-the-Sun Road. This is a great hike if you are traveling east on the road and your legs are ready for a stretch. The trail is self-guided and leads you to Baring Falls, which drop 30 feet into St. Mary Lake, creating an inspiring scene. If you want to see another waterfall, head 0.7 mile farther to Virginia Falls.

Trail of the Cedars Nature Trail is an easy 0.8-mile loop hike near Avalanche Campground along the Going-to-the-Sun Road. This trail is self-guided and leads hikers through a stand of old-growth cedars and eventually to Avalanche Gorge. During late spring or early summer the rush of water through the gorge will get your adrenaline pumping. If you want to extend your hike you can take a 2-mile spur trail to Avalanche Lake; however, this spur trail is not handicapped accessible.

HORSEBACK RIDING Glacier National Park allows private horse owners to ride on most of the trails. Horses are not allowed on paved roads. If you are planning a trip with your own horses, you must check with the Park Service for the latest information and regulations before bringing your horse. For an up-to-date list of outfitters and guides who offer private horseback riding in and around the park, please contact any of the visitor centers or any local chambers of commerce.

PADDLING/FLOATING With the abundance of lakes in Glacier, paddlers will have many options for exploration. For the most easily accessible lakes, see *To Do–Boating* in this section. But for more adventurous paddlers (those who are willing to hand-carry their craft), Glacier provides some great options for solitude while paddling. One of my favorites is **Trout Lake** near Lake McDonald. Begin from the Trout Lake Trailhead at the north end of Lake McDonald. Hike up and over (the ascending switchbacks can be tough, but certainly doable with a kayak or light canoe) 2.5 miles to Trout Lake. Another large lake requiring a hike is **Logging Lake.** Leave from the Logging Lake Trailhead on the Inside North Fork Road. The lake is 4.25 miles in, after a relatively easy hike. For more information on paddling/floating, check with a visitor center.

Flathead River. In Glacier the North and Middle Forks of the Flathead provide nearly all of the floating opportunities. The Middle Fork forms much of the southern border of the park and the North Fork forms the western border. Both rivers provide ample whitewater floating options, but due to their relatively wild nature (logjams, high runoff, and cold water) floating them is best left to experienced paddlers. Or plan to hire the services of a licensed outfitter or guide. The Middle Fork has more serious paddling for whitewater enthusiasts—several Class IIs, IIIs, and IVs are scattered throughout the river.

SNOW SPORTS **Glacier National Park** is truly a winter wonderland. Cross-country skiing and snowshoeing are enjoyed by many locals and winter visitors. The Park Service grooms only a few of the trails, but many will have already been explored by previous skiers or snowshoers. Before venturing out in winter it is always a good idea to tell someone else your plans and your expected return time.

UNIQUE ADVENTURES **Glacier Park Red Bus Tours** (406-892-2525; www .glacierparkinc), run by **Glacier Park, Inc.** Take a ride back in time while you view the sites of Glacier National Park in style on one of the historic red buses. These vintage motor coaches, built by the White Motor Company, travel over the Going-to-the-Sun Road and link all of the hotels and inns within the park. The bright red coaches have roll-back canvas tops, which allow for spectacular views. **Glacier Park, Inc.,** also offers horseback riding, guided fishing, whitewater rafting trips, and multi-day adventures into Glacier and the surrounding area.

✳ Lodging and Eating Out

BED & BREAKFASTS

East Glacier Park

Bison Creek Ranch (406-226-4482; www.angelfire.com/mt/bisoncreek), Box 144. This rustic B&B is 2 miles east of East Glacier on US 2. The accommodations are on a large ranch and provide easy access to the park's east-side highlights. Guests can stay in an A-frame chalet for $90 a night or in one of a few cabins that start at $45 and up. All of the options are nestled in the trees and make for a fun place to start or end your day of exploring.

West Glacier Park

Paola Creek Bed & Breakfast (406-888-5061; www.paolacreek.com), P.O. Box 97. From mile marker 172 on US 2 E., go 0.25 mile on Paola Creek Road. This place is luxurious, with a handcrafted log house (made mostly from timber from Montana) that includes four bedrooms, each with a queen-size bed and private bath. There is a king suite with a private bath and a whirlpool. They have a great stone fireplace and a 1,000-volume library—so why leave? Well, you will find out this place is close to everything in Glacier. Kelly Hostetler, who owns the B&B with her husband, Les, will make you a full breakfast before your day of adventure. And, for a reasonable price, Kelly will also make you a tasty and filling dinner as well. Rates $120 and up.

A Wild Rose Bed & Breakfast
(406-387-4900; www.awildrose.com), 10280 US 2 E. Located in a peaceful mountain setting just 6 miles from spectacular Glacier Park, they offer four immaculate and richly detailed rooms that are beautifully decorated with a Victorian flair. There are deluxe mattresses, all natural linens, hair dryers, Neutrogena bath amenities, and plush robes to use. The romantic Victorian whirlpool suite is perfect for a special occasion or just relaxing after a day on the hills of Glacier. Rates $110 and up.

LODGES, CHALETS, AND OTHER OPTIONS

East Glacier Park

♿ **East Glacier Motel & Cabins** (406-226-5593; www.eastglacier.com), 1107 MT 49; 10 miles west of East Glacier on US 2. With six spacious new units and 11 cozy cabins, this is a fine place to base out of while exploring Glacier. The owner stresses cleanliness and guest comfort. Within walking distance you will find the spectacular Glacier Park Lodge and golf course, swimming, horseback riding, bicycling, and hiking. AMTRAK is located just three blocks away and pick-up service is available. A few miles by car, and you are at scenic Two Medicine Lakes or Marias Pass. An excellent full-service restaurant is located just across the street. Inquire, as rates vary seasonally.

Glacier Park Lodge & Resort
(406-892-2525; www.glacierparkinc.com), downtown East Glacier. Located in East Glacier, this grand lodge, built at the turn of the 20th century, is a fun place to stay. Huge Douglas fir pillars over 40 feet high and 40 inches in diameter form the supports in the impressive lobby that welcomes you to the lodge. The Blackfeet Indians, awed by the size of the timbers, called it *Omahkoyis*, or "Big Tree Lodge." With a heated outdoor swimming pool, nine-hole golf course, and close proximity to Glacier National Park, Glacier Park Lodge is a wonderful Montana destination resort.

Summit Station Lodge (406-226-4428; www.summitstationlodge.com), 10 miles west of East Glacier on US 2. Built in 1906 by the Great Northern Railway, Summit Station Lodge is a wonderful place to experience the incredible beauty of the surroundings. It is located on the Continental Divide at the top of Marias Pass, the lowest route across the Divide in the United States. They are just a footstep away from the wilderness of Glacier National Park. Most of the rooms offer breathtaking views. The lodge can also arrange just about any adventure into Glacier imaginable, from horseback rides to helicopter tours. Rates $150 and up.

Essex
Izaak Walton Inn (406-888-5700; www.izaakwaltoninn.com), 290 Izaak Walton Inn; on US 2 between West and East Glacier. Known more as a cross-country ski lodge, this inn is ideally situated for exploring Glacier. It is listed on the Historic Register and is fun place for kids to stay. It also serves as a great home base for day trips. The dining room at the inn serves fine meals and the bar is an enjoyable place to soothe aching muscles after hiking or driving all day. Rates vary seasonally.

Glacier National Park
Apgar Village Lodge (406-888-5484; www.westglacier.com), P.O. Box 410. At the junction of US 2 and Going-to-the-Sun Road near the west entrance, this lodge is open May through October. This is a unique historic lodge offering motel-style rooms and cabins. Rates vary according to season and room style but are very reasonable. The adjacent **West Glacier Restaurant and Lounge** provides family-style American dining

with a varied menu that has something for everyone.

Granite Park Chalet (406-387-5555; www.granitparkchalet.com), P.O. Box 333. Open July through September; reservations required. This is one of the most amazing places to stay in Glacier—because it requires a 7-mile moderate hike along the Highline Trail, which starts about the midway point on Going-to-the-Sun Road. The chalet is listed on the Great Northern Railway Buildings National Historic Landmark. Built in 1914, this lodge offers very comfortable accommodations for hikers, and optional linen service and packaged meals for anyone in the backcountry for an extended period of time. A night spent here, or in **Sperry Chalet** (see below), truly is an unforgettable experience. Rates $80 and up.

&. **Many Glacier Hotel** (406-892-2525; www.glacierparkinc.com) is located west of the Many Glacier entrance. Open mid-June through mid-September; rates vary with room-type, so please inquire. This hotel was built in 1920 and has undergone various renovations through the years. Today it has more than two hundred rooms, making it the largest facility in the park. The views are fantastic, the décor is traditional Swiss-themed, and Glacier National Park is literally out your front and back doors. There are several dining options on the property, including **Ptarmigan Dining Room** (handicapped access and fine dining, including breakfast, lunch, and dinner), **Swiss and Interlaken Lounge** (drinks and bar food), and **Heidi's Convenience Store** (hot dogs, pre-made sandwiches, and desserts).

Sperry Chalet (406-387-5654; www.sperrychalet.com), P.O. Box 188.

Open mid-July through mid-September; reservations required. Similar to **Granite Park Chalet,** this historic building is accessible only by foot via a steady 6.7-mile hike (you will gain 3,300 feet in elevation) from Lake McDonald Lodge. The chalet is listed on the Great Northern Railway Buildings National Historic Landmark. Built in 1913, this stone lodge offers very rustic lodging for hikers—as no running water or electricity are available to guest or to lodge staff. Rates, which start at $170 per person, include breakfast, lunch, and dinner. A night spent here will not soon be forgotten.

&. **Lake McDonald Lodge** (406-892-2525; www.glacierparkinc.com), is 11 miles inside the west entrance. The lodge is a National Historic Landmark and located on the shore of Lake McDonald. Built in 1913, it was originally a hunting lodge, but today it has a variety of lodging options, from cabins to motel and lodge rooms. Rates vary based on room type and season, so inquire. Guests will find a cozy lodge with a rustic atmosphere and three restaurants on-site— **Russell's Fireside Dining Room** (handicapped accessible and fine dining, including breakfast, lunch, and dinner); **Jammer Joe's Grill and Pizzeria** (casual dining, including lunch and dinner); and the **Stockade Lounge** (drinks and bar food). A gift shop, a camp store, and access to many park attractions round out the excitement of Lake McDonald Lodge.

St. Mary

Johnson's of St. Mary (406-723-5565; www.johnsonsofstmary.com), located 0.25 mile from the St. Mary entrance to Glacier National Park. If you are RVing or camping, Johnson's

is the place to stay. But they also have a nice bed & breakfast as well. The Johnson family has been in the hospitality business for over 50 years and through three generations. The RV park offers a variety of campsites. There are 75 tent sites and 82 RV sites. Camping can be in a thicket of trees, in a grassy meadow, or at sites with a panoramic Glacier view. The view from Johnson's campground is one of the most amazing you'll ever encounter. Rates vary seasonally, as do their dates of operation (generally late May through November), so please inquire. They have a **restaurant on-site** that serves breakfast, lunch, and dinner. The breads are great and the tasty food is served family style. Johnson's also provides laundry facilities, a gift shop, high-speed Internet, and more.

&. **The Resort at Glacier St. Mary Lodge** (406-732-4431; www.glc park.com), US 89 and Going-to-the-Sun Road. Open mid-April through October. Rates vary seasonally and according to room type, so please inquire. They offer motel-style rooms and cabins. There are many things here, including a grocery store, gas station, and laundry facilities. There is an abundance of dining options as well, from fine dining to bar food to fudge to an espresso bar.

West Glacier

Belton Chalet & Lodge (406-888-5000; www.beltonchalet.com), located at the west entrance on US 2. Rates start at $140 and go up from there based on room style and season. After going through a substantial remodel in the past few years, the Benton is back to its former railroad glory. Although you won't find railroad tycoons gracing the hallways of this hotel, you will find clean rooms, a family environment, and a restaurant, a day spa, and a tap room on-site. If you need to take a break from adventure, you will be more than happy relaxing around the hotel. Most rooms have great views of Glacier Park and all have a private balcony.

The Cabins at Glacier Raft Company (406-888-5454; www.glacier -anglers.com), on US 2 five miles west of West Glacier. The log cabins provide all the comforts of home along with breathtaking views of the mountains of Glacier National Park. They're conveniently located just half a mile from the park's west entrance and offer separate sleeping and living areas, a complete kitchen, full bath, television (local stations only), covered deck, gas grill, and a gas fireplace to warm you on a cool Montana night. According to one guest, "This is the best base camp at Glacier." And I am inclined to agree. If these folks are booked, there are many other great options as well. Cabins $280 and up.

DINING OPTIONS Below are some of my favorite places in the Glacier National Park area to refuel. However, this is not a complete list *and* many of the lodging options previously listed have food on-site or are adjacent to dining. Additionally, all of the lodging within Glacier has food on-site. Keep in mind that the towns near Glacier are quite small and most dining and lodging options are within walking distance of each other.

East Glacier Park
& **The Great Northern Steak and Rib House** (406-892-2525; www .glacierparkinc.com); downtown East Glacier. The Great Northern main-

tains a western theme in its menu of choice beef, barbecued ribs, and chicken and fish entrées. A full breakfast buffet, lunch, and dinner are available. Enjoy a frosty pint of Montana microbrew beer or glass of wine during lunch and dinner. The restaurant seats on a first-come, first-served basis and does not accept reservations. Casual attire is required, so come and enjoy western cuisine with traditional local influences.

Firebrand Food & Ale (406-226-9374), 20629 US 2; downtown East Glacier. This may be the best place to have a cold pint north of the Missouri River and east of Minneapolis. Firebrand Food & Ale is named after Firebrand Pass, seen out of the west-facing windows. In 1910, a forest fire on the west side of the Rocky Mountains burned north up the Ole Creek drainage and brands of fire blew over the pass, igniting the east slope. The restaurant/bar has been in operation for 30 years and offers a full and varied menu of steaks, seafood, pasta, ribs, sandwiches, pizza, etc. It also offers over 50 different beer labels and a well-balanced wine selection.

& **Glacier Village Restaurant and Buzz's Brew** (406-226-4464), 304–308 US 2 East; downtown East Glacier. The Glacier Village Restaurant opens at 6 A.M. and is the place in town for a big, special breakfast and homemade pastries. For lunch, try any of the cold sandwiches; loaded with meat, they are quite good. For dinner, the buffalo ribs are lip-smacking good. The wine list is very accommodating and they have a wide selection of cold beers. Next door, Buzz's Brew Station will serve all of your espresso and tea needs. The same family has owned the place for nearly 50 years; be sure to spend some time looking at the pictures adorning the walls.

Essex

&. **The Dining Room at the Izaak Walton Inn** (406-888-5700; www .izaakwaltoninn.com), 290 Izaak Walton Inn; on US 2 between West and East Glacier. The food here, matched by the settings, is certainly worth sampling. Many of the entrees carry a "Montana signature," in that they are prepared using ingredients such as wild huckleberries, topnotch beef, quality buffalo meats, Rocky Mountain elk, and rainbow trout. The desserts are scrumptious, especially the huckleberry pie. The menu is varied and has full-course dinners and pub-style meals for less money. For breakfast, especially if you are heading out for a long hike or paddle, you must have the huckleberry pancakes. The reputation of the food here has spread and reservations are recommended, however, you can often pop in and still get a seat at the Flagstop Bar. If you ask nicely you might be able to order off the dining room menu and not just the bar menu.

West Glacier

Cajun Mary's Café (406-387-4134), 12070 US 2. Cajun Mary's is a really fun place for families to eat. Born in the heart of Cajun/Creole country, Mary learned to cook at the elbows of her French mother and grandmothers in New Orleans, Louisiana. Mary came to Montana to work the resorts in the summer of 1990. While here, the vast beauty of the land and the people captured her heart. Cajun Mary's Cafe was founded on the idea of serving guests great flavors at a reasonable price—and she's perfected it. Mary's charm and passion for cooking blends the southern flavors with the ambiance of the West. The setting, among the tall ponderosa pines, is unique. Be sure to save room for the bread pudding.

&. **West Glacier Restaurant** (406-888-5359), 200 Going-to-the-Sun Road. The West Glacier Restaurant offers casual family dining for breakfast, lunch, and dinner. They have something for every taste, including homemade soups, pies, and baked goods. Their special huckleberry treats—ice cream, pie, soda, tea, and lemonade—are the best around. At the end of the day, prop up your feet and enjoy a cocktail with your meal and relax in the nonsmoking lounge. Come as you are here, even if you are still wet from wading the Middle Fork of the Flathead.

South-Central
Montana:
Yellowstone
Country

SOUTH-CENTRAL MONTANA: YELLOWSTONE COUNTRY

Beginning just west and north of Yellowstone National Park and stretching east for nearly 200 miles and north for about 130, Yellowstone Country is Montana's smallest tourism region. But don't let that fool you—framed by the Madison River on the western boundary, Yellowstone Park and the Beartooths on the southern edge, the Yellowstone River on its northern boundary, and the Clarks Fork River on the eastern edge, this region is by far the largest in terms of recreation pursuits. No matter the season, Yellowstone Country has outdoor excitement (and, of course, some fine indoor pursuits as well) for every season, every ability, and every interest. Whether you came to Montana to fly-fish, downhill ski, RV camp, bird-watch, climb a mountain (the state's tallest peak is in this region, Granite Peak at 12,799 feet), tackle Class V rapids, see dinosaur fossils, or relax by a pristine stream, Yellowstone Country truly has it all.

Just take a quick look at some of the names and numbers: Gallatin National Forest, 1.8 million acres; the Absaroka-Beartooth Wilderness Area, 920,000 acres; Lee Metcalf Wilderness Area, 260,000 acres; six mountain ranges (including the Absarokas with 65 peaks over 10,000 feet and Beartooth Range with nearly 30 peaks over 12,000 feet); the Beartooth Ranger District of Custer National Forest, nearly 600,000 acres; hundreds of thousands of acres of BLM and state lands; six major rivers, thousands of lakes and streams; four downhill ski resorts; hundreds of trails crisscrossing the mountains, forests, and streams; and much more. This region provides phenomenal access for hikers, mountain bikers, horseback riders, walkers, Nordic skiers, snowmobilers, snowshoers, with miles and miles of well-maintained trails and open backcountry. Because there are so many options, this guide is only able to list a limited number of favorites. But keep in mind that often times the best adventures are found by inquiring locally or by just heading out on your own—after being aware, of course, of all the necessary precautions such as changes in weather, interactions with wildlife, etc.

If you are only looking for information about scaling Granite Peak on your own or tackling the rapids of Yankee Jim Canyon or the Stillwater River, perhaps this is not the guidebook for you. In fact, I have purposely omitted many of the more challenging adventures in this book. This doesn't mean that outdoor

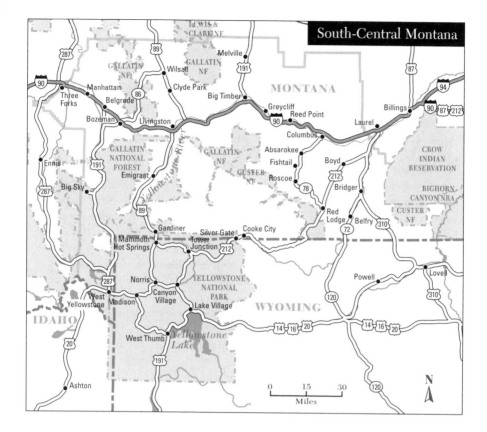

experts won't be able to use this book, quite the contrary. The lodging and dining options, museum and historical highlights, and the amount of contact information contained in the following pages will no doubt aid in the planning of your trip. And even folks who believe they only have a moderate ability to partake in some exciting adventures will be pleasantly surprised in the availability and abundance of professional guides, outfitters, and other service provider in this region who can safely ensure you are able to enjoy a mountain trek, fly-fishing adventure, horseback-riding expedition, whitewater float, rock climb, ice climb, backcountry ski venture, cattle drive, and the list goes on. By hiring the services of a licensed professional you are getting expertise, safety, and insider knowledge that will only enhance a trip. In many of the listings I have included private, licensed professionals who can take you on a trip or help you plan a trip or a specific activity. Keep in mind, however, that the professionals listed here are not the only service providers available for a particular adventure or region. For a complete, current list, contact any of the local chambers of commerce. From years of experience venturing in Montana, I've learned that money spent on an outfitter or guide should be viewed as an investment in a safe and enjoyable time. For many of these folks, showing people an enjoyable time has been part of their family's history for generations.

This region is also packed with history, directly influenced by Native American and pioneer cultures. If you need a break from the hills and rivers, you can plan a visit to any of a number of historical museums, monuments, landmarks, highways, parks, and sites throughout the region. Lewis & Clark buffs can stop at Headwaters State Park, where the Corps came across the headwaters of the Missouri and Sacagawea met up with her tribe. You can literally walk along their footsteps and trace the path they took as they named the Jefferson, Madison, and Gallatin Rivers. On his return, Clark followed the Jefferson and then the Yellowstone River to eventually meet with Lewis near where the Yellowstone and Missouri Rivers join. Clark's trail is highlighted in many roadside markers.

In Bozeman the Museum of the Rockies chronicles everything from dinosaurs to wolves to early pioneer life. Outside of Bozeman, near Headwaters State Park, visit the Madison Buffalo Jump State Park, a site once used by Native American tribes to hunt and harvest buffalo. An interpretive exhibit guides you through the rugged countryside as you learn about a traditional method of hunting buffalo. Farther east in Livingston, the Depot Museum chronicles the role railroads had in opening the West and in providing access to Yellowstone National Park, and you can learn the history of Livingston—a town the railroad basically built. At the Crazy Mountain Museum in Big Timber you can learn about the region's unique ties to Scandinavian culture and about the current ranching lifestyle.

But much of this fascinating history is overshadowed by the region's main draw—its proximity to Yellowstone National Park. In fact, three of the park's five main entrances (and the administrative headquarters) are located in this region. Many visitors to Yellowstone Country visit Yellowstone National Park on their trip; however, the region is overflowing with other adventures for all ages and abilities. Take my word for it: I have spent my whole life in Yellowstone Country and there are still adventures that I haven't yet experienced.

So does Yellowstone Country offer anything beyond adrenaline-filled adventure? You bet. This region is home to many places to relax and unwind. Whether this means enjoying the sunset over the Tobacco Root Mountains from the front porch of the Sacajawea Hotel in Three Forks or soaking that horseback ride out of your muscles in the all-natural Chico Hot Springs, you will find plenty of options for physical and soulful rejuvenation. If the whole family is along on the trip you might try a cowboy cookout, a dogsled adventure, or a dinner hay-, sleigh-, or snowcat ride. Or hop in the car and take any number of scenic drives in the region, most notably the Beartooth Scenic Byway. You can travel to Hailstone National Wildlife Refuge or Halfbreed Lake to picnic and watch wildlife. Try your hand at fly-fishing on any of the easily accessible rivers in the area, but first sign up for a free fly-casting lesson at the Federation of Fly Fishers' Fly-Fishing Discovery Center and Museum in downtown Livingston. The kids will enjoy the commercialized attractions in West Yellowstone, such as the Yellowstone IMAX Theater and the Grizzly & Wolf Discovery Center. If traveling to or from Yellowstone National Park, be sure to visit Gardiner and drive through the original entrance to Yellowstone—the Roosevelt Arch.

And while we are talking about Yellowstone, a visit to the nation's first park from Montana will ultimately take you through Gardiner at the north entrance, Silver Gate and Cooke City at the northeast entrance, or West Yellowstone at the west entrance. These towns and their surrounding communities are ideal jumping-off points for venturing into Yellowstone. Many of the service providers listed in this guidebook are also licensed to operate in the park. Where appropriate, I've included adventures into the park, but it is always good to do a little research before heading out on your own or with a licensed professional. And while planning, keep in mind that the area surrounding Yellowstone has just as many options for exploration as the park itself.

The entire Yellowstone Country region is full of adventure, history, and culture. The hard part is deciding which ones are right for you, your family, and perhaps the time of year. The information below should get you started.

GUIDANCE **Belgrade Chamber of Commerce** (406-388-1616; www.belgrade chamber.org), 10 East Main Street, Belgrade 59714.

Big Sky Chamber of Commerce (406-995-3000; www.bigskychamber.com), P.O. Box 160100, Big Sky 59716. The office is located on Pine Drive in the West-fork Meadows complex near Big Sky Western Bank. Look for the blue visitors sign.

Big Timber/Sweet Grass Chamber of Commerce (406-932-5131; www.big timber.com), P.O. Box 1012, Big Timber 59011; located near I-90 Exit 367.

Bozeman Area Chamber of Commerce (406-586-5421; www.bozeman chamber.com), 2000 Commerce Way, Bozeman 59715. The office is located just off I-90 and North 19th Avenue.

Bridger Chamber of Commerce (406-662-3651), P.O. Box 99, Bridger 59014.

Cooke City Chamber of Commerce (406-838-2495; www.cookecitychamber .com), P.O. Box 1071, Cooke City 59020.

Gardiner Chamber of Commerce (406-848-7971; www.gardinerchamber .com), P.O. Box 81, 222 Park Street, Gardiner 59030.

Livingston Area Chamber of Commerce (406-222-0850; www.livingston chamber.com), 308 E. Park Street, Livingston 59047.

Manhattan Chamber of Commerce (406-284-4162; www.manhattan montana.com), P.O. Box 606, 105 South Broadway, Manhattan 59741.

Red Lodge Area Chamber of Commerce (406-446-1718; www.redlodge .com), P.O. Box 988, 601 North Broadway, Red Lodge 59068.

Stillwater County and Area Chamber of Commerce (406-322-4505; www .stillwater-chamber.org), P.O. Box 783, Columbus 59019. The office is located in Columbus, just off the I-90 exit.

Three Forks Chamber of Commerce (406-285-4753; www.threeforks montana.com), P.O. Box 1103, Three Forks 59752. The visitor center is housed in an Old Milwaukee Railroad Caboose at the south end of Milwaukee Railroad Park, which you will see as you come into town off I-90 Exit 278.

West Yellowstone Chamber of Commerce (406-646-7701; www.westyellow stonechamber.com), 30 Yellowstone Avenue, P.O. Box 458, West Yellowstone 59758.

Yellowstone Country (406-556-8680; www.yellowstone.visitmt.com), 1822 Lincoln, Bozeman 59715.

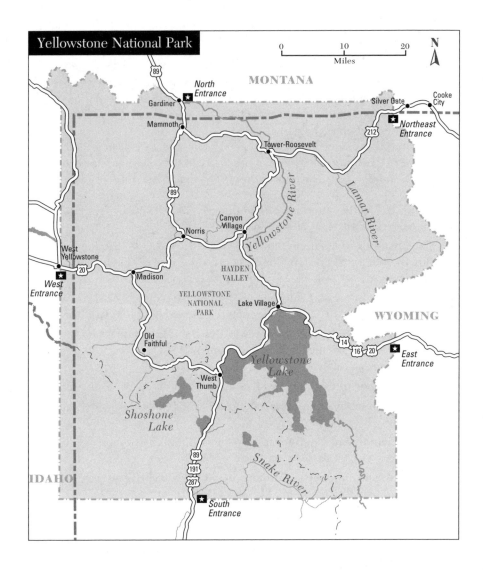

Yellowstone National Park

GETTING THERE From west to east, Three Forks, Manhattan, Belgrade, Boze-man, Livingston, Big Timber, Columbus, and Park City lie along I-90. South from I-90 near Belgrade lie Gallatin Gateway, Big Sky, and West Yellowstone along US 191. West Yellowstone can also be accessed by US 287 south from Three Forks. Gardiner lies south of Livingston via US 89. Red Lodge is accessible via MT 78 through Columbus or US 212 from Laurel, near Billings. Cooke City is accessed via Gardiner or Red Lodge and the Scenic Beartooth Highway (US 212).

See also *Airports* and *Bus Service* in "What's Where in Montana."

BEAUTIFUL VIEWS ABOUND IN YELLOWSTONE COUNTRY

MEDICAL EMERGENCIES **Beartooth Hospital and Health Center** (406-446-2345), 600 W. 20th Street, Red Lodge.

Bozeman Deaconess Hospital (406-585-5000), 915 Highland Boulevard, Bozeman.

Clinic at West Yellowstone (406-646-7668), 236 Yellowstone Avenue, West Yellowstone.

Livingston Memorial Hospital (406-222-3541), 504 S. 13th Street, Livingston.

Pioneer Medical Center (406-932-4603), W. 7th Avenue N., Big Timber.

Stillwater Community Hospital (406-322-5316), 44 W. 4th Avenue N., Columbus.

✳ To See

TOWNS **Big Sky,** on US 191 less than 50 miles north of the west entrance to Yellowstone National Park and 40 miles south of Bozeman, is a summer and winter recreation paradise. It is a tad on the spendy end of the spectrum, but if you have more time than money there is an abundance of public camping in the area. The hiking, fishing, snow skiing, and general exploring near Big Sky are hard to beat anywhere in Montana. There are two full-size ski resorts near Big Sky, over 30 eating establishments, and many lodging options.

Cooke City and **Silver Gate** are twin towns located 5 miles apart on US 212 at the northeast entrance to Yellowstone Park. Cooke City is slightly larger than Silver Gate (meaning it has 10 square blocks, while Silver Gate has 5) and was founded in the 1870s as a mining camp. Cooke City and Silver Gate are ideal places for more hardcore adventurers as the backcountry surrounding these two towns is some of the best in the Lower 48. The towns also offer unique and fun alternative lodging to West Yellowstone and Gardiner for those venturing into Yellowstone. Silver Gate could also be the only town in the nation where every structure is made from logs or other native materials—in fact, it's a requirement there.

Gardiner is on US 89 at the north entrance to Yellowstone Park. This is the only entrance open year-round to vehicle traffic. The original 1903 stone arch, dedicated by President Theodore Roosevelt and known as **Roosevelt Arch,** marks the entrance to Yellowstone Park. Gardiner is also a destination for whitewater rafters, big game hunters, anglers, and folks heading into the backcountry of Yellowstone. The **Yellowstone River** tumbles through town and the US 89 bridge right in town provides an exhilarating view of the river below.

Livingston is 25 miles east of Bozeman on I-90. This town was actually the first entrance town to Yellowstone Park, at a time when motor coaches met trains coming from east and west and took visitors south to Yellowstone. Surrounded by four mountain ranges, nearly every view from Livingston is scenic. The Yellowstone River flows through town and **Sacajawea Park** offers families a fun place to picnic. There is plenty of history, arts, museums, and culture in Livingston as well.

Red Lodge was founded as a mining town and today lies on US 212 at the doorstep of the Beartooth Mountains. This tiny mountain town is a great place for outdoor pursuits, including, but not limited to, skiing, horseback riding, fishing, golf, whitewater rafting, and mountain biking. The main drag, Broadway, is one long street with a few unique shops and dining options. There is an enjoyable walking tour with maps available from the chamber (see *Guidance*).

Three Forks is one of the more history-steeped towns in the region: Headwaters State Park is 5 minutes away, Parker Homestead is 5 minutes away, Madison Buffalo Jump is 20 minutes away, etc. And this small community lies along the Jefferson River and is at the location where Sacagawea provided horses for the Lewis & Clark Expedition.

West Yellowstone is reached by US 191 south of Bozeman, US 287 south of Ennis, US 20 from Idaho, or from the west entrance of Yellowstone Park. This town is quite a contrast to some of the smaller, sleepier towns of this region. With many businesses catering to tourists, it is hard to not get caught up in the curio shops, but once outside of town the natural world dominates the landscape. West Yellowstone is a good place for families as there are lots of things for kids to enjoy, including the **Grizzly & Wolf Discovery Center** (see *For Fami-*

lies); however, since this exhibit is so close to Yellowstone some folks might find it hard to justify paying for something that with a little time and effort might be seen in the wilds of Yellowstone Park.

See also **Historic Downtown Bozeman** under *Historic Landmarks, Places, and Sites.*

MUSEUMS &. **American Computer Museum** (406-587-7545; www.compu story.com), 2304 N. 7th Avenue, Suite B, Bozeman. Open daily June through August, 10 A.M.–4 P.M., Thursdays until 8 P.M.; September through May, Tuesday, Wednesday, Friday, Saturday, 12 P.M.–4 P.M. and Thursday, 4 P.M.–8 P.M. Rates vary by season and there are discounts for children. Computers drive nearly everything today. But a computer museum in Montana? Well, we've also got pig races, testicle festivals, and a few other head-scratchers, so it is not that far-fetched. The award-winning American Computer Museum brings together 20,000 years of technology through thousands of artifacts displayed in a visitor-friendly environment. The exhibits are designed to appeal both to the novice and technology expert. See scores of exhibits, everything from original Babylonian clay tablets, historic Bible leaves, and Isaac Newton's writings to the telegraph, telephone, radio, television, slide rules, and of course computers—including the ENIAC and Apple 1. Open to the public since 1990.

Carbon County Historical Society & Museum (406-446-3667), 224 N. Broadway, Red Lodge. Open Memorial Day through Labor Day, Monday through Saturday, 10 A.M.–5 P.M.; in winter, open Tuesday through Friday, 10 A.M.–5 P.M., Saturday, 11 A.M.–5 P.M. Admission $3 adults, $2 students, free for children 5 and under. The Carbon County Historical Society & Museum highlights the historic Carbon County area, including the Greenough and Lin-derman family (rodeo legends) collection, the Waples family historic gun and Indian artifact collections, interactive coal and hard-rock mine exhibits, and much more. The museum also houses the Carbon County archives and assists with genealogical and historic research. The museum is housed in the first Labor Temple built in Montana. This three-story brick building is at the beginning of the historic commercial district, when entering Red Lodge from the north.

&. **Clarks Fork Valley Museum** (406-668-7650), P.O. Box 274, 101 East River Street, half a block from US 310 at the caution light in Fromberg. Open June through September, daily, 11:30 A.M.–3:30 P.M. This is a fun little side trip if you're visiting Red Lodge. This museum displays the history of the Clarks Fork Valley. It is in one of the last class four (small, rural) area railroad depots in the country. The depot, which is listed on the National Register of Historic Places, is over a hundred years old. Exhibits include a one-room doctor's office and a tra-ditional homesteader's cabin.

&. **Crazy Mountain Museum** (406-932-5126; www.sweetgrasscounty.com/museum), south of I-90 via Exit 367; next to the cemetery and the only tall pine trees on the south side of the interstate. Open Memorial Day through Labor Day, Tuesday through Saturday, 10:30 A.M.–4 P.M. and Sunday, 1–4:30 P.M. Home to several exhibits, this museum is an interesting place in which to explore Mon-tana's past. It is a historical museum featuring exhibits that reflect the history of

Sweet Grass County and the surrounding area. A few of the exhibits include: "Sheep and Wool," the story of sheep ranching and its great importance to Sweet Grass County and the American West, and "The Norwegian Stabbur," in memory of the huge impact Norwegians had on Sweet Grass County. This separate building includes Norwegian artifacts, a one-room schoolhouse, and a Lewis & Clark exhibit. An archives room provides information for research on county history and its people. Head outside to enjoy the Lewis & Clark Native Plant Garden, which has a wonderful assortment of plants with interpretive signs relating to the plants and other interesting facts of Clark's journey through here in July of 1806.

 **Federation of Fly Fishers' Fly-Fishing Discovery Center** (406-222-9369; www.livingstonmuseums.org/fish), 215 E. Lewis Street, Livingston. Open year-round, June 15 to October 1, Monday through Saturday, 10 A.M.–6 P.M., Sunday, noon–5 P.M.; October 2 to June 14, Monday through Friday, 10 A.M.–4 P.M. Admission $3 adults, $1 children 7–14. Any angler headed to Montana should plan for a stop here. Not only are there free fly-casting lessons with equipment provided every Tuesday and Thursday during the summer season (inquire for times), but this place is home to several exhibits on the history of fly-fishing, living fish displays, artwork, and more. Casual visitors will enjoy the center's Fish of Lewis & Clark Exhibit, detailing the role that Montana's fish and rivers played in the historic expedition. Serious fly-fishers will be captivated by the extensive collection of flies and equipment and all visitors will enjoy the live fish, resource

MAJESTIC LOWER FALLS IN YELLOWSTONE NATIONAL PARK

displays, and artwork. Featured in many national publications, the Federation of Fly Fishers' Fly-Fishing Discovery Center offers a unique opportunity to explore the sport that has captured the attention of the world.

♿ **Gallatin Historical Society Pioneer Museum** (406-522-8122; www .pioneermuseum.org), 317 Main Street, Bozeman. Open June through August, Monday through Saturday, 10 A.M.–5 P.M.; September through May, Tuesday through Saturday, 11 A.M.–4 P.M. Admission $3 adults, free to children 12 and under. The museum offers a unique glimpse into the area's past. Together with jail cells and a hanging gallows, the museum's displays depict pioneers who settled the valley. For example, there's a reconstructed log cabin, a model of old Fort Ellis, the infamous Big Horn Gun, Indian artifacts, five generations of wedding dresses from the Accola-Spain family, and even a porcelain doll that belonged to a girl who came to Bozeman by wagon in 1864. There's also a new display on Lewis & Clark in southwest Montana. The museum also boasts a photo archive with more than 12,000 historic images. There's a research library that includes a special Lewis & Clark collection and files on many Gallatin County communities and families. There is also a bookstore selling many hard-to-find historical materials.

♿ **Headwaters Heritage Museum** (406-285-4778), corner of Cedar Street and Main Street, Three Forks. Open June through September 30, daily, 9 A.M.–5 P.M.; winter months by appointment. The year 2008 will be a big one for the Headwaters Heritage Museum as Three Forks will celebrate its centennial. The museum contains a vast and fascinating array of artifacts from the Missouri River Headwaters area. An anvil from an 1810 fur trapper's trading post at the Missouri River headwaters, Montana's largest brown trout weighing in at 29.5 pounds, an extensive barbwire collection, a dugout canoe used in a Lewis & Clark TV documentary, and a log cabin from Gallatin City built in the 1860s are but a few of the interesting exhibits.

♿ **Livingston Depot Center** (406-222-2300; www.livingstondepot.org), 200 West Park, Livingston. Open mid-May through late-October, Monday through Saturday, 9 A.M.–5 P.M., Sunday, 1 P.M.–5 P.M. Admission $3 adults, $2 children and seniors. Located in a beautifully restored 1902 Northern Pacific Railroad station, this center has various exhibits throughout the year and also hosts concerts, art shows, performing arts, and other local activities. The art exhibits change seasonally, so be sure to contact the center during your visit.

♿ **Museum of the Beartooths** (406-332-4588), 440 E. 5th Avenue N., Columbus. Open May through September, 12 P.M.–5:30 P.M. Free. The center is housed in a new building and its focus is on highlighting Stillwater County's role in the shaping of Montana's history. Exhibits include historic washing machines, artifacts relating to the second Crow Agency (1875–1882), the Albert Johnson vintage home furniture, 1895 Line Drug Company pharmaceutics, a military section featuring a tribute to native Donald J. Ruhl, one of Montana's seven Congressional Medal of Honor recipients (earned by his death on Iwo Jima). Other notable displays tell the story of the 1938 Frank Robideau hanging in Columbus and offer a timeline of mining activities culminating in the current Stillwater Mining Company platinum/palladium mine, the only one in America.

Many photos have been identified and much information is available on families that live or have lived in Stillwater County.

&. ✐ **Museum of the Rockies** (406-994-2251; www.museumoftherockies.org), 600 W. Kagy Boulevard, Montana State University, Bozeman. Open June through August, daily, 8 A.M.–8 P.M.; September through May, Monday through Friday, 9 A.M.–5 P.M., Sunday, 12:30 P.M.–5 P.M. Admission $8 adults, $4 children 5–18, free to children 4 and under. This is a relatively large museum on the campus of Montana State University, but the exhibits are so well thought out that you feel like you are in several first-class personal museums. They also maintain the **Montana Dinosaur Trail** (www.mtdinotrail.org). Once in the museum you'll travel through four billion years of Earth's history beginning in the "Landforms and Lifeforms" hall. The next stop is "One Day 80 Million Years Ago," a re-creation of the dinosaur nesting colonies discovered by Jack Horner, the museum's Curator of Paleontology. Travel on through exhibits about Montana's Native Americans and the state's recent history. For a unique experience, visit the Taylor Planetarium. During the summer, visit a living history farm and experience life a century ago on a Montana homestead. Each summer, the museum features a new exhibit. My favorite exhibit is "West of Wonder: The Natural History of Lewis & Clark." Often thought of as America's great adventure story, the Lewis & Clark Expedition should also be thought of as America's first great scientific endeavor. The museum also hosts many activities for children and has a great gift shop and ample parking for RVs.

Yellowstone Gateway Museum (406-222-4184; www.livingstonmuseums.org), 118 W. Chinook Street, Livingston. Open Labor Day through September, daily, 10 A.M.–5 P.M.; October through May by appointment. Admission $4 adults, $3.50 seniors, $3 children 6–12, free children 6 and under. Housed in a restored 1906 schoolhouse, which is on the National Register of Historic Places, this museum has some unique things to offer, including one-of-a-kind artifacts from the 1860s–1940s. These include stagecoaches, W. H. Jackson chromolithographs, the Fort Yellowstone bell, and artifacts relating to Calamity Jane, Buffalo Bill Cody, the Plummer Gang, the Texas Rangers, and the Goodnight-Loving cattle trail. There are also displays from three nationally important sites in Park County, including the 11,500-year-old Anzick burial site and the largest Clovis cache ever found, along with many more interesting exhibits and artifacts.

&. **Yellowstone Historic Center Museum** (406-646-1100; www.yellowstone historiccenter.org), 104 Yellowstone Avenue, West Yellowstone. Open mid-May to October, daily, 9 A.M.–9 P.M. On your way to or from Yellowstone, a stop in West Yellowstone is usually in order. While venturing in Yellowstone Park you are not always exposed to the exciting history of the park. A stop here will fix that. Located in the historic Union Pacific Depot at West Yellowstone, the museum showcases the history of visitation and transportation to our nation's first national park. The museum contains displays on stagecoach and railroad companies that brought tens of thousands of visitors to the park, wildlife of the area (the animal dioramas are entertaining), and an exhibit detailing and explaining the benefit of the epic fires of 1988.

HISTORIC DOWNTOWN BOZEMAN IS A MIX OF THE TRENDY AND THE TRADITIONAL

HISTORIC LANDMARKS, PLACES, AND SITES Historic Crail Ranch (406-995-2160), Spotted Elk Road (2 miles west of US 191 on MT 64, then right on Little Coyote to Spotted Elk Road), Big Sky. Open weekends July through August and the first weekend in September, noon–3 P.M. Free admission. This collection of buildings, all of which are listed on the National Register of Historic Places, transports visitors back in time to life on the frontier. Frank Crail's family—Big Sky's original homesteaders—began ranching here in 1902, on 160 acres.

✿ **Historic Downtown Bozeman** (406-522-8122; www.pioneermusuem.org), 317 W. Main Street (Gallatin Historical Society Pioneer Museum), Bozeman. Guided walking tours take place June through September, Monday through Wednesday at 11 A.M. and 6 P.M. Free admission. Beginning at the Pioneer Museum, this 90-minute tour takes you along Main Street and then meanders through downtown Bozeman—where some 700 structures are listed on the National Historic Register. Your guide will showcase the buildings you shouldn't miss. While traveling on Main Street you will actually be walking the path of the Bozeman Trail (which was a cattle-herding trail in the 1800s). As with many volunteer-led tours, always be sure to call ahead to confirm time and place.

Madison Buffalo Jump State Park (406-994-4042; http://fwp.mt.gov/lands/site_281935.aspx), 23 miles west of Bozeman of I-90 to Exit 283, and then 7 miles south on Buffalo Jump Road (gravel but suitable, yet quite bumpy, for cars). Open year-round for day use; free for residents, $5 per vehicle for non-residents. There is certainly something special about this place. Not only is it one of a kind in Montana, but this is a place where the culture of the past can easily be seen. Historically, this area was used by various Native American tribes for

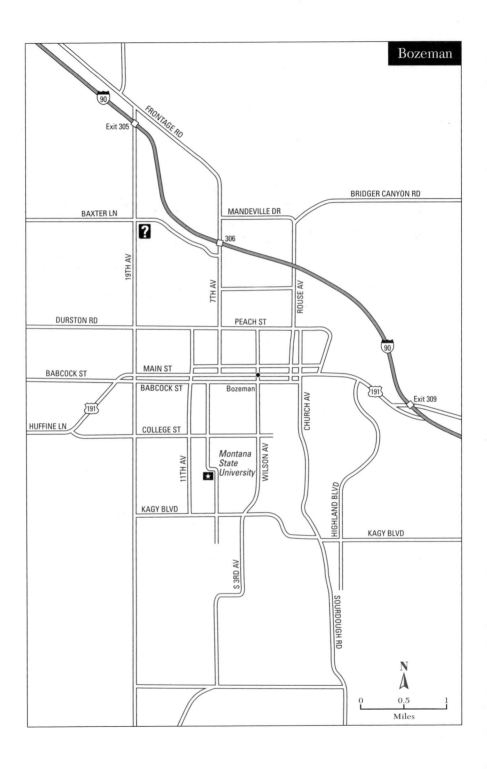

hunting and harvesting buffalo. There are several self-guided walks depicting exactly how the tribes would chase the buffalo off a cliff edge or drive them down a narrow wash, where other tribesmen would be waiting to finish the job. This site was utilized for nearly 2,000 years. Once horses were introduced, buffalo jumps were of little use. But the area's arid climate has preserved the site to this day.

Oregon Short-Line 1903 Train Car (406-646-7365; www.doyellowstone.com/restaurant.htm), 315 Yellowstone Avenue, West Yellowstone. Open year-round; free. The Oregon Short-Line Railroad once brought travelers to Yellowstone in style and comfort. Today, the 1903 executive car has been restored to museum quality and sits in the heart of the West Yellowstone Conference Hotel. It serves as the theme for the Oregon Short-Line Restaurant. A full year has been spent on restoration of the car. The furniture and appointments are original. Railroad history experts have commented that it is the most perfectly preserved executive rail car in the world today.

Parker Homestead State Park (406-287-3541; http://fwp.mt.gov/lands/site_281960.aspx), 8 miles west of Three Forks on US 287. Open year-round, day use only; free. This is the state's smallest state park, but also one of the more intriguing. There are no services, but for history buffs this park is sure to delight. The 1-acre park preserves a simple sod-roofed log cabin built in the early 1900s. Pioneers across Montana accepted the hardships, limits, and opportunities of such frontier homes. Here you can step into one family's past. The site also offers great photo opportunities.

FOR FAMILIES ✿ **Big Timber Waterslide** (406-932-6570; www.bigtimberwaterslide.com), Exit 377 on I-90, 9 miles east of Big Timber. Open June through Labor Day, 10 A.M.–7 P.M.; $15.95 ages 13 and up, $11.95 ages 4–12; half-day rates available. This is Montana's first waterpark and the only one in this region. For the little dudes (under 4 feet tall), there is the Tadpole Pool with floatable animals, the Frog Slide, and the Munchkin Run. For the not so little and yet not so big there is the Zipper and the Hurricane. Then for the big kids there is the Suicide and the Typhoon. They also feature Oldfaceful, where the big kids can take the little ones; up to four people can ride, perhaps the whole family. On the Lazy River ride everyone can relax. The Wave Pool provides an easygoing soak as well. They also have nice picnic facilities on-site and are adjacent to a KOA Kampground, so it is possible to spend a day or two relaxing and splashing.

& ✿ **Children's Museum of Bozeman** (406-522-9087; www.cmbozeman.org), 234 E. Babcock Street, Bozeman. Open Monday through Thursday, 10 A.M.–5 P.M., Friday, 10 A.M.–8 P.M., Saturday, 10 A.M.–5 P.M., Sunday, noon–5 P.M.; $3 adult or child, and all children must be accompanied by an adult. Visitors will engage all of their senses while exploring everything from pioneers to sports figures. A special Lewis & Clark area is a hit with the kids and parents and kids are encouraged to make noise, bang whatever they want in the Busy Bee Corner, and just plain explore things together as a family. On Friday nights admission is free and pizza is for sale for a buck a slice. The center also hosts special events.

&. ♂ **Grizzly Wolf & Discover Center** (406-646-7001; www.grizzlydiscovery ctr.org), 201 S. Canyon, West Yellowstone. Open year-round during daylight hours; $10 adults, $9 seniors, $5 children 5 and older, free children 4 and under. Here you can come face-to-face with wolves and grizzly bears. The thing I like about this place is that it is accredited by the American Zoo and Aquarium Association, and the center is a nonprofit and does many things to educated visitors on the conservation of these two species. Children have the opportunity to help staff hide food for the bears and learn proper food storage while in bear country. In early morning and evening visitors may witness the active wolf pack as they howl majestically. Live birds of prey and other presentations by a Karelian bear dog delight young and old visitors. Take a stroll through the museum exhibit "Bears: Imagination and Reality." Another interesting fact about the bears here is that they had to be removed from the wild because they were becoming dangerously comfortable around humans. Their stories help share a valuable lesson of how humans can take proper steps to ensure bears stay forever wild. The wolves at the center are ambassadors, providing a greater understanding of this predator in the Yellowstone ecosystem. Admission is good for two consecutive days, so you'll have the time to experience it all.

&. ♂ **Rare Earth Unlimited, Inc.** (406-646-9337; www.wyellowstone.com/ rareearth), 111 W. Yellowstone Avenue, West Yellowstone. Open May through October 9, A.M.–10 P.M.; December through March, 10 A.M.–6 P.M. This place is really a rock shop and gift shop; however, in the back of the store the Yellowstone Mining Company (creatively titled to entice visitors) offers customers the opportunity to mine for real Montana gems, including sapphires and garnets, as well as gold. This is done via an operational sluice. This is a fun activity to do with the whole family as you all hope to strike it rich as you and the kids learn how miners used to work. The most fun part is that your success is guaranteed, so you will at least bring back something even if it isn't the mother lode.

&. ♂ **Yellowstone IMAX Theater** (406-646-4100; www.yellowstoneimax.com), 101 S. Canyon, West Yellowstone. Show times vary seasonally so be sure to inquire before visiting. Prices vary according to show and show times. Much like any other IMAX in the world, this one provides a fantastic viewing experience. This is a fun late-evening event in West Yellowstone when you want to sit and relax after a long day of exploring.

SCENIC DRIVES There is only one designated scenic drive in Yellowstone Country, which is too bad because nearly every drive is scenic. I have included a few drives worth taking, as well as the designated route.

Beartooth Scenic Byway, 64 miles on US 212 from Red Lodge to Cooke City or vice versa. Closed seasonally, inquire locally as to road conditions. Deemed the most beautiful highway in America by many sources, this may also be the most "wild" highway in America—a massive 2005 landslide damaged and closed much of the highway. Because the highway is such a tourist draw the federal government moved extremely fast and had the road open the following year. The highway was first opened in 1936, connecting Yellowstone National Park to Red Lodge, via Cooke City and the Beartooth Plateau. This highway is breathtaking,

ATOP THE BEARTOOTH PLATEAU, WITH MONTANA'S BIG SKY OVERHEAD

with endless views from the "top of the world" at its highest point of 10,974 feet. Designated a National Scenic Byway in 1989, visitors are attracted to its proclaimed splendor and are amazed at the raw beauty of the Beartooth Mountains. The ragged rock peaks and sheer walls that plunge to talus slopes and canyon bottoms are a spectacular sight.

Columbus to Red Lodge via Roscoe. This drive takes you from the Yellowstone River, along the Stillwater River, up to the foothills of the Beartooth Mountains, and then into the historic resort town of Red Lodge. Begin on MT 78 and head south out of Columbus for 14 miles until you reach the small ranching town of Absarokee and then continue on MT 78. Spectacular views of the north face of the Beartooth Mountains can be had, as well as views of the High Plains to the east and south. You can make a loop of the trip by traveling on US 212 north from Red Lodge, back to I-90.

Gallatin Gateway to West Yellowstone via Big Sky. Head south from Gallatin Gateway on US 191 and you will travel along the Gallatin River and through the Gallatin Canyon. Anglers will especially enjoy this drive, as the highway provides easy and substantial access to the Gallatin River—the river Robert Redford chose for many of the scenes from his movie *A River Runs Through It*, despite the fact that much of the fishing in Norman Maclean's book took place on the Blackfoot River near Missoula. Redford thought this canyon was more scenic. And scenic it is, as the hillsides are blanketed in pine trees and the river tumbles by high rock walls. The drive finishes as it heads into West Yellowstone, and there are some great views of Hebgen Lake and Yellowstone Park.

Raynolds Pass via MT 87 north of Yellowstone. Drive through the same gap in the Horn Mountains through which mountain man Jim Bridger guided a group of scientists back in 1860. Led by Captain W. F. Raynolds of the U.S. Army Corps of Engineers, the expedition chronicled peaks and various wildlife. This pass can be accessed by US 20 west of West Yellowstone or south of US 287 just past **Quake Lake.** Look for the Raynolds Pass fishing access sign as MT 87 crosses the Madison River, where US 287 ventures up the pass.

NATURAL WONDERS Devils Slide, along US 89 north of Gardiner near Corwin Springs. This is a 200-million-year-old geologic formation. The vantage point is well marked about 6 miles north of Gardiner. If you're coming from the south it is obvious on the west side of the Yellowstone River, as a reddish slash of decomposing basalt creates a distinct channel down the south slope of Cinnabar Mountain.

Granite Peak (406-446-2103; www.fs.fed.us/r1/custer/recreation/granitepeak .shtml), 45 miles south of Columbus. At nearly 13,000 feet (12,799 to be exact) this is Montana's tallest mountain. Located in the Beartooth Mountain Range, the climb to the summit is for more experienced hikers and climbers, and many experts agree that this may be the toughest state summit in the Lower 48. There are three trails to the summit and all require some basic mountaineering skills and planning. To put it bluntly, this is not a climb for weekenders or inexperience climbers. If you plan to attempt it please check in with the Beartooth Ranger Station (listed above) before embarking on your trip. You could also consider hiring a guide to ensure your safety. (See Rock Climbing and Ice Climbing under *To Do–Unique Adventures* for more information.)

✪ **Grasshopper Glacier** (406-446-2103; www.fs.fed.us/r1/custer/recreation/ grasshopper/shtml), 2 miles east of Cooke City on US 212 to Lulu Pass–Goose Lake Road (FR 6493), a very rough road for high-clearance, four-wheel-drive vehicles in the dry season of late July and August only. Take the road as far you can and then hike the remaining 4 miles on the well-marked trail. The glacier, which sits at 11,000 feet in the heart of the Beartooth Mountains, takes its name from the millions of grasshoppers embedded within it. A study done by scientists in 1914 estimated that the grasshoppers had been extinct for two hundred years. More recently, entomologists have identified the hopper as a species of migratory locust commonly called the Rocky Mountain locust. This place is certainly a natural wonder.

Natural Bridge Falls (406-932-5131; www.bigtimber.com), about 30 miles south of Big Timber via MT 298. Open year-round for day use only; free. If you had been around in 1988 you could have seen the actual natural bridge; however, in that year it tumbled into the Boulder River below. Today there is still a breathtaking 100-foot waterfall, and in some years (depending on water flows) you may even see three falls. There are plenty of interpretive signs on the site that guide you through the geology and the surroundings. This is a fun place to picnic and for the more adventuresome types the 5.5-mile **Green Mountain Trail** (#94) departs from here. For anglers the **Boulder River** provides exhilarating fishing and floating.

Quake Lake–Madison Canyon Earthquake Area and Visitor Center (406-823-6961), located on US 287 25 miles from West Yellowstone. Open Memorial

Day through mid-September 8:30 A.M.–6 P.M. For anyone who has an appreciation for the natural powers of the earth this area will be a wonder. On August 17, 1959, a massive earthquake literally moved a mountain, blocking the Madison River and creating Quake Lake. The quake measured 7.5 on the Richter scale. The slide moved at 100 miles per hour and in less than a minute it dumped more than 80 million tons of rock into the narrow canyon. The visitor center sits on the site of a campground, where several people were killed in the massive wall of earth that slide from the mountain. The visitor center offers interpretive programs and views of the slide. The drive along the shore of Quake Lake is always interesting, as you can see the old roadbed and where it buckled with the earthquake. But more eerie are the dead trunks of hundreds of trees now half submerged by the waters of the lake.

See also Gallatin Petrified Forest under *To Do–Hiking.*

✳ To Do

BICYCLING **Bangtail Ridge Trail,** north of Bozeman on MT 86, then east on FR 480 (Stone Creek Road). This trail is located within Gallatin National Forest and begins at the gated parking area at the end of FR 480. This is a singletrack trail, suitable for intermediate riders. Once you reach a few of the higher points on the 26-mile trek, you will have views of the six surrounding mountain ranges (the Big Belts, Crazies, Absarokas, Hyalites, Bridgers, and Tobacco Roots). Some improvements to the trail in 2003 make viewing wildflowers possible, and there are a few exhilarating downhill sections. The surrounding area (mainly considered the Bozeman area) is a fat-tire rider's dream, as there are several nearby mountain bike trails with varying degrees of difficulty. Any of the local bike shops can provide ample riding information. Two of our favorites are **Bangtail Bicycle Shop** (406-587-4905; www.bangtailbikes), 508 W. Main Street in Bozeman, and **Chalet Sports** (406-587-4595; www.chaletsportsmt.com), 108 W. Main Street in Bozeman..

Big Sky provides easy access to hundreds of miles of serious mountain biking trails. Anyone who thought that Big Sky was merely a winter destination just hasn't spent enough time in the area during the summer. In addition to the trails maintained by the Gallatin National Forest (a few are outlined below), the friendly folks at **Big Sky Resort** offer numerous roads and singletracks to get your legs and heart pumping. A place for everything mountain biking (and plenty of other outdoor gear) is **Grizzly Outfitters** (406-995-2939; www.grizzly outfitters.com), 145 Center Lane Unit H, Big Sky. These folks will gladly provide free information or fully outfit you with your own bike or a rental bike for whatever kind of ride you wish. One nice local trail is the **Grizzly Loop near Big Sky.** Park at Buck's T-4 Lodge (406-995-4111; www.buckst4.com), south of Big Sky on US 191. This trail is great for beginners and intermediate riders—the section that gets a little hairy is easily avoided. The trail starts across from the parking lot (across US 191, actually) at Buck's. Pass through a fence, take the first right, and hop on the singletrack. You will parallel the Gallatin River for nearly 2 miles and then cross over it. In 0.5 mile you will reach a parking area. Here, beginners should turn around and head back to Buck's T-4. More experienced riders can continue on a 5.5-mile loop ride back to the second parking area and then ride back to Buck's.

Gardiner is thought of more as a gateway to Yellowstone National Park, but cyclists and mountain bikers will find a plethora of peddling pursuits in the area. For road cyclists, the best opportunity is to travel north of Gardiner to MT 540 (E. River Road) and follow this paved highway to **Chico Hot Springs.** This easy, 20-mile peddle includes views of two mountain ranges, the Yellowstone River, and some unique geologic formations. Once at Chico you can rest your muscles in one of their hot pools. For mountain bikers, there are several trails of varying abilities in the Gardiner area. For a heart-pounding climb, head north from town by car 3 miles on Jardine Road. Leave your car at the Eagle Creek Campground and pedal on Jardine Road for another 6 miles until you get to the old mining town of Jardine. This ride is on a well-maintained dirt road, but it offers some amazing views south into Yellowstone Park. If you want to see wildlife, try biking the old Gardiner-Mammoth Road. The trail starts (or ends if you want to travel only downhill) at the north entrance to Yellowstone Park just outside of Gardiner. The trail climbs 5 miles to Mammoth Hot Springs. Be on the lookout for antelope, bighorn sheep, buffalo, elk, deer, bear, and various birds. This trail is entirely in Yellowstone National Park.

West Yellowstone is another town offering a range of rides for mountain bikers and road cyclists, and it's home to one of the coolest bike and ski shops in the state, **Freeheel and Wheel** (406-646-7744; www.freeheelandwheel.com), 40 Yellowstone Avenue, West Yellowstone. They offer all kinds of rentals, great advice, and a latte that a Seattle barista would be proud of. From West Yellowstone, mountain bikers will enjoy the **Rendezvous Ski Trails** just south of town. These trails are maintained and offer a wide degree of riding abilities. A favorite ride of locals is to follow the South Fork of the Madison River along FR 1700 (at the junction of Yellowstone Avenue and Iris Street).

Meeteetse Trail is located 0.75 mile south of Red Lodge on US 212, then east across Rock Creek onto a gravel road. This is a historic four-wheel-drive road that runs 19 miles to meet up with MT 72. If you do not mind biking on highways, continue on MT 72 south to Wyoming onto WY 120. But if biking on highways is not your cup of tea, then just turn around at any point on the four-wheel-drive trail and venture back to Red Lodge. The Meeteetse Trail began as an army supply trail in 1881 that started at Meeteetse, Wyoming, went through Red Lodge and continued on to Coulson (now Billings). The trail brought the first mail, supplies, and settlers the 100-mile distance from Meeteetse to Red Lodge, and was originally called the "100 Mile Route." Several years after its opening, stagecoaches began to travel the Meeteetse regularly. The views of the High Plains and Beartooth Mountains are spectacular.

See also Fat Tire Frenzy and Mountain Bike and Fine Arts Festival under *Special Events.*

BOATING ♿ **Cooney Reservoir State Park** (406-445-2326; http://fwp.mt.gov/lands/site_283293.aspx), Exit 434 off I-90, then south 22 miles to Boyd, then east on an access road for 8 miles. Open year-round; day use free for residents, $5 for nonresidents; camping for a nominal fee. This is a large irrigation reservoir near Red Lodge and Columbus. Despite its size at 780 acres, the summer months can be busy on the weekends when the folks from nearby Billings need a place to boat. The nice thing about the park is that they have nearly 80 campsite and 100 picnic tables, so you can usually find a place to crash or dine. Anglers will find walleye and rainbow trout and in winter there are a few cross-country ski trails.

& **Dailey Lake,** south on US 89 from Emigrant (35 miles south of Livingston), then west on Chico Road for 1 mile, then south on US 89 for 3 miles, then south on Sixmile Creek Road to the lake. This may be one of the more scenic lakes in the region, as it sits at the base of Emigrant Peak and also affords views of the Hyalite Mountains to the northwest. This lake is usually quieter than some others in the area, as motorboats over 10 horsepower are not allowed. The lake is 206 acres in size and is home to rainbow trout and walleye. There are 35 primitive campsites with a $12 nightly fee.

& **Hebgen Lake,** 8 miles west of West Yellowstone via US 20, then north on Hebgen Lake Road for 4 miles. You can also access the north end of the lake via US 287, 8 miles north of West Yellowstone. The south and east shores of Hebgen Lake can be accessed by FR 291. At 6,500 feet, this large reservoir is susceptible to high winds, fast-moving thunderstorms, and unpredictable weather. It is highly encouraged that only skilled boaters in well-maintained craft utilize Hebgen's waters. Anglers will find rainbow trout, brown trout, and a few chubs.

& **Hyalite Reservoir,** 17 miles south of Bozeman via MT 345 to FR 62. Popular with boaters in the summer and snowmobilers and ice fishermen in the winter, this reservoir for the city of Bozeman and Gallatin Valley is accessible year-round (a little tricky in winter unless the road is plowed). Motorized boats must follow a no-wake rule, and anglers will find arctic grayling (catch-and-release only), brook trout, and Yellowstone cutthroat trout. This is also a popular jumping-off place for mountain bikers, hikers, and cross-country skiers to explore the Hyalite Mountain Range.

CAMPING There are many private campground and RV parks in this region. For those who want to rough it, there are endless possibilities for pitching a tent, as most fishing access sites, state parks, national forest lands, and BLM lands allow overnight camping. You can rest assured that at any public site there will be signs stating whether overnight camping is allowed. If in doubt read all posted signs, especially if you are unclear about the need to pay a fee.

Carbella Recreation Site (406-533-7600), 16 miles north of Gardiner via US 89. Open year-round; free. This is a very primitive BLM campsite with pit toilets and access to the Yellowstone River. This is a nice option for campers who want a bare-bones camping experience close to Yellowstone Park. This site is also less visited than others that are closer to Yellowstone, so some solitude can often be found here.

Custer National Forest Beartooth Ranger District (406-446-2103; www.fs .fed.us/r1/custer/recreation/D2.shtml), HC 49 Box 3420, Red Lodge. The Beartooth Ranger District has 16 campgrounds in this region, most of which provide disabled access. Six of these campgrounds are on US 212 (Beartooth Scenic Byway) and are open May through September. The **M-K Campground** is free for overnight stays. Three campgrounds lie south of Red Lodge on the West Fork of Rock Creek, and three are northwest of town on FR 177, the road to East Rosebud Lake. Two lie on West Rosebud Road, the road to West Rosebud Lake and the Mystic Lake trailhead. Two lie on Nye Road (MT 419) in the Stillwater Valley. These campgrounds are open year-round and are either free or charge a nominal fee for camping from Memorial Day through September. Many of these campgrounds have campsites that can be reserved in advance by contacting **ReserveUSA** (1-877-444-6777; www.reserveusa.com). A few of these campgrounds have immediate access to fishing areas. In summer, the forest also rents out **Lime Creek Cabin** ($20), 66 miles south of Red Lodge.

& **Gallatin National Forest** (406-587-6701; www.fs.fed.us/r1/gallatin), P.O. Box 130, Bozeman. With five ranger districts and nearly 40 developed campgrounds, this national forest offers a wide range of camping opportunities, including several with facilities for the disabled. The Gallatin National Forest Web site is a great resource for planning a trip. The **Big Timber Ranger District** (406-932-5155) has nine year-round campgrounds with various fee structures (most are free), so please inquire before venturing out. Most of the campgrounds are south of the Yellowstone River in the Beartooth Mountains or adjacent areas. The two exceptions are Half Moon Campground and Shields River Campground. The **Bozeman Ranger District** (406-522-2520) has 11 seasonal campgrounds (most are open May through September) with various fees (most are free). The campsites are located off MT 86 north of Bozeman along the Bridger Mountains, along or just off US 191 south of Bozeman in the Gallatin Canyon, or along FR 62 in Hyalite Canyon. The **Gardiner Ranger District** (406-848-7375) has eight campgrounds (some seasonal, some year-round) with various fees (some free). They are all located north of Gardiner on Jardine Road, US 89 near Yankee Jim Canyon, and near Cooke City on US 212. The **Hebgen Lake Ranger District** (406-823-6961) is home to seven seasonal campgrounds ranging from free to $20. These are located on or just off US 191 north of West Yellowstone, on or just off US 287 northwest of West Yellowstone, or on Hebgen Lake Road via US 20 west of West Yellowstone. The **Livingston Ranger District** (406-222-1892) has three seasonal campgrounds ranging from free to $10. They are located off US 89 south or north of Livingston. They are all close to fishing areas. (See also Gallatin National Forest Cabins under *Lodging–Other Options.*)

Itch-Kep-Pe Park (406-322-4505), south of Columbus via MT 78, is a city-run park on the banks of the Yellowstone River. Open April 1 through October 31; free, but donations are appreciated. There are 30 campsites available, with a boat ramp and the town of Columbus nearby. This is a nice place when you want to be close to town for a few days.

FISHING This region of Montana might be the most visited by traveling anglers. Within Yellowstone Country, dozens of creeks and rivers draw anglers from around the globe. And for very good reason: not only are many of these rivers in beautiful settings, but they also contain wild trout, and most are easily accessible.

The Boulder River (406-247-2940; http://fwp.mt.gov/fishing/guide/q_Boulder _River__1099233458529.aspx - 34k) begins south of Big Timber in the Beartooth Mountains and flows for nearly 70 miles before it joins with the Yellowstone River near Big Timber. The river is easily accessed by county and forest roads as it tumbles, turns, and whirls its way north. It is home to brook trout, brown trout, mountain whitefish, rainbow trout, and Yellowstone cutthroat trout (which much be released). The Gallatin National Forest Big Timber Ranger District has numerous campgrounds along the river, many of which offer overnight camping for free or for a nominal fee, and most provide access to the river.

The Clarks Fork of the Yellowstone (406-247-2940; http://fwp.mt.gov/fishing/ guide/q_Clarks_Fork_Yellowstone_River) begins in the heart of the Beartooth Mountains and flows out of Wyoming and into Montana along MT 72 and US 310 east of Red Lodge, ending south of Laurel where it meets the Yellowstone. This is a lesser-known river and a good place to go if you desire solitude. Species include brown trout, burbot, mountain whitefish, and rainbow trout. The primitive Bridger Bend Fishing Access Site is 30 miles south of Laurel on US 310 to Bridger and then 13 miles south on MT 72.

The Gallatin River (406-444-2535; http://fwp.mt.gov/fishing/guide/q_Gallatin _River__1114924459385.aspx) flows out of the northwest corner of Yellowstone National Park and continues for nearly 100 miles before it meets the Jefferson and Madison Rivers near Three Forks. Access is plentiful and the trout are rambunctious and hungry. The river is home to brown trout, rainbow trout, and mountain whitefish. US 191 follows the river for much of its length and provides access to several state fishing access sites and Gallatin National Forest campgrounds. For those desiring guided fishing, the towns of Bozeman, Big Sky, and West Yellowstone offer dozens of licensed professionals to ensure you have a good experience on the Gallatin.

Rock Creek (406-247-2940; http://fwp.mt.gov/fishing/guide/q_Rock_Creek __1088211455237.aspx) is a fast-moving freestone tumbler flowing out of the Beartooth Mountains south of Red Lodge. Flowing for nearly 65 miles before it meets the Clarks Fork of the Yellowstone, this river is best accessed by US 212 and FR 71 west of Red Lodge. It is home to brook trout, brown trout, mountain whitefish, rainbow trout, and Yellowstone cutthroat trout. Custer National Forest has several access sites that offer camping, and only one (Water Birch) requires a fee.

The Stillwater River (406-247-2940; http://fwp.mt.gov/fishing/guide/q_Still water_River__1092800456391_0_69.6240005493164.aspx) rushes out of the Absaroka-Beartooth Wilderness and flows 70 miles to meet the Yellowstone at Columbus. This river is home to brook trout, brown trout, mountain whitefish, rainbow trout, and Yellowstone cutthroat. There are eight access points along the river and all allow overnight camping, most for free. Cliff Swallow Fishing Access Site 10 miles north of Absarokee on MT 420 has easy access for the disabled, including a fishing pier and toilets.

The Yellowstone River (406-247-2940; http://fwp.mt.gov/fishing/guide/q _Yellowstone_River__1039825479787_15.3889999389648_570.177001953125

.aspx) is the region's namesake and a world-famous river for its fishing and scenery. Its fishable water runs nearly 170 miles once in Montana, after exiting Yellowstone National Park. For its first 60 miles, the river is best accessed by US 89. At Livingston the river turns eastward, and then I-90 and its frontage road provide most of the access. This river is the longest free-flowing (undammed) river in the Lower 48, as it flows for 670 miles from its source to its confluence with the Missouri River just inside the western boundary of North Dakota. Species include brown trout, burbot, channel catfish, mountain whitefish, paddlefish, rainbow trout, sauger, smallmouth bass, walleye, and Yellowstone cutthroat trout (which must be released). There are dozens of access points along the river, many of which allow free overnight camping, and most with boat ramps to launch a raft or driftboat.

GOLF **Big Sky Golf Course** (406-995-5780; www.bigskyresort), Big Sky Spur Road (2 miles west of US 191), Big Sky; 18 holes.

Bridger Creek Golf Course (406-586-2333; www.bridgercreek.com), 2710 McIlhattan Road, Bozeman; 18 holes.

Columbus Stillwater Golf Course (406-322-4298), 1203 E. 3rd Avenue S., Columbus; nine holes.

Cottonwood Hills Golf Course (406-587-1118; www.cottonwoodhills.com), 8955 River Road, Bozeman; 18 holes.

Headwaters Golf Course (406-285-3700), 225 7th Avenue E., Three Forks; nine holes.

Livingston Country Club (406-222-1100), 44 View Vista Drive, Livingston; nine holes.

Overland Golf Course (406-932-4297), Exit 367 off I-90, Big Timber; nine holes.

Red Lodge Mountain Golf Course (406-446-3344; www.redlodgemountain .com/golf), 828 Upper Continental Drive, Red Lodge; 18 holes.

Riverside Country Club (406-587-5105; www.riverside-country-club.com), 2500 Springhill Road, Bozeman; 18 holes.

Valley View Golf Club (406-586-2145), 302 E. Kagy Boulevard, Bozeman; 18 holes.

HIKING Yellowstone Country is home to some of the best and most varied hiking in Montana. With glaciers, mountain peaks, rivers, and High Plains all accessible, hikers of all abilities will find enjoyment near every town. I have listed a few of the designated trails here and a few not-so-well-known hikes, but there are hundreds of options for hikes in this region and the best way to find them is with a little research and some local information.

Basin Lakes National Recreation Trail (#61) is reached by FR 71 west of Red Lodge. This 4.8-mile route leads to Upper and Lower Basin Lakes, which are popular fishing destinations. The trail follows an old horse-logging road and is relatively easy, but the last 0.75 mile is a leg-burner. However, the reward is some beautiful mountain scenery and some good fishing. If you are interested in more exploring continue on Trail 12, **Timberline Trail,** to Lake Gertrude and Timberline Lake. Or you can make a loop on Trail 1 and finish at the end of FR 346 near Black Pyramid Mountain south of Red Lodge.

Blue Lake Trail is accessed via Trails 119 or 118 from the Half Moon Trailhead on the east side of the Crazy Mountain Range north of Big Timber. Follow the trail along Big Timber Creek for 4 miles to the lake. The lake sits just above 8,000 feet and lies in a beautiful basin with high peaks on all sides. Bring your fishing rod, as there are feisty rainbow trout and few people make the hike so the fish are hungry and stupid.

Confluence Trail is an easy hike and will be enjoyed by Lewis & Clark history buffs. The trail departs from the campground at **Missouri Headwaters State Park** (see *Wilder Places–Parks*). This 4.1-mile hike leads you, with interpretive signs along the route, to the confluence of the Jefferson and Madison Rivers. This trail is mostly flat and you will have great opportunities to see various birds and plenty of deer.

Gallatin Petrified Forest is accessed via Tom Miner Road, 17 miles north of Gardiner off US 89. The ride from US 89 to the petrified forest will take about half an hour on a fairly bumpy but very scenic drive. Most of the land along the road is private, so please wait to venture out of your car until you reach the trailhead. Once at the well-marked trailhead, a 0.5-mile interpretive hike guides you to some petrified remains of a forest that lived between 35 and 55 million years ago. A few of these prehistoric remains are still in the upright position, a rarity for petrified trees.

Ġ **Palisade Falls National Recreation Trail** is a very accessible hike for folks of nearly every ability. The trailhead lies 17 miles south of Bozeman via MT 345 (S. 19th Avenue) to FR 62 (Hyalite Canyon Road), then south past Hyalite Reservoir for 2 miles to the well-marked trailhead. For its entire length, the 1.2-mile round-trip trail is paved, but a little steep in places. There are plenty of interpretive signs along the trail and the reward is a stunning 98-foot waterfall in an interesting geologic location.

Pine Creek Falls and **Pine Creek Lake.** It is an easy 1-mile hike to the beautiful waterfall, but the lake is a serious hike for more fit hikers. The trail leaves from the Pine Creek Campground south of Livingston via MT 540 (East River Road). The trail is well maintained and the hike to the falls is for all abilities. From there, it is another 4 miles to the lake—not that far, but almost straight up. The rewards for reaching the lake are some amazing views of Paradise Valley and large and hungry Yellowstone cutthroat trout in the lake.

West Rosebud Lake–Mystic Lake–Island Lake are accessible via MT 78 to W. Rosebud Road (FR 2702) southwest of Columbus. The first lake, West Rosebud Lake, can be seen from the road, but the other two must be reached via Trail 19. The trail leads you along the shore of Mystic Lake (which is the largest lake in the Beartooths at just over 400 acres), then on up to Island Lake in the Absaroka-Beartooth Wilderness. From the trailhead to Island Lake (around Mystic Lake) is 12-miles round-trip. The fishing in either lake is very good for rainbow trout.

EMERALD LAKE LIES HIGH IN THE MOUNTAINS

HORSEBACK RIDING ✍ **Broken Hart Ranch** (406-763-4279; www.broken hartranch.com), 73800 Gallatin Gateway. A great place for kids, as they have all sorts of livestock as well as horses for kids to look at and pet. These folks are great for day trips if you are in the Bozeman area. Kids and adults will enjoy their evening hay rides. They even offer an evening cookout ride on which guests can enjoy a steak or a freshly caught trout. Please inquire for rates and reservations.

✍ **Hells-A-Roarin' Outfitters** (406-848-7578; www.hellsaroarinoutfitters.com), Jardine Road, Gardiner. Located near Gardiner and Yellowstone Park. The Johnson family provides fully guided pack trips in the Absaroka-Beartooth Wilderness and Yellowstone Park. They also offer hourly horseback rides and all-day fishing trips on horseback. Beautiful, secluded log cabins are for rent during the summer months. They can also arrange guided fishing and Saddle-and-Paddle trips in the mountains and then on the thrilling whitewater of the Yellowstone River near Gardiner. Please inquire for rates as they vary seasonally.

✍ **Medicine Lake Outfitters** (406-388-4938; www.packtrips.com), 3246 Linney Road, Bozeman. Since 1973 Tom and Joan Heintz have been running day rides and overnight horse-packing trips in Yellowstone Country. They offer a variety of trips for all levels of ability. Advance reservations are highly recommended. Their trips may take you into the Madison, Bridger, Gallatin Mountains or Yellowstone National Park. They also offer single-day horseback fly-fishing trips, where a guide will ride with you and your horse to a remote stream or lake for some fishing. Please inquire about rates.

Montana Horses (406-285-3541; www.montanahorses.com), 9700 Clarkston

Road, Three Forks. The team of Kail Mantle and Renee Daniels-Mantle provides an abundance of horse services, but their specialty lies in providing some of the best horses in the region for rent or lease. So if you are looking to take a horse-packing adventure and have the necessary experience but not the horses, they can hook you up. For even the more adventuresome sort, they offer a wrangling school each spring. Advance reservations are required, and please inquire for rates as they vary seasonally.

✔ **Paintbrush Adventures** (406-328-4158; www.paintbrushadventures.com), 86 Stillwater Road, Absarokee. For rides into the Absaroka-Beartooth Wilderness or just the Beartooth Mountains, these folks can do it for you whether it is a day- or weeklong adventure. They also offer a Saddle-and-Paddle trip, which is a horseback ride and then a whitewater float trip on the Stillwater River. They also can arrange guided fishing trips and guided hikes, drop camps and wilderness pack trips. Please inquire for rates as they vary seasonally.

✔ **320 Guest Ranch** (406-995-4283; www.320guestranch.com), 205 Buffalo Horn Creek, Big Sky. Located just off US 191 south of Big Sky, the 320 is in the middle of some of the best Yellowstone Country has to offer. Their horseback rides take you deep into the Gallatin National Forest for either a day or a week. They have evening cookouts, hay rides, sleigh rides, kids-only rides, and family outings. This is a complete guest ranch, but their horseback-riding services are some of the most varied and enjoyable in the region. Please inquire for rates as they vary seasonally.

See also Ranch Vacations under *To Do–Unique Adventures.*

HOT SPRINGS **Bozeman Hot Springs** (406-586-6492; www.bozemanhotsprings .com), 8 miles west of Bozeman on US 191. Open daily, year-round; hours and rates vary so please inquire. They recently underwent a massive renovation and they got it right—it is clean, comfortable, and family friendly. There are several pools, ranging from a cold pool to a steaming hot pool. This is a locals' hangout, especially on the weekends, but there is always space in the pools. The pools are chemical free and also have wet and dry saunas. There is even a fitness center, and massages are available with advance reservations. Recently they have added a day-care center in case you want to soak without the kids for once.

✔ **Chico Hot Springs Resort and Day Spa** (406-333-4933; www.chicohot springs.com), 1 Old Chico Road, 31 miles north of Gardiner on US 89 or 30 miles south of Livingston on US 89. Watch for the signs, as the directions on how to get from Chico from US 89 are well marked, but the resort lies off the main highway a few miles. Open daily year-round; rates vary depending on season and services selected. If you are planning to stay the night you must make your reservations in advance, sometimes as much as six months to a year ahead if you want to stay over on a weekend. Chico has become a Montana institution over the past 30 years. They have two pools: one hot and one warm. The dining room serves excellent food, and rooms are reasonable as well. There is a day spa on-site and advance reservations are a must. Chico has its own character that is hard to define and you must visit to truly understand how this place works—it is unique to Montana and the West. (See also the listing under *Lodging–Other Options.*)

PADDLING/FLOATING **The Boulder River** south of Big Timber on MT 298 (Main Boulder Road) offers some incredible paddling above Natural Bridge for very experienced whitewater kayakers and rafters. This water should be taken very seriously and not suitable for the casual floater. The water below Natural Bridge is a tad more mellow, but the abundance of boulders and low water as early as July make it a tough go. There are a few access points downstream of Natural Bridge, and they are well marked and easy to see from the river. Above the bridge there are few access points and anyone floating this stretch must not float past Falls Creek Campground. There is a bridge about 0.25 mile above the campground. If you are planning to float anywhere on the Boulder River it would be a good idea to seek some local knowledge before venturing out.

The Gallatin River begins in the northwest corner of Yellowstone National Park and flows in the park for its first few miles. Floating is prohibited in the park and few paddlers spend time above Big Sky outside the park as the river is mainly a boulder-strewn obstacle course. A few miles downstream from Big Sky floaters finally turn their attention to the river. For the next 20 miles from here the river's whitewater ranges from Class II to IV. Similar to some other rivers in the region, the section from Big Sky to the Squaw Creek Bridge should only be floated by very experienced paddlers. Once the river passes under Squaw Creek Bridge, it flows out of the canyon and into the Gallatin Valley. Floaters will find a mix of logjams but little in the way of rapids from Squaw Creek to where the river meets the Missouri near Three Forks. Several companies operate guided floats on the Gallatin, and one of my favorites is **Montana Whitewater** (1-800-799-4465; www.montanawhitewater.com). They offer a wide array of whitewater trips; please call for pricing information as rates vary.

THE BOULDER RIVER

THE GALLATIN RIVER NEAR BIG SKY

The Stillwater River flows off the north slope of the Beartooth Mountains near Absarokee. The name must have been a joke because even at its headwaters the river barely has a still stretch of water. This river, even in its lower reaches, is one that should only be run by very experienced floaters or with a professional guide or outfitter. The upper reaches include some of the most exciting rapids in Montana, and several guides and outfitters provide safe, fun whitewater trips here. Two of my favorites in the area are **Adventure Whitewater** (406-446-3061; www.adventurewhitewater.com) in Red Lodge and Absarokee and **Beartooth Whitewater** (406-799-3142; www.beartoothwhitewater.com).

The Yellowstone River has the most accessible, and beginner friendly, whitewater of all the rivers in this region, and it also has the most miles of lazy and relaxing floating. Originating from Yellowstone Lake in Yellowstone National Park, the river tumbles out of Yellowstone (where floating the river becomes legal) at the town of Gardiner. For the next 20 miles the river is a mix of rock gardens, drops, and riffles. In these 20 miles there is a mix of Class II and III rapids (and perhaps a IV during high flows). Only one section of the river ought to be left to experts and that is the water in Yankee Jim Canyon. This section begins at the Joe Brown/Yankee Jim Gallatin National Forest access at the south end of the canyon. Once the river leaves the canyon, it flows relatively smoothly all the way to Billings. From here the river is wide, access plentiful, and the scenery spectacular. Many whitewater rafting companies work the Gardiner/Yankee Jim area, but my favorite (and the one that has been around the longest) is the **Yellowstone Raft Company** (1-800-858-7781; www.yellowstoneraft.com). They offer several trips and are one of four companies that can utilize a special Park Service put-in, ensuring that you can float some of the best rapids on the river.

See also Gallatin Whitewater Festival under *Special Events.*

THE EXCITING WHITEWATER OF YANKEE JIM CANYON ON THE YELLOWSTONE RIVER

SNOW SPORTS

Ice Skating

Bozeman Recreation Department's Ice Skating Rinks (406-587-4724), located in Southside Park (S. 5th and College), Bogart Park (Church St. and Olive) and Beall Park (N. Black and Villard). Open around Christmas, closed in spring (weather dependent). The city of Bozeman has several parks where ice skating is available. When the cold weather stays for good, the parks listed have free ice skating.

Skiing

Big Sky Resort (406-995-5000; www.bigskyresort.com), 1 Lone Mountain Trail, Big Sky. With more than 150 named trails and 11,166-foot Lone Peak at the top of it all, Big Sky Resort and Lone Mountain offer skiers a remarkable abundance of options. There are 3,600 acres (nearly 5,500 once you add in adjoining Moonlight Basin), a run of 6 miles, and thousands of feet of vertical. The resort is also a great place for kids (I skied many of these runs by the time I was four years old) because if you have two paying adults, children 10 and under are free. And skiing is not all that can be had here. Summer or winter, there are plenty of things to do, including dinner sleigh rides, a kids' club, horseback riding, day care, snowshoeing, fly-fishing, a full-service spa, and lots more. *Lifts:* 1 tram, 1 quad, 1 gondola, 4 triples, 4 high-speed quads, 6 doubles, 3 handle tows. *Terrain:* 150 trails—17 percent beginner, 25 percent intermediate, 37 percent advanced, 21 percent expert; 4,350 feet of vertical. *Snowmaking:* 10 percent coverage. *Average annual snowfall:* 400 inches. *Facilities:* large base lodge with various restaurants and restrooms. *Snow sports school:* available for all ages and ability levels of skiers and snowboarders. *For children:* day care for ages 6 months to 8 years, Small Fry Try for ages 3–4, Mini Camp for ages 4–6, Ski Camp for ages 6–12, Teen Mountain Experience for ages 13–17. *Rates:* adults 18 to 70—$75 for just Big Sky, $89 for Lone Peak Pass, which includes Moonlight Basin; adults 70 and over, $65; juniors 11–17, $55; children 10 and under free with 2 paying adults; inquire about half-day and multi-day rates.

✦ **Bohart Ranch Cross-Country Ski Center** (406-586-9070; www.bohart ranchxcski.com), 16621 Bridger Canyon Road, 16.6 miles north of Bozeman via MT 86. Located in Bridger Canyon, this ranch is designed for the Nordic skier. They offer regularly groomed trails perfect for classic tracks or skating. Some of the views on their trails are fantastic and the quiet nature of Nordic skiing lends itself to seeing wildlife. Lessons are offered in classic and skate skiing for all ages and abilities. Rental equipment is available from an extensive pro shop. I also enjoy the biathlon course when I'm feeling inclined to get a workout and then try some shooting practice. *Trails:* 25 kilometers, varied terrain with plenty of beginner and expert terrain, and some snowshoeing trails as well. *Rates:* adults $15, children 7–12, $8, 6 and under free, seniors 70 and over free.

&. ✦ **Bridger Bowl Ski and Snowboard Resort** (406-587-2111; www.bridger bowl.com), 15795 Bridger Canyon Road, 16 miles north of Bozeman via MT 86. Explore a big mountain with short lift lines, long runs, and big bowls. Though well known for its incredible cold-smoke powder, they groom nearly a third of the runs. The best thing about this place is its world-class skiing at small-town rates. This nonprofit community ski area is ranked consistently as one of the top values in the nation and is only 20 minutes from downtown Bozeman. *Lifts:* 1 quad, 2 triples, 4 doubles. *Terrain:* 71 trails—25 percent beginner, 35 percent intermediate, 40 percent expert; 2,000 feet of vertical drop. *Average annual*

LONE PEAK TOWERS OVER BIG SKY SKI RESORT

BRIDGER BOWL SKI AREA NEAR BOZEMAN

snowfall: 350 inches. *Snowmaking:* 4 percent coverage. *Facilities:* three cafeterias, a slopeside bar and grill, plus a midmountain lodge with food, beer, and wine. *Ski school:* Available for all ages and abilities and guided skiing, please inquire. *Rates:* adults 13–64, $43; seniors 65–71, $35; children 6–12, $15; children 5 and under free; seniors 72 and over free. Inquire about half- and multi-day rates.

& ✇ **Moonlight Basin Ski Resort** (406-993-6000; www.moonlightbasin.com), past Big Sky on MT 64, Big Sky. This is Montana's newest ski resort, open since 2003. Adjacent to Big Sky Ski Resort, this resort opens up most of the north side of Lone Peak. With one pass, skiers can access both Moonlight Basin and Big Sky Ski Resort, creating the largest ski area in North America—the amount of terrain between the two is amazing. This is a full-service destination resort complete with slopeside lodging, spa, several options for food, a fitness center, dogsledding, snowshoeing, ice skating, a hot tub, and a heated outdoor pool. *Lifts:* 1 triple, 1 six-person, 1 double, 3 quads, 1 kids' conveyor. *Terrain:* 76 trails—23 percent beginner, 41 percent intermediate, 36 percent expert; 4,166 feet of vertical drop. *Facilities:* full-service restaurant and bar at the base lodge, food at two other restaurants; *Ski school:* customized instructions, please inquire. *Rates:* adults, $51; college student with ID, $46; seniors 70+, $46; juniors, 11–17, $39; military, $39; children 10 and under free. Inquire about half- and multi-day rates.

& ✇ **Red Lodge Mountain Resort** (406-446-2610; www.redlodgemountain .com), US 212 in Red Lodge. The family-friendly atmosphere at Red Lodge Mountain is hard to beat. The mountain has some surprisingly good skiing for it being "off the radar," so to speak, in relation to the other areas in this region, but for many skiers that is just fine. I love the powder here and the views of the

Beartooth Mountains. The ski area is only five minutes from the town of Red Lodge, which is a fun little western town; it reminds me of what Montana was like 20 years ago. *Lifts:* 1 triple, 2 high-speed quads, 4 doubles, 1 handle tow. *Terrain:* 71 trails—14 percent beginner, 29 percent intermediate, 57 percent expert; 2,400 feet of vertical drop. *Average annual snowfall:* 250 inches. *Snowmaking:* 30 percent. *Facilities:* one full-service bar/restaurant and two cafeterias on the mountain. *Ski school:* available for all ages and abilities of skiers and snowboarders. *For children:* day care for ages 1–4, Wrangler Ski Program for ages 4–6 (private instruction for ages 3–6 available), Trailblazer Learn to Ski and Skillbuilder Program for ages 7–12. *Rates:* adult, $45; junior 13–18, $39; children 6–12, $15; free for children 5 and under and for seniors 70 and over. Inquire about half- and multi-day rates.

Red Lodge Nordic Center (406-446-9191; www.beartoothtrails.org), 3 miles west of Red Lodge on MT 78 off Fox Road. Red Lodge Nordic Center is nestled at the base of Beartooth Mountains only 3 miles away from downtown Red Lodge. Ski from Thanksgiving through March on 15 kilometers of machine-groomed trails, from open meadow trails to rolling loops through the aspen trees. *Trails:* 4 kilometers are easy, 7 kilometers more difficult, 4 kilometers most difficult. *Rates:* adults $5, children 13 and under $3. There is a sign-in and money box at the entrance.

Rendezvous Ski Trails (406-823-6961; www.rendezvousskitrails.com), just south of West Yellowstone. These trails are operated and maintained by the West Yellowstone Chamber of Commerce. This Nordic trail system winds 42 kilometers through the Gallatin National Forest next to Yellowstone National Park. The trail system includes a wide skating lane and diagonal stride tracks. The U.S.

MOONLIGHT BASIN, ONE OF THE STATE'S NEWEST SKI RESORTS, IS RIGHT NEXT TO BIG SKY

Nordic and biathlon teams train here during the month of November. Hundreds of other race enthusiasts converge on West Yellowstone for weeks of early season training. Dogs and snowmobiles are prohibited. *Trails:* 42 kilometers of beginner, intermediate, and expert terrain. *Rates:* $5, except for November when passes are $10. These can be purchased at the trailhead or at Free Wheel and Heel in West Yellowstone. (See also Yellowstone Ski Festival under *Special Events.*)

Snowmobiling

When the snow starts to fall in this region, snowmobilers are getting their sleds tuned, routes planned, and hoping for even more snow. The massive amounts of snow that fall here and the wide array of public land translate to plenty of places to run a snow machine. In the **Gallatin National Forest** alone there are nearly 150 miles of groomed trails accessible from the area around **West Yellowstone.** West Yellowstone is also the jumping-off point for most of the snowmobiling into Yellowstone National Park. Near **Cooke City,** sledders can find trails heading off US 212. Because of heavy snow and changing weather it is a good idea to check locally for specific trail conditions. In the **Custer National Forest** on the north slope of the Beartooth Mountains, there are dozens of groomed snowmobile trails leading into and around these majestic mountains. Snowmobiles are fairly easy to operate and you will find many options for snowmobile rentals in Cooke City, Red Lodge, West Yellowstone, and the Bozeman area.

UNIQUE ADVENTURES Absaroka Dogsled Treks (406-222-4645; www .extrememontana.com), based out of Chico Hot Springs, 36 miles south of Livingston off US 89. Available every day except Christmas Day from Thanksgiving through March, weather permitting. With a sled drawn by a team of Alaskan and Siberian huskies, Absaroka Dogsled Treks offer you quite the adventure. Along with an experienced guide, bundle up the kids and mush a six-dog team. Enjoy the serenity of Mill Creek Canyon as you explore the Absaroka-Beartooth Mountains. For a longer adventure, take it all in on an 18-mile "Denali trek" overlooking mountain summits. Dine on buffalo steak and trout grilled to order. Or enjoy a picnic on a half-day "Yukon trek." If time is limited, get a taste of dogsledding on the 2-hour, 6-mile "Tenderfoot trek." Please inquire for rates; advance reservations are highly recommended.

✍ 🐎 **Chuckwagon BBQ, Hay, and Dinner Horse Rides at the 320 Guest Ranch** (406-995-4283; www.320ranch.com), 11 miles south of Big Sky on US 191, just across the Gallatin River from the highway. You do not have to be an overnight guest at the ranch to enjoy their activities. Whether summer, winter, fall, or spring, the wranglers and ropers at this well-run guest ranch are great at planning enjoyable trail rides and rides with a purpose—for dinner, breakfast, and just plain fun. Their chuckwagon dinner ride is one of my favorites, but I also enjoy the winter sleigh ride, where there is always a good chance to see some elk migrating out of Yellowstone Park. Either of these trips is great for children, as the staff at the 320 is great with kids. Inquire about rates since so many options exist. Additionally, advance reservations are highly recommended.

Lone Peak Tram (406-995-5000; www.bigskyresort.com), 1 Lone Mountain Trail, Big Sky. Whether you are an expert skier or hardcore hiker, taking a trip up the Lone Peak Tram is a unique experience. Built in the late 1990s, this tram cost nearly $3 million dollars, holds 15 passengers, and takes people to the summit of 11,150-foot Lone Peak. In winter, skiers can access some of the best double-black diamond terrain in Montana. In summer, hikers have spectacular views and quad-burning descents. If you want to rest your body you can simply enjoy the ride back down and stay in the comfort and safety of the tram.

✐ **Moonlight Dinners** (406-995-3880; www.moonlightdinners.com), Moonlight Basin Ranch, 1 mile past Big Sky Mountain Resort. The name says it all— dinners by moonlight at Moonlight Basin Resort. The professional guides at **Montana Backcountry Adventures** (www.skimba.com) will organize, pack a scrumptious dinner, and take you on snowcats (what they use to groom trails, basically a giant car on treads) for a journey through the snow-covered woods. After about 30 minutes you will leave the snowcat and dine in a warm and toasty yurt (a small, cabinlike structure about 30 feet in diameter). Menu items include filet mignon, cedar-plank salmon, and other tasty delights. This is certainly roughing, though in style. Rates $95 per person (price includes tax and gratuity), children ages 10 and under are $85. This trip is uniquely Montana and worth the price.

RANCH VACATIONS Montana is home to more than one hundred first-class guest ranches. These ranches range from working cattle and sheep ranches to luxurious pampering dude ranches where guests relax and unwind at their leisure. The abundance and diversity of ranch vacations are reflective of Montana—there is always something for every taste. Below is a listing of some

THE LONE PEAK TRAM

of my favorites, but this list is by no means complete. And in order to find the ranch that best suits your tastes and desires, it is always a good idea to contact them directly. They are listed here in alphabetical order: **Crazy Mountain Cattle Company** (406-222-6101; www.montanaworkingranches.com/crazy _mountain_cattle_company.htm), Big Timber; **G Bar M Ranch** (406-686-4423; www.gbarm.com), Clyde Park, north Livingston; **Hawley Mountain Guest Ranch** (406-932-5791; www.hawleymountain.com), McLeod south of Big Timber; **Lazy E-L Working Guest Ranch** (406-328-6858; www.lazyel.com), Roscoe; **Lonesome Spur Ranch** (406-662-3460; www. onesomespur.com), Bridger; **Parade Rest Ranch** (406-646-7217; www.paraderestranch.com), West Yellowstone; **Rocking Tree Ranch** (406-932-5057; www.rockingtreeranch.com); **S-Bar Shepherd Ranch** (406-326-2327; www.shepherdranch.com), Reed Point; **Sweet Grass Ranch** (406-537-4477; www.sweetgrassranch.com), Big Timber; **WD Ranch** (406-537-4452; www.thewdranch.com), Melville, north of Big Timber.

ROCK CLIMBING AND ICE CLIMBING Not to be taken lightly, rock climbing and ice climbing opportunities abound in this region. It is strongly advised that you hire the services of a professional guide service if you want to rock or ice climb in Yellowstone Country. There are several reasons for this, but one is the remote nature of many of the climbing opportunities—should an accident happen, the nearest hospital will most likely be hours away. Here is a listing of a few of the climbing guides in the region: **Beartooth Mountain Guides** (406-446-9874; www.beartoothmountainguides) in Red Lodge offers everything from day climbs to overnights to their unique Snow School. If you want to summit **Granite Peak** (see *To See–Natural Wonders*) these folks have been doing it for years. Another good resource is **Barrel Mountaineering** (406-582-1335; www.barrelmountaineering.com) in downtown Bozeman. They can assist with guides, climbs, safety, trail conditions, gear, and more. They also offer ice climbing instruction in Hyalite Canyon near Hyalite Reservoir.

WILDLIFE SAFARIS This sounds like something reserved for regions of Africa, but this part of Montana, and south into Yellowstone National Park, is home to hundreds of species of unique wildlife. Many of the wildlife in the region can be spotted by taking any of the scenic drives listed in this section. Additionally, a few companies offer guided wildlife-viewing adventures, most notably **Safari Yellowstone** (406-222-8557; www.safariyellowstone.com) in Livingston. These folks have created guided trips: In the comfort of specially-designed vans and snowcats, you will enjoy viewing many of the region's wildlife.

✳ Wilder Places

PARKS ♿ **Greycliff Prairie Dog Town State Park** (406-247-2940; http://fwp .mt.gov/lands/site_283312.aspx), Exit 378 off I-90 at Greycliff, east of Big Timber near **Big Timber Waterslide.** Open for day use only, April through October. Perhaps before or after a trip to the waterslide, grab your camera and hop off I-90 at Greycliff to delight in the playful, curious black-tailed prairie dogs that

live here. Interpretive signs provide information on the important role of these
entertaining animals. There are no amenities here (expect for a pit toilet), but it
is a quick stop and a nice place for a picnic while watching the goofy animals.

& **Missouri Headwaters State Park** (406-994-4042; http://fwp.mt.gov/lands/
site_281910.aspx), Exit 283 from I-90, then east on MT 205, then 3 miles north
on MT 286 (the directions from I-90 are well marked). Open year-round for day
use; free for residents, $5 for nonresidents; camping only allowed May 1 through
September 30, $12. Three major rivers come together here (the Jefferson, Madi-
son, and Gallatin) to form the headwaters of the Missouri River. You can walk in
the footsteps of Lewis & Clark along the **Confluence Trail** (see *To Do–Hiking*).
The park is also a great place to camp, fish, picnic, boat, and hike.

See also Madison Buffalo Jump State Park and Parker Historic Homestead State
Park under *To See–Historic Landmarks, Places, and Sites.*

FORESTS Custer National Forest, Beartooth Ranger District (406-446-
2103; www.fs.fed.us/r1/custer/recreation/D2.shtml), HC 49 Box 3420, Red
Lodge. This ranger district is home to most of the Beartooth Mountains, four
national recreation trails (an abundance of other great trails), the Beartooth
Scenic Highway (possibly the most stunning drive in the Lower 48), 345,000
acres of the **Absaroka-Beartooth Wilderness,** and lots more. This district is
also home to **Red Lodge Mountain Ski Resort** and **Granite Peak.** Recreational opportunities include boating, bicycling, camping, fishing, horseback riding, paddling/floating, rock climbing, ice climbing, cross-country skiing,
snowmobiling, snowshoeing, picnicking, and wildlife viewing.

Gallatin National Forest (406-587-6701; www.fs.fed.us/r1/gallatin), P.O. Box
130, Bozeman 59771. There are 1.8 million acres in the Gallatin National Forest
and all of them are in this region. This forest is home to six mountain ranges,
two designated **wilderness areas** (**Lee Metcalf** and **Absaroka-Beartooth,**
both crown jewels of the nation's wilderness areas), hundreds of miles of well-
maintained trails, and lots more. Recreational pursuits are endless but include
boating, hiking, fishing, horseback riding, rock climbing, ice climbing, snow skiing (the forest is home to three world-class ski resorts in **Bridger Bowl, Moonlight Basin,** and **Big Sky**), snowmobiling, and more.

WILDERNESS AREAS Absaroka-Beartooth Wilderness (406-587-6701;
www.fs.fed.us/r1/gallatin or 406-446-2103; www.fs.fed.us/r1/custer/recreation/
D2.shtml), managed by the Gallatin and Custer National Forests, this wilderness
area is nearly 1 million acres in size. It was created in 1975 and named after the
Crow Indians (*Absaroka* being an Indian name for "Crow") and one mountain
peak's likeness to a bear's tooth. This area is home to hundreds of lakes, several
glaciers, and an abundance of wildlife.

Lee Metcalf Wilderness Area (406-587-6701; www.fs.fed.us/r1/gallatin) is
located west and south of the Gallatin Valley and managed by the Gallatin
National Forest. With almost 300,000 acres, this wilderness is a vital chunk of
habitat in the land northwest of Yellowstone National Park. This area is home to
numerous jagged mountain peaks and some of the most beautiful scenery in

ABSAROKA-BEARTOOTH WILDERNESS

Montana. It is easily accessed from the Bozeman and Big Sky areas and provides visitors and locals a place to truly get away from the hustle and bustle.

WILDLIFE REFUGES AND WILDLIFE MANAGEMENT AREAS ✒ **Beartooth Nature Center** (406-446-1133; www.beartoothnaturecenter.org) in Coal Miners Park on 2nd Avenue E. (US 212), Red Lodge. Open daily mid-May through mid-October, 10 A.M.–5 P.M.; daily mid-October through mid-May, 10 A.M.–2 P.M. Admission $6 adults, $5 adults 55 and over, $2.50 children ages 5–15. This is the only public refuge in Montana to house native animals that cannot be returned to the wild due to injury or habituation to humans. They care for 75 animals and birds, many placed here by the Montana Department of Fish, Wildlife & Parks, including wolves, mountain lions, black bears, bison, elk, antelope, bobcat, fox, coyote, eagles, hawks, owls, and many more. The center offers visitors an unparalleled chance to learn about these and other animals by observing them at close range and through interpretive displays.

Dome Mountain Wildlife Management Area (406-247-2940; http://fwp.mt .gov/lands/site_281152.aspx), south on US 89 for 21 miles, then west on Chico Road at Emigrant for 1 mile, then south on MT 540 (East River Road) for 3 miles, then 8 miles south on Sixmile Creek Road. This area is adjacent to Dailey Lake and is probably the best place to view herds of elk in the winter.

Hailstone National Wildlife Refuge and **Halfbreed Lake National Wildlife Refuge** (406-538-8706), north of Columbus via MT 306 to Rapelje, then east of Rapelje on the Molt-Rapelje Road. This complex of wildlife refuges

ends in the south with the state-managed **Eastlick Pond–Big Lake Wildlife**
Management Area. This is not a developed recreation area by any means, but more for waterfowl and migratory birds. Bird-watching and wildlife viewing are the extent of the activities here. However, solitude and some rare animal sightings are possible.

YELLOWSTONE NATIONAL PARK Yellowstone (307-344-7381; www.nps.gov/yell) is open year-round, but with seasonal road and service closures, so be sure to check locally. Although the majority of the nation's first national park lies in Wyoming, the park also extends into Montana and Idaho. Created before any of the three states were actually part of the Union, Yellowstone is a remarkable place. In fact, the majority of its visitors enter the park through one of three Montana entrances, so it is important to include Yellowstone National Park in this region. The park's 2.2 million acres were established in 1872 by an act of Congress, creating the world's first national park. The park is home to a large variety of wildlife, including grizzly bears, wolves, bison, and elk. Preserved within Yellowstone National Park are Old Faithful and a collection of the world's most extraordinary geysers and hot springs and the Grand Canyon of the Yellowstone, among many other extraordinary sites. And from hiking to guided snowmobile tours, visitors will not find a lack of recreational opportunities, or providers. Lodging and camping are available in the park (406-344-7381; www.nps.gov/yell/planyourvisit/lodging-in-yellowstone.htm) and in its gateway communities. For most visitors, a trip to Yellowstone Country wouldn't be complete without a stop in Yellowstone National Park.

✳ Lodging
BED & BREAKFASTS

Absarokee
 ♿ **Brookside Bed & Breakfast**
(406-328-4757), 103 Brook Street. Nestled in the little town of Absarokee is a perfect place to relax after a day exploring the nearby mountains and rivers. There is a large family-style common room, a hot tub (which is nice after fishing or hiking all day), and a filling breakfast each morning. There are four bedrooms: one queen, one queen and double (these two rooms share a bathroom), one double and twin on the main floor (this room has a private bathroom), and one double upstairs with a nice sitting area outside the room. Rates $80 and up.

Stillwater Lodge (406-328-4899; www.stillwaterlodge.net), 28 South Woodard Avenue. They have six distinctive rooms, each with a different décor and theme, all with native lodgepole beds (which are sometimes hard to get out of because they are so comfy), antiques, and fine paintings and prints. The lodge is great for people seeking a variety of Montana adventures and assists with arrangements for fly-fishing, backpacking, horseback riding, and river rafting. In winter, guests enjoy miles of cross-country ski trails, and for downhill powder fans, Red Lodge Ski Resort is nearby. For the less adventuresome, there are many fine-dining establishments, antique, gift, and art shops, and legendary watering holes within minutes of the lodge. Rates $70 and up.

Big Sky

&. **Big EZ Lodge** (406-995-7003; www.bigezlodge.com), 5.8 miles from US 191 on Beaver Creek Road. In just a few short years, this place has evolved into one of the most exclusive and intimate lodges in the Rocky Mountains. This extraordinary retreat blends the finest in American antiques and original fine-art appointments with the tradition of the 19th-century Arts & Crafts period. The Big EZ dining room serves superb cuisine with a specialty in wild game and organically grown produce. Service throughout the lodge is attentive without being intrusive. Constructed at a cost of $12 million, the lodge's 12 luxurious guest rooms and the Lone Star Suite feature individually decorated accommodations, several with river-rock fireplaces. If you must stay connected while on vacation, each room offers high-speed Internet access through T1 lines. Please inquire for rates.

Big Timber

Big Timber Inn Bed & Breakfast (406-932-4080; www.finditlocal.com/bigtimber/lodging.htm), P.O. Box 328. Take Exit 370 off I-90, then go east on the northside Frontage Road for roughly 1.5 miles to the second house at the end of the drive. Located on the Yellowstone River approximately 3 miles northeast of Big Timber, this B&B offers seclusion and privacy. The views of the Yellowstone River, the Crazy Mountains to the north, and other mountain ranges are breathtaking. The guest accommodations are found in the lower portion of the home and provide two spacious bedrooms, a full bathroom, and a large comfortable sitting room with a wood-burning stove and a television. Rates $60 and up.

The Grand Hotel and Bed & Breakfast (406-932-4459; www.thegrand-hotel.com), 139 McLeod Street. The Grand Hotel is a gem of a historic hotel with a fabulous restaurant. The rooms are sunny and spacious, exquisitely decorated in Victorian themes, the wine list is award-winning, and visitors are treated with gracious hospitality. The Grand boasts of serving cattlemen, cowboys, sheepherders, and travelers since 1890. Rates $59 and up.

Bozeman

The Fox Hollow Bed & Breakfast (406-582-8440; www.foxhollowbandb.com), 545 Mary Road, west of Bozeman near Cameron Bridge on the Gallatin River. Located in relative seclusion, they have luxury accommodations, panoramic mountain views, wide-open spaces, and hospitality unique to Montana. The country-style custom home offers a relaxed atmosphere surrounded by the peace and quiet of a country setting. It is minutes to the Gallatin River, downtown Bozeman, and some inviting open country. Settle into one of five spacious air-conditioned guest rooms, each with beautiful furnishings, mountain views, and private bath. View the sunset, the stars, or the shocking blue of the Montana sky from the wraparound deck. Their hot tub is a great place to rest your knees after a day of hiking or sliding down the slopes at Bridger. Rates $100 and up.

Lehrkind Mansion Bed & Breakfast (406-585-6932; www.bozemanbedandbreakfast.com), 719 N. Wallace Avenue, downtown Bozeman.

This 1897 Queen Anne–style Victorian mansion is listed on the National Register of Historic Places. Inside, the décor includes period antiques, an abundance of plant life and comfy chairs, and an atmosphere that encourages relaxation. There is also a hot tub to round out the options for relaxation. A full gourmet breakfast is served daily and fuels you up for a walking tour of historic downtown Bozeman, which is only a few blocks away.

Voss Inn (406-587-0982; www .bozeman-vossinn.com), 319 S. Willson, downtown Bozeman. There are six bedrooms at the immaculate mansion. In this restored 120-year-old Victorian, you will be only three blocks from downtown Bozeman, six blocks from Montana State University, and less than half an hour from a variety of recreational opportunities. The breakfasts are scrumptious and filling (they will even bring it to your room if you would like). After breakfast, and before your day of adventure, you can amble through their Victorian rose garden. Or for a nice afternoon respite, enjoy a spot of tea in the garden as well. Rates $100 and up.

Emigrant

Johnstad's Bed & Breakfast (406-333-9003; www.johnstadsbb.com), 03 Paradise Lane. This lovely B&B on 5 acres is surrounded by some of the region's most beautiful scenery. Views of the Yellowstone River, Absaroka Mountains, Emigrant Peak, and the Hyalite Mountains can be had from nearly every room. They have three guest rooms, all with private baths. There is also a log cabin for folks who want more privacy. Rates $85 and up.

& **Paradise Gateway Bed & Breakfast** (406-333-4063; www.paradise gateway.com), Box 84, located 25.5 miles south of Livingston on US 89 between mile markers 26 and 27. Paradise Gateway has magnificent views of the Absaroka Mountains and is about a half-hour from Yellowstone National Park. The hosts, Pete and Carol Reed, have been in the valley for over 40 years and are great resources for local information. There are magnificent rooms in the B&B, but for larger groups the Reeds also have a cabin overlooking the Yellowstone and two riverside homes. The cabin is decorated in a western motif and it should be called a "luxurious retreat," as "cabin" does not do it justice—but the rates are very reasonable. The riverside homes sit on 20 acres, so they are great for families or groups who desire a little extra room to stretch their legs. Rates $85 and up.

Gardiner

♪ **The Gardiner Guest House** (406-848-7314; www.gardinerguest house.com), P.O. Box 196, Main Street and US 89 one block south of the Yellowstone River High Bridge. Owned by Richard and Nance Parks, who also own Parks Fly Shop, the Gardiner Guest House is an ideal spot for folks who want comfort and cleanliness, but don't need posh, chic, Victorian, or log cabin. The four rooms are themed and the house sits on the banks above the Yellowstone River. Nance's breakfasts are exactly the sustenance anyone needs before heading out for a day exploring Yellowstone Park or the surrounding area. In fact, they are literally one block from the park. While in Gardiner, you will quickly see the town may have come up with the slogan, "Come as you are." The Gardiner Guest House is pleasantly informal and a great option. Rates $75 and up.

♂ ♿ Headwaters of the Yellowstone Bed & Breakfast (406-848-7073; www.headwatersbandb.com), 9 Olson Lane, 6.4 miles north of Gardiner off US 89. Across the river from Yellowstone Park and 5 miles from the park boundary, there are few places as ideally situated (both for adventure and views) as Merv and Joyce Olson's B&B. They have five guest rooms in their main house and two riverside cabins. This is a great place for any anglers traveling with the family because they have river access and the family can enjoy the view while someone fishes. The Olsons can arrange whitewater float trips, horseback rides, and more.

Yellowstone Suites B&B (406-848-7937; www.yellowstonesuites.com), right past the Yellowstone River High Bridge onto Stone Street to Fourth Street; from there, follow the signs. Three blocks from the Roosevelt Arch and North Gate to Yellowstone National Park, this historic 1904 home is nestled in a quiet neighborhood off the main highway and next to the Yellowstone River, where the sounds of the river lull you to sleep and views of Electric Peak and the surrounding mountain ranges entice you to explore. Four guest rooms, two with private baths and a suite with a kitchenette, are arranged for comfort and privacy on the second and third floors. A large shaded porch and a beautifully landscaped woodland garden help to relax your bones after a day in the park. Before you start your day, a full country breakfast is served family style and includes an egg dish, meat, hot/cold cereals, seasonal fresh fruit, yogurt, fresh-baked pastries, and a wide assortment of beverages. My favorite is the apple-pecan custard coffee cake—but be sure to let it settle before you take too big a hike. Breakfasts-to-go are available for early morning anglers, hunters, birders, or wildlife watchers. Packed lunches or gourmet picnic items can also be purchased. Rates $80 and up.

Livingston

♿ Blue Winged Olive Bed & Breakfast (406-222-8646; www.bluewingedolive.net), 5157 US 89; 3 miles south of Livingston on US 89 (if you get to the East River Road turnoff you've gone too far). Owned by a local fly-fishing outfitter, this place is not just for anglers. Their large, ranch-style breakfast is hard to beat and one of the best breakfasts around. They have four rooms, all nonsmoking and all with private baths and private decks—a great feature for long summer days. A unique feature of the Blue Winged Olive is that they offer horse boarding on the property; however, they do not allow pets. Rates $90 and up.

Mission Creek Bed & Breakfast (406-222-8290; www.missoncreek bandb.com), 10 Mission Creek Road. Take Exit 343 east of Livingston; you can't miss this place. This beautiful ranch is located 10 miles east of Livingston on Mission Creek and offers views of the north slope of the Absarokas and the Crazy Mountains. They have three rooms, all with private baths, and a very nice suite with a spectacular view. They can arrange just about every activity. Mission Creek runs through the property and offers visitors a chance to relax by rippling waters or perhaps catch a trout on a fly. Rates $110 and up.

Red Lodge
Gallagher's Irish Rose Bed & Breakfast
(406-446-0303; www
.irishrosehost.com), 302 South Broadway, downtown Red Lodge. Nestled close to the Beartooth Mountains and Red Lodge Mountain and in the heart of historic Red Lodge, this is a nice base when exploring the area. A few of the rooms have spa tubs and fireplaces—both essential for unwinding after a day in the local wilds. There are three distinctive rooms, each with a private bath. The Emerald Room has a two-person spa tub and a shower, plus a cozy gas fireplace. The Irish Rose room has a cozy gas stove and an oversize shower. The Limerick Room has a spa tub/shower and can accommodate adults with children. Artist Leah Gallagher's original artwork, plus the work of other artists, adorns this elegant, lovingly restored, stately home (ca. 1910). Each room has been individually decorated to create a special place in your home away from home. The breakfasts here are plentiful and will fuel you up for a big day of whatever you are about to do—rafting the Stillwater River, fly-fishing Rock Creek, summiting Granite Peak, or swishing down the slopes at Red Lodge Mountain. Rates $80 and up.

Weatherson Inn Bed & Breakfast
(406-446-0213; www.weathersoninn
.com), 314 North Broadway, downtown Red Lodge. This charming 1910 Victorian home is just two blocks from downtown Red Lodge—providing gracious European-style accommodations with a Montana twist. The West Room is an elegant and spacious room featuring a queen bed and a private bath with spa tub and shower. The Suite consists of a bedroom, sunny sitting room, and large private bath with claw-foot soaking tub and large tiled shower. Furnished with a queen bed and a daybed with trundle, the Suite can accommodate up to four people or provide a luxurious retreat for one or two. Both rooms have a TV and VCR. Enjoy breakfast in the sunroom or on the deck, customized to suit your tastes, featuring fresh-baked goods and delightful entrees. Rates $89 and up.

Reed Point
The Bunkhouse Bed & Breakfast
(406-932-6537; www.bunkhouse.biz), Exit 384 off I-90 between Greycliff and Reed Point. Follow Bridger Creek Road south 3.6 miles and then follow the signs. This unique place is private, quiet, and completely western. Nestled in the foothills of the Beartooth Mountains along the shores of Bridger Creek, the Bunkhouse sits on 47 acres complete with wildlife and great views. The cabin is the only option available (so book early), but it comes complete with a refrigerator, toaster oven, hot plates, dishes, and utensils. There is one log double bed, one twin bunk bed, and a child's pull-out bed. For special guests (and of course every guest is special), there is one room in the main house. There are plans for a future cabin, so inquire about that when contacting these friendly folks. Rates $125 and up for the cabin.

Silver Gate
Log Cabin Cafe and Bed & Breakfast
(406-838-2367), US 212 West; you can't miss it. The owners have operated the restaurant since 1977 and in the early 1990s they purchased adjoining cabins and decided to operate a small B&B. The cabins,

built in the 1930s, have been refurbished by the owners and local crafters. Each cabin has two log double beds with easy access to the shower house and bathroom. The cabins are literally a mile from Yellowstone National Park. This is a nice place to stay if you want some quiet while visiting Yellowstone. Rates $85 and up.

West Yellowstone

&. **West Yellowstone Bed & Breakfast** (406-646-7754; www.westyellowstonebandb.com), 20 Crane Lane; 6 miles west of West Yellowstone on US 20, on the north side of the highway just after you cross the South Fork of the Madison. Scott and Deborah Clark have built a beautiful B&B minutes west of West Yellowstone. Each room is beautifully decorated and with very comfortable log beds, which Scott made himself. Scott also milled the wood and built the entire lodge as well. The rooms also come with private bath. This place is ideal for outdoor enthusiasts as it is an easy walk to some great fly-fishing and in winter provides access to ski trails or snowmobile trails. There is plenty of food for breakfast, and you even have a few choices each morning. Rates $135 and up.

LODGES, GUEST RANCHES, AND HOTELS/MOTELS

Big Sky

&. ✈ ✪ **Buck's T4 Lodge** (406-995-4111; www.bucksT4.com), P.O. Box 160279; 3 miles south of Big Sky on US 191. This is a very reasonably priced hotel in the heart of Gallatin Canyon. Hop on US 191 and you have your pick of some of the best hiking in the state. You are 10 minutes from Big Sky and Moonlight Basin and 30 minutes from Yellowstone Park. The food at Buck's T4 is some of the best around. The staff is very professional, the rooms are clean, and the bar is a great mix of atmosphere, good beer, and conversation. They have a large outdoor hot tub and swimming pool, which are open late so you can enjoy a long soak after your day of adventure. Rates $115 and up.

🍽 **The Motel at the Corral Steakhouse** (406-995-4249), 42895 Gallatin Road, 8 miles south of Big Sky on US 191. Across the highway from the Gallatin River and close to Yellowstone Park, the rooms here are simple, yet they're some of the most reasonably priced rooms in the area. This place is ideal for folks who want a clean, safe, and cheap place to stay while exploring the Big Sky area. Plus, they offer a large hot tub for soaking your muscles. If chocolates on your pillow and 600-thread-count sheets are a must for your vacation, than stay someplace else. But if you want quality rooms and reasonable prices, then this is the place. Rates $60 and up.

&. **Rainbow Ranch** (406-995-4132; www.rainbowranch.com), 42950 Gallatin Road; 10 miles south of Big Sky on US 191. Riverside cabins, great food, and easy access along US 191 make this an ideal location. The folks at the Rainbow Ranch can arrange any activity from fishing to dogsledding. The location is matched (and perhaps surpassed) by the 16 immaculate rooms that surround the main lodge. Each room comes with a private bath and Jacuzzi tub, and most have private decks with fabulous forest views. A few of the rooms even have fireplaces—great for those winter nights after days on the slopes.

For a large group or more social guests, they have a 12-person hot tub on-site. Their restaurant is one of the best in the area (see *Dining Out*) and is worth trying whether you are staying here or not. Rates $185 and up.

&. **River Rock Lodge** (406-995-4455; www.riverrocklodging.com), 3080 Pine Drive. In the middle of Big Sky's action (ski hill and golf course), the lodge is well appointed and meticulously thought out. The breakfast is more continental than hearty, but there is plenty of it and it is quite tasty. They have 29 rooms and the down comforters are great for snuggling. Rates $160 and up.

&. ☌ **Lone Mountain Ranch** (406-995-4644; www.lmranch.com), P.O. Box 160069; located 4.5 miles west of US 191 on the way to Big Sky. Lone Mountain Ranch is a summer family guest ranch and winter ski resort. Summer activities focus on appreciating nature through naturalist-guided walks, Yellowstone Park interpretive trips, riding, mountain biking, canoeing, special evening presentations, outdoor youth adventures, barbecues, and just about anything else. They also offer guided fly-fishing. In winter they offer 50 miles of professionally groomed ski trails for all levels of ability, packed snowshoe trails, and alpine skiing at Big Sky Ski Resort just 10 minutes away. Lone Mountain Ranch (LMR) has comfortable, cozy cabins, a beautiful log dining lodge, dependable snow, and top-quality ranch gourmet meals. One of my favorite things at LMR is the Sleigh Ride Dinner. Guests take a 20-minute sleigh ride through winter woods to the North Fork Cabin, where a prime rib feast awaits you. Musical entertainment rounds out the evening with folk/cowboy tunes. Reservations required and various packages are available, so it is best to inquire.

&. ☌ ☯ **320 Guest Ranch** (406-995-4283; www.320ranch.com), 205 Buffalo Horn Creek; 10 miles south of Big Sky on US 191. The 320 Guest Ranch caters to everyone—you can stay a day, a week, a month and they will take care of you with a smile. The ranch's historical journey began in 1898, when Sam Wilson homesteaded 160 acres along the Gallatin River. In 1900, Sam's father, Clinton, claimed an adjoining 160 acres and they combined their two properties, naming the stunning parcel the Buffalo Horn Resort. Today, guests can sample some true Montana traditions while also enjoying new activities. You can ski, fish, hike, horseback ride, or just relax in your cabin. Their location along the banks of the Gallatin River, close to Big Sky and Yellowstone, provides guests with ample options for exploring. For accommodations they have small cabins, large cabins, and luxury log homes, all of which are affordably priced. They offer dinner and wintertime sleigh rides, private events, and weddings. For a single cabin, rates are $90 and up.

See also Big Sky Resort and Moonlight Basin Ski Resort under *To Do–Snow Sports*.

Bozeman/Belgrade

Gallatin River Lodge (406-388-0148; www.grriverlodge.com), 9105 Thorpe Road; 5 miles south of Belgrade or 10 miles west of Bozeman. This lodge is nestled on the banks of the Gallatin River. The views from this lodge are to die for. The morning sunrises against the peaks of the Bridger Mountains and the evening sunsets amid the Tobacco Roots are amazing enough that friendly host Steve Gamble could charge even more for them (but he doesn't). A large heron rookery is nearby, with eagles, osprey, and sandhill cranes as neighbors. Whitetail deer, beaver, mink, muskrat, fox, and pheasant inhabit this riparian treasure. All six suites have elegant oak Mission-style furniture and a private bath containing a large Jacuzzi tub and shower. A king- or queen-size bed, large comfortable settle (Mission-style couch), beautiful fir floors, Tiffany lamps, satellite TV, and western artwork adorn each suite. Large windows offer super views of the mountains and river terrain.

Cooke City

Soda Butte Lodge (406-838-2251; www.cookecity.com), 210 US 212. This is more of hotel/motel than a lodge, but it's ideal for exploring Grasshopper Glacier, Yellowstone Park, and the forests around Cooke City. They have 32 rooms, a Jacuzzi suite, family suites, HBO, phones, hot tub, free wireless Internet, and public laundry. The fireplace in the grand lobby is pretty cool and a great place to trade stories at the end of the day. They also have an on-site restaurant, the Prospector, which overlooks the upper reaches of Soda Butte Creek. Rates $75 and up.

Big Moose Resort (406-838-2393; www.bigmooseresort.com), 715 US 212, 3 miles east of Cooke City. Big Moose Resort consists of cabin lodging surrounded by acres of national forestlands among lodgepole pines. Excellent access to fly-fishing, hiking, horseback riding, and winter activities. They have various cabins with private bath/shower, kitchenettes, satellite TV, and heating that are com-

fortable and clean. And they now offer wireless Internet access and massage. Their country atmosphere makes for a nice relaxed place to spend your vacation days and evenings. Rates $75 and up.

See also Buns 'N' Beds Deli and Cabins under *Eating Out*.

Emigrant

Chico Hot Springs (406-333-4933; www.chicohotsprings.com), #1 Chico Road; 36 miles south of Livingston in Emigrant. Head to Emigrant, then follow the signs. Chico is a Montana institution. From its hundred-year-old main lodge to the newer cabins with oversized bathrooms, this rustically romantic resort is unique to Paradise Valley. Chico boasts two open-air mineral hot springs pools. The small pool averages 104 degrees, and the large one averages 96 degrees. Guests can soak their cares away from 6 A.M. until midnight, every day of the year. Weekends book up well in advance, so plan ahead. You can eat cheap or dine with the movie stars in the dining room (Chico is that well known), but be sure to pack an attitude for fun because this place is distinctly laid back. Reservations are strongly suggested; inquire about rates as they have lots of options.

The Trout House and Guest Cabin (406-333-4763; www.thetrouthouse.com), 23 miles south of Livingston on US 89 to Emigrant. Call for specific directions. This is a private streamside mountain retreat, exquisitely furnished with all the comforts of home. Three bedrooms and two full baths accommodate up to eight guests in this handsome log home. Nestled in the cottonwoods at the base of 11,000-foot Emigrant

Mountain, the Trout House incorporates a vaulted great room, stone fireplace, a well-stocked gourmet kitchen, large deck with outdoor spa, fire ring, and picnic area into the perfect place for friends, family, or a romantic getaway. The Guest Cabin will accommodate up to four and is beautifully appointed with a western flair. Amenities include private sundeck, gear and rod racks, creek fishing, streamside fire ring and picnic area, horseshoes. They are minutes from Chico Hot Springs, midway between Livingston and Yellowstone National Park, and the Yellowstone River is at the end of the road. Inquire early about rates and reservations as they book up early.

Gallatin Gateway

♿ **Gallatin Gateway Inn** (406-763-4672; www.gallatingatewayinn.com), P.O. Box 376; US 191 fourteen miles south of Four Corners. "The Gateway" is only five minutes from the Gallatin River, 30 minutes from Big Sky, and 20 minutes from the Bozeman airport. The inn has been fully restored to its original 1920s splendor and is now among the finest historic inns in the Rocky Mountain West. Designed as the Chicago, Milwaukee & St. Paul Railroad's most elegant hotel, its palatial structure features arched windows, Spanish-style corbels, and carved beams. The original railroad clock still keeps accurate time in the lobby. Rooms and suites are decorated in warm tones of the West and offer amenities required by today's busy traveler. The inn's restaurant, the Porter House, a local favorite, is well known for its fine American and western cuisine. An on-site conference room and banquet facilities are also available, and there is a heated outdoor swimming pool and outdoor hot tub for guests.

Gardiner

♿ **Absaroka Lodge** (406-848-7414; www.yellowstonemotel.com), US 89. Absaroka Lodge is located on the banks of the Yellowstone River with a spectacular view of the river and of several peaks in Yellowstone. Each room has its own balcony directly overlooking the river. Sit on the lawn (unless the elk have beat you to it) or your balcony and kick back, relax, and enjoy the scenery. They offer quiet, clean, comfortable, air-conditioned rooms, including eight fully-equipped suites. There are queen-size beds, cable TV, phones, and smoking and nonsmoking rooms, and the lodge is within walking distance of restaurants, lounges, and shops. The friendly, helpful staff will help with information about Yellowstone National Park, area activities, and guides. Rates $90 and up.

Livingston

♿ ✸ **The Murray Hotel** (406-222-1350; www.murrayhotel.com), 201 W. Park Street. Their slogan, "Even cowboys need big, fluffy pillows," about sums up the Murray—very comfortable western-style lodging in intriguing downtown Livingston. Since its grand opening in 1904, the Murray Hotel's guest registry has been more like a who's who of Hollywood. Celebrities such as Buffalo Bill and Calamity Jane have graced the threshold of what was once *the* elegant railroad hotel. The Murray was also home to Walter Hill, son of railroad tycoon James J. Hill. More recently, colorful personalities like motion-picture director Sam Peckinpah rented what had been the largest suite in the place, built originally for an heir to the Burlington railroad fortune. The Murray also played host to other notables such as the Queen of Denmark and humorist Will Rogers. Despite all of the glitz, glamour, and wealth that has passed through the Murray, it still remains truly a "come as you are" hotel with a friendly staff. The large rooms all have great views, and you will be within walking distance of some of Montana's best food, bars, and art galleries. Guests would be hard-pressed to find a hotel in Montana, or the world, for that matter, that has the charm, friendliness, and unique touches of the Murray. Rates $75 and up.

Red Lodge

♿ **The Pollard** (406-446-0001; www.pollardhotel.com), 2 N. Broadway. Built in 1893 and known to have lodged Buffalo Bill Cody and Calamity Jane on more than one occasion, this hotel is more than just a historic icon to the Old West. In 1994 the owners did a massive renovation, and today the hotel is one of the better known in Montana. There are 39 guest rooms and suites and they offer varying degrees of luxury and amenities. All guests enjoy access to an on-premises health club and an on-site restaurant that serves great food. **Red Lodge Mountain Ski Resort** is less than 10 minutes away and the plethora of recreational opportunities in the Beartooth Mountains are close by as well. Rates $85 and up.

♿ ⚲ **Red Lodge Reservations** (406-446-1272; www.redlodgereservations.com). The folks here can arrange and book every type of lodging in the area. This truly is a one-stop place for hotels/motels, B&Bs, and vacation rentals. They also offer special packages. Rates vary, so please inquire.

Three Forks

♿ ⚲ ✦ **The Sacajawea Hotel** (406-285-6515; www.sacajaweahotel.com), 5 North Main Street. Ideal for exploring **Headwaters State Park** or **Madison Buffalo Jump State Park,** the Sacajawea Hotel offers gracious accommodations in 31 guest rooms, each with TV, private bath, and telephone. The hotel was named after the famous Shoshone guide who led the Lewis & Clark Expedition through the area in 1805. It was founded in 1910 by John Q. Adams (no relation to the former president) to serve the passengers and crew of the Milwaukee Railroad. When rail service to Three Forks was discontinued, the Sacajawea found itself in the unenviable position of being a railroad hotel without a railroad. However, today the hotel is still the focal point of the small community of Three Forks. The bar is one of the best in Montana, the food is served with a smile, and the rooms have a historical uniqueness that is hard to find anymore.

West Yellowstone

♿ ⚲ **Faithful Street Inn** (406-646-1010; www.faithfulstreetinn), 120 N. Faithful Street, downtown West Yellowstone. A few blocks from the west entrance to Yellowstone National Park, the Faithful Street Inn provides cabins and townhomes for multinight rentals. All of the cabins are individually decorated and anyone will feel right at home. Being in the heart of West Yellowstone, the Faithful Street Inn is a nice option for traveling families. The rates are considerably less in the spring and fall months as the busy tourist seasons are June–July and December–February.

OTHER OPTIONS ❦ **Gallatin National Forest Cabins** (406-587-6701; www.reserveamerica.com), P.O. Box 130, Bozeman. People are always surprised at the availability and abundance of Forest Service rental cabins. The cabins are in various locations throughout the forest, and some sleep only two people while others can handle groups of 10 or more. The prices are very reasonable (some for as little as $25/night), but most are also very primitive, offering only pit toilets and no running water in winter. However, each cabin is different so do the appropriate homework. Some offer vehicular access, some do not. The bottom line is this: If you want some adventure and don't mind putting forth a little effort in researching a cabin (and then getting there) these places offer a truly unique lodging experience. (See Gallatin National Forest under *To Do–Camping* for contact information for individual ranger districts and Gallatin National Forest under *Wilder Places–Forests.*)

Montana Vacation Homes (406-586-1503; www.montanavacation home.com), Intermountain Property Management, Inc., 1807 W. Dickerson, Suite A, Bozeman. Various vacation rentals—private homes, second homes, cabins, etc.—are available for short- and long-term stays nearly all over Yellowstone Country. The folks at Montana Vacation Homes have a substantial list of such properties. To include them all here would be impossible, so contact them for more information. Most accommodations offer a nice blend of luxury and value. Be sure to inquire and make reservations early, as most vacation properties in this region book up fast.

Mountain Home–Montana Vacation Rentals (406-586-4589; www .mountain-home.com), P.O. Box 1204, Bozeman. Mountain Home represents more than 60 very special vacation homes and cabins around Yellowstone Country. All of the offerings are carefully screened—they have charm and character, they are well maintained, and they are in great vacation locations. The homes are completely stocked with high-quality bed and bath linens, laundry and dish soap, complete kitchen equipment and essentials, and **Mountain Home** signature hand soaps. You simply bring your gear and the groceries and they take care of the rest. Inquire about rates and reservations early, as these homes book up fast.

Yellowstone National Park
♿ ❦ **Xanterra Parks and Resorts** (307-344-7311, 1-866-GEYSER-LAND; www.travelyellowstone), P.O. Box 165, Yellowstone National Park. Xanterra owns and operates all lodging in Yellowstone National Park. To book any accommodations in Yellowstone Park, with the exception of backcountry campsites, you must do so through Xanterra. The best place to stay for geyser watching is the Old Faithful Inn. The inn is the largest and oldest entirely log structure in North American. The lobby is a great place for people watching after a day spent watching geysers. For wildlife viewing in the northeast section of the park, rent a cabin at Roosevelt Lodge. For enjoying Yellowstone Lake, book one of the deluxe rooms at Lake Lodge. With a view of Yellowstone Lake, these rooms are as inspiring as they are comforting. Xanterra also has a wide selection of other

accommodations throughout the park. Be sure to inquire locally for the best lodging to match your party.

✳ Where to Eat

DINING OUT

Big Sky

⚡ **The Dining Room at Buck's T4 Lodge** (406-995-4111; www.bucks T4dining.com), P.O. Box 160279, 3 miles south of Big Sky on US 191. The dining experience at Buck's T4 is, for lack of a better word, phenomenal. They have worked extremely hard to train and retain a great team of servers, the wine list is one of the best in the area, and the menu that chef Scott Peterson has created could be at home in San Francisco or Paris, but he's put a fabulous Montana twist on it. The prices are not cheap, but excellent food, wine, and service is worth splurging on every now and then. The bar is intimate and relaxed—you won't find many hardcore rocksters in this bar. It has a dark, yet inviting feel, and once you're in, it is hard to leave. The music is at the right volume and it is an ideal place for conversation without feeling like you have to yell to the person next to you.

⚡ **Rainbow Ranch Lodge** (406-995-4132; www.rainbowranch.com), 42950 Gallatin Road, 10 miles south of Big Sky on US 191. The food here is fantastic and the setting is hard to beat—alongside the Gallatin River. The Rainbow has a great wine list and Chef Donohue is always creating twists on "new western" cooking. Deemed one of the best meals in the Rockies, this is the ideal place for visitors with a refined palate. The food is worth the price, but the riverside location is priceless.

Big Timber

⚡ 🐕 ⚙ **City Club Lanes & Steak House** (406-932-5485), 202 Anderson, downtown Big Timber. Many head butchers at the various grocery stores across Montana contend that the best steak in Montana is at the City Club Bowling Alley & Steak House. Yep, that's right, a bowling alley and steak house. The latter was added on to the existing bowling alley and the taste buds of local folks have been thankful ever since. Prime rib is the house specialty and you can enjoy it seven nights a week. They will also charbroil your favorite cut of steak in any size, and the menu runs the gamut from prawns to broiled chicken, but steaks are the specialty. They also offer burgers and a kiddy menu.

See also the Grand Hotel under *Lodging–Bed & Breakfasts*.

Bozeman

⚡ **John Bozeman's Bistro** (406-587-4100), 125 W. Main St., downtown Bozeman. The original owners, it has since sold, opened this Bozeman institution back in the early 1980s. At that time is was *the* place in town for a fabulous meal with good service. Today it remains one of the better places in town to refuel while delighting the palate. What sets the Bistro apart from Bozeman's thriving restaurant scene is the exciting risks they take in creating a menu—and it pays off handsomely. The food is in a class by itself, the wine list is solid, and the service is quality.

Cooke City

Beartooth Café (406-838-2475), US 212. The first thing you will notice are the unique logs used to build this place. The next thing will be the varied menu. After that it will be the great beer and wine selection or the view of Silver Gate Mountain as you dine. The Beartooth Café has a near cult following of visitors, and for good reason. The food is very good and the location just outside Yellowstone National Park can't be beat.

Emigrant

ᕕ The Dining Room at Chico Hot Springs (406-333-4933), #1 Chico Road, 21 miles south of Livingston in Emigrant. Head to Emigrant, then follow the signs. For exquisite meals such as beef Wellington or pine-encrusted halibut, or perhaps a celebrity sighting, head to the dining room at Chico. The wine list is spectacular and the service is often some of the best in Montana. Dining at Chico is a special experience. For dessert you must try the Flaming Orange.

Livingston

ᕕ ⌀ Montana's Rib and Chop House (406-222-9200), 305 E. Park, downtown Livingston. Because the food and service were so popular the "Chop House," as locals call it, moved to a larger location a few years back— and you still have to wait for a table most nights. They were awarded "Best Restaurant" from the local readers of the *Park County Weekly* and most Montanans take pride in knowing good food when they eat it. The Chop House is a prime example of how good food, quality service, and a nice setting can rope in hungry people on a regular basis.

ᕕ ⌀ The Northern Pacific Beanery (406-222-7288), 108 West Park, downtown Livingston, adjacent to the Livingston Depot and across the street from the Murray Hotel. The Northern Pacific Beanery, formerly

Martin's Cafe, has been serving good food for over one hundred years. A local icon in the heart of historic downtown Livingston, adjacent to the Livingston Depot Center, the Beanery was recently purchased and renovated. Originally founded as the Northern Pacific Lunchroom, the restaurant was the eatery for the NP railroad workers, locals, and the traveling public who first rode the NP Lines to visit the newly designated Yellowstone National Park. The Beanery's owner, Mary Hagemeyer, expects to offer dinners as well. Her breakfast sandwich is hard to beat.

Logan

ᕕ Land of Magic Steakhouse (406-284-3794), 11060 Front Street. Take I-90 Exit 283 and head into Logan. Logan used to be a bustling railroad hamlet but has been reduced to not much more than a handful of modest homes along the lower Gallatin River. The Land of Magic, however, continues to thrive despite its relative distance from the major population centers of the valley. This is due to the great steaks one can have at the Land-O, as most area patrons call it. Housed in a wonderful log building, the Land-O is famous for steaks, their homemade twice-baked potatoes, and a cozy bar. If you are around on the first Saturday in May be sure to take in the annual branding party.

Red Lodge

ᕕ ⌀ Bridge Creek Backcountry Kitchen and Wine Bar (406-446-9900), 116 S. Broadway. Whether you have been hiking, fishing, skiing, biking, or just driving your car through Yellowstone Park and over the Beartooth Highway, relaxing hospitality and great food await you at this friendly place in downtown Red

Lodge. Offering familiar yet innovative cuisine combined with the finest selection of beer, wine, and liquor, Bridge Creek has more than food and beverages. They offer a place for relaxation, socialization (a popular gathering place for locals and tourists alike), entertainment (occasional live music and related events), education (frequent beer and wine tasting), and adventure (the chance to try new things). For javaheads, they are also the exclusive source for Starbucks coffee in Red Lodge. The coffee bar opens daily at 7 A.M.

Three Forks

& **The Dining Room at the Sacajawea Hotel** (406-285-6515), 5 North Main Street, downtown Three Forks. The Sac, as locals call it, has one of the best barrooms in the state. Originally catering to railroad passengers and workers, the bar is ideal for conversations after a long day of adventure. The food at the Sac is a fine complement to the historic building and inviting bar. Try your steak topped with the chef's special gorgonzola cheese butter spread.

West Yellowstone

& ✐ **Bullwinkle's Saloon and Restaurant** (406-646-7974), 19 Madison Avenue, downtown West Yellowstone. Bullwinkle's is a West Yellowstone landmark. With a wide selection of entrees ranging from sandwiches to seafood, there is something for everyone at Bullwinkle's. There is also a full bar with a great selection of beer and wine. Bullwinkle's is half a block from the Madison River trailhead, so it makes a great après hiking or skiing spot.

& **Sydney's Mountain Bistro** (406-646-7660), 38 Canyon Street, downtown West Yellowstone. Very friendly service, reasonably quick meals, and fabulous food make Sydney's a must for anyone looking for a good meal and glass of wine while in West Yellowstone. Compared to other restaurants in town, they have a very diverse menu, and the food is some of the best in Montana, no joke. The steaks are great, the salmon is wild, and if you need to fill up for a long day cross-country skiing or fishing, their biscuits and gravy is a hard-core hit with the locals. The place is small, so get there early to snag a table, but the food is worth the wait if you are a straggler.

EATING OUT

Belgrade

& ✐ **Bar-3 BBQ** (406-388-4545), 11 W. Main Street, downtown Belgrade. The South, Midwest, and Texas are all known for great barbecue *and* having enough people around who love to eat it. Well, the folks at Bar-3 BBQ have found both, too—great food and a local following. The menu is substantial, with fried pickles, pulled pork, chicken, and lots of other great goodies. They have a great bar, good service and are very close to the airport and Bridger Bowl Ski Resort. If you are looking for a pleasant experience at a very reasonable price this is the place; in fact, many folks would choose Bar-3 BBQ over higher-priced meals in the valley. If you are pressed for time get your order to go.

& **The Mint Bar and Café** (406-388-1100), 27 E. Main St., downtown Belgrade. The Mint has been through several makeovers in the past 20 years. The last one occurred in the late 1990s, and they hit a home run. The cool thing about the Mint is how you're thrust into Belgrade's agricultural past: large sepia photographs of local ranchers along with Hereford and longhorn cattle mounts. The place was built on the site of the 1904 Mint Bar and is now where ranchers and tourists mingle. They like to believe they have something for everyone. And they do—besides a 28-ounce T-bone, you can get barbecued shrimp or salmon with a blueberry beurre blanc, and one of the best Caesar salads in Montana.

Big Sky

ﾎ ✿ **Corral Steakhouse** (406-995-4249), 42895 Gallatin Road, 8 miles south of Big Sky on US 191. This is a very tasty and affordable option for a meal in the area. If you need a lunch break while hiking, cross-country skiing, or snowmobiling, you can have a good burger or a great cut of steak. The service is always friendly and the location right on US 191 makes this a perfect spot for explorers. Try the buffalo burger and their homemade fries with their own special spices—tasty.

ﾎ ✿ **Dante's Inferno** (406-995-3999), 1 Lone Mountain Trail. Ski-slope views and family atmosphere make this one of the best places on the mountain for the whole family to enjoy a quick bite. Mostly American and Italian cuisine, there is something for every taste. For the adults in the family, there are 10 beers on tap and more than three-dozen bottle options, plus wine. This is also a nice choice for dinner and après-ski fare, as you can order a great steak while the little ones pick something from a well-thought-out kids' menu.

Big Timber

See the Grand Hotel under *Lodging*.

Bozeman Area

ﾎ ✿ **La Parilla** (406-586-2100), 1533 W. Babcock. Whenever I'm in Bozeman I usually stop here for a quick snack or a wrap to go—and that is pretty much their specialty, various wraps with everything under the sun in them. They have a wide selection of meats (organic buffalo, wild salmon, tuna, and more) and you have your choice of veggies, beans, salsas and sauces, and more, all wrapped in an assortment of tortillas. Their homemade soups and chilis are also very good. In spring, summer, or fall their porch gets ample sunshine and is a nice place to watch the world go by.

✿ **The Cat Eye Café** (406-587-8844), 23 N. Tracy, downtown Bozeman. Although they serve lunch and dinner, the breakfasts are what put them on the Bozeman-area dining map. With mostly local ingredients, the food has a home-cooked feel with enough contemporary elements so that it feels like a real treat. You may sit in comfy booths or at a bar where you can watch them cook up the goodies. The booths are an ideal place to plan a day's adventure while sipping great coffee.

ﾎ ✿ **Mackenzie River Pizza Company,** locations in Belgrade (406-388-0016; 409 W. Main Street), Bozeman (406-587-0055; 232 E. Main Street), and Gallatin Gateway (406-763-4600; US 191 two miles south of Four Corners). They have some of the best pizzas in the state and the salads and sandwiches are good as well. You can always expect quality food and friendly service. Pizzas range from classic pepperoni to gourmet varieties with choice of styles and flavors of crusts. Each location in the Gallatin Valley has a bar that will serve late. For two hungry adventurers, a Taos salad and large pizza make a perfect meal.

The Western Café (406-587-0436), 443 E. Main Street, downtown Bozeman. Despite Bozeman's affluence and influx of new wealth, the Western Café has not changed one bit. Breakfasts at the Western are the main attraction. Step into this place and you will feel like you are back in the Montana of the 1960s and '70s. A small radio still sits on top of the cabinet, but the conversations of ranchers, friends, and original Bozeman folk drown out the twang of old-time country singers. The Western is known for its large cinnamon rolls and bottomless cups of coffee. One of these rolls will keep anyone going long after lunchtime. Other menu items are tasty, too, and you will not leave hungry.

Cooke City

Buns 'N' Beds Deli and Cabins (406-838-2030), 201 US 212. Grab a sandwich to go—or spend the night in one of their log cabins—before you head out in the wilds around Cooke City. They bake the bread daily, have surprisingly good barbecue (a rarity in Cooke City), and even a few vegetarian selections. If you plan to pack these sammies bring a large pack, as they will fill your tummy and then some.

Emigrant

The Old Saloon and Livery Stable (406-333-4688), US 89; 36 miles south of Livingston in Emigrant, just west of the flashing yellow light. The Old Saloon has Old West atmosphere in the original interior of the saloon. With a pool table, swinging doors, and a great mirror behind the bar, an out-law would feel at ease here. Burgers are good and the pool table is usually open, even during the busiest weeks of the year. If heading out for a day of horseback riding begin with the biscuits and gravy and you'll be galloping all day long.

Gardiner

♦ ✑ **K-Bar Café and Pizza** (406-848-9995), P.O. Box 28, US 89 and Main Street. This is truly a hidden gem among small-town pizza joints. Granted, making good pizza is not that hard, but making great pizza and serving it with a smile is difficult, and when you find a place that can make great pizza with great service, it's really something special. The K-Bar is that place. What makes the K-Bar even better is that it lacks the masses of obnoxious tourists that often gravitate to pizza places in small tourist towns. Its relatively homely atmosphere turns off most people who peek in the door, which is unfortunate for them because the pizza is some of the best in the state.

♿ ✑ **Sawtooth Deli** (406-848-7600), 220 West Park Street, downtown Gardiner, overlooking Yellowstone Park. This is perhaps the best place for outdoor dining in Gardiner and a favorite locals' hangout. The breakfast and lunch menu stays the same year-round, but the dinner menu changes daily. Be sure to call or check the board out front to see what they've got cooking that night. They have a nice beer selection and their porch is a great place to watch the tourists stroll Front Street or the antelope play in a meadow across the road.

♿ ✑ **Helen's Corral Drive Inn** (406-848-7627), US 89. You would be hard-pressed to find a better burger in the state, period. The menu is simple—burgers, fried chicken fingers, fries, and a few other things you might find at a drive-in fast-food place. The Corral Drive Inn sits right on the main drag in Gardiner, US 89, and all of the seating (except for three tables) is outdoors on a wood-covered patio. Tourists heading to Yellowstone can watch you sink your teeth into a burger that is as big as your head. Do not expect to get your burgers fast, as something this large takes time. The buffalo burgers are the best thing on the menu, and coupled with a basket of fries will keep you full for days. The only downside: it is BYOB as Helen's doesn't have a beer and wine license, but the state liquor store and local grocery store is only a block away.

Livingston
&. 𝄢 **Mark's In & Out** (406-222-7744), 300 Park Street, downtown Livingston. A classic 1950s drive-in serving great beefburgers, fries, and shakes made fresh to order, always cooked and dressed to your desire. They have weekend carhops during the summer. Serving Livingston since 1954, and currently operating seasonally March through October.

&. **The Pickle Barrel** (406-222-5469), 131 S Main Street, downtown Livingston. Fresh-made deli sandwiches as big as your head, and bigger. At first, the prices may seem high, but you are getting several pounds of food. One sandwich will keep you going for nearly a day, but take plenty of napkins with you because the sammies overflow with ingredients. If you like hot subs try a cheesesteak or mushroom steak. For folks on the go or on a budget, this is the place for a great sandwich.

Red Lodge
&. 𝄢 **Bear Creek Saloon** (406-446-3481), 7 miles east of Red Lodge on MT 308. It is too bad that the food here takes a backseat to the swine—yes, the pigs. This is the only place (that I know of) in the world where you can legally bet on pigs. Since 1988 the Bear Creek Saloon has been home to pig races—the owners have built a race track and guests place bets on which pig will win. All the money goes to local scholarships for high school students, so it is for a good cause. You don't need to worry if your pig comes in last because there is no pig on the menu at all—mainly steaks, chicken, and seafood, and it is all very good.

𝄢 **Bogart's Restaurant** (406-446-1784), 11 S. Broadway, downtown Red Lodge. With a varied menu, this is a good place to take the entire family. Bogart's Restaurant features legendary food in rustic comfort, with warm and friendly service. It has been under the same management since 1984. Bogart's is Red Lodge's busiest restaurant; a must stop. Pizza, Mexican food, margaritas, and lots of atmosphere. Worth the trip alone.

See also the Pollard under *Lodging*.

Silver Gate
See Log Cabin Cafe and Bed & Breakfast under *Lodging*.

West Yellowstone
&. 𝄢 **Canyon Street Grill** (406-646-7548), 22 Canyon Street. A fun place to eat for the whole family—as they have styled it after a 1950s milkshake shack. In addition to the shakes, the burgers are great, they have huge, tasty steak fries, and they even offer a handful of vegetarian sandwiches. However, this is not a fast-food place,

so expect to relax and enjoy the atmosphere.

&. ✆ **Ernie's Bakery and Deli** (406-646-9467), 406 US 20, on the western edge of West Yellowstone. Their sack lunches pack quite a wallop, with fresh-baked bread, a giant cookie, and your choice of chips. However, it is their breakfast sandwiches that I really like. If you are heading out of West Yellowstone for a day of adventure this is the only place you need to stop at in the morning, and if you're heading to Hebgen Lake they are right on the way.

✆ **Freeheel and Wheel** (406-646-744), 40 Yellowstone Avenue, downtown West Yellowstone. The women who run this store are hip and with it—but they are neither pretentious nor unwilling to divulge information. In fact, this may be one of the friendliest places in town. They make great espresso drinks and lunches, whether enjoyed outside watching the tourists pass by or out on the trail (they offer tasty lunches to go); this place is a must-visit while in West. Plus they are one block from the entrance to Yellowstone National Park.

✴ Special Events

January: ✆ 🐾 **St. Nick's Nordic Festival,** Big Sky. A day filled with outdoor winter fun for the whole family. Recently named the #1 Nordic ski center in the country, Lone Mountain Ranch holds its annual festival geared at getting everyone out and enjoying the trails on cross-country skis or snowshoes. A $5 entry fee allows for the use of ski trails, as well as ski or snowshoe rentals and lessons throughout the day.

February: ✆ 🐾 **Wild West Winterfest,** Bozeman. Grab your galoshes and head to the Wild West Winter-Fest. Some of the activities include horse-drawn wagon rides, a kids' special Roundup Rodeo, McLien's FFA Farm Barn, a working horse & driver contest, and a horse sale. Dog events include agility, terrier races, conformation, pet tricks, and a keg-pulling contest. There is also a packer's scramble, an elk bugling contest, and a chili cook-off. For kids there is a children's arts and crafts show, a quilt show, and even a photography show.

✆ **Winter Carnival,** Red Lodge. Winter Carnival is a much anticipated three-day themed event in Red Lodge for kids and adults. Events include the cardboard classic parade and race, Mini-Griz Skin-to-Win race, King and Queen of the Mountain race, Bogart's Jalapeno-Eating Contest, live music, and the Torchlight Parade and Fireworks Show.

March: ✆ **Big Sky Winterfest,** Big Sky. A day of Nordic and snowshoe races, team races, children's activities, and live music.

June: **Gallatin Whitewater Festival,** Gallatin Gateway. During runoff on the Gallatin—one of Montana's most popular whitewater rivers—rafters, kayaks, and onlookers gather for canoe and kayak races.

June and July: ✆ 🐾 **Red Lodge Mountain Man Rendezvous,** Red Lodge. This is a large living history re-creation of an 1830s fur-trapper encampment, with family events, costume contests, storytelling, educational seminars, camping, and lots more.

July: ✆ 🐾 **Jim Bridger Day,** Bridger. An annual event to celebrate the town's namesake, mountain man Jim Bridger. Events include a parade, car show, barbecue, dancing in the streets, and more.

🖉 **Livingston Roundup and Rodeo,** Livingston. Perhaps the most anticipated rodeo in the region, complete with some of the best cowboys in the nation and topped off with dances and a large fireworks display the night of the 4th.

Fat Tire Frenzy, Red Lodge. An annual mountain biking event held outside Red Lodge that attracts some of the best riders in the country.

August: **Bite of Bozeman,** Bozeman. They close off Main Street to cars and open it to the many restaurants in the area for outside dining—quite the treat for the taste buds.

September: 🖉 🌸 **Running of the Sheep,** Reed Point. One of my favorite traditions in the region. On Labor Day weekend they run hundreds of sheep down the small town's main street, and there are even beauty contests for various sheep; a street dance finishes this crazy weekend of family fun.

🖉 🌸 **Belgrade Fall Festival,** Belgrade. A parade, BBQ, dance, and unique arts festival to celebrate the changing season.

Mountain Bike and Fine Arts Festival, Rapelje (north of Columbus). This event includes several races, a costume contest, and children's activities.

October: **Old Faithful Fall Cycle Tour,** West Yellowstone. Ride from West Yellowstone to Old Faithful. Enjoy the fall colors of Yellowstone National Park as the 60-mile round-trip takes you past geysers, thermal features, bison, and bugling elk. If you are looking for a shorter ride, they will shuttle you and your bike

back from Old Faithful, or shuttle you in so you can ride back. After the day's ride there is a spaghetti dinner at 6 P.M. There is a limit of 300 riders, so register early at www.cycleyellow stone.com.

November: 🖉 **Feasts for the Beasts,** Red Lodge. A great cause and great food for the animals of the Beartooth Nature Center, including a silent auction and dancing.

🖉 **Yellowstone Ski Festival,** West Yellowstone. An annual Nordic festival at Rendezvous Ski Trails, featuring races, clinics, pro demos, and children's programs.

December: 🖉 🌸 **Christmas for the Critters,** West Yellowstone. Share in the joy of the season by donating food for the bears and wolves at the Grizzly and Wolf Discovery Center. Donations will provide tasty enrichment and hours of enjoyment for the animals. The Christmas list for the bears includes jars of peanut butter, jam, honey, corn oil, and unsalted nuts. The wolves enjoy hamburger, spices, extracts, and perfumes in their stockings. To ensure the safety of the animals, please bring only unopened items.

🖉 🌸 **Christmas Stroll,** Bozeman. The town closes Main Street and it is a five-block citywide stroll and party as the shops stay open late, food and music is plentiful, and a good time is had by all. There are fireworks, hayrides, and a dance.

🖉 🌸 **Christmas Stroll,** Red Lodge. Features free wagon rides, Santa Claus, candy for kids, music, and refreshments such as hot cider and roasted chestnuts. Many specials offered by Red Lodge businesses.

✐ 🏵 **Three Forks Winter Stroll,** Three Forks. Experience Three Forks at its finest during its annual Winter Stroll. Enjoy visits with Santa, horse-drawn wagon rides, arts and crafts, delicious food, and retail specials and sales.

✐ 🏵 **Festival of Lights,** Belgrade. The Festival of Lights is a community Christmas celebration with crafts,

hayrides, music, art exhibits, sleigh rides, and Santa. Stores are open late for shoppers.

✐ 🏵 **Old Saint Nick Day,** Joliet. Annual celebration held the first Sunday of December, including horse-drawn sleigh rides, a chili feed, a hot dog and marshmallow roast, and more.

North-Central Montana: Russell Country

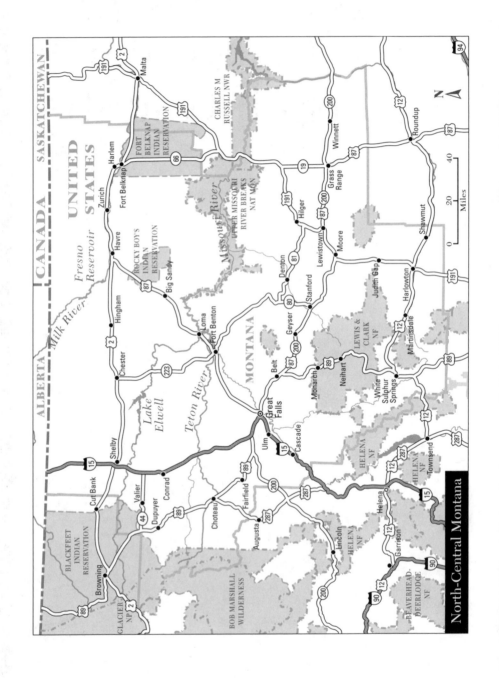

North-Central Montana

NORTH-CENTRAL MONTANA: RUSSELL COUNTRY

This region of Montana embodies the phrase "From the Mountains to the Prairies." With majestically rugged Rocky Mountain Front along the western boundary, the dramatic and distant Upper Missouri River Breaks National Monument bisecting the region, the Belt and Snowy Mountains along the southern boundary, and the vast grasslands and prairie along the northern and eastern boundary, Russell Country is the most diverse region of Montana. It is also the largest region, although in population, it is sparse. Except for Great Falls with its nearly 70,000 people, the entire region is blanketed by open spaces and dotted with small towns. These small towns all have services for visitors and all offer surprisingly interesting attractions, accommodations, and places to dine. Just because Russell Country is rural and rugged doesn't mean it lacks quality services and inviting towns. A huge part of Russell Country's charm is its rural feel—visitors to this region get a true sense of the soul of Montana.

Much of this region remains similar to how Lewis & Clark found it over two hundred years ago. In fact, the Corps of Discovery spent more time in this region than any other in Montana. One area that remains nearly untouched and wild is the Missouri River corridor, designated a National Wild and Scenic River. The 150 miles of river from Fort Benton to the James Kipp Recreation Area in the Charles M. Russell National Wildlife Refuge represent only a small portion of the Upper Missouri River Breaks National Monument. Nearly 400,000 acres surrounding the river are managed by the Bureau of Land Management. Much of this area is rugged—sandstone cliffs and coulees reminiscent of South Dakota's badlands, but nearly 10 times the size. This area can be explored by car on the Missouri Breaks National Backcountry Byway, by paddling on the river itself on a multi-day adventure, by keelboat, by horseback, or on foot. Many service providers offer a variety of ways to enjoy this region.

West of Great Falls and the Missouri River area is the expansive and breathtaking Rocky Mountain Front. It is often called the Serengeti of North America because it is one of the few areas on the continent with such an abundance of game: grizzly bear, wolf, elk, mountain lion, deer, antelope, bighorn sheep, and more. Stretching for nearly 250 miles, the mountains are the source of four major rivers (Dearborn, Sun, Teton, and Marias) and make up the Lewis & Clark National Forest and the Bob Marshall Wilderness. In winter you can enjoy downhill skiing at one of the more remote ski areas in the state, hundreds of miles of cross-country ski trails, snowmobiling, snowshoeing, and ice fishing. During warmer months, hiking, camping, fishing, horseback riding, mountain biking, and more are available in and along "the Front." Visitors can even dig for dinosaur fossils in one of the largest digs in North America.

In the southern portion of Russell Country you'll find the Big and Little Belt Mountains and the Snowy Range. Similar to the Front in their relative isolation, these mountains also offer abundant recreation opportunities. The small towns of Lewistown, Harlowton, and White Sulphur Springs offer all types of services for exploring the mountains.

For cyclists, many country roads are gravel or dirt, but most are maintained on a regular basis. Cyclists and mountain bikers will encounter little traffic, but lots of great scenery. If you want to venture even farther off the beaten path by pedal power, the Lewis & Clark National Forest maintains hundreds of miles of trails. Ability and desire are really your only limiting factors when it comes to exploring this region from a bike seat.

If rivers and lakes are your thing, Russell Country provides a lifetime of opportunities. Along with the Upper Missouri River, numerous other rivers flow through this region. These rivers offer whitewater, angling, solitude, camping, birding, and more. A highlight of this region is the Smith River, which flows for nearly 60 miles through a limestone canyon with walls towering nearly 1,000 feet. Scattered throughout Russell Country are easily accessible lakes and reservoirs that offer boating, fishing, ice fishing, bird-watching, and sightseeing. For paddlers seeking solitude, a little local research will unearth some small bodies of water that are not mentioned in this book.

If exploring the countryside grows old, then you can partake in some Montana art, culture, and history in this region's largest (and only) major city, Great Falls. This city is home to the Lewis & Clark National Historic Trail Interpretive Center, the Charles Russell Museum, a Sunday summer art series, and more. The small town of Lewistown offers a few small museums and the Charlie Russell Chew-Choo, where you can enjoy a scenic train ride with a mouth-watering meal served in your cabin. White Sulphur Springs offers a natural hot springs and some interesting Montana history.

From the jagged peaks of the Rocky Mountain Front to the sweeping grasslands of the Hi-Line to the sandstone cliffs of the Upper Missouri, Russell Country offers the most intriguing mix of scenery and history in all of Montana.

GUIDANCE Big Sandy Chamber of Commerce (406-378-2418; www.bigsandy mt.com), P.O. Box 411, Big Sandy 59520.

Chester/Liberty County Chamber of Commerce (406-759-4848; www .libertycountycc.com), 30 Main Street, Chester 59522.

Chinook Chamber of Commerce (406-357-3160; www.chinookmontana.com). Visitor information available at the **Blaine County Museum** (406-357-2590), 501 Indiana Avenue, P.O. Box 744, Chinook 59523.

Chippewa Cree Business Committee (406-395-4282; www.rockyboy.org), RR1 Box 544, Box Elder 59521.

Choteau Chamber of Commerce (406-395-4282; www.choteaumontana.com), 35 1st NW, P.O. Box 897, Choteau 59422.

Conrad Area Chamber of Commerce (406-271-7791; www.conradmt.com), 702 S. Main Street, Suite 1, Conrad 59425.

Dupuyer Community Club (406-472-3241), P.O. Box 135, Dupuyer 59432.

Fairfield Area Chamber of Commerce (406-467-2531), Drawer 9, Fairfield 59436.

Fort Belknap Tourism Office and Information Center (406-353-8471; www.fortbelknapnations-nsn.gov), RR1, Box 66, Harlem 59526.

Fort Benton Chamber of Commerce (406-622-3864; www.fortbenton.com), 11421 Front Street (in the Information Center), P.O. Box 12, Fort Benton 59442.

Great Falls Chamber of Commerce (406-761-4434; www.greatfallschamber .org), 710 1st Avenue N., Great Falls 59401.

Harlowton Chamber of Commerce and Agriculture (406-632-4694; www .harlowtonchamber.com), P.O. Box 694, Harlowton 59036.

Havre Area Chamber of Commerce (406-265-4383; www.havremt.com), 518 1st Street, Havre 59501.

Judith Basin Area Chamber of Commerce (406-566-2238; www.judithbasin .com), P.O. Box 102, Stanford 59479.

Lewistown Area Chamber of Commerce (406-538-5436; www.lewistown chamber.com), 408 NE Main Street, Lewistown 59457.

Meagher County Chamber of Commerce (406-547-2250; www.meagher chamber.com), P.O. Box 356, White Sulphur Springs 59645.

THE ONCE PROUD GREAT FALLS OF THE MISSOURI

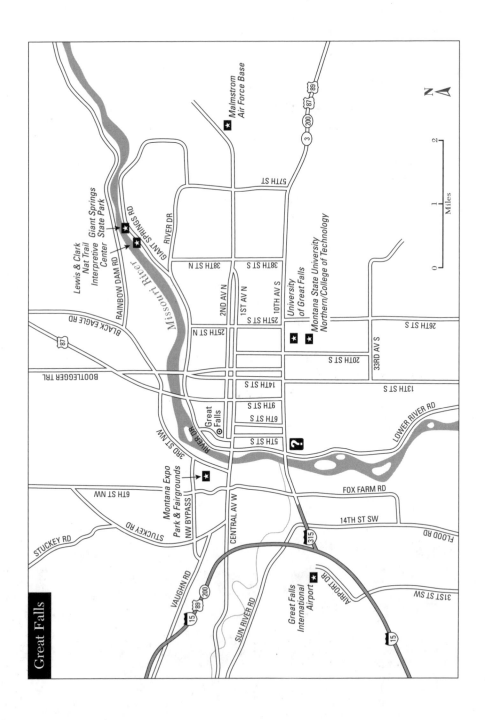

Great Falls

Monarch Area Community Association (www.monarchmt.org), P.O. Box 126, Monarch 59463.

Rocky Boy's Indian Reservation *See* Chippewa Cree Business Committee.

Russell Country, Inc. (1-800-527-5348; www.russell.visitmt.com), P.O. Box 3166, Great Falls 59403.

Shelby Area Chamber of Commerce (406-434-7184; www.shelbymt chamber.org), 102 Main Street, Shelby 59474.

Valier Area Development Corporation (406-279-3561; www.valier.org), P.O. Box 568, Valier 59486.

GETTING THERE Because of the size of this region, most highways in Montana run through Russell Country at some point. Great Falls lies at the junction of I-15, US 87, and US 89. Shelby, Chester, Havre, Chinook, and Harlem lie from west to east on US 2. Shelby is located at the junction of US 2 and I-15. Conrad is between Shelby and Great Falls on I-15. Cut Bank, Valier, and Choteau all lie northwest of Great Falls on US 89. White Sulphur Springs is south of Great Falls on US 89. Lewistown is at the juncture of US 87 and US 191.

See also *Airports* and *Bus Service* in "What's Where in Montana."

MEDICAL EMERGENCIES **Basin Medical Center** (406-566-2773), 76 Central Avenue, Stanford.

Benefis Healthcare (406-455-5200), 1101 26th Street S., Great Falls.

Big Sandy Medical Center (406-378-2188), 3 Montana Avenue, Big Sandy.

Central Montana Medical Center (406-538-7711), 408 Wendell Avenue, Lewistown.

Liberty County Hospital (406-759-5181), MT 223 and Monroe, Chester.

Marias Medical Center (406-434-3200), 640 Park Drive, Shelby.

Missouri River Medical Center (406-622-3331), 1501 Charles Street, Fort Benton.

Mountainview Medical Center (406-547-3321), 16 W. Main Street, White Sulphur Springs.

Northern Montana Hospital (406-262-1201), 30 13th Street W., Havre.

Pondera Medical Center (406-271-3211), 805 Sunset Boulevard, Conrad.

Teton Medical Center (406-466-5763), 915 4th Street N.W., Choteau.

Wheatland Memorial Hospital (406-632-4351), 530 3rd Street N.W. Harlowton.

✳ To See

TOWNS **Augusta** is a rural ranching community that provides access to some spectacular recreation in the **Lewis & Clark National Forest,** the **Bob Marshall Wilderness,** and the lands along the Rocky Mountain Front. For wildlife-viewing enthusiasts, the **Sun River Game Range** will delight. For anglers and boaters, **Gibson Reservoir, Willow Creek Reservoir, Bean Lake,** and **Nilan Lake** offer places to wet a line or stroke a paddle.

Choteau lies in the shadow of the Rocky Mountain Front, about a 1.5-hour drive from Great Falls. There are camping facilities in town, a public swimming pool, golf course, and plenty of shopping and lodging options. The town lies on the **Montana Dinosaur Trail** and is home to a few museums. Outdoor recreation abounds near Choteau. Contact the **Choteau Ranger Station** to learn about the **Ear Mountain Trailhead, the Nature Conservancy's Pine Butte Swamp Preserve, the Bob Marshall Wilderness,** and the **Lewis & Clark National Forest.**

Fort Belknap is located at the junction of US 2 and MT 66 on the **Fort Belknap Indian Reservation.** Stop at the Fort Belknap Tourism Office and Information Center for information about the recreational and cultural activities on the reservation, which is inhabited by the Assiniboine and Gros Ventre tribes. The information center and rest area also have a campground and the staff can guide tours as well. The surrounding area and reservation is home to a 10,000-acre **buffalo preserve, tepee rings, Mission Canyon, the Natural Bridge,** and **Devil's Kitchen**, among other sites.

Fort Benton is northwest of Great Falls on US 87 and the Missouri River. This historic town marks the western border of the Upper Missouri National Wild and Scenic River. Established as a crossroads for fur trading and river barging in the late 1840s by the American Fur Company, Fort Benton's history is colorful and varied. As the jumping-off point for most gold seekers and the embarkation point for steamboats during that era, this little town grew from a few wooden shacks to rowdy hotels, gambling halls, and more overnight. Most of the buildings constructed in the 1800s still stand today and the downtown is a **National Historic Landmark District,** which includes the remains of **Old Fort Benton**

THE ROCKY MOUNTAIN FRONT NEAR CHOTEAU

THE GREAT NORTHERN GOAT, THE ORIGINAL LOGO OF THE GREAT NORTHERN RAILWAY, WELCOMES YOU TO THE HAVRE RAILROAD STATION

in City Park. This is also the last place to get any supplies if you are planning a multi-day trip on the Missouri River.

Great Falls is the largest city in this region. Its namesake is a series of waterfalls along the Missouri River. Dams have diminished the beauty of the falls, but the town still has lots to offer. Three of the best museums in Montana are here: the **Lewis & Clark National Historic Trail Interpretive Center,** the **Charles M. Russell Museum,** and the **Paris Gibson Museum of Art.** For outdoor pursuits, Great Falls is a jumping-off point for adventures in the **Big Belt Mountains, the Rocky Mountain Front,** and the **Missouri River.** For trout lovers, **Giant Springs State Park** provides a scenic spot on the banks of the Missouri River from which to view a rearing pond for trout and enjoy views of the falls on the Missouri River.

Harlowton is at the junction of US 191 and US 12. It's a tiny town, but home to some interesting railroad history, and it has breathtaking views of the east side of the Crazy Mountains. Travelers can camp, fish, or picnic at **Chief Joseph Park.** The **E057B Electric Train Park,** which pays homage to the longest stretch of electric railroad in the world, is in Harlowton. The **Upper Musselshell Museum** is also in town. Within 30 minutes of town are numerous trails, streams, and lakes; most notably **Deadman's Basin Recreation Area,** which has camping, a boat ramp, and seasonal ice skating.

Havre is located on what Montanan's call the Hi-Line, the area along the northern border of Montana. Havre lies on US 2 about two hours northeast of Great Falls. The town's roots are in agriculture and the railroad, and it's the largest city along US 2. The **Bears Paw Mountains** lie to the southeast and the **Milk**

River runs through town. Outdoor enthusiasts will find unique opportunities and broad vistas, while history buffs will enjoy the region's past.

Lewistown, southeast of Great Falls along US 87, lies in the geographical center of Montana—Fergus County. This small town with big character and even larger outdoor recreation pursuits is slowly being discovered. Near the **Judith, Moccasin, Little Belt,** and **Snowy Mountains,** this town is a paradise for hikers, hunters, and anglers. And it is still uncrowded when compared to the rest of Montana (which, of course, is still uncrowded by non-Montana standards). Home to the first Montana residence of Charles M. Russell, art and history buffs will enjoy the **Lewistown Art Center** (406-538-8278), the **Central Montana Museum** (406-538-5436), and the historic **Silk Stocking District,** northeast of downtown. Contact the chamber of commerce (see *Guidance*) for more information.

Shelby is north of Great Falls at the junction of I-15 and US 2. It was one of the original stopping points along the Great Northern Railroad, as it made its way to Glacier National Park, as well as a point of departure for anyone headed to Canada (the border is only 40 miles to the north). Today **AMTRAK** passengers board and rest in Shelby. An official **Montana Visitor Center** is located in Shelby near the junction of US 2 and I-15. **Marias Museum of History and Art** (406-434-2551) provides exhibits on local and regional history.

MUSEUMS & **Castle Museum** (406-547-2324), 310 2nd Avenue, White Sulphur Springs. Open May 15 through September 15, 10 A.M.–6 P.M.; free. The Castle is an imposing mansion (worth a visit in its own right) and is now home to the

THE JAMES HILL STATUE IN HAVRE

Meagher County Museum. Built in 1892 by Bryon Roger Sherman, the mansion has 12 rooms, all laid with hardwood floors and covered with Belgian and Oriental rugs. In the bathrooms were washbowls and stands of Italian marble, and the light fixtures were of crystal and brass. The Victorian landmark is made of hand-cut granite blocks hauled by oxen from the nearby Castle Mountains. The museum is complete with period furniture, mineral samples, clothing, and artifacts from the region's past.

C. M. Russell Museum (406-727-8787; www.cmrussell.org). Open all year May through September, seven days a week, 9 A.M.–6 P.M.; winter, Tuesday through Saturday, 10 A.M.–5 P.M. and Sunday, 1 P.M.–5 P.M. Adults $9, seniors $7, students $4, kids 5 and under free. Established in 1953, the C. M. Russell Museum owns the most complete collection of Charles Russell art and personal objects in the world. The permanent collection comprises over 12,000 artworks and objects. View one of the nation's finest collections of western art and history in spacious, modern surroundings. In addition to Russell art and artifacts, the museum has outstanding pieces from Russell contemporaries such as O. C. Seltzer, J. H. Sharp, E. E. Heikka, E. I. Couse, Winold Reiss, Olaf Wieghorst, and others. The museum shop offers many unique gifts such as jewelry, Russell prints, and fine western books. The complex also includes the former home and log cabin studio of Montana's famous cowboy artist. Preserved as it was in the early 1900s, the studio includes displays of Russell's personal objects used as props and references for accuracy.

♿ **Fort Benton, Montana's Heritage Complex** (406-622-5316; www.fort benton.com/museums), 1205 20th Street and/or Old Fort Park, Fort Benton. Inquire for specific hours and rates. This complex is actually a collection of museums in the Fort Benton area. Home to many Montana firsts, Fort Benton is full of history and has the museums to back it up. The **Museum of the Northern Great Plains** (1205 20th Street) details the story of human life on the plains in the 19th century; the **Museum of the Upper Missouri** (Old Fort Park) covers the unique role this area played in the migration of people to Montana and the West; **Old Fort Benton** is the remaining monument of a fur-trading post; and the **Upper Missouri River Breaks Interpretive Center** highlights the natural and cultural history of the region. Boating information for those floating the Wild and Scenic Upper Missouri River is available, as well as hands-on exhibits about the land, the wildlife, and culture of the area.

♿ **H. Earl Clack Memorial Museum** (406-265-4000; www.theheritagecenter .com), 306 3rd Avenue, Havre. Open all year: Labor Day–Memorial Day, Tuesday–Saturday 1 P.M.–5 P.M.; Memorial Day–Labor Day, daily, 11 A.M.–6 P.M., and Sunday, 12 P.M.–5 P.M. The museum offers interpretive displays correlated with archaeological findings in the nearby Wahkpa Chu'gn bison kill site. In addition to the exhibits, daily guided tours at the archaeological site and of historic Fort Assiniboine are available. The museum also houses an exhibit of dinosaur eggs and embryos found nearby that are 75 million years old. The Clack Museum is one of the attractions along Montana's Dinosaur Trail.

♿ **Lewis & Clark National Trail Interpretive Center** (406-727-8733; www .fs.fed.us/r1/lewisclark/lcic), 4210 Giant Springs Road, Great Falls. Open all year:

Memorial Day–September 30, 9 A.M.–6 P.M.; October 1–Memorial Day, Tuesday–Saturday, 9 A.M.–5 P.M., and Sunday, 12 P.M.–5 P.M. Adults 16 and older $5 and children 15 and under free. Sitting on a bluff overlooking the Missouri River, the setting for this substantial place is as unique as the exhibits inside. Relive the 1804–1806 Lewis & Clark Expedition's 8,000-mile journey across western North America in the comfort of the Lewis & Clark National Historic Trail Interpretive Center. Start your indoor journey with the introductory video by acclaimed filmmaker Ken Burns in the 158-seat theater with six wheelchair-accessible seats and open captioning. Then join a ranger for a program or explore the many hands-on exhibits in the center operated by the Forest Service since 1998. (See also Museum Sunday Sampler under *Special Events.*)

& **Old Trail Museum** (406-466-5332), 823 N. Main Street, Choteau. Open Memorial Day–Labor Day, daily, 9 A.M.–5 P.M. This small, but unique, museum reflects the rich natural and cultural history of Montana's pristine Rocky Mountain Front region. Explore fossils, dinosaurs, Native American artifacts, grizzly bears, and the diverse and colorful local history. Other exhibits include A. B. Guthrie Jr., Old Agency on the Teton, Jesse Gleason's art studio, the Old North Trail, Métis people, and Choteau's last hanging. Don't miss "Dinosaurs of the Two Medicine," the Old Trail Museum's new paleontology gallery, as this museum lies on the **Montana Dinosaur Trail.** Next door is an ice-cream parlor, and it's fun to enjoy a cone while watching action along Main Street.

& **Paris Gibson Square Museum of Art** (406-727-8255; www.the-square.org), 1400 1st Avenue N., Great Falls. Open all year, Monday–Friday, 10 A.M.–5 P.M., Saturday, noon–5 P.M., and Tuesday evenings, 7 P.M.–9 P.M. This cultural center is located in a Nationally Registered Landmark Building, built in 1895. The Square, as it's called, now houses this contemporary art museum, a historical society exhibit, galleries, restaurant (the **Bistro at the Square,** and it is quite tasty), and a shopping area. Tours, classes, lectures, art workshops, and performances are offered on a regular basis. Paris Gibson Square is free and open to the public year-round.

HISTORIC LANDMARKS, PLACES, AND SITES Bear Gulch Pictographs (406-428-2185; www.beargulch.net), 2749 Fairview Road, Forest Grove (27 miles southeast of Lewistown via MT 238). Open May through November, daily tours start at 10 A.M. Tours are $15 per person, but the entire family is only $30. If a picture is worth a thousand words, then you'll discover hundreds of ancient stories when you visit the Bear Gulch pictographs. Among the 2,000 pictographs (paintings) and petroglyphs (etchings), you'll see figures of warriors holding shields and clubs and ochre-red elk and bison, along with other designs drawn by Native Americans depicting scenes from their lives.

Bear Paw Battlefield (406-357-3130; www.nps.gov/nepe), 16 miles south of Chinook via MT 240. Open year-round dawn to dusk; free. On September 29, 1877, eight hundred men, women, and children made camp on Snake Creek, 40 miles from the Canadian border. At dawn the next day, the U.S. Army attacked the camp, beginning a siege that would last until October 5, when Chief Joseph surrendered. This quiet and compelling site is sacred ground for all who fought here and looks much the way it did in 1877. This is the site where Chief Joseph gave his immortal speech: "From where the sun now stands, I will fight no more forever." In nearby Chinook, the handicapped-accessible **Blaine County Museum** (406-357-2590) has exhibits and an audiovisual presentation on the battlefield and the Nez Perce Indians. Open Memorial Day through Labor Day, 8 A.M.–noon and 1 P.M.–5 P.M.; open Labor Day through Memorial Day, Thanksgiving, Christmas, and New Year's Day, 1 P.M.–5 P.M. Free admission.

Cascade County Courthouse (406-454-6810; www.co.cascade.mt.us), 415 2nd Avenue N., Great Falls. Open Monday through Friday, 8 A.M.–5 P.M.; free. This is one of the more grand historic buildings in the state. Built from 1901 to 1903, the building features a copper dome raised on columns, as well as four polished granite columns at the entrance. It is certainly worth a visit if you are in downtown Great Falls.

Fort Assiniboine Historic Site and Northern Agricultural Research Center (406-265-4000; www.ag.montana.edu/narc.fort.htm), 6 miles southwest of Havre on US 87. Open June through September for tours by appointment only. Fort Assiniboine Historic Site was constructed in 1879, and it became the largest military fort west of the Mississippi River. The post had 104 buildings and was contained within a 40-mile-long, 15-mile-wide military reservation. The fort originally had 700,000 acres, taking in the Bears Paw Mountains and extending to the Missouri River. Several of the original buildings still stand. It became a state agricultural experiment station in 1911 and continues so today. The primary mission of the fort's garrison was to prevent attacks from the some 5,000 Lakota

THE FERGUS COUNTY COURTHOUSE

Sioux Indians, led by Sitting Bull and other chiefs, who had fled to the safety of Canada after the Battle of the Little Big Horn. The most famous soldier to serve at the fort was John J. Pershing, who was assigned to the post in 1896. He commanded H Troop, the black Buffalo Soldiers of the 10th Cavalry. Guided tours are available on an appointment basis. Tours originate at the H. Earl Clack Museum, located at the corner of the Holiday Village Mall in Havre. Otherwise, entry to the fort grounds for historical sightseeing is not allowed.

Havre Beneath the Streets (406-265-8888; www.havremt.com/attractions/beneath_the_streets.htm), 120 3rd Avenue, Havre. Tours daily in summer, 9 A.M.–5 P.M.; tours in winter, Monday through Saturday, 10 A.M.–4 P.M. Adults $10, seniors $9, students $7, and reservations are required. Havre Beneath the Streets (Historical Underground Tour) is a re-creation of Havre's history. When fire destroyed most of the city, business owners moved underground to carry on their business until the town could be rebuilt. Step back in time into the Sporting Eagle Saloon, a turn-of-the-last-century honky-tonk where cowboys gambled, kicked up their heels, and drank good old-fashioned frontier rotgut. Saunter along the streets beneath Havre and see an opium den (one of three known to have existed in the early days), a Chinese laundry, an ethnic restaurant, and of course, a bordello. Tours depart from the **Havre Railroad Museum,** which offers a brief history of the railroad in Havre, with complete model railroad trains running daily. An original handcart and working block signal is on display. There is no charge to visit the railroad museum.

Havre Residential Historic District (self-guided walking tours from downtown Havre) is a 36-block residential area listed on the National Register of Historic Places. Begin at 306 3rd Avenue. Free walking maps are available at the Havre Historic Preservation Office (by appointment only, 406-265-6233) located in the Heritage Center. Free guided tours are offered by the Heritage Center on Saturdays at 7 P.M. during the summer.

Historic Carter, McClelland, and Virgelle Ferries. These historic river crossings on the Missouri provide "ride at your own risk" thrills for travelers wanting a true frontier experience. **Carter Ferry** (406-454-5840), 26 miles north of Great Falls via US 87 to Carter, and then south on 3rd Avenue (Carter Ferry Road) to the crossing at Carter; **McClelland Ferry** (406-462-5513), north of Winifred on CR 300; **Virgelle Ferry** (406-378-3110), at Virgelle, northeast of Fort Benton and southwest of Big Sandy via US 87. Inquire locally before venturing out as seasonal closures due to ice or high water may close the service. Once at the crossing, ring the buzzer to call the ferry operator, and then watch as your car is hooked and hitched for secure passage.

Lewistown Area Ghost and Mining Towns (406-538-5436; www.lewistown chamber.com), coordinated by the Lewistown Chamber of Commerce in downtown Lewistown. The area around Lewistown features several ghost towns, reminiscent of a rough-and-tumble bygone era. Visit the chamber in Lewistown for directions and self-guided tour instructions. South of Utica on MT 239 you will find the former towns of Yogo City and Hoover City. Near here in 1877 gold was discovered and an onslaught of seekers soon followed. Gold was never in great supply, but in 1894 the discovery of sapphires kept settlers here, and from 1895 to 1923 this area produced the highest quality sapphires in the world. Today sapphires are still mined and cut. The area northeast of Lewistown is home to more ghost towns as well, such as Gilt Edge, Kendall (known as one of the roughest in old Montana), and Maiden. Today all you will find are a few buildings in various states of disrepair, but a stroll in the vicinity of these buildings is a sure reminder of an exciting time in Montana's history.

State of Montana's Lewis & Clark Memorial (406-622-3864; www.fort benton.com/l&c/index.htm), River Front Park, Fort Benton. Commissioned by artist Bob Scriver, this is the official state of Montana memorial to the Corps of Discovery and their time in Montana. The sculpture depicts the two leaders, along with Sacagawea, seeking to find their way to the Pacific Ocean.

Ulm Pishkum/First Peoples Buffalo Jump State Park (406-866-2217; http: //fwp.mt.gov/lands/site_282807.aspx), 10 miles south of Great Falls on I-15. A visitor center and interpretive trails tell the story of this prehistoric bison kill site, one of the largest in the United States. For over six hundred years, Indians stampeded buffalo over the mile-long cliff. Now, the top of the jump gives you panoramic views of the Rocky Mountain Front, the Missouri River valley, and the buttes and grasslands that characterized this High Plains setting. Plan at least a two-hour stop in this day-use-only park.

Tower Rock State Park (406-454-5840; http://fwp.mt.gov/lands/site_6844284 .aspx), approximately 30 miles south of Great Falls on I-15. This 136-acre site is accessed by a small parking area, with hiking trails and interpretive signs. Tower Rock State Park is a significant historic landmark referenced in the Lewis & Clark journals. Meriwether Lewis loved it here. As he wrote in his journal on

THE MISSOURI RIVER AT FORT BENTON

July 16, 1805, "At this place there is a large rock of 400 feet high wich stands immediately in the gap which the Missouri makes on it's passage from the mountains. . . . This rock I called the tower. It may be ascended with some difficulty nearly to it's summit and from it there is a most pleasing view of the country we are now about to leave. From it I saw that evening immense herds of buffaloe in the plains below.[sic]"

Wahkpa Chu'gn Archaeological Site (406-265-6417; www.buffalojump.org), 3993 6th Street W., Havre. Open June 1 through Labor Day for daily one-hour tours, 10 A.M.–5 P.M. and 7 P.M. (except Sunday); open by appointment only the remainder of the year. Adults $6, students $3, seniors $5, and children under 6 free. Tours are operated by the H. Earl Clack Memorial Museum (see *Museums*). This well-preserved site takes you back two thousand years when Native Americans first used this area as a kill and slaughter site for buffalo. Exhibits include layers of campsites, arrowheads, and buffalo remains. There is also evidence that several tribes used this area as a hunting and harvesting grounds.

FOR FAMILIES ✿ **Children's Museum of Montana** (406-452-6661; www .childrensmuseumofmt.org), 22 Railroad Square (behind the Civic Center), Great Falls. May through September, open Tuesday–Saturday, 9:30 A.M.–5 P.M.; October through April, Wednesday–Saturday, 9:30 A.M.–5 P.M. and Thursday, 9:30 A.M.–8 P.M. Admission is $3 for anyone over age 2, seniors $1. Catering strictly to kids, they have designed exhibits that encourage touching, poking, climbing, feeling, and other "hands-on" experiences. Children are encouraged to engage themselves without risk or being too loud or too touchy. Education and interaction are stressed here.

✿ **Electric City Waterpark** (406-771-1265; www.ci.great-falls.mt.us/people _offices/park_rec/ecwp/index.htm), 100 River Drive S., Great Falls. Inquire locally for seasons and hours; typically opens the first weekend in June. Rates vary as well. Enjoy several slides, a wave rider (one of only eight in the United States), and the largest heated public outdoor pool in Montana.

✿ **Gibson Park** (406-771-1265; www.ci.great-falls.mt.us/people_offices/park _rec/gibson.htm), along Park Drive between Central Avenue and 6th Street, Great Falls. This is a nice park for the kids to run off a little steam if you've been at the **Lewis & Clark National Historic Trail Interpretive Center,** but there is also something for adults in the 1884 Vinegar Jones Cabin. For walkers and joggers, a path links to the River's Edge Trail (see *To Do–Bicycling*); in winter a duck pond provides ice skating. Gibson Park is also home to summertime flower gardens and a year-round coffeehouse, **Park & Ponder Coffeehouse.** This is an enjoyable place for the whole family.

SCENIC DRIVES This region has several scenic drives, but only two nationally designated routes. Defined by broad vistas stretching for hundreds of miles and several mountain ranges, Russell Country is a region where just driving is an invigorating experience.

Havre Badlands, 5 miles along CR 534 northwest of Havre and north of the Milk River. View the Havre area's version of the badlands on this short scenic jaunt. Along this route you will also discover the Rookery Wildlife Management Area. Venturing off the road here is nearly impossible as most of the surrounding land is private, but it's very scenic and a great place for viewing wildlife.

Kings Hill National Scenic Byway, 71 miles on US 89 from its junction with US 12 to its junction with US 87. This drive takes you, twisting and turning, through the **Little Belt Mountains.** Exploring beyond the road on most of this route is relative easy as ample trails and side roads exist off US 89. Most of the land lies within the **Lewis & Clark National Forest,** where you'll find opportunities for camping, fishing, mountain biking, snowmobiling, cross-country skiing, and downhill skiing.

Missouri Breaks National Backcountry Byway, 80 miles total in very rugged and remote terrain. Do not attempt this drive in wet or poor weather conditions and be sure to stock up on fuel and some food in Winifred as there is little, if anything, along the way. The byway begins in Winifred along MT 236 (38 miles north of Lewistown) and loops with Knox Ridge Road and Lower Two Calf Road with an access road (NWR 200) to US 191, which puts you at the **James Kipp Recreation Area** in the **Charles M. Russell National Wildlife Refuge.** At the junction of Knox Ridge Road and Lower Two Calf Road, visit the information kiosk for details on the route and the scenery. Another interesting highlight of this drive is that the northern portion travels along the **Upper Missouri River National Wild and Scenic River,** and this portion also lies along the **Lewis & Clark National Historic Trail,** including two of their campsites. (See also Upper Missouri River Breaks National Monument and Wild and Scenic River under *To See–Natural Wonders.*)

NATURAL WONDERS & **Giant Springs State Park** (406-454-5840; http://fwp .mt.gov/lands/site_282690.aspx), 4600 Giant Springs Road, Great Falls. Open

AN OLD JAIL NEAR SQUARE BUTTE

year-round, day use only; free for residents, nonresidents $5 per vehicle. Lewis & Clark first noted this massive spring on their journey in 1805. Today it remains one of the largest known freshwater springs, pumping nearly 156 million gallons of water per day at a constant temperature of around 55 degrees F. There are 15 miles of trails for hiking or biking (some of which are handicapped accessible). You can also access the Rainbow Falls Overlook. The park includes a visitor center, state fish hatchery, playground, and picnic area.

Square Butte (406-538-7461), MT 80 to Square Butte (you can't miss it), then 2.5 miles on a signed county road. Designated a National Natural Landmark, this flat-topped butte is a banded igneous formation that rises over 2,000 feet from the High Plains. The unique thing about Square Butte is that the grasslands atop the butte have remained nearly untouched by humans; nearly 80 mountains goats make their home on the butte. A 1-mile hike will take you to the top. The views are breathtaking.

Upper Missouri River Breaks National Monument and Wild and Scenic River (406-538-7461; www.blm.gov/mt/st/en/fo/lewistown_field_office/UM.html). This rugged and beautiful centerpiece of Russell Country begins at Fort Benton near US 87, then spans 150 miles to end at the Fred Robinson Bridge on US 191 across the Missouri River. The Missouri River flows unimpeded for the length of this stretch and is remote and inaccessible most of the way. The river and surrounding countryside look much the same as it did when Lewis & Clark traveled here over two hundred years ago. The best way to experience this area is to plan a multi-day canoe or kayak expedition. You will see abundant wildlife, including herds of elk and bighorn sheep, prairie dog towns, raptors, antelope, deer, and various birdlife. The monument also includes 375,000 acres of public land administered by the Bureau of Land Management. Recreational pursuits include floating/paddling, camping, fishing, hiking, picnicking, and scenic drive.

✳ To Do

BICYCLING **River's Edge Trail** (406-788-3313; www.thetrail.org), 25 miles along the Missouri River near Great Falls. The trail travels from Oddfellows Park (southwest) to Cochrane Dam (northeast). It's ideal for biking, but also good for skating, jogging, or walking, with spectacular views of Black Eagle Falls, Rainbow Falls, Crooked Falls, and the Great Falls of the Missouri. Portions of the trail are paved and wheelchair accessible. Once out of downtown Great Falls, the trail passes a boxcar and caboose display and Black Eagle Falls and enters **Giant Springs State Park.** New tunnels and trail segments link to the **Lewis & Clark National Historic Trail Interpretive Center.** The trail continues through the park to interpretive overlook areas at Rainbow and Crooked Falls. The south-shore trail continues as a singletrack and doubletrack to Cochrane Dam. An 11-mile stretch of the trail on the north shore along the reservoirs links to several singletrack loops and a native plant interpretive walk loop. The first 5.5 miles is gravel with relatively gentle grades. The next 5.5 miles is a singletrack through native lands with some steep and technical sections. The River's Edge Trail provides great views of the rugged canyon, the reservoirs, the native plains, and distant mountains, as well as year-round opportunities to view

SHOWDOWN SKI AREA IN THE LITTLE BELT MOUNTAINS

abundant bird and wildlife. The trail is open year-round during daylight hours. Much of the urban trail is plowed during the winter.

Showdown Ski Area Mountain Bike Trails (406-236-5522; showdown montana.com). These trails lie in the heart of the Little Belt Mountain's mountain biking trail system. Hundreds of miles of trails and fire roads spiderweb out from Showdown, creating an amazing array of opportunities for riders of all abilities. These trails and rides will take you through some of the finest wild country that Montana has to offer, and the best part is that you will have it all to yourself because few mountain bikers have yet discovered the great riding available here.

See also Windy Mountain Trail under *Hiking;* Beaver Creek County Park and Sluice Boxes State Park under *Wilder Places–Parks;* and Lewis & Clark National Forest under *Wilder Places–Forests.*

BOATING &. **Fresno Reservoir** (406-266-2927; http://fwp.mt.gov/fishing/guide/ q_Fresno_Reservoir__1099707486400_0_1.aspx), 14 miles west of Havre via US 2; follow the signs. With nearly 7,000 acres of surface water and 65 miles of shoreline, this reservoir provides ample space to roam. There is a concrete boat ramp with a few campsites nearby. Water sports, swimming, picnicking, and fishing are popular. Fish species include northern pike, perch, and walleye.

&. **Lake Elwell and Tiber Dam State Recreation Area** (406-454-5840; http: //fwp.mt.gov/fishing/guide/q_Tiber_Reservoir__1111912483707_0_1.aspx), 10 miles south of Chester via MT 223, then 5 miles west on an unpaved road; follow the signs. Numerous access roads run from US 2 to the shoreline, but be aware of private property. There are four boat ramps and 181 miles of shoreline to the 17,678 acres of surface area. This is the largest reservoir in Russell Country and it's a boater's paradise. Aside from the usual water sports and activities, anglers will find carp, ling, northern pike, perch, sauger pike, trout, and walleye. Ice fishing is growing in popularity as well. There are a few handicapped-accessible campsites around the reservoir.

✦ **Lake Frances** (406-454-5840; http://fwp.mt.gov/fishing/guide/q_Lake _Frances__1122656482913_0_1.aspx), six blocks south of Valier on MT 44 via Teton Avenue–Lake Frances Road. This 3,618-acre natural lake provides year-round fun for boaters, anglers, ice skaters, and snowmobilers. Anglers will find northern pike, walleye, and yellow perch. (See also Lake Frances Ice Derby under *Special Events.*)

Pishkun Reservoir (406-454-5840; http://fwp.mt.gov/fishing/guide/q_Pishkun _Reservoir__1124651476907_0_1.aspx), lies 20 miles southwest of Choteau on Pishkun Reservoir Road; follow the signs in Choteau. This reservoir is 1,518 acres in size and sits at nearly 4,400 feet in elevation. Boaters will find some room to roam and gorgeous vies of the Rocky Mountain Front. Anglers will find northern pike, rainbow trout, and yellow perch.

See also the Missouri River and Willow Creek Reservoir under *To Do–Fishing;* Upper Missouri River Keelboat Company under *Unique Adventures;* Ackley Lake State Park and Beaver Creek County Park under *Wilder Places–Parks.*

CAMPING There are many private campground and RV parks in this region. If you want to rough it, there are probably a hundred places to pitch a tent as most fishing access sites, state parks, and BLM lands allow overnight camping. You can rest assured that at any public site there will be signs stating whether or not overnight camping is allowed. If in doubt read all posted signs, especially if you are unclear on the need to pay a fee.

THE MARIAS RIVER TUMBLES FROM TIBER DAM

☞ **Choteau City Park** (406-466-2510). Turn east off Main Street in Choteau at the blinking light and proceed two blocks. Open year-round; $10. In summer, water and picnicking are available. There is a three-night camping limit. Fishing can be had in Spring Creek. This is a safe, quiet place to stay despite the fact that it's just off Main Street in Choteau.

Coal Banks Landing Recreation Site (406-538-7461; www.blm.gov/mt/st/en/ fo/lewistown_field_office/recreation/coal_banks.html), north of Fort Benton and south of Big Sandy off US 87 toward Virgelle. Open year-round; free, but water is available in the summer months. There are 5 acres of camping space, as well as picnic tables, hiking trails, RV sites (but no hook-ups), fishing, a boat ramp, and floating access. This is the main launch point for floaters headed into the Upper Missouri River Breaks National Scenic Monument.

♿ **James Kipp Recreation Site** (406-538-7461; www.mt.blm.gov/ldo/rec reation/docs/kipp.html) is the eastern terminus of the **Missouri River Breaks Backcountry Scenic Byway.** Here NWR 200 meets US 191, and that is about it in this lonely, yet scenic countryside. Open April 1 through December, camping is $6 ($10 for use of RV dump station). This area in the **Charles M. Russell National Wildlife Refuge** is the most popular take-out point and camping site for paddlers on the Upper Missouri River. There are several single and group sites, a warming hut, a boat ramp, maintained restrooms, fishing access, and hiking trails.

Judith Landing Recreation Area (406-538-7461; www.blm.gov/mt/st/en/fo/ lewistown_field_office/recreation/judith.html) is 26 miles northwest of Winifred via MT 236. The campground is open May 15 through October 15; the rest of the site is open year-round with no facilities. This is a unique place to camp as it is on the National Register of Historic Places as a designated Historic District. Among the many historic events here are a Lewis & Clark campsite, May 28, 1805; Fort Chardon Trading Post, 1844–1845; Isaac Stevens 1855 Lame Bull Treaty; Camp Cooke (first military post in Montana), 1866–1870; PN Cable Ferry, 1880–1908. This is also a popular take-out point for paddlers and floaters finishing a trip through the Upper Missouri River area. There are tent sites, RV sites (no hook-ups), boating, fishing access, picnicking, and a few hiking trails.

☞ **Lake Shel-oole Campground** (406-434-5222), 0.5 mile north of Shelby on I-15. Open May 1 through September 30; $15. This small site is popular with locals and their kids. There are over 40 campsites with water, electricity, a playground, a fishing access, and some walking trails. In winter ice skating and ice fishing are popular pursuits. Near this campground, a little farther from Shelby, is the **Williamson Park Campground,** 7 miles south of Shelby on the I-15 Frontage Road.

Lewis & Clark National Forest (406-791-7700; www.fs.fed.us/r1/lewisclark), 1101 15th Street N., Great Falls. The bulk of this forest lies west of Great Falls. The forest is divided into divisions and districts. In the **Rocky Mountain Division** there are 10 campgrounds in this region managed by the forest. Three are handicapped accessible, and most of them lie west of Augusta or Choteau and are accessed off US 287. The northernmost campground lies 12 miles west of

East Glacier on the border of Glacier National Park. Many of the campgrounds in this division have trails leading into the **Bob Marshall Wilderness,** as well as fishing areas such as the Teton or Sun Rivers. Most of the campsites require a fee and it is best to contact the division office before heading out. The **Jefferson District** is home to 14 campgrounds, of which five are handicapped accessible. These campgrounds are scattered throughout the forest lands south and east of Great Falls, many along US 89 (see also Kings Hill National Scenic Byway under *To See–Scenic Drives*), and can be found with a good map. Most require a fee and are usually open only in summer or fall. The forest also rents five cabins with varying amenities, but still relatively primitive. Rates vary, so please inquire with the Forest Service office.

FISHING **Big Spring Creek** (406-454-5840; http://fwp.mt.gov/fishing/guide/ q_Big_Spring_Creek__1096415472029.aspx), along MT 466 and MT 238 southeast of Lewistown, and along MT 426 northwest of Lewistown. It runs northwesterly 30 miles, mainly between the Big Snowy and Judith Mountains, and enters the Judith River west of Brooks, Montana. Enclosing the large spring at the head of the creek, giant willows and cottonwoods shade a park and wildlife-viewing area. There are five state fishing access sites along the creek, two southeast of Lewistown and three northwest. The creek is home to brown trout, mountain whitefish, and rainbow trout. The first 20 miles are the most productive; after that, the numbers of trout per mile decrease.

The Marias River (406-454-5840; http://fwp.mt.gov/fishing/guide/q_Marias _River__1104910479289.aspx) flows for nearly 200 miles from the Rocky Mountain Front to the Missouri River. The river also creates Lake Elwell/Tiber Reservoir. Not known as a great fishery, this river offers solitude and enough fish to keep most folks busy. The river, however, boasts some historical significance as Lewis & Clark nearly went up the Marias on their way west. There is one state fishing access site (with a boat ramp) near the Loma Bridge off US 87. The river is home to brown trout, burbot, channel catfish, mountain whitefish, northern pike, rainbow trout, sauger, shovelnose sturgeon, and walleye. Other than the access at Loma, getting to the river is difficult as most of it flows through private land.

The Missouri River (406-538-7461; http://fwp.mt.gov/fishing/guide/q_Missouri _River__1039825479786_1586.77905273438_2312.46704101563.aspx). The river in Russell Country has two distinct sections, each with a different feel. South of Great Falls (from Holter Dam to Cascade) and along I-15, the river is a prolific coldwater trout fishery. Downstream from Cascade for nearly 200 miles, the river is a warmwater fishery and provides more sightseeing and solitude than angling opportunities. From Holter Dam to Cascade there are more than a dozen state fishing access sites, some with camping and boat ramps and handicapped access. This section of the river is world famous among trout anglers. North of Cascade, several state fishing access sites are spaced along the remaining 200 miles. Anglers visiting the Missouri can expect to find black crappie, brown trout, burbot, channel catfish, lake whitefish, mountain whitefish, northern pike, paddlefish, rainbow trout, sauger, shovelnose sturgeon, smallmouth bass, walleye, and yellow perch.

&. **The Smith River** (406-454-5840; http://fwp.mt.gov/parks/recreation/smith river/default.html) flows for 121 miles from south of White Sulphur Springs to its confluence with the Missouri River about 10 miles south of Great Falls. Access to the river is limited, difficult, and mostly managed by Montana Fish, Wildlife & Parks. However, it's possible to float and/or fish the river with some advanced planning—and it is worth it. The river's best fishing occurs in its spectacular canyon between Camp Baker and Eden Bridge, both state fishing access sites. But due to private land the only way to experience the canyon's fishing (unless you know someone who has a cabin on the river with drive-in access) is to float the river. And the only way to float the river is to apply for a permit and hope you get one. Advance planning (and lots of luck) is essential in getting a permit for the prime floating and fishing seasons of May, June, and July—the fishing and scenery are just so great that many people want to enjoy the river during this season. If you do not want to take your chances in the permit application/lottery you can hire a professional outfitter. A list of licensed Smith River outfitters is available from Montana Fish, Wildlife & Parks at the number above.

Willow Creek Reservoir (406-454-5840; http://fwp.mt.gov/fishing/guide/q _Willow_Creek_Reservoir__1117033457046.aspx) is 5 miles west of Augusta on Sun River Road. Though technically in the Gold West Region of Montana, this small reservoir is very close to Pishkun and within an hour of Great Falls, so it deserves mention in Russell Country. There is a boat ramp and camping facilities. Species include kokanee salmon and rainbow trout.

GOLF **Anaconda Hills Golf Course** (406-761-8459), East Smelter Avenue, Great Falls; 18 holes.

Arrowhead Meadows Golf Course (406-547-3993), US 89 south of White Sulphur Springs; nine holes.

Beaver Creek Golf Course (406-265-4201), 5 miles west of Havre on US 2; nine holes.

Chinook Golf Course (406-357-2112), north of Chinook (you cannot miss it); nine holes.

Choteau Country Club (406-466-2020), just east of Choteau on Airport Road; nine holes.

Eagle Falls Golf Club (406-761-1078), 29 River Drive N., Great Falls; 18 holes.

Emerald Greens Gold Club (406-453-4844), 1100 American Avenue, Great Falls; 18 holes.

Gannon Ranch Golf Course (406-727-1206), 240 Sunflower Lane, Great Falls; 18 holes.

Harlem Golf Course (406-353-2213), on US 2 south of Harlem; nine holes.

Harvest Hills Golf Course (406-467-2052), just south of Fairfield on US 89; nine holes.

Jawbone Creek Golf Course (406-632-4206), N. Main Street, north of Harlowton; nine holes.

Judith Shadwows Golf Course (406-538-6062), US 87 east of Lewistown; 18 holes.

Marias Valley Golf and Country Club (406-434-5940), 5 miles south of Shelby on I-15; Exit 358, then follow signs along Golfcourse Road; 18 holes.

Meadow Lark Country Club (406-454-3553), 300 Country Club Boulevard, Great Falls; 18 holes.

Pine Meadows Golf Course (406-538-7075), south on Spring Creek Road, 9 miles south of Lewistown; nine holes.

Pondera Golf Club (406-278-3402), west of Conrad; nine holes.

Signal Point Golf Club (406-622-3666), northeast of Fort Benton on MT 387; nine holes.

HIKING **A. B. Guthrie Memorial Trail** is located on the Nature Conservancy's **Pine Butte Swamp Preserve** (406-466-2158; www.nature.org/wherewework/ northamerica/states/montana/preserves/art342.html). To reach this short, scenic, and easy trail, travel via US 89 five miles north of Choteau, then west on Teton Canyon Road for 17 miles, then south across the Teton River, then another 3.5 miles, following the signs for the preserve. The path leads you to a fantastic vista of the Rocky Mountain Front. For more hiking and adventure, consider a stay at the **Pine Butte Guest Ranch.**

Clary Coulee Trail is a moderate to difficult 6-mile loop trail (Trail #177) with great rewards—views of the Rocky Mountain Front and High Plains. To access the trailhead, travel west from Choteau on Canyon Road. Follow the signs to Teton Pass Ski Area and you will see the sign just inside the Lewis & Clark National Forest boundary.

Crystal Lake Shoreline Loop Trail is an easy 1.7-mile interpretive hike (Trail #404). Take US 87 west of Lewistown for 8.7 miles, then continue south on Crystal Lake Road for 16 miles (follow the signs), then south on FR 275 for 8.5 miles to **Crystal Lake Campground** (handicapped accessible; $10). After some twists and turns in getting here, the trail skirts around 100-acre Crystal Lake (itself a popular destination). For a fun place to spend the night, try booking (well in advance) the **Crystal Lake Forest Service Cabin.** For a shorter hike, try the **Jack Milburn Trail,** which begins at the campground. This trail is handicapped accessible. The campground is also the beginning and ending point for numerous hiking and horseback-riding trails, including the popular **Uhlorn Trail** (Trail #493), a 16-mile round-tripper that takes you to some exciting year-round ice caves.

Decision Point Overlook is more like a historic walk than a hike, as you wander on an easy 0.5-mile round-trip path. The trail is 11 miles north of Fort Benton along US 87. Once at the vantage point, you will be in the exact location where Lewis & Clark pondered which of the two rivers—Marias or Missouri—was actually the Missouri. There are interpretive signs along the way that tell more of the story.

Dry Wolf Trail is a 5.2-mile loop that starts at the Dry Wolf Campground, which is accessible from FR 251 southwest of Stanford (follow the signs). This hike ambles to high meadows on Jefferson Divide. This is an easy hike on a well-maintained trail. Wildlife and wildflower viewing are abundant.

Memorial Falls Trail is an easy 3-mile round-trip hike accessible via US 89, north of White Sulphur Springs (just north of Neihart). The trailhead is well marked. If you are driving the **Kings Hill Scenic Byway**, this is a nice respite from the car. The trail (#438) follows a creek to two waterfalls.

Sluice Boxes State Park is located 8 miles south of Belt via US 89. This is a fun hike for families as the geology and creek are sure to keep kids entertained. The hike follows Belt Creek from the bridge near the mouth of Logging Creek to the parking area at Riceville at the north end of Sluice Boxes State Park. The distance is approximately 7 miles, along a well-maintained trail.

Windy Mountain Trail-Briggs Creek Trail. These two trails form a moderate 6.5-mile loop hike. Take US 89 east from Great Falls, then travel on MT 228 toward Highwood for 14 miles. Follow the signs for **Thain Creek Campground** (handicapped accessible). Once at the campground, hydrate and be ready for a climb as your hike up Arrow Peak on your way to Windy Mountain. Up on top, the vistas will make the effort worthwhile. The return route will take you along the Briggs Creek Trail back at the campground.

See also River's Edge Trail under *To Do–Bicycling* and Beaver Creek County Park under *Wilder Places–Parks*.

HORSEBACK RIDING ✒ **Bull Run Guest Ranch** (406-731-3263; www.bullrun guestranch.com), 719 Sheep Creek Road, Cascade. The friendly folks here offer packaged ranch vacations and nightly cabin rentals during the summer, along with daily horseback-riding trips. Rates start at $35/person for 1.5-hour rides and go up from there based on length and number of riders. A daylong ride with a gourmet dinner is a fun thing for the family, or perhaps rent a cabin and enjoy a self-service cookout.

✒ **Grizzly Trails Ranch** (406-472-3301) is west of Dupuyer, 4.8 miles off US 89 at the rest stop via Swift Dam Road; follow the signs. The setting here is hard to beat—at the foot of the Rocky Mountain Front. From a working ranch vacation to a daylong horseback ride, guests can enjoy working with livestock, hiking, wildlife watching, fishing, sightseeing, or just relaxing and enjoying the breathtaking scenery in the peace and quiet of a country atmosphere. Reservations are recommended; please inquire about rates.

✒ **Hitch'n Rail Ranch** (406-378-2571; www.trailridemontana.com), south of Big Sandy and downriver from Coal Banks Landing Recreation Site. From here you can take a riding tour of the **Upper Missouri River Breaks**. They also offer hour, half-, and full-day rides, or multi-day expeditions. This is the place for anyone who wants to mix Lewis & Clark history with horseback riding. Because of the customized nature of their trips, please inquire for rates and reservations.

✒ **Sourdough Ranch Adventures** (406-462-5422; www.sourdoughranch adventures.com), 106 3rd Avenue N., Winifred. These folks offer full-day rides, with instruction and on-trail lunch and dinner cooked over a campfire. The rides occur in the area explored by Lewis & Clark and offer a fun family experience in a remote part of the state. Sourdough Ranch Adventures also offers weekend or weeklong adventures.

HOT SPRINGS **Spa Hot Springs Motel** (406-547-3366; www.spahotsprings .com) 202 W. Main Street, White Sulphur Springs. On US 89 and US 12 in White Sulphur Springs, this small-scale hot springs resort is open year-round. There are two pools (both fed by natural hot springs) open to the public, one indoors and one outdoors. The guest rooms have private baths and are very reasonably priced. The springs were long thought by Native Americans to have healing powers and are the namesake for the town, White Sulphur Springs. The springs were once owned by John Ringling (of circus fame), who planned to make them a lavish grandiose resort. But the Great Depression hit and those plans were, well, history—all that remains of Ringling's plans are the small town of Ringling a few miles south of White Sulphur. A nice thing about these springs: They are chemical free and drained, cleaned, and refilled each night.

PADDLING/FLOATING **Missouri River Breaks National Monument—Wild and Scenic River** (406-538-7461; www.blm.gov/mt/st/en/fo/lewistown_field _office/UM.html) begins near Fort Benton on US 87 and continues 150 miles downstream to end at the Fred Robinson Bridge at US 191. This section of the nation's longest river has many appeals: Lewis & Clark history, solitude, scenery, fishing, camping, and more. Much of the terrain remains untouched by humans (or at least has that feel) and is mostly accessible only by floating or paddling. There are hundreds of interesting sites, historical locations, and wildlife-viewing opportunities along the paddle. The Web site above, maintained by the BLM, is a good resource for planning a trip through this region. If you want to leave the details to someone else, there are many excellent outfitters and guide services who can assist or take care of everything for you. A complete list of all service providers can be obtained by contacting the BLM office listed above. These providers rent equipment (canoes, kayaks, tents, stoves, etc.), offer shuttle services, and more.

SNOW SPORTS

Ice Fishing
Russell Country is one of the more popular destinations in Montana for ice fishing. You'll need to inquire locally for the best locations, but here are a few well-known places: Willow Creek Reservoir, northwest of Augusta, and Bynum Reservoir and Eureka Reservoir northwest of Choteau.

Ice Skating
Ice skating in Russell Country can be had anywhere a pond or lake freezes over. Just exercise caution if skating in an unimproved area. Most small towns in the region have a community skating rink. Here are a few ideas among the many available: Gibson Park in Great Falls, Lake Frances northwest of Havre, and Ackley Lake State Park near Lewistown.

Skiing

✍ **Bear Paw Ski Bowl** (406-265-8404; www.skibearpaw.com), 29 miles south of Havre via Beaver Creek Road to BIA 123 (follow the signs) on the Chippewa Cree Recreation Area within the Rocky Boy's Indian Reservation. During ski season (which varies based on snow conditions), they are open on weekends. This is a real affordable option and a fun place for a day of skiing with the family. *Lifts:* one double, one handle tow. *Terrain:* 25 trails—25 percent beginner, 25 percent intermediate, 50 percent expert; 900 feet of vertical. *Average annual snowfall:* 140 inches. *Facilities:* On-site concession stand, lodging in nearby Havre. *Ski school:* certified ski school. *Rates:* Adults $18, students $15, seniors 80 and over and children 8 and under free.

♿ ✍ **Showdown Montana Ski Area** (406-236-5522; www.showdownmontana .com), 8 miles south of Niehart on US 89 (Kings Hill National Scenic Byway; see *To See–Scenic Drives*). Open Wednesday through Sunday in-season. Situated in the Little Belt Mountains of the Lewis & Clark National Forest, Showdown is Montana's oldest ski area. They offer downhill skiing plus 12 kilometers of groomed cross-country trails. *Lifts:* 1 triple, 2 doubles, 1 conveyor lift. *Terrain:* 34 trails—30 percent beginner, 40 percent intermediate, 30 percent expert; 1,400 feet of vertical drop. *Average annual snowfall:* 240 inches. *Facilities:* lodging in Neihart, White Sulphur Springs, and Monarch; plenty of food and drink options on the mountain. *Ski school:* alpine, snowboard, telemark, and snowbike; group or private lessons; kids' Snowmonsters and Little Shredders programs. *Rates:* magic carpet (conveyor) free, child 5 and under free, juniors 6–13 all area $19; beginner chair only $19; senior 70+ all area $23; college student with college ID $28; adult all area $33.

Silver Crest Ski Trail (406-236-5511; www.fs.fed.us.r1/lewisclark), 7 miles south of Neihart on US 89 (Kings Hill National Scenic Byway). Park in the Kings Hill Recreation Area parking lot on US 89. This trail system has four loops (13.8 kilometers total) of varying degrees of difficulty. They are groomed weekly and offer solitude among the winter wonderland that is the Kings Hill area. There are also several warming huts along these trails.

Teton Pass Ski Area (406-466-2209; www.skitetonpass.com), 27 miles west of Choteau via US 89 to Teton River Road. A remote ski area in the Rocky Mountain Front offering downhill skiing, cross-country skiing, and snowmobiling. *Lifts:* 1 single, 1 double. *Terrain:* 26 trails—10 percent beginner, 35 percent intermediate, 46 percent expert; 1,010 feet of vertical drop. *Average annual snowfall:* 300 inches. *Facilities:* base lodge has food and drink, nearest lodging is in Choteau. *Ski school:* ski and snowboard lessons available for all ages and abilities; special workshops in racing, bumps, and powder; Dinos for ages 3–6; Teton Rangers for ages 7–12. Sessions are all day and include snack and lunch. *Rates:* kids under 6 $7, seniors 66+ $16, child 6–12 $16, student (up to age 20 with a student ID) $21, and adult $27.

For additional cross-country skiing opportunities, see Beaver Creek County Park under *Wilder Places–Parks* and Lewis & Clark National Forest under *Wilder Places–Forests.*

THE AMAZING VIEW FROM TETON PASS SKI AREA

Snowmobiling

The most popular snowmobiling spots in Russell Country are the trails off the Kings Hill Scenic Byway along US 89 south of Great Falls. Nearly 200 miles of trails branch out from the Kings Hill Recreation Area parking lot. These trails are maintained by the Lewis & Clark National Forest. Snowmobiles can be rented from **Montana Snowmobile Adventures** (406-236-5358) at Showdown Ski Area. There are also hundreds of miles of trails to explore in other parts of Russell Country.

UNIQUE ADVENTURES ⚓ **Charlie Russell Chew-Choo** (406-538-8721; www .montanacharlierussellchewchoo.com/). The office is in downtown Lewistown, but the train runs 11 miles north of town via US 191 for 3 miles, then 8 miles west on MT 346. Open in summer only and for special events during the holiday season, this is an evening dinner ride. Wildlife abounds on this scenic 56-mile round-trip journey, with a plentiful supply of antelope, eagles, deer, hawks, and coyotes. Be sure to watch out for masked bandits, as rumor has it holdups can occur when you least expect them—something the kids will love. Crossing three historic trestles and passing through a half-mile-long tunnel, the 3.5-hour trip in climate-controlled, nonsmoking coaches includes a full-course prime rib dinner and dessert, plus a full bar. Advance reservations are encouraged.

Missouri River Breaks Tours (406-386-2486; www.fortbenton.com/mrbtours/ index.htm), located in Big Sandy. Gary Darlington and his guides can take you on a variety of tours. It is best to contact them directly for rates and schedules. You will see lots of wildlife, Indian artifacts like pictographs and tepee rings,

Lewis & Clark historical sites, and more. This area is certainly worth seeing and these are good folks to venture out with.

Missouri River Canoe Company (406-378-3110; www.canoemontana.com), 7485 Virgelle Ferry Road. These folks offer every service for those wanting to explore the Upper Missouri River area. From bed & breakfast rooms to ATV adventures, cabins, and canoe expeditions, these folks know what it takes to have an enjoyable experience in this remote section of Montana. They even offer a Paddle to Saddle trip for a true Missouri Breaks experience. Trips can range in duration from a single hour to 10 days. Because of the customized nature of the trips it is best to contact them for rates and the seasonal schedule.

Ranch Vacations. A vacation in Montana is not complete without a visit to or stay at a working Montana ranch. And Russell Country has some of the most genuine vacation ranches in the state. A typical ranch vacation will include anything from herding cattle, sheep, or other livestock to branding livestock, cutting hay, breaking horses, and more. The time spent working versus relaxing is up to the ranch owners or hands, but also you—remember this is your vacation. All of the ranches listed below include horseback riding, lodging, meals, and more as part of an all-inclusive package. This is only a small sample of the many ranch vacations available: **Sky View Ranch** (406-378-2549), Big Sandy; **Bull Run Guest Ranch** (406-468-9269), Cascade; **Bonanza Creek Country Guest Ranch** (406-572-3366), Martinsdale; **Why Lazy Tree Ranch** (406-788-0365), Stockett; **Homestead Ranch** (406-423-5301), Hobson; **Pine Butte Guest Ranch** (406-466-2158), Choteau; **Seven Lazy P Ranch** (406-466-2044), Choteau; **Grizzly Trails Ranch** (406-472-3301), Dupuyer; **Careless Creek**

THE CHARLIE RUSSELL STATUE IN GREAT FALLS

Ranch Getaway (406-632-4140), Shawmut. For a complete list, visit the Russell Country Web site (www.russell.visitmt.com).

⚓ **Timescale Adventures** (406-469-2211; www.timescale.org), 120 2nd Avenue S., Bynum near Choteau. Guests will join an active dinosaur dig with full-time paleontologists. Rates vary, so please inquire. The site is located in what is referred to as the "Two Medicine Formation," which is one of the most paleontologically significant rock layers in the world. From its sediments have come discoveries of the first dinosaur eggs in North America, the first nest of dinosaur babies in the world, and the closest dinosaur/bird relative in North America. The Two Medicine Dinosaur Center is located in the heart of this formation, only a few miles from where these discoveries were made. The center is a nonprofit research and educational institution whose main focus is the dinosaurs of the Two Medicine Formation. Timescale offers adventures by the hour or by the week. You will learn not only about dinosaurs but about local history, wildlife, fossil finding and preparation, and more. Reservations are required and advance planning is a must.

Upper Missouri River Keelboat Company (406-739-4333; www.mrkeelboat .com), 4 miles east of Loma along US 87. Experience this beautiful area from the comfort and peacefulness of the keelboat, *General Wm. Ashley*. It's a 38-foot replica of the keelboats that plied the fur and robe trade on the Upper Missouri before the days of the steamboats. The *General Wm. Ashley* was designed specifically for the shallow waters of the Upper Missouri River and is extremely maneuverable and stable in all conditions. An experienced and caring crew (all in period dress) man the boat. Six to 12 guests can be seated comfortably in the midships cabin, or experience hands-on keel boating to further enhance this one-of-a-kind experience. Guests will have the opportunity to experience living history presentations and primitive skills demonstrations from a direct descendent of one of the area's first settlers. Short scenic hikes to vantage points and historical sites are offered as well. Discover what the river looked like at the time of Lewis & Clark's visit in 1805. Camp in comfort at places where the Corps of Discovery encamped over two hundred years before. Discover the rich history of the river with every turn of the bend. Inquire about rates and schedule.

✳ Wilder Places

PARKS ♿ **Ackley Lake State Park** (406-454-5840; http://fwp.mt.gov/lands/site _282450.aspx), 5 miles south of Hobson on MT 400, then 2 miles southwest to the park entrance. Open year-round; free. There is a small lake here stocked with rainbow trout. The lake provides swimming and paddling in summer, as well as ice skating and ice fishing in winter. Camping and picnicking are also available.

Beaver Creek County Park (406-395-4565), 20 miles south of Havre via Beaver Creek Road (MT 234). Open year-round. With 10,000 acres managed by the county, this could be the largest county park in the country. There are campsites (for a fee), hiking and biking trails, fishing, boating, and picnicking. In winter snowmobiling, cross-country skiing, and ice fishing can all be had. Its location at the foot of the Bears Paw Mountains affords ample wildlife-viewing opportunities as well.

Sluice Boxes State Park (406-454-5840; http://fwp.mt.gov/lands/site_282818 .aspx), 8 miles south of Belt on US 89, then 0.5 mile to park entrance. Open year-round; free. This is an interesting park with lots to explore. Summer is a better time than winter. In summer there are hiking trails, fishing on Belt Creek, and wildlife viewing. The canyon here is a limestone canyon that any armchair geologist will love.

FORESTS **Lewis & Clark National Forest** (406-791-7700; www.fs.fed.us/r1/ lewisclark), 1101 15th Street N., Great Falls. With nearly 1.8 million acres (most of which are in Russell Country), the Lewis & Clark National Forest provides much of the outdoor recreation in this region. The forest has two major divisions. The 680,000-acre **Rocky Mountain Division,** west of Great Falls, abuts Flathead National Forest, Lolo National Forest, and Helena National Forest. The **Great Bear, Bob Marshall, and Scapegoat Wildernesses** make up about 380,000 acres of this division as well. The **Jefferson Division** includes more than 1 million acres of mountains and the prairie that surrounds them— creating, in essence, a few "islands" of mountains such as the Highwood Mountains. In all, there are six mountain ranges in the forest, providing recreational opportunities that include mountain biking, fishing, hiking, boating, camping, horseback riding, paddling/floating, skiing, snowmobiling, picnicking, and wildlife viewing.

WILDERNESS AREAS **Bob Marshall, Scapegoat, and Great Bear Wilderness Areas** (406-587-6701; www.fs.fed.us/r1/lewisclark). All three of these areas

THE FERRY BOAT AT CARTER CROSSING ON THE MISSOURI RIVER

THE BEARS PAW MOUNTAINS

are accessible via lands in Russell Country. To get to these areas you will most likely travel US 89 or US 87 via Augusta, Choteau, or Dupuyer.

WILDLIFE REFUGES AND WILDLIFE MANAGEMENT AREAS **Benton Lake National Wildlife Refuge** (406-727-7400; http://bentonlake.fws.gov), 922 Bootlegger Trail (12 miles north of Great Falls via MT 225). Open year-round Monday through Friday, 7:30 A.M.–4:30 P.M.; free. The 5,000-acre Benton Lake and surrounding marsh is a wetland home to hundreds of thousands of migratory birds, including ducks, geese, eagles, swans, and peregrine falcons. The lake has a unique history—it was carved by North America's last inland glacier. Aside from birds, there are plenty of other wildlife-viewing opportunities as well. This is best done by the 9-mile **Prairie Marsh Wildlife Drive.**

Freezeout Lake Wildlife Management Area (406-467-2646; www.fwp.state .mt.us/habitat/wma/freezeout.asp), 40 miles west of Great Falls on US 89. Open year-round; free. This is a fantastic place in which to view hundreds of thousands of migratory birds, including the famous snow geese migration, where up to 300,000 birds pass through. Additional birds include tundra swans, raptors, shorebirds, upland game birds, and plenty of waterfowl. Hunting is permitted in-season.

Judith River Wildlife Management Area (406-454-5840; www.state.mt.us/ habitat.wma/Judith.asp), 9 miles southwest of Utica. Take a gravel road north of Judith River to Sapphire Village, then go right on the first road after the village; follow the signs. Open May through November; free. An area more dedicated to protecting winter grazing for elk and other animals, this is a nice place to view antelope, deer, and smaller mammals. Raptors and other birds can be spotted as well. The nearby Judith River offers some fishing opportunities as well.

See also Charles M. Russell National Wildlife Refuge under *Wildlife Refuges and Wildlife Management Areas* in chapter 6.

✳ Lodging

BED & BREAKFASTS

Big Sandy
Raven Crest Bed & Breakfast (406-378-3121), 3002 Winchester Road, 10 miles west and north of Big Sandy on MT 432. Rustic and away from the small town of Big Sandy, this place is a location to get away from it all. On a clear night the stars are amazing and the inn's location, near the White Cliffs of the Upper Missouri, offers proximity to outdoor recreation. The house is on a working ranch and has two guest bedrooms with a shared bath. The biscuits at breakfast are grand. Rates are very reasonable and this place books up quickly. Please inquire for specific rates and seasons of operation.

Chester
& **Great Northern Bed & Breakfast** (406-759-5900; www.great northernbandb.com), 14 Monroe Avenue E. This would be a grand B&B anywhere in the country—the catch is that they only have one room. The breakfasts are fantastic, and for music lovers, you are next door to the recording studio of well-known Montana pianist Phillip Aaberg. The cottage was built in 1909 and features some art from the original Empire Builder rail line. Rates $80 a night per couple.

Choteau
See Styren Ranch Guest House *under Lodges, Guest Ranches, and Hotels/Motels.*

Dupuyer
& **Inn Dupuyer Bed & Breakfast** (406-472-3241; www.3rivers.net/~inndupyr/), 308 Morton Avenue. Built over one hundred years ago (with plenty of updating), this unique place is en route to or from Glacier National Park along US 89. Most of the logs in the house were hand-hewn and the floors were built by the original homesteaders. There are five guest rooms, plus a bunkhouse and loft. Each has its own bath. A plentiful breakfast is served each morning. They also offer horse boarding and tepees for more adventuresome types. Rates $65 and up.

Fairfield
Riverbend Bed & Breakfast (406-622-5601; www.riverbendbb.com), P.O. Box 602. Five miles west of Fort Benton on US 87, this country place offers two bedrooms and full continental breakfast. They are located near the Missouri River, where Lewis & Clark traveled. This is a good jumping-off place for venturing down the Upper Missouri River. Please inquire for current rates.

& **Vixen Lane Guest House and Fox Cottage** (406-733-6791), 47 Vixen Lane, 14 miles south of Fort Benton in the small town of Shonkin. Open March through November; reservations are required. You can choose to join the host family in one of the bedrooms in the main house or stay in the private three-bedroom Fox Cottage. Breakfasts will fill you up for your day of adventure in the area. Rates vary seasonally, so please inquire.

Great Falls

Charlie Russell Manor (406-455-1400; www.charlierussell.com), 825 4th Avenue N. This 7,000-square-foot mansion offers guests several choices. There are five bedrooms in all, each with private bath. Two of the rooms form a suite that can share a Jacuzzi, the other has a fireplace. The nice thing about the manor is the abundance of common spaces, including a large den with a big-screen television. A full breakfast is served each morning. Rates $95 and up.

Collins Mansion Bed & Breakfast (406-452-6798; www.collinsmansion.com), 1003 2nd Avenue N.W. Built in 1894 in the Victorian Queen Anne style, this building is on the National Register of Historic Places. In 1998 the owners did a full restoration on the inside and the grounds—creating a historic and enjoyable place to stay. There are five distinctly different guest rooms, a veranda, and great views of the city and the surrounding mountains. A gourmet breakfast is ready each morning. Rates $95 and up.

Havre

&. **Our Home Bed & Breakfast** (406-265-1055; www.hi-line.net/~donagh). This place is just as the name implies—someone's home, and they do a fine job with their two guest rooms. The rooms feature a Native American décor and great views of the Bears Paw Mountains to the south. The breakfasts are made to order and the hosts, the McDonaghs, are very inviting and accommodating. Rates $55 and up.

Lewistown

○ **Pheasant Tales Bed and Bistro** (406-538-6257; www.pheasanttales.biz). Owned and operated by Chris and Rick Taylor, this modern place serves great evening dinners along with the breakfasts each morning. There are six rooms, all with private bath and access to a hot tub. Hunters and anglers will enjoy the décor here, and the fact that Chris will serve up a gourmet meal with the day's quarry. There is plenty of space to roam, a great deck, and they often have various puppies (they breed English setters) to provide entertainment. Rates $85 and up.

✎ **Snowy View Bed & Breakfast** (406-538-5538; www.snowyview.com), 1145 Timber Tracts Road. Only 10 miles south of Lewistown at the base of the Snowy Mountains, this is a great spot for the outdoor enthusiast, hunter, or angler. There is a spacious queen suite with a great porch and a full private bath. Rates $95 and up.

Symes–Wicks House Bed & Breakfast (406-538-9068), 220 W. Boulevard. In the heart of historic Lewistown's Silk Stocking District, this restored 1909 mansion is on the National Register of Historic Places. There are distinctive shingle-style arts in the architecture and Tiffany pieces and period antiques inside the house. There are three bedrooms (two with private baths), and a full breakfast is served each morning with tea in the afternoon. Rates $80 and up.

Valier

Stone School Inn Bed & Breakfast (406-279-3796; www.stoneschoolinn.com), 820 3rd Street. Constructed in 1911, this stone house is on the National Register of Historic Places. It was built primarily as a schoolhouse, but after a serious makeover a few years back it now serves as a unique place to spend the night. There are five bedrooms, all with private baths. There is a nice common area downstairs with a complete kitchen. A continental breakfast is offered each morning. Please inquire for rates.

White Sulphur Springs
Foxwood Inn Bed & Breakfast (406-547-2106; www.foxwoodinn .com), 52 Miller Road. This 1890 Victorian home is quite large for a B&B—14 rooms, all with a distinct personality, some with private baths, most with shared baths, but all decorated in period antiques with modern beds. This a fun place to stay if you're heading out to the Smith River or planning a ski trip to Showdown. Rates $60 and up, but please inquire as to seasonal rates.

See also Montana Sunrise Lodge under *Lodges, Guest Ranches, and Hotels/Motels.*

LODGES, GUEST RANCHES, AND HOTELS/MOTELS

Choteau
Styren Ranch Guest House (406-466-2008; www.styrenguesthouse .com), 961 20th Road N.W. This three-bedroom guest house is 10 miles north of Choteau (with great views of the Rocky Mountain Front). You can book each room separately or rent the entire house. It sits on a family ranch and guests can enjoy ranch activities or just relaxing on the grounds. The full kitchen is well stocked, and there is even a laundry room. Rates $500 per week and up.

Fairfield
Rusty Spur Guest House and Gallery (406-467-2700; www.rusty

spur.net), 221 10th Lane S.W. This place is basically a gallery where you sleep. All of the art on the walls is for purchase, and many guests enjoy the idea of the place so much that they plan a stay here anytime they're in the area—just to see the newest art adorning the walls. They can house up to five guests in the house, and there is a full kitchen, laundry, and satellite TV. They also offer facilities for horses. Rates $70 per night and up.

Fort Benton
✔ **Pioneer Lodge** (406-622-5441; www.pionnerlodgemt.com), 1700 Front Street. This 10-room hotel, built in 1916, was originally the Pioneer Mercantile. Today the interior provides guests with modern rooms with private baths and cable television. Each room is decorated with a piece of local history, so guests still feel part of the past. Rates are very reasonable at $60 a night and up.

&. **Franklin Street Guest House** (406-733-2261; www.fortbenton.com/ franklin/index.htm), 1105 Franklin Street. A single house in downtown Fort Benton, available for the night, week, or month. There are three bedrooms that can accommodate up to six people in this quiet house within walking distance of Fort Benton's historic downtown area. The kitchen is large and well stocked for cooking your own meals. Please inquire for rates and availability.

&. ✪ **Grand Union Hotel** (406-622-1882; www.grandunionhotel.com), 1 Grand Union Square. Built in 1882 and listed on the National Register of Historic Places, this is Montana's oldest operating hotel. Restored and renovated, it's a true piece of Montana history. But do not let the historic

THE GRAND UNION HOTEL IN HISTORIC FORT BENTON

nature fool you. This place has plenty of amenities, so a stay here is the perfect blend of history and modern-day convenience. There are 26 rooms and rates start at $85, but inquire because they adjust rates seasonally. The **Union Grille** offers fine dining (try the roasted huckleberry chicken) and a great wine list.

Great Falls

Russell Country Inn (406-761-7125; www.russellcountryinn.com), 2516 4th Avenue N. This small space is actually a lower-level guest house in a residential area of Great Falls. It is quiet and very convenient to the art museums and historical highlights of the city. There is a bedroom and full kitchen, and the place can sleep two to four people comfortably. The owners also let guests use a canoe and two bicycles. Rates $80 per night or $290 per week.

Lewistown

Duvall Inn (406-538-7063; www.lewistown.net/~duvalinn), 612 Limekiln Road. After you have explored the mountainsides or Big Spring Creek, come to this western lodge and discover one of the best kept secrets: their home-baked breads and hot delicious soups. They are the best around these here parts and in most of Montana. The rooms are also very nice and feature queen beds and private baths. One of the favorite hangouts is in front of the stone fireplace in the common area. You also can partake in the daily full breakfast or venture out in Lewistown. Rates $85 a night and up.

Historic Hotel Calvert (406-538-5411; www.tein.net/~calvert), 216 7th Avenue S. Once a dormitory for the rural kids who went to Fergus County High School, this large hotel is listed on the National Register of Historic Places. There are 45 rooms and none of them are fancy by any means, but it is fun to sleep in this historic place. The prices are very reasonable and to say you stayed here is a good enough reason to spend the night. Rates $18 a night and up. A room with a double bed and private bath is $24—see, I wasn't kidding about it being very reasonable.

Leininger Ranch Log Cabins (406-538-5797; www.logcabinatlewistown.com), 5754 Lower Cottonwood Creek Road. These cabins were recently sold, so please inquire about rates and availability. But the new owners plan to rent out the cabins—all with a full kitchen, covered deck, hot tub, and great views. These cabins are great for families who want to explore some on their own.

♿ **Montana Bunkhouse and Paradise Cabin** (406-538-5543; www.montanabunkhouse.com), 23 miles south of Lewistown in the Big Snowy Mountains. The bunkhouse and cabin are located on a 4,000-acre ranch. Here you can hike the mountains, view elk, bear, and other wildlife, roast marshmallows around the campfire, or just relax on the comfy porch and enjoy a gentle breeze. The bunkhouse is handicapped accessible and can sleep up to four people. The Paradise Cabin has two bedrooms, a full kitchen, a large bathroom, and a laundry. Please inquire about rates and seasonal availability.

Martinsdale

♿ **Crazy Mountain Inn** (406-572-3307; www.crazymountaininn.com), 112 Main Street. The rustic, yet historic accommodations make this a fun adventure. And the hosts, Peter and Cheryl Marchi, might be some of the friendliest folks in Montana. The inn, built nearly one hundred years ago, only accepts cash or check. If you want a true sampling of small-town Montana lodging, where no one cares whether you make one dollar a month or a million, this is the place. The on-site restaurant claims to have the world's best chicken-fried steak, and yes, it is very good; however, make sure you finish it off with a piece of their sour cream lemon pie. Rates $25 a night and up.

White Sulphur Springs

Grassy Mountain Lodge (406-547-3357; www.grassymountain.com), 100 Grassy Mountain Road. If you are looking for more of a ranch vacation the folks at Grassy Mountain have created a beautiful lodge. They can arrange horseback rides, fishing on a children's trout pond, and various other activities. They have four log cabins with three separate rooms per cabin. Each room has a wood-burning fireplace, desk, dresser, walk-in closet, and in-room coffee. Choose from a room with a queen bed or a double and single bed. Adjoining rooms are available. The food here is also quite good and the servings are plentiful—great if you have a large family. The view from the cabins is certainly picture-worthy. Please inquire about rates and seasonal availability.

Montana Sunrise Lodge (406-685-6343; www.montanasunriselodge.com), 2063 US 89. Located 25 miles north of White Sulphur Springs and a great base for skiing at Showdown Ski Area or exploring the Little Belt Mountains, this large (seven bedrooms), luxurious rental is a great place for a group of friends or a family retreat. There are four bathrooms, a full kitchen, laundry facilities, and a monster television with satellite TV. Rates $300 and up per night.

See also Spa Hot Springs Motel under *To Do–Hot Springs* and Ranch Vacations under *To Do–Unique Adventures.*

OTHER OPTIONS ❧ **Lewis & Clark National Forest Cabins** (406-791-7700; www.fs.fed.us/r1/lewisclark/recreation/cabin-rentals/cabin_index.shtml). Renting a historic fire lookout or backcountry cabin is a unique way to experience the outdoors. These rustic cabins and lookouts are in remote, yet spectacular settings in the Lewis & Clark National Forest. Recreation cabins and lookouts are rented on a first-come, first-served basis and may be reserved through the National Recreation Reservation system. To check availability and reserve a facility, visit http://www.reserveusa.com or call 1-877-444-6777.

✳ Where to Eat
DINING OUT

Cascade
The Missouri Inn (406-468-9243), 2474 Old US 191 (also called Recreation Road); just off I-15, 10 miles north of Craig. The Missouri Inn, locally called Rosie's, is a fun place to eat. They have a varied menu ranging from soups to steaks to homemade ice creams. For lunch, try one of their soups, homemade every day. This is one of the larger places on the river and a good spot for families because they have a more developed kids' menu than some of the other places. Rosie's is a great spot for lunch during a fall float on the Missouri—the bar is warm and inviting.

Fort Benton
See Grand Union Hotel under *Lodging–Lodges, Guest Ranches, and Hotels/Motels.*

Great Falls
♿ ✎ **Bar S Supper Club** (406-761-9550), US 87, 5 miles from downtown. A favorite among the surf-and-turf crowd in Great Falls, with nightly beef specials and steaks on the menu over 2 pounds. You will not leave here hungry, as they have a large salad bar, homemade soups, and fresh-baked breads. This is also a good place for kids because the children's menu is complete with chicken strips and shaped fries.

Beargrass Grill (406-453-1760), 518 Central Avenue, downtown Great Falls. This fine establishment offers a pleasant dining experience with a Montana atmosphere. With all seafood flown in daily from Hawaii, the finest wine cellar around, and 100-percent, Montana-raised beef, the Beargrass Grille is a refreshing choice while in Great Falls.

Bert and Ernie's (406-453-0601), 300 1st Avenue, downtown Great Falls. Established in 1977, Bert and Ernie's is a Great Falls tradition. The restaurant is comfortable, with an atmosphere they refer to as "rustic elegance." They serve a variety of wonderful, homestyle foods that run the gamut from hearty soups and salads to grilled seafood and eclectic pasta dishes. They also offer the largest selection of microbrewed beers in the city, featuring at least 10 Montana brews at all times. The desserts are baked in-house.

Clark and Lewie's (406-454-2141), 17 7th Street S., downtown Great Falls. Enjoy a plentiful meal at this full-service restaurant. A large menu of tempting, tasty treats awaits you, along with a wide selection of micro-brews and wines. The ribs are the best in town and the chili has won some local awards. They hand batter their own secret recipe fish and chips and serve them with beer-battered fries.

Dante's Creative Cuisine (406-453-9599), 1325 8th Avenue, downtown Great Falls. Dante's is in a beautiful old brick building that was built in 1908 as an ironworks. The building is now called Ironworks Square. Dante's features Italian, Southwest, seafood, prime rib, steak, and nightly features. All meals include a tasty signature gorgonzola salad and sourdough bread, served with roasted garlic. The food is elegant, but the atmosphere is casual and relaxed.

♿ ☌ ◉ **3D International Restaurant and Lounge** (406-453-6561), 1825 Smelter Avenue, Black Eagle just north of Great Falls. Family owned and operated since 1946, the menu includes steaks, seafood, Italian, a Mongolian grill, prime rib, veal, and a children's menu. There is also a full-service bar and lounge. They also feature some unique art deco surroundings in historic Black Eagle. Open for lunch Monday through Friday and dinner seven days a week.

Havre

♿ **The Duck Inn's Mediterranean Room and Vineyard** (406-265-6111), 1300 1st Street. The only real place in Havre for a fine-dining experience, this place would be a popular place in any town in Montana, small or large. The salad bar is impressive; in fact, they call it a "salad garden," and there are enough items in it to

have a meal just from the garden. The beef here is some of the best in the region, but their pastas and chicken are also impressive. If you want a more casual environment try the **Vineyard,** which has a more relaxed atmosphere and a more bar-food-type menu. Both places have a fine wine list and a broad selection of micro-brews. You can order from a children's menu at either place.

Lewistown

The Mint Bar and Grill (406-535-9925), 113 4th Avenue. The building was originally built for a car dealership in the 1940s, but a decade later it was sold and became the Mint. In 1998 the Mint was remodeled into what we know it as today. The menu features steaks, seafood, pasta, and ribs, complemented by savory sauces that are made in-house and change daily. Save room for dessert; they are made in-house and are scrumptious. They also offer a full bar, wine list, and several micro drafts.

See also Charlie Russell Chew-Choo under *To Do–Unique Adventures.*

EATING OUT

Belt

Harvest Moon Brewery (406-277-3188), 7 5th Street S. Known more for their beer—and all beer lovers should make a stop here—they do offer a limited pub-fare menu. When traveling to or from Great Falls, it is always a good idea to plan a stop here.

Choteau

Buckaroo Eatery and Coffeehouse (406-466-2667), 202 North Main Avenue. As far from Choteau as you could go in a culinary sense—a hip and trendy menu with fresh-baked goods and creative salads. The coffee is always fresh and they serve the best lattes in town.

Elk Country Grill (406-466-3311), 309 10th Avenue N.E. A small-town steakhouse and family eatery, this place is great for thick and juicy steaks and various seafood and chicken options. They specialize in authentic Dutch-oven meals, worth a try when you need a break from a dinosaur dig or a day of adventure along the Rocky Mountain Front.

Fort Benton

Bob's Riverfront Restaurant (406-622-3443), 1414 Front Street. They offer a wide menu and three meals a day, but it's the blackberry cobbler that keeps folks coming back to this local place.

✦ Expedition Pizza Company (406-622-5102), 1050 22nd Street. Named after the Lewis & Clark Expedition, this friendly pizza joint has something the whole family will enjoy. The pizzas are made fresh, and they make their own sauce as well. Or try one of the many sandwiches, broasted chickens, or calzones. With a wide variety of fine wine, microbrews, and Italian sodas, there is a beverage here to complement any of the fine pizzas.

Great Falls

✦ 5th Street Diner (406-727-1962), 500 Central Avenue, downtown Great Falls. The 5th Street Diner takes you back to the 1950s. It's centerpiece is an original F. W. Woolworth lunch counter, all stainless steel and 65 feet in length. No one is certain, but it may be the last one in operation in the entire country. A section just like this one sits in the Smithsonian in Washington, D.C. Along with the counter are enough booths, tables,

and chairs to accommodate everyone's taste. The menu is 100 percent comfort food, from burgers and shakes to hot meatloaf.

& ✦ The Breaks Ale House and Grill (406-453-5980), 202 2nd Avenue, downtown Great Falls. One of Great Falls's newer establishments, you can get a fresh pint of local microbrew or a tasty sandwich. The atmosphere is fun and friendly. They have great baby back ribs, and a more adventuresome eater can try the lobster won tons. They also have large custom salads and homemade desserts. They are new but will be in Great Falls for a long time.

Penny's Gourmet To Go (406-453-7070), 815 Central Avenue, downtown Great Falls. This place is a nice respite from the normal food scene in Great Falls. They feature healthful, fresh, gourmet food. Items are prepared daily, including soups, salads, sandwiches, quiche, hot entrees, pizza, vegetarian specialties, fresh-baked breads, and terrific desserts. Espresso, cappuccino, and latte specialty coffee drinks are available, as well as a juice bar serving smoothies and fresh fruit and vegetable juices.

Harlowton

& Snowy Mountain Coffee and Slow Rise Bakery (406-632-6838), 124 N. Central Avenue. They tout themselves as having a passion for perfection, and even in itty bitty Harlowton they come close. They feature daily lunch specials of gourmet wraps, sandwiches, or soups. Not hungry for lunch? Try a jet tea or waffle cone with a scoop of Wilcoxson's hard ice cream. And with the Slow Rise Bakery you can enjoy fresh-baked breads, pastries, biscotti, cinnamon rolls, and cookies.

Havre

The Coffee Hound (406-265-8105), 4 First Street. The best coffee in Havre is here, along with chai, teas, and an assortment of fresh-baked goodies. This is a good place to enjoy a morning cup and catch up with some of the locals.

PJs Restaurant and Casino (406-265-3211), 15 Third Avenue. The menu here is diverse, with something for everyone. They serve breakfast, lunch, and dinner. The dining room is separate from the casino and smoke free. Kids will enjoy a large children's menu and adults can try steak, seafood, chicken, pasta, and a few daily specials.

& ✍ **Wolfer's Diner** (406-265-2111), 220 3rd Avenue, #401, in the Atrium Mall. This is the place for old-fashioned comfort food and big portions. One nice thing about Wolfer's is that all the beef is locally raised and cut each morning—it doesn't get any fresher than at Wolfer's. And the pies are scrumptious.

Lewistown

& ✍ **Ruby's 100 Percent Montana Burgers** (406-538-7450), 501 E. Main Street. The name says it all—a taste of local cuisine. The beef comes from cattle born and humanely raised in Montana. Experience the exquisite taste of all-natural beef. No growth hormones or antibiotics are used in the cattle you will eat. In addition to the specialty burgers, they offer a variety of items including espresso, breakfast dishes, moo-lattes, smoothies, salads, hot dogs, chicken strips, cheese fries, onion rings, and over 50 flavors of shakes and sundaes.

& ✍ ✪ **The Whole Famdamily** (406-538-5161), 206 W. Main Street. Friday nights are the best nights to dine here, but if you are not that lucky the regular menu—with sandwiches, homemade soups, salads, and more—has plenty of good offerings. The children's menu is varied and healthy, but tasty.

White Sulphur Springs

Dori's Café (406-547-2280), 112 East Main Street. Dori's offers clean, friendly service in an area known for its scenery and recreational opportunities. The menu is basic, small-town Montana, with a twist. Curious? You will have to visit to see why. They serve up plenty of food, and if you want a nice breakfast before heading out for a horseback ride or Smith River float trip this is the place to go in White Sulphur Springs.

Happy Days Café (406-547-2223), 307 3rd Avenue S.W. This is a unique and fun Montana café where you will certainly be eating with a cross-section of small-town Montana folks—maybe a vehicle shuttler, a rancher, or kids playing hooky from school. The 1950s and '60s decorating (hence the name) adds charm, but burgers are the highlight here, touted by truckers and river guides as the best in the state. Ask for extra cheese and extra napkins.

✳ Special Events

January: ✍ ✿ **Montana Winter Fair** (406-538-8841; www.centralmontana fair.com), Lewistown. A statewide annual fair featuring livestock, a horse show, free Sunday breakfast, chili cook-off, Death by Chocolate competition, flea market, and much more.

February: ✍ ✿ **Lake Frances Ice Derby**, Valier. An annual ice-fishing competition to benefit local emergency services. Anglers target northern pike, perch, and trout.

March: ♪ **C. M. Russell Auction and Exhibitors Show,** Great Falls. Named after the famous cowboy artist, this auction benefits the local C. M. Russell Museum. The event includes two major auctions, a fixed-price art sale, Chuckwagon Brunch, three receptions, and two Quick Draws. Free admittance to the 100-plus artist exhibitor rooms, seminars, and an artist autograph party. All artist exhibitor rooms have original art for sale.

April: ♿ ♪ **Museum Sunday Sampler,** Great Falls. The Lewis & Clark Interpretive Center presents special programming as part of the annual Museums Sunday Sampler program with other members of the Great Falls Museums Consortium from noon–5 P.M. Other participating venues include the Children's Museum of Montana, C. M. Russell Museum, Galerie Trinitas, High Plains Heritage Center, Malmstrom Air Force Base Museum, Paris Gibson Square Museum of Art, Ulm Pishkun State Park, and the Ursuline Centre. Free admission.

May: ♪ **Black Powder Shoot,** Havre. The annual spring Black Powder Shoot, with shooters of all ages competing in numerous match events. Tomahawk- and knife-throwing competitions and a pancake race are part of the fun. Primitive dress is encouraged but not required, and camping is available. A long-range black powder cartridge event is included, along with 35 other shooting events.

June: ♪ 🐎 **Rodeos,** various locations. Enjoy a real Montana pastime in Belt, Augusta, Chinook, Chester, and other small towns.

Lewis & Clark Festival. The annual festival highlights the Lewis & Clark Expedition during their stay in the Great Falls area in 1806. You will observe reenactors in historic dress, taste the foods the expedition ate, smell the burning campfires, and understand the adventure along the banks of the Missouri River. Learn how the men worked and what they found. Tours of Lewis & Clark sites, demonstrations, children's activities, exhibits, float trips, and a kids' relay race. Observe artists as they paint along the banks of the Missouri River during the Lewis & Clark Outdoor Art Gala, an evening filled with a sumptuous dinner, live and silent auctions, and a lively Quick Draw.

Whoop-Up Days and Rhubarb Festival, Conrad. Activities include a children's carnival and a rodeo Calcutta, a free pancake breakfast, parade, and a rodeo. The newly added Rhubarb Festival (formerly the Ulm Rhubarb Festival) includes rhubarb pies, cinnamon rolls, jellies, cookies, bars, and ice cream.

July: ♪ **Rocky Boy's Annual Powwow,** Rocky Boy. The powwow is an event of Indian heritage and tradition. Dance, costume, and drumming competitions are the featured events. Competitions last throughout the weekend, with all ages participating. Exciting, excellent cultural demonstrations, as well as ethnic and traditional food offered daily.

August: ♪ 🐎 **Montana State Fair,** Great Falls. Experience culture and history in the heart of Montana. Superstar entertainment, the Mighty Thomas Carnival, live horse racing, four nights of pro rodeo, 40 food vendors, livestock shows, stage acts, Native American art, quilts, floral and cooking exhibits, and more.

September: ♪ **Liberty County Harvest Festival,** Chester. The event includes a chili cook-off and fun for the kids. Prizes are awarded for Judges' Choice and People's Choice. Contestants are also encouraged to enter the pie contest. Prizes are awarded for first-place through fourth-place winners in each category. There are plenty of arts and craft vendors, as well as game booths and food booths. There is also a cakewalk throughout the day.

October: ♪ **Sugar Beet Festival,** Chinook. A great way to close out the harvest and enjoy the fall season. Activities planned include kids' games in a sugar beet theme, a sugar mall featuring by-products of sugar, a motorcycle and car show, local musicians in the parks, results of the sugar beet growing contest, a parade with a barbecue, and a street dance.

December: ♪ 🐟 **Charlie Russell Chew-Choo New Year's Eve Train,** Lewistown. Enjoy central Montana's wide-open spaces on a special New Year's Eve train, with hot hors d'oeuvres and music, a prime rib dinner back at the Yogo Inn, and a New Year's Eve dance.

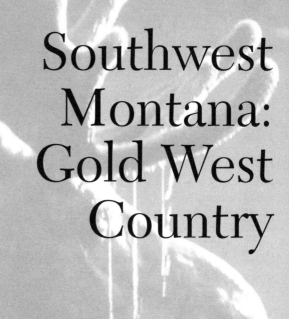

Southwest Montana: Gold West Country

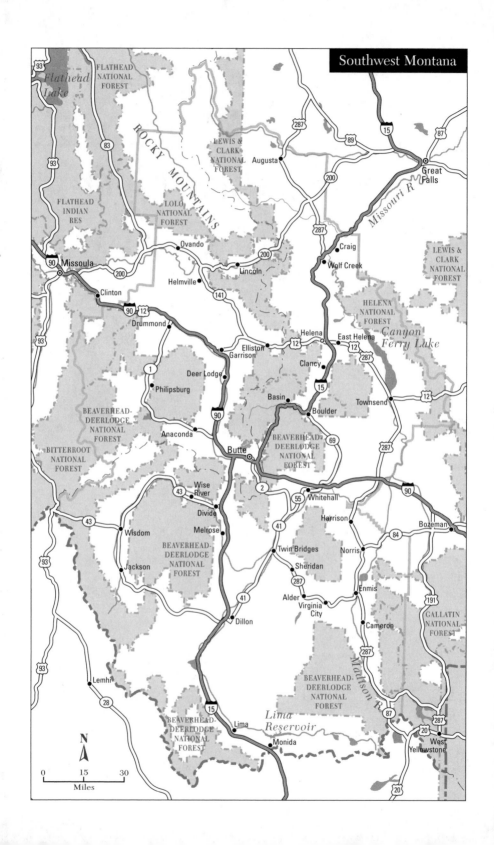

Southwest Montana

SOUTHWEST MONTANA:
GOLD WEST COUNTRY

Tucked into a small corner of Montana is the home of a large part of the state's history: vast valleys dotted with ranches and trout-filled rivers, and mountain ranges that rise from the valley floors for thousands of feet. Geographically, this is the smallest region of Montana, but what it lacks in size it makes up for in friendliness, scenery, and a wide array of interesting sites and outdoor activities.

Gold West Country is best known for its mineral wealth, more past than present, although a few operations still exist. Most any route through this region provides evidence of Montana's history with minerals, from Butte's "richest hill on earth" to the millionaire mansions of Helena to the 15 ghost towns that are scattered across the region.

Beginning in the mid- to late 1800s, this region was home to a vibrant mining culture as discoveries of gold, copper, and sapphires brought in thousands of immigrants from all over the world. Like most gold rushes, only a few actually struck it rich, but the ones who found glory in Gold West Country have left a visible legacy. Mining is not nearly as culturally important here as it was a hundred years ago, although economically speaking the industry is still a vital player.

Gold West Country is home to two major towns: Helena and Butte. Helena is the state capital, while Butte was the grandiose crown jewel of Montana for nearly 75 years, from the late 1800s until the late 20th century. In the mid-1800s, once gold mining in the various gulches of Gold West Country played out, silver mining became prominent. However, it wasn't until a massive copper mine in Butte found a large strike that mining had its greatest impact on Montana history. About the same time the copper lode was found, the smelting process allowed for more production of ore. Railroads were already prevalent in the state, and electricity was readily available and reasonably priced. So conditions were ripe for a massive mining operation. In comes Marcus Daly and the Copper Kings—copper magnates who created 24-hour-a-day mining operations. Quickly Butte and the surrounding area had a population of over 100,000 people. At the time, it was by far *the* place to be in Montana. Today, it's home to nearly 40,000 people and relics of its past mining greatness are still the cornerstones of its cultural attractions. Additionally, in the past several years Butte has seen a resurgence in its fine arts culture.

BUTTE'S COPPER KING MANSION

While in Butte, mining related sites to visit include the Berkeley Pit. This massive waterlogged pit is an ominous reminder of the environmental impact of early mining practices. In fact, the pit is filling with highly toxic water at a rate fast enough that environmental engineers are studying what to do when the pit begins to overflow. Water in the pit is one thing, but what you cannot see is even more amazing—nearly 3,000 miles of tunnels located almost a mile below ground so miners could harvest the copper ore. For more mining history, be sure to visit the World Museum of Mining and the Copper King Mansion, the former residence of William A. Clark, one of Montana's more prominent Copper Kings. There are also many other mining-related sites and historical attractions in Butte.

Butte's Uptown District is home to several unique art galleries, shops, and restaurants—proof that despite Butte's mining past it is going through a bona fide resurgence.

Another place steeped in history is the small town of Anaconda. This tiny town was home to the Anaconda Copper Mining Company's well-known smelter stack. The brief history of the smelter goes like this: Marcus Daly sought a location for the construction of an enormous smelter for the copper mined in Butte. In 1882 he chose Anaconda. From then until 1980, the smelter provided jobs and a boon to the economy. However, the environmental impacts of the massive smeltering operation are still being felt in the surrounding area, but that should in no way stop anyone from visiting this unique area. In fact, some of the state's best fishing and skiing are within 30 minutes of Anaconda.

The Anaconda-Pintler Scenic Highway provides a stunning trip, with such highlights as Georgetown Lake, Discovery Basin Ski Area, the Jack Nicklaus Old Works Golf Course, and much more.

Helena also had its share of mining drama, and it was eventually made the state capital. Many consider Helena one of the most attractive cities in the country, nestled in Last Chance Gulch beneath the forested hillsides of Mounts Ascension and Helena.

Last Chance Gulch was the site of a very prolific gold mine—in fact, the gulch produced more than $3 billion in only 20 years of operation. That is $3 billion in 21st-century dollars. At one point the small gulch that was Helena had more millionaires per capita than any city in the world. During that time the city was prominent and the territorial capital was moved from Virginia City (begrudgingly) in 1875; in 1898 Helena was named the state capital.

Today Helena is home to many historic landmarks and sites, great fishing, mountain biking, art galleries, and several nearby lakes for boating enthusiasts. These include the original Governor's Mansion, the State Capitol, and St. Helen Cathedral. Outdoor pursuits include the Missouri River below Holter Dam, boating on Hauser and Holter Lakes and Canyon Ferry Reservoir, and hundreds of miles of hiking and biking trails in Helena National Forest. Helena is also home to the state's largest city park, Mount Helena City Park.

Of course, Gold West Country has much more to offer than just past mining glory. Lewis & Clark spent considerable time here. Their path can be traced by visiting any of the following: Beaverhead Rock State Park, Lewis & Clark Caverns, Clark's Lookout State Park, Clark Canyon Reservoir, Gates of the Mountains, and the Beaverhead County Lewis & Clark Festival.

THE SCENIC ANACONDA-PINTLER BYWAY

HISTORIC LAST CHANCE GULCH IN HELENA

This region also is blessed with an abundance of outdoor recreational opportunities, from world-famous fly-fishing on its many rivers to jaw-dropping whitewater on the Madison River in Bear Trap Canyon. There are three downhill ski areas in this region and hundreds of miles of cross-country ski trails, along with many snowmobile trails in the Helena and Deer Lodge National Forests.

Many Native American tribes traditionally lived and hunted in Gold West Country's broad valleys. This region also saw the Nez Perce Indians make their historic flight along what is now the Nez Perce Nee-Me-Poo Trail. Along this trail is the infamous Big Hole National Battlefield, where in early August 1877 a historic battle occurred between the U.S. military and the Nez Perce tribe.

From mining grandeur to big brown trout to ghost towns to hot springs (there are six in Gold West Country), this region is truly a gem in Montana's crown. Among the many other exciting things to do, you can dig for sapphires, pan for gold, view wildlife, go on a ghost hunt at the Old Montana Prison, and much more. While exploring, be sure to watch the scenery but also keep your eyes on the road, and always be on the lookout for relics and historical markers that reveal Montana's exciting past.

GUIDANCE **Anaconda Chamber of Commerce** (406-563-2400; www.anaconda mmt.org), 306 E. Park Street, Anaconda 59711.

Beaverhead Chamber of Commerce and Dillon Visitor Information Center (406-683-5511; www.beaverheadchamber.org), 125 S. Montana, P.O. Box 425, Dillon 59725.

Butte-Silver Bow Chamber of Commerce (406-723-3177; www.butteinfo .org), 1000 George Street, Butte 59701.

Ennis Chamber of Commerce (406-682-4388; www.ennischamber.com), Main Street, P.O. Box 291, Ennis 59729.

Gold West Country (406-846-1943; www.goldwest.visitmt.com), 1155 Main Street, Deer Lodge 59722.

Greater Ruby Valley Chamber of Commerce and Agriculture (406-683-5511; www.rubyvalleychamber.com), P.O. Box 134, Twin Bridges 59754.

Helena Chamber of Commerce (406-447-1530; www.helenachamber.com), 225 Cruse Avenue, Suite A, Helena 59601.

Lincoln Valley Chamber of Commerce (406-362-4949; www.lincolnmontana .com), P.O. Box 985, Lincoln 59639.

Philipsburg Chamber of Commerce (406-859-3388; www.philipsburgmt .com), in the historic **Courtney Hotel** at 135 S. Sansome Street, P.O. Box 661, Philipsburg 59858.

Powell County Chamber of Commerce (406-846-2094; www.powellcounty montana.com), 1171 Main Street, Deer Lodge 59722.

Townsend Chamber of Commerce and Agriculture (406-266-4101), 415 Front Street, P.O. Box 947, Townsend 59644.

Virginia City Chamber of Commerce (406-843-5555; www.virginiacity chamber.com), P.O. Box 218, Virginia City 59755.

Virginia City Depot Information Center (406-843-5247; www.virginiacitymt .com), west end of Wallace Street (MT 287), P.O. Box 338, Virginia City 59755.

Whitehall Chamber of Commerce (406-287-2260; www.whitehallmt.com), P.O. Box 72, Whitehall 59759.

THE ORIGINAL MONTANA TERRITORIAL PRISON

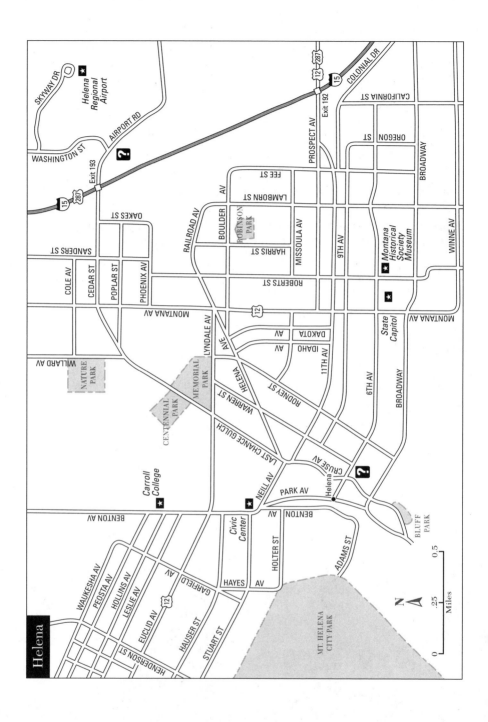

Helena

GETTING THERE Butte is located at the junction I-15 and I-90, 80 miles west of Bozeman and 100 miles east of Missoula. Helena is at the junction of I-15 and US 287/12, 60 miles north of Butte and 80 miles south of Great Falls. Anaconda is west of Butte via I-15 and MT 1 or MT 48. Deer Lodge is on I-15, 30 miles north and west of Butte. Dillon is 65 miles south of Butte via I-15 and the junction of MT 41. Ennis is southeast of Butte and Helena on US 287.

See also *Airports* and *Bus Service* in "What's Where in Montana."

MEDICAL EMERGENCIES **Anaconda Community Hospital** (406-563-9644), 115 W. Commercial Avenue, Anaconda.

Barrett Hospital and Health Care (406-683-3000), 1260 S. Atlantic Street, Dillon.

Broadwater Health Center (406-266-3186), 110 N. Oak Street, Townsend.

Granite County Medical Center (406-859-3271), off MT 1, Philipsburg.

Liberty County Hospital (406-759-5181), MT 223 and Monroe, Chester.

Madison Valley Hospital (406-682-4222), 217 N. Main Street, Ennis.

Powell County Medical Center (406-846-2212), 1101 Texas Avenue, Deer Lodge.

Ruby Valley Hospital (406-842-5453), 220 E. Crofoot, Sheridan.

St. James Hospital (406-723-2500), 400 S. Clark Street, Butte.

St. Peter's Hospital (406-442-2480), 2475 Broadway, Helena.

THE CAPITOL BUILDING IN HELENA

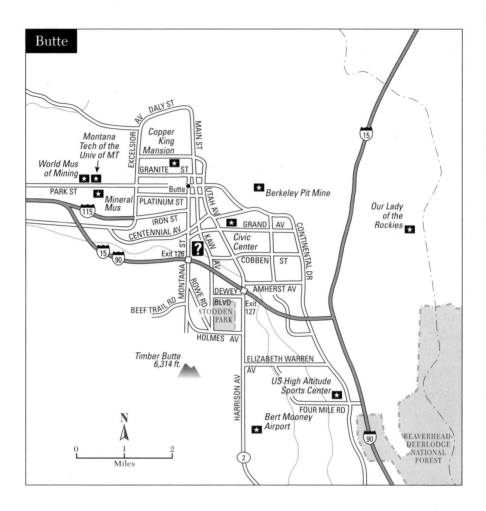

Butte

Montana Tech of the Univ of MT
World Mus of Mining
Copper King Mansion
DALY ST
EXCELSIOR AV
MAIN ST
GRANITE ST
PARK ST
Butte
Mineral Mus
PLATINUM ST
UTAH AV
Berkeley Pit Mine
Our Lady of the Rockies
115
IRON ST
CENTENNIAL AV
KAW ST
GRAND AV
Civic Center
CONTINENTAL DR
15 90
Exit 126
COBBEN ST
MONTANA ST
ROWE RD
DEWEY
AMHERST AV
BEEF TRAIL RD
BLVD
STODDEN PARK
Exit 127
HOLMES AV
Timber Butte 6,314 ft.
ELIZABETH WARREN AV
HARRISON AV
US High Altitude Sports Center
FOUR MILE RD
N
Bert Mooney Airport
0   1   2
Miles
2
90
BEAVERHEAD-DEERLODGE NATIONAL FOREST

❋ To See

TOWNS Anaconda is the core of the **Anaconda-Pintler Scenic Route.** The town boasts three National Historic Districts and one of the finest golf courses in the Northwest, the **Old Works Course.** There is a fascinating **self-guided walking tour, Copper Village Museum, Anaconda Stack,** and much more history to explore. Outdoor recreation includes fishing on the **Big Hole River, Georgetown Lake,** and other waters. And there are miles of trails around town for hiking or biking. The **Discovery Basin Ski Area** is minutes away, and snow-mobile and cross-country trails are easily accessed from Anaconda.

Dillon is about 60 miles south of Butte on I-15. It is the county seat of Montana's largest county—Beaverhead. Dillon dates back to the gold-rush era, when it served as an important point for shipping goods south to Utah and farther down the line. The **Beaverhead County Museum** (406-683-5027; 15 S. Montana Street) provides insight into the area's role in the history of Montana. The downtown area is well preserved and provides easy access to an abundance of recreational pursuits.

Ennis sits at the base of the majestic Madison and Tobacco Root Mountain Ranges. Only 75 miles from Yellowstone National Park, Ennis sees more visitors than many places in Gold West Country. Native American tribes, including the Bannack, Flathead, and Shoshone, hunted the massive herds of elk and buffalo that used to graze on the valley's fertile grasses. The discovery of gold in **Alder Gulch** changed much of that, and in 1863 William Ennis settled here and founded the town that bears his name. Today Ennis is a destination for families, anglers, and folks headed to Yellowstone National Park. Attractions include the **Madison River**, as well as the **Ennis National Fish Hatchery** (406-682-4847), 12 miles southwest of town, and the **Wildlife Museum of the West** (406-682-7141), at 121 W. Main Street.

Deer Lodge sits on I-15 in the upper Clark Fork Valley about 20 miles south of Anaconda. This small ranching community is home to **Grant Kohrs Ranch,** the **Old Montana Prison,** and the **Montana Auto Museum.**

Lincoln is 60 miles northwest of Helena on MT 200. This mountain hamlet is the perfect place if you want to leave what little urban life there is in Montana and get away from it all. The **Scapegoat Wilderness Area** lies just to the north, while the **Blackfoot River** flows through town and offers floating and fishing. South of Lincoln is **Stemple Pass,** home to several cross-country ski trails, as well as the **Great Divide Ski Area.** Snowmobiling is very popular in and around Lincoln—there are over 250 miles of groomed trails.

RELICS OF A BYGONE ERA IN BUTTE

Philipsburg is northwest of Anaconda on MT 1 (the **Pintler Scenic Route**). Known locally as P-Burg, it was established in the 1860s as a mining settlement for sapphire and silver. In fact, this area had some of the largest concentrations in the world. The town was named after Philip Deidesheimer. He invented square-set mine timbering, a now-universal technique. The downtown, newly renovated, is a National Historic District. The buildings are impressive and include a jailhouse, opera house, and school. The **Granite County Museum and Cultural Center** (406-859-3020) in the historic **Courtney Hotel** is worth a visit. There are also many ghost towns in the area (contact the P-Burg Chamber of Commerce under *Guidance* at the beginning of this chapter).

Virginia City and **Nevada City** are approximately 12 miles east of Ennis on MT 287. Virginia City was once the territorial capital of Montana during the gold rushes of the 1860s. A visit to either of these two towns is like stepping back into the gunslinging days of the past—they often have actors in full period dress having gun fights on Main Street. The gunfights and fully restored buildings are two of the many reasons that most of Virginia City (and a good chunk of Nevada City) is a National Historic Landmark. They even have wooden boardwalks. This is great place for live theater. **The Brewery Follies** is a cabaret and skit show at the H. S. Gilbert Brewery, and there is a 19th-century melodrama presented by the **Virginia City Players** (406-843-5218; reservations are highly recommended) at the Opera House.

MUSEUMS ⟋ **Arts Chateau** (406-723-7600; www.artschateau.org), 321 W. Broadway, Butte. Open April through October, 10 A.M.–4 P.M.; $4 adults, $3 seniors, $2 children. Built in 1898 as a home for Charles Clark, son of Copper King William A. Clark, this unique residence-turned-artifact is both an art center and museum. On display in the mansion are thousands of historic artifacts, including

THE BLAIR MANSION NEAR MARTINSDALE, EAST OF WHITE SULPHUR SPRINGS

textiles, books, vintage clothing, and accessories. The wonderful entryway combines beveled glass windows, ornate wrought iron, sandstone, and a vaulted brick ceiling. The interior features a freestanding spiral staircase, 26 rooms adorned with exotic woods from around the world, hand-painted wallpaper by Marshall Field, several stained-glass windows, and a redwood-paneled fourth-floor ballroom. The museum is run by the Butte–Silver Bow Arts Foundation, which also runs the **Butte–Silver Bow Art Center** at 124 S. Main Street.

& **Copper Village Museum and Arts Center** (406-563-2422), City Hall Cultural Center, Anaconda. Open year-round, 10 A.M.–4 P.M.; free. This historic structure was saved from demolition, renovated, and is currently on the National Register of Historic Places. The Museum and Arts Center features visual arts exhibitions of tradition and heritage arts, world arts, and Montana contemporary artists. Also located in the City Hall Cultural Center are the **Marcus Daly Historical Society Museum and Archives** and a retail gift shop.

Dumas Brothel Museum (406-494-6908; www.thedumasbrothel.com), 45 East Mercury Street, Butte. Open April through September, 9 A.M.–5 P.M. You cannot feature a region known for miners and gunslingers and not have a museum devoted to brothels. Well, in Butte, they have created one. The Dumas, built as a brothel in 1890, was open as a house of prostitution continuously until 1982, making it the longest-running enterprise of its kind in the country. The Dumas is the only preserved building in what was once Butte's thriving red-light district. Saved from demolition by Butte native Rudy Gieck, who bought the building and began its restoration in 1990, the Dumas is open as a museum featuring an old-time photography studio and tours.

& **The Mineral Museum** (406-496-4414), located on the campus of Montana Tech on 1300 West Park Street, Butte. Open daily Memorial Day through Labor Day, 9 A.M.–6 P.M.; winter hours Monday through Friday, 9 A.M.–4 P.M.; open weekends in May, September, and October, 1 P.M.–5 P.M. If you would like to see a fantastic mineral collection or need advice on where to look for your own mineral specimens in the region, this is the place to visit. Over 1,300 specimens are on display from around the world, with exhibits specifically devoted to Butte and Montana minerals and the area's mining history. Included in the collection are the 27.8-ounce gold nugget found in 1989 in the Highland Mountains south of Butte and a 400-pound smoky quartz crystal also from the area. Butte's rich mining history is exhibited through an impressive array of fine-quality mineral specimens from the underground mines. The Fluorescent Room, always a favorite, contains ordinary earth-toned minerals that radiate vibrant shades of pink, orange, or blue when exposed to ultraviolet light. The Earthquake Studies Laboratory is situated in the museum with operating seismographs for visitors to see.

Montana Historical Society or "Montana's Museum" (406-444-2694; www .his.state.mt.us), 225 North Roberts, Helena. Open Monday through Friday, 9 A.M.–5 P.M., Thursday until 8 P.M., Saturday, noon–5 P.M.; $5 adults, $1 children, $12 per family. The Montana Historical Society houses the Montana Homeland exhibit, which traces 12,000 years of history under the Big Sky. Its Mackay Gallery has one of the premier Charles M. Russell art collections. Special exhibits are rotated regularly. The Society library, archives, and photo archives are a draw for historians and genealogists. The MHS archives contain manuscript collections containing such topics as business and finance, mining, homesteading and ranching, the pioneer era, and social organizations. The archives also have oral history recordings. The Society publishes *Montana: The Magazine of Western History* and history books. The museum store has a wide collection of western books and gifts.

Powell County Museum (406-846-3111; www.pcmaf.org), 1106 Main Street, Deer Lodge. Open daily Memorial Day through Labor Day, noon–5 P.M. This county museum features exhibits on local history, including a massive gun collection with weapons dating from frontier days to World War II. There are thousands of photos, an old jukebox; a slot machine collection, and more. The museum is part of a larger complex in Deer Lodge that includes the **Old Montana Prison.** The prison was built by convict labor in the late 1800s. It was the first territorial prison in the western United States. The gray sandstone walls of this immense structure are 24 feet high and buried 4 feet deep to prevent escape by tunneling. You can visit the enclosed courtyard where the convicts exercised and walk through their austere cell blocks and feel the chills of maximum-security cells. The last prisoners were moved in 1979, after which the facility was opened to the public. For a real adventure, join a real live "ghost hunt" in the prison, run by TSI (www.tsimt.net), a well-known, legitimate paranormal investigative company. For more museums in the area, visit the **Montana Law Enforcement Museum, Frontier Museum, Montana Auto Museum, Yesterday's Playthings, Desert John's Saloon Museum,** and **Cottonwood City.**

&. ✎ **World Museum of Mining** (406-723-7211; www.miningmuseum.org), 155 Museum Way, Butte. Open April through October, 9 A.M.–to whenever they feel like closing. Nestled beneath the towering head frame of the once-active Orphan Girl underground mine is one of Butte's most popular attractions, the 44-acre World Museum of Mining and Hell Roarin' Gulch. An 1890s mining town with displays both inside and outdoors, this museum will appeal to the whole family. Stroll along the brick-lined streets of Hell Roarin' Gulch and marvel at over 750 exhibits carefully arranged with artifacts from that era. Be amazed at the unique displays, including the Chinese laundry, the sauerkraut factory, the funeral parlor, the ice house, and of course, the school, the general store, and the saloon. Visit the hoist house and view the massive hoist that raised and lowered men and material into the mine and the air compressors that were the heart of the mine.

HISTORIC LANDMARKS, PLACES, AND SITES Anaconda Smelter Stack State Park (406-542-5500; http://fwp.mt.gov/lands/site_280918.aspx); the smelter is visible from MT 1 just east of Anaconda. The viewing site for the Anaconda Stack is located at the junction of Park Street (MT 1) and Monroe Street at the eastern edge of Anaconda, adjacent to Goodman Park. Access is limited to the viewing/interpretive area only. Open year-round; free. You can see the smelter from nearly 30 miles or more away, but it is not until you are standing relatively near it (you can only view it from about 0.5 mile away) that you truly feel how massive it was. The smelter stack, completed on May 5, 1919, is one of the tallest free-standing brick structures in the world at 585 feet, 1.5 inches. The inside diameter at the bottom is 75 feet and at the top, 60 feet. The stack may be viewed and photographed only from a distance. The site is listed in the National Register of Historic Places.

Archie Bray Foundation (406-443-3502; www.archiebray.org), 2915 Country Club Avenue, Helena. Listed on the National Register of Historic Places, this unique arts and ceramics center is worth a visit. Archie Bray founded what was known as the Western Clay Manufacturing Company, dedicated to the enrichment of the ceramic arts and providing an atmosphere of creative excellence for ceramic artists since 1951. Ceramic artists from around the world travel to Helena to work and study as they enrich their creative and artistic talents. The foundation is also near **Spring Meadow State Park.**

& **Bannack State Park** (406-834-3413; www.bannack.org), I-15 three miles south of Dillon, then 20 miles west on MT 278, then 4 miles south of MT 5 (Bannack Road). Follow the signs. Open year-round: fall through spring, 8 A.M.–5 P.M.; summer, 8 A.M.–9 P.M. Free admission. Come walk the deserted streets of Bannack and discover the best preserved of all Montana ghost towns. Bannack State Park is a Registered Historic Landmark and the site of Montana's first major gold discovery on July 28, 1862. This strike set off a massive gold rush that swelled Bannack's population to over three thousand by 1863. As the value of gold steadily dwindled, Bannack's bustling population was slowly snuffed out. Over 50 historic log and frame structures line Main Street, recalling Montana's formative years. **Bannack Days** (see *Special Events*), with historic displays, activities, and events, is held the third weekend in July each year. The visitor center does tours and is open from Memorial Day through Labor Day. A tepee is available to rent from the center. The park is 5,800 feet in elevation and covers 1,254 acres. The campground has 28 sites and a group picnic site. A 14-day camping limit is in effect. The campgrounds include vault toilets, grill/fire rings, firewood, picnic tables, trash cans, drinking water, and access to Grasshopper Creek for fishing.

Beaverhead Rock State Park (406-834-3413; http://fwp.mt.gov/lands/site _281875.aspx), 14 miles south of Twin Bridges on MT 41. In 1805 Sacagawea recognized Beaverhead Rock, which resembles the head of a swimming beaver, while traveling with Lewis & Clark. It can be viewed and photographed from a distance, but it's not directly accessible. The site is listed in the National Register of Historic Places. **Clark's Lookout State Park** (406-834-3413; http://fwp.mt .gov/lands/site_281963.aspx) is nearby and has a scenic overlook and an interpretive exhibit. Projecting above the dense cottonwoods and willows along the Beaverhead River, the overlook provided an opportunity for members of the Lewis & Clark Expedition to view the route ahead. You can drive to the site, located just 1 mile north of Dillon off US 91, park right next to it, and walk the trail to the top.

& **Berkeley Pit** (406-723-3177; www.pitwatch.org), Continental Drive (at the east end of Park Street), Butte. The pit is closed to the public, but the viewing stand is open from March until November, with a $2 charge. Begun in 1955, this was a large truck-operated open-pit copper mine until 1982. By 1980 nearly 1.5 billion tons of material had been removed from the Pit, including more than 290

THE ENTRANCE TO THE INFAMOUS BERKELEY PIT

million tons of copper ore. The pit enabled Butte to claim the title, the Richest Hill on Earth. The pit is 7,000 feet long, 5,600 feet wide, and 1,600 feet deep from the high wall on the north side just below the Kelley mine. Present-day visitors can view the mine from a platform located above it. The viewing stand offers a look at the Berkeley Pit, which is filling with water.

& **Big Hole National Battlefield** (406-689-3155; www.nps.gov/biho), 10 miles west of Wisdom on MT 43. Open Memorial Day through Labor Day, 10 A.M.–6 P.M., and 10 A.M.–5 P.M. the remainder of the year; free. The Battle of the Big Hole on August 9 and 10, 1877, was a turning point during the flight of the Nez Perce. This is one of 38 sites in Montana, Idaho, Oregon, and Wyoming in the **Nez Perce National Historic Park** (www.nps.gov/nepe). After five months in which U.S. Army forces tried to place one third of the Nez Perce tribe on a reservation, the fighting began in White Bird Canyon in Idaho and had a dramatic ending in the Bears Paw Mountains of north-central Montana. Self-guiding tours take you to many points on the Big Hole battlefield. A short drive to the lower parking area connects with foot trails to the Nez Perce Camp, the Siege Area, and the Howitzer Capture site. The walks each take about an hour. Ranger-conducted programs are offered in summer; introductory presentations and exhibits are available year-round.

Copper King Mansion (406-782-7580; www.copperkingmansion.com), 219 W. Granite Street, Butte. Open year-round. Built for William A. Clark, one of the principle developers of copper mining in Butte, the Copper King Mansion was constructed from 1884 to 1888. More money was spent on the mansion construction in 1884 than on the original courthouse in 1883. This mansion is listed on the National Historic Register and was Montana's first State Historic Place. Rooms featured in this Elizabethan-style mansion include a 64-foot ballroom, a billiards room, a chapel, and a library. In addition, many of the rooms showcase hand-carved and customized mantelpieces, each designed by European craftsmen especially for the mansion, and each from a different wood. For anyone interested in living like a Copper King, the mansion is available as a **bed & breakfast** year-round.

Elkhorn Ghost Town and State Park (406-495-3260; http://fwp.mt.gov/lands/site_281892.aspx). Take Exit 164 off I-15 at Boulder, go 7 miles southeast on MT 69, then 11 miles north on FR 258; follow the signs. Free and open year-round. Backcountry roads settle you into a 19th-century mining landscape before you reach historic **Fraternity Hall** and **Gillian Hall,** nestled within the privately owned town of Elkhorn. Bring your camera when you visit these two picturesque structures from the early days of this silver-mining ghost town. Each has been recorded in the Historic American Buildings Survey. These are the only two buildings in the town of Elkhorn that are open to the public. All of the other buildings are privately owned and visitors should not trespass without permission.

Granite Ghost Town State Park (406-542-5500; http://fwp.mt.gov/lands/site_280883.aspx). To find this undeveloped park, take MT 10-A east of Philipsburg, go south on Fanfone Street, and turn east on the gravel road opposite Center Street. Proceed about 4 miles to the townsite. Open May through September; free. This is perhaps the best ghost town in Montana. At one point it was the richest silver mine on Earth, and it may never have happened because the mine's backers thought the venture was hopeless and ordered an end to its operation. But the last blast on the last shift uncovered a bonanza that yielded $40 million. In the silver panic of 1893, word came to shut the mine down. It was deserted for three years, and never again would it reach the population it once had of three thousand miners. Today there is no one living in the camp, but the shell of the Miners' Union Hall still stands. The roof supports have caved to the bottom floor, and the third-floor dance hall, second-floor union offices, and ground-floor saloon/café are about to collapse together. The company hospital still stands.

🚶 ✎ **Grant-Kohrs Ranch National Historic Site** (406-846-2070; www.nps .gov/grko), 266 Warren Lane, Deer Lodge. Open year-round, 9 A.M.–5:30 P.M. Memorial Day through Labor Day, and 9 A.M.–4:30 the rest of the year; free. The 1,500-acre historic ranch illustrates the development of the Northern Plains cattle industry from the 1850s to recent times. The ranch was the headquarters of one of the largest open-range ranches in the country. Today the ranch house, bunkhouse, and outbuildings are much as they were during ranch operations from the 1860s through the 1960s. Guided tours of the house, self-guiding walks, and exhibits are available. Vehicles are left at the visitor center and visitors must walk 0.25 mile on a paved trail to the ranch. As you walk around the ranch, you'll see activities that recall the days of old-time cowboys as well as modern ranchers. Kids can rope a calf model, bale some hay, and more.

Historic Uptown Butte (406-723-3177; www.butteinfo.org), anywhere "up on the hill" in downtown Butte. One of the better-kept secrets in Montana is the culture and architecture of Uptown Butte. Many of the buildings are listed on the National Register of Historic Places and have plaques detailing their past histories and present-day renovations. Few downtowns in the West have the colorful history of Butte—and are restored to evoke feelings of yesteryear. Historic sites include the **Arts Chateau** and the **Copper King Mansion,** as well as the **First Presbyterian Church** and **St. Lawrence O'Toole Church,** among other attractions. (See also Old No. 1 Trolley Tours under *To Do–Unique Adventures.*)

Marysville (406-442-4120). Travel northwest out of Helena on MT 279 (Lincoln Road) for 7 miles off I-15 at Exit 200. Turn southwest on Marysville Road and drive for 8 miles. Marysville was once a thriving gold camp. Now it's a small community with several buildings listed on the National Historic Register. The town is far from being deserted, and some mining still goes on, although it's nothing like the riproaring period when Irishman Tommy Cruse's magnificent Drumlummon Mine poured out $50 million. In the 1880s and 1890s Marysville was said to have been the leading gold producer in the world. Tommy Cruse sold the mine for $1.5 million to an English syndicate. They went bankrupt and sold the mine to Nathan Vestal, who eventually sold it and also went bankrupt. Today the town sits in a scenic draw and is a fun place to dine or drink after a day on the slopes at nearby **Great Divide Ski Area.**

Montana State Capitol (406-444-2694; www.montanahistoricalsociety.org), 225 N. Roberts, Helena. Open daily, 9 A.M.–5 P.M., for self-guided tours; free. Guided tours are available hourly May through September. The schedule varies based on legislative sessions, so it is best to inquire. The main section of the Capitol was completed in 1902. The two wings were completed in 1912 and the building is constructed of sandstone and granite. A statue depicting Liberty sits atop the copper dome. A walk through the Capitol will allow you to view many beautiful paintings, including Charles M. Russell's magnificent historical depiction of Lewis & Clark meeting the Indians at Ross's Hole on September 5, 1805.

Original Governors Mansion (406-444-4789; www.montanahistoricalsociety .org), 304 N. Ewing, Helena. Open May through September, Tuesday–Saturday, noon–4 P.M., and October through April, Saturday only, noon–4 P.M.; $4 adults, $1 children, $8 per family. Tours are available during summer; please inquire for the specific schedule. Despite what you may think, the mansion was not constructed for the original governor of Montana. It was built for entrepreneur William A. Chessman. Chessman built the mansion in 1888 for his family, and several other families called the mansion home before the state of Montana acquired the house. In 1913 it then became the home for Montana's governors until 1959. During that time nine governors and their families called it home.

&. **St. Helena Cathedral** (406-442-5825; www.sthelenas.org), 530 N. Ewing, Helena. Open year-round; free. Daily Mass in cathedral, Monday and Friday at 7:15 A.M. and Tuesday through Thursday at 7:15 A.M. and noon. Weekend masses are on Saturday at 5:15 P.M. and Sunday at 7:30 A.M., 9 A.M., and 11 A.M. Constructed at the turn of the century during the episcopate of Bishop John Carroll,

it's an outstanding example of Geometric Gothic architecture, patterned after
the Votive Church of the Sacred Heart in Vienna, Austria. Stained-glass windows, white marble altars, statues carved of the purest Carrara marble, and genuine gold leaf decorate the sanctuary. The pews and woodwork are all done in hand-carved oak. The magnificent lighting fixtures are of hand-forged bronze with a special lacquer finish. Outside, majestic twin spires rise 230 feet above the street.

FOR FAMILIES ❧ See World Museum of Mining under *To See–Museums;* Blacktail Ranch and Rocking Z Guest Ranch under *To Do–Horseback Riding;* Fairmont Hot Springs Resort under To Do–Hot Springs; Yellowstone Raft Company under *To Do–Paddling/Floating;* Montana Fishing Outfitters under *To Do–Unique Adventures;* Discovery Basin Ski Area, Great Divide Snowsports and Ski Area, and Maverick Mountain under *To Do–Snow Sports;* Alder Gulch Short-Line Railroad, Old No. 1 Trolley Tours, Gates of the Mountains, Sapphire Mining, and Wagon-Ride Dinners at the Moose Meadows Tipi under *To Do–Unique Adventures;* Crystal Park under Wilder Places–Parks; The Sweet Palace under *Where to Eat–Eating Out;* and Governor's Cup Road Race, Last Chance Stampede and Fair under *Special Events.*

SCENIC DRIVES **Anaconda-Pintler Scenic Highway.** This spectacular 63-mile drive takes you from Exit 153 on I-90, along MT 1 through Philipsburg and Anaconda and the upper Rock Creek and the Flint Creek valleys, and eventually back to the Clark Fork River valley. You will enjoy **Philipsburg, Granite Ghost**

A BOAT SLIDES ACROSS GEORGETOWN LAKE BENEATH THE PEAKS OF THE ANACONDA-PINTLER WILDERNESS

Town State Park, Anaconda, and more, along with the **Skalkaho Highway, Discovery Basin Ski Area,** and **Georgetown Lake** and its surrounding countryside and recreational opportunities. You can take side trips to the **Anaconda-Pintler Wilderness,** the **smelter stack** in Anaconda, and more.

Big Sheep Creek Backcountry Byway is a 50-mile scenic route that starts at Exit 23 off I-15 at Dell; follow the signs. This two-lane gravel road (conditions vary seasonally, so drive with caution) traverses some Montana ranch countryside before cutting through a scenic canyon and then circling north back to **Clark Canyon Reservoir**, at Exit 44 on I-15. On this rustic drive you will see plenty of wildlife and have opportunities for fishing, camping, hiking, and more. You may even get to see **bighorn sheep,** as well as scenic vistas. If you have the car for it, take an adventure on any of the many side roads off the main route—just be sure to exercise good judgment and always know how to fix a flat tire.

Pioneer Mountains Scenic Byway is a 50-mile, partially paved, partially gravel road through the mountains, high prairies, and valley bottom. It starts on MT 43 (east of Divide at Exit 102 on I-15) near **Wise River** and continues on FR 484 to MT 278. This byway takes you the length of the **Pioneer Mountain Range** and reaches elevations of 7,800 feet. You can partake in fishing, hiking, and biking (both road and mountain). You will also drive through **Elkhorn Hot Springs,** past **Maverick Mountain Ski Area,** and by many campgrounds in the **Beaverhead-Deerlodge National Forest.** Hikers and bikers can try the **Blue Creek Trail** or **Crystal Park.**

Skalkaho Highway is a 55-mile journey along MT 38 from about midway through the **Anaconda-Pintler Scenic Highway,** just north of Georgetown Lake, to its junction with US 93 near Hamilton. It is hard to keep your eyes on the road while making this drive. You will pass through the **Beaverhead-Deerlodge National Forest** and **Bitterroot National Forest,** while visiting the **Sapphire Mountains, Skalkaho Falls,** and **Skalkaho Pass.** Fantastic fishing opportunities are available along the drive, as are chances for wildlife viewing, camping, hiking, and biking.

NATURAL WONDERS ✐ **The Gates of the Mountains** (406-458-5241) are located on the Missouri River (actually Holter Lake) and can only be reached by boat via two marinas—the marina at **Holter Lake** (406-444-2535; http://fwp .mt.gov/fishing/guide/q_Holter_Reservoir__1119588469424_0_1.aspx) and the private marina at **Gates of the Mountains.** This unique rock formation was aptly named by Lewis & Clark as they traveled upstream on their journey. The rock walls, as one travels up to them, appear to open up like gates. Once on the water in the Gates of the Mountains, you can access primitive camping sites and hiking trails and find ample wildlife-viewing opportunities.

⚲ **Humbug Spires Wilderness Study Area** (406-533-7600; www.blm.gov/ mt/st/en/fo/butte_field_office/recreation/humbug.html) is accessible via Exit 99 off I-15. This 11,775-acre roadless area is a great place to enjoy some rock climbing and hiking. Part of the geologic formation known as the **Boulder Batholith** (which is a sudden upthrust of granite formations and boulders that stretches for nearly 80 miles), this area has rock outcroppings that rise to over

600 feet. An easy 3-mile (one way) hike starts at the parking area and winds along the creek through an old-growth forest, and then climbs a ridge and eventually reaches the Wedge, one of the more prominent spires. Recreational opportunities include hiking, fishing, rock climbing, primitive camping, wildlife viewing, and horseback riding. It is best to pick up an area map and brochure before you head out. You can get one at any of the outdoor recreation stores in Butte or by contacting the BLM office at 106 N. Parkont, Butte 59701.

& **Lewis & Clark Caverns State Park** (406-287-3541; http://fwp.mt.gov/lands/ site_281895.aspx), 19 miles west of Three Forks on MT 2. Campground and cabins open year-round and tours available May through September; $10 adults, $5 children ages 6–11. Tours last about two hours and require a 2-mile hike. Lewis & Clark Caverns State Park is Montana's first and best-known state park, featuring one of the largest known limestone caverns in the Northwest. Naturally air-conditioned, these spectacular caves, lined with stalactites, stalagmites, columns, and helictites, are electrically lighted and safe to visit. Above ground, a self-guided nature trail provides opportunities to understand the natural surroundings. Also available is a 40-space campground, three camping cabins, tepee, picnic sites, firewood, flush and vault toilets, showers, group-use area, RV dump station, public phone, grills/fire rings, picnic tables, trash cans, drinking water, and a food, beverage, and gift concession. The cabins are handicapped accessible and sleep four comfortably (maximum occupancy is six people). Shower facilities are located 20 feet away.

Refrigerator Canyon is located in the **Gates of the Mountains Wilderness** in the **Helena National Forest,** accessible by Beaver Creek Road (FR 138) northeast of Helena. This is a steep, isolated canyon with some amazing geological features—one being that it can maintain a temperature approximately 20 degrees cooler than the temperature outside the canyon, even on the hottest days of the year. The hike to the canyon is short, but if you want some more adventure try Trail #260 (at the 2-mile mark on the Refrigerator Canyon Trail). It will take you to Sheep Mountain and deeper into the Gates of the Mountains Wilderness.

See also Lost Creek State Park under *Wilder Places–Parks.*

✳ To Do

BICYCLING **Mount Helena Ridge–National Recreation Trail** (406-449-5490) is a 6-mile trail in Mount Helena City Park and the Helena National Forest that takes pedalers through forests and over rolling hills. There are some steep climbs, so this is not the best trail for beginners, but the rewards are some great views and a good workout.

Pear Lake Trail (Trail #72) is located north of Dillon; take I-15 to Exit 74, then go west on Birch Creek Road (CR 801) to the trailhead on the right. In the Beaverhead-Deerlodge National Forest, this 12-mile out-and-back trail takes you mainly along an old four-wheel-drive road up to a remote and gorgeous mountain lake. There are a few rocky and strenuous sections along the way, but nothing too scary and beginners will do just fine.

BOATING &. **Canyon Ferry Reservoir** (406-475-3310; www.usbr.gov/gp/mtao/canyonferry/index.cfm), along US 287/US 12 between Townsend and Helena. The east shore is accessed by MT 284. Created in 1955 and managed by the Bureau of Reclamation, this large reservoir covers nearly 35,000 acres and is roughly 25 miles in length. Boaters will find plenty of boat ramps and three marinas. Anglers will enjoy fishing for rainbow and brown trout, walleye, perch, and burbot. There are opportunities to see deer, bald eagles, osprey, and more. There is also ample hiking, picnicking, camping, and swimming available.

Clark Canyon Reservoir (406-683-6472; www.usbr.gov/gp/mtao/clarkcanyon/index.cfm) is 11 miles southwest of Dillon along I-15. Managed by the Bureau of Reclamation, this reservoir has 17 miles of shoreline and up to 5,000 acres of surface water, depending on levels. Boaters will find many concrete boat ramps and a marina. There are nine camping areas scattered around the reservoir. Anglers will find brown and rainbow trout and burbot. For hikers, the **Cattail Marsh Nature Trail** is an interpretive trail in the Cattail Marsh Recreation Area on the north end of the reservoir. The area has some historical significance as well—Lewis & Clark named the surrounding area Camp Fortunate, as this is the approximate area where Sacagawea was reunited with her Lemhi Shoshone tribe.

Georgetown Lake is in the Beaverhead-Deerlodge National Forest, west of Anaconda and south of Philipsburg on MT 1, the Anaconda-Pintler Scenic Highway. This is a very popular lake, for good reason—fantastic scenery and great fishing. It is also easily accessible but feels quite remote. There are nearly 3,000

THE AREA AROUND GEORGETOWN LAKE IS A SNOWMOBILER'S DREAM

acres of surface water and several boat ramps along the shoreline. Anglers will find brook and rainbow trout and kokanee salmon. In wintertime snowmobiling is a popular pastime, and there are many groomed trails in the area.

&. **Hauser Lake and Black Sandy State Park** (406-495-3270; http://fwp.mt .gov/fishing/guide/q_Hauser_Lake_1118211466843.aspx) can be reached via MT 453 northeast of Helena. Open year-round; free for residents, $5 for nonresidents. Camping is available for $15. The state park lies on the western shore of Hauser Lake. The lake has 3,700 acres of water to explore and there are many boat ramps in the area. **Lakeside Marina** (406-227-6413) provides a nice marina and supplies for boaters. The bar and restaurant offer a scenic place to enjoy a cold one and a nice meal. In fact, dining at the Lakeside Marina is a very tasty experience. Anglers can fish year-round for brown, brook, and rainbow trout, kokanee salmon, and walleye. Other activities include swimming, interpretive displays, camping, and wildlife viewing.

Holter Lake Recreation Area (406-533-7600; www.blm.gov/mt/st/en/fo/butte _field_office/recreation/holter.html) is reached by I-15 Exit 226, 35 miles north of Helena at the small town of Wolf Creek; follow the signs. Open year-round; $2 per vehicle to enter, camping is $10. Fees are only charged May through October. Holter Lake Recreation Area consists of four areas—**Holter Lake, Log Gulch, Departure Point,** and **Holter Dam.** Only the Holter Dam site is not on the lake; instead, it is at the outlet of the dam on the Missouri River. There are many campsites around the lake, but most are primitive. Anglers will find kokanee salmon, brown and rainbow trout, perch, and walleye. There are plenty of hiking and horseback-riding trails in the area. Swimmers and wildlife viewers will have ample opportunity to enjoy the area as well. Additionally, Holter Lake is the body of water used to access the **Gates of the Mountains.** The area also adjoins the **Sleeping Giant Wilderness Study Area,** a popular hiking, primitive camping, and wildlife-viewing area.

CAMPING There are many private campgrounds and RV parks in this region. If you want to rough it, there are probably a hundred possible places to pitch a tent, as most fishing access sites, state parks, and BLM lands allow overnight camping. You can rest assured that at any public site there will be signs stating whether or not overnight camping is allowed. If in doubt read all posted signs, especially if you are unclear about the need to pay a fee.

&. **Beaverhead-Deerlodge National Forest** is south of Helena, east of Missoula, and west of Bozeman, covering more than 3.2 million acres of land over eight counties. There are seven ranger districts with over 50 developed campgrounds. Many of these sites can be reserved through the **National Recreation Reservation System** (1-877-444-6777; www.reserveusa.com). For more information on the various ranger districts and locations, contact the main office (406-683-3900; www.fs.fed.us/r1/bdnf/). They can help with campgrounds, hiking trails, and more. Additionally, the forest has more than **25 rentals cabins** that can be reserved via the National Reservation System. Some of the more popular camping areas are **Lodgepole Campground** (Pintler Ranger District, 406-846-1770), 11 miles south of Philipsburg on MT 1, and **Spring Hill Campground** (Pintler Ranger District), 11 miles west of Anaconda on MT 1.

&. **Bureau of Land Management, Butte and Dillon Field Offices** (Butte: 406-533-7600, www.mt.blm.gov/bdo; Dillon: 406-683-2337, www.mt.blm.gov/dfo). In the Butte district the BLM manages seven campsites. In the Dillon region there are several campsites, most notably the undeveloped **Ruby Reservoir Site** (south of Alder on MT 257; free) and the **South and West Madison Campgrounds** on the Madison River south of Ennis (both provide boat ramps and fishing access sites and camping for a nominal fee). In the Butte district all of the campsites are free except for **Divide Bridge Campground,** which is $5 per night from May to October. For more information, contact the Butte Field Office or visit their Web site.

&. **Helena National Forest** (406-449-5201; www.fs.fed.us/r1/Helena) has nearly a million acres in the vicinity of the city of Helena. There are three ranger districts, all of which offer camping and recreation. To contact the districts directly, call the Helena office at the number listed above or visit their Web site. Some of the more popular campgrounds are **Cromwell Dixon Campground,** 15 miles west of Helena off US 12, and **Skidway Campground,** 20 miles east of Townsend off US 12. The forest also has **seven rental cabins** that can be reserved through the National Recreation Reservation System (1-877-444-6777 or www.reserveusa.com).

FISHING Gold West Country could very well be named "Fishing Country" due to the abundance of large rivers and small creeks with great fishing—by far the best fishing of any region in Montana. These rivers are all very accessible, and nearly every river is serviced by several topnotch fly and tackle shops and outfitters. If you have a little time on your trip and are looking to do some fishing, try wetting a line in any of these rivers. And it would be a great decision to enlist the services of one of the region's many qualified outfitters.

The Beaverhead River (406-994-4042; http://fwp.mt.gov/fishing/guide/q _Beaverhead_River__1123386455677_0_74.9.aspx) begins at the outflow of Clark Canyon Reservoir south of Dillon on I-15 and flows for 69 miles to its confluence with the Big Hole, where the Jefferson River is born. There is some fishing on the river above Clark Canyon Reservoir, but this is mostly private property and access is nearly impossible. The river above Dillon is characterized by a tight channel meandering through densely covered willow banks. From Dillon, the Beaverhead flows through a broad, open agricultural valley for 50 miles before reaching Twin Bridges. Its channel is restricted through a narrow canyon during part of its lower journey near Point of Rocks. The water in the Beaverhead is comparatively cold, except in areas subject to dewatering, mainly in the lower river. Fish cover primarily consists of submerged and overhanging bank vegetation, undercuts, and long, deep pools. Fish species include brown and rainbow trout and mountain whitefish.

The Big Hole River (406-994-4042; http://fwp.mt.gov/fishing/guide/report .aspx?llid=1123386455678) originates at Skinner Lake high in the Beaverhead Mountains. It then flows north along MT 278, east along MT 43, and south along I-15 before making a large turn back north to where it meets the Beaverhead River near Twin Bridges. There are ample fishing access sites along the Big

Hole. Early explorers and settlers were drawn to the Big Hole by the sheer size, beauty, and richness of the high-elevation valley, or hole, as the trappers called it. The river remains free flowing for its entire course, adding to its unique charm. The Upper Big Hole contains the last stream-dwelling population of arctic grayling in the Lower 48. This has prompted many significant private partnerships and cooperative efforts to ensure the protection of this valuable population. In addition to grayling populations, brown and rainbow trout dominate, along with mountain whitefish.

The Jefferson River (406-994-4042; http://fwp.mt.gov/fishing/guide/q_Jefferson _River__1115074459268.aspx) begins where the Beaverhead and Big Hole meet just north of Twin Bridges and then flows northeast for 80 miles to join the Madison and Gallatin Rivers to form the Missouri River. The river is home to brown and rainbow trout and mountain whitefish. In addition to fishing, the Jefferson River and its floodplain provide opportunities for waterfowl hunting, trapping, floating, sightseeing, and asparagus picking.

The Madison River (406-994-4042; http://fwp.mt.gov/fishing/guide/q_Madison _River__1115074459269_0_131.90299987793.aspx) begins in Yellowstone National Park at the junction of the Firehole and Gibbon Rivers and flows in a northerly direction for 140 miles to Three Forks. There it joins the Jefferson and Gallatin Rivers to form the Missouri River. The Madison is interrupted by several impoundments: Hebgen Reservoir, Ennis Reservoir, and Quake Lake, a natural lake formed by a major earthquake in 1959. From Ennis Reservoir, the river flows through Bear Trap Canyon before entering the lower Madison River valley for its final 18 miles. Due to its famous reputation, heavy fishing pressure,

QUAKE LAKE WAS CREATED IN 1959, WHEN AN EARTHQUAKE TRIGGERED A MASSIVE LANDSLIDE

good access, high scenic value, and excellent wild trout populations, it has been classified as a Blue Ribbon trout stream. The Madison is also the birthplace of wild trout management—the results of a controversial study in the early 1970s led to a shift in management emphasis nationwide, from stocking trout to population monitoring, harvest regulation, and habitat protection for wild trout. Fish species include rainbow and brown trout and mountain whitefish.

The Missouri River (406-444-2535; http://fwp.mt.gov/fishing/guide/q_Missouri _River__1039825479786_1586.77905273438_2312.46704101563.aspx) begins where the Jefferson, Madison, and Gallatin all meet near Three Forks. From there until the river exits Holter Dam at Holter Lake, the fishing is primarily done on one reservoir and two lakes: **Canyon Ferry Reservoir, Hauser Lake,** and **Holter Lake.** Fishing on the river section from the headwaters to below Holter Dam is sporadic at best for brown and rainbow trout, carp, and mountain whitefish; however, once the river leaves Holter Dam it becomes one of the most consistent trout fisheries in the state. Species include brown and rainbow trout, mountain whitefish, and carp. It is a good place for first-time anglers to experience the excitement of fishing in Montana (see *Unique Adventures– Montana Fishing Outfitters*).

The Ruby River (406-994-4042; http://fwp.mt.gov/fishing/guide/q_Ruby_River __1123453455129.aspx) begins high in the Gravelly Range south of Alder, but doesn't really become a viable fishery until it leaves **Ruby Reservoir.** Much of the land along the Ruby is private and most landowners deny access, but there are a few public access points along MT 287. Species include brown and rainbow trout and mountain whitefish. Floating anglers should exercise caution as

TREES POKING THROUGH THE WATER GIVE QUAKE LAKE A SPOOKY QUALITY

the river is very windy and often quite shallow; it's often best to float with a licensed outfitter.

GOLF Anaconda Country Club (406-797-3220), #1 Country Club Lane, Anaconda; nine holes.

Beaverhead Country Club (406-683-9933), 1200 MT 41 N., Dillon; nine holes.

Bill Roberts Golf Course (406-442-2191), 2201 N. Benton Avenue, Helena; 18 holes.

Butte Country Club (406-494-3383), 3400 Elizabeth Warren Avenue, Butte; 18 holes.

Deer Lodge Golf Club (406-846-1625), W. Milwaukee Avenue, Deer Lodge; nine holes.

Fairmont Hot Springs Resort Golf Course (406-797-3241), 1500 Fairmont Road, Fairmont (Exit 211 off I-90 between Butte and Anaconda); 18 holes.

Fox Ridge Golf Course (406-227-8304), 4020 Lake Helena Drive, Helena; 18 holes, plus a nine-hole, par-three course.

Green Meadow Country Club (406-442-1420), 2720 Country Club Avenue, Helena; 18 holes.

Highland View Golf Course (406-494-7900), 2903 Oregon Avenue, Butte; nine holes.

Madison Meadows Golf Course (406-682-7468), 110 Golfcourse Road, Ennis; nine holes.

Old Baldy Golf Course (406-266-3337), Delger Lane, 1.5 miles northeast of Townsend; nine holes.

Old Works Jack Nicklaus Signature Golf Course (406-563-5989), 1205 Pizzini Way, Anaconda; 18 holes.

HIKING Bear Trap National Recreation Trail (406-683-2337). To reach the trailhead, travel 8 miles east of Norris on US 287 and then 3 miles south on the Red Mountain Campground gravel road. This 9-mile, one-way hike parallels the Madison River as it tumbles through Bear Trap Canyon. It is a great early season hike or an enjoyable hike if you want to get in some fishing (see Madison River under *To Do–Fishing*). Avoid this hike in late July and August unless you plan to take plenty of water as the south-facing slopes the trail traverses can be hot and dry in late summer.

Cherry Creek Trail (#123) is accessible via Exit 93 on I-15 at Melrose. Head west on Trapper Creek Road for 1.5 miles, then about 9 miles southwest on Cherry Creek Road to FR 1011, which eventually drops you at the trailhead. Depending on the road conditions, the last mile or so could be passable only with a four-wheel-drive vehicle. This hike is a climb, but worth it as you will pass an old miner's cabin, travel along Cherry Creek, and make it to Cherry Lake. And if you want to climb even more there's a side trail of about 0.25 mile to Granite Lake.

Hanging Valley National Recreation Trail (#247) is accessible via Trout Creek Road east of Helena. This trail climbs moderately to a ridge along some spectacular limestone cliffs and spires. The views along the ridge are breathtaking, and once you climb the first 3 miles it is relatively flat. The trail eventually drops down into a secluded valley with old-growth Douglas firs, and on the return you get some amazing views of the Helena Valley and the Continental Divide in the distance.

Lake Louise National Recreation Trail (#168) is accessible via MT 359 at Exit 256 (east of Butte at Cardwell) off I-90. Head southwest on S. Boulder Road for about 17 miles to Bismarck Reservoir, where you will find the trailhead. This may seem like a tough climb, but the switchbacks are easy and it is worth it once you reach the reservoir. Plan a mid- or late summer hike here as the snowpack can last until late June. A fun side jaunt is the **Lost Lake Cabin Trail** (#150). A little less steep than the main trail, this 5-mile add-on takes you through some old-growth forests; you may even see a mountain goat.

Mount Helena City Park borders the city of Helena to the south and west. Many trailheads lead from various streets in town, so it's best to inquire locally about the nearest trailhead. There are 20 trails in this 620-acre city park, which borders even more acreage in the Helena National Forest. For fantastic views of the city and valley, try to reach the summit. The most traveled is the **1906 Trail,** which involves an easy (yet a little steep) climb around the west side of the mountain, providing more vistas.

Nez Perce Nee-Mo-Poo Trail is a designated National Historic Trail along the 1,170-mile journey of the Nez Perce from Wallowa Lake in Oregon to the

MOUNT HELENA WATCHES OVER DOWNTOWN HELENA

THE BIG HOLE RIVER NEAR THE BIG HOLE NATIONAL BATTLEFIELD

Bear Paw Battlefield near Chinook. During the Nez Perce War of 1877, the Indians fled as they fought to retain what few freedoms remained for them and to maintain their traditional way of life. In this region, the trail passes through the **Big Hole National Battlefield.** At the battlefield, the trail is accessed by several interpretive walks.

& **Sheepshead Mountain Recreation Area** lies in the Beaverhead-Deerlodge National Forest and is accessible via Exit 138 8 miles south of Butte. From there, you head northwest on FR 442 for 13 miles. This is an interesting recreation area that is largely handicapped accessible. There are 4.5 miles of paved trails, including a nice 0.75-mile saunter around Maney Lake. These trails provide opportunities to see elk, deer, waterfowl, and more. There is a fishing access that is wheelchair accessible, picnic tables, and views for all to enjoy.

Upper Rattlesnake Trail is accessible via I-15, Exit 74, 8 miles north of Dillon. Take CR 801 west until it changes to FR 98/Mule Creek Road; follow the signs. This is a hike for experienced and fit hikers, but the rewards are grand. It is a 5-mile loop trail that will take you past five lakes. A few sections offer views of the vast Beaverhead Valley, but not many people make the long journey to the trailhead so you'll find plenty of solitude and wildlife.

See also Pioneer Mountains Scenic Byway under *To See–Scenic Drives;* Humbug Spires Wilderness Study Area, Lewis & Clark Caverns State Park, and Refrigerator Canyon under *To See–Natural Wonders;* Wade Lake Ski Trails under *To Do–Snow Sports;* Gates of the Mountains under *To Do–Unique Adventures;* Lost Creek State Park under *Wilder Places–Parks;* Beaverhead-Deerlodge National Forest, Helena National Forest, and Lincoln State Forest under *Wilder Places–Forests;* Red Rock Lakes National Wildlife Refuge and Mount Haggin

Wildlife Management Area under *Wilder Places–Wildlife Refuges and Wildlife Management Areas.*

HORSEBACK RIDING ✍ **Blacktail Ranch** (406-235-4330; www.blacktailranch .com), 4440 South Fork Trail, Wolf Creek. The drive into the Blacktail Ranch is enough to excite anyone. They offer single- and multi-day rides along the eastern edge of the Continental Divide. The Blacktail Ranch is an 8,000-acre jewel, located at the base of the Continental Divide, where the Rockies meet the prairie. The South Fork of the Dearborn River flows through the center of the ranch, feeding rich meadows and deep, lush aspen groves. Above the riverbed, unspoiled acres of pine and fir roll into broad fields of native grasses and wildflowers. Please inquire about specific rates and seasons.

✍ **Broken Arrow Lodge and Outfitters** (406-842-5437; www.brokenarrow lodge.com) is located near Alder. Because of their remote location, please contact them for specific directions. Ideal for single- and multi-day rides, the folks here have easygoing horses and rides that will take you to some of the most breathtaking scenery in this region. They also offer river swimming, scenic rides, wildlife viewing, and late-night campfires.

✍ ✪ **Rocking Z Guest Ranch** (406-458-3890; www.rockingz.com) is 20 miles north of Helena via Exit 216. From there, travel 2 miles on Sieben Canyon Road; follow the signs. The hosts here (and their horses and scenery) are a real treat. Zach and Patty Wirth are fourth-generation Montanans who are rooted in horses and make all of their guests feel at home. Their horses are gentle and this family-run operation is close enough to Helena that a two-hour ride is easy to fit in while you're enjoying other sites. Please contact the ranch for current rates.

✍ **Virginia City Overland Stagecoach & Horseback** (406-843-5200; www .virginiacitystagecoach.com), located at the north end of Virginia City near Wallace Street. The folks here can treat you to an old-fashioned stagecoach ride (be on the lookout for stagecoach robbers in costume and gunslingers—this is Virginia City, after all) or an afternoon horseback ride. On either tour you will see some restored buildings, great scenery, and get a feel for what life was like in the Old West. Stagecoach rides take about half an hour, while the horseback rides can last as long as you like, although most are an hour or so.

HOT SPRINGS ♿ **Boulder Hot Springs Inn and Conference Center** (406-225-4339; www.boulderhotsprings.com), 3 miles south of Boulder on MT 69, easily spotted. Located on nearly 300 acres in a scenic little valley, this unique place is somewhat off the beaten path, but worth the extra effort to get here. The entire building is on the National Register of Historic Places, and this hot springs has been a destination for centuries. They have an outdoor pool, two plunge pools, and steam rooms. Lately they have added spa services along with the hot pools and steam rooms. Overnight rooms are comfortable and clean and come with a full breakfast. This is also a nice place for kids; the entire inn and hot springs are alcohol and smoke free.

♿ **Elkhorn Hot Springs** (406-834-3434; www.elkhornhotsprings.com) is 13 miles north of MT 278 on the Pioneer Mountains Scenic Byway (FR 484). This is a year-round resort, but only car-accessible in summer. They have two outdoor pools and one indoor wet sauna. They also offer lodging in cabins and in a few rooms in the main lodge. A deluxe continental breakfast is served each morning and dinner is offered on weekends. This resort is a great jumping-off point for outdoor pursuits in the Beaverhead-Deerlodge National Forest. In winter, snow-mobiling, cross-country skiing, downhill skiing at nearby Maverick Mountain, and snowshoeing are popular here.

&. ✍ **Fairmont Hot Springs Resort** (406-797-3241; www.fairmontmontana .com), 1500 Fairmont Road, Fairmont (Exit 211 off I-90 between Anaconda and Butte). This year-round full-service resort is a destination in itself. Drawing visitors from all over the Northwest, they have two Olympic-size swimming pools (one indoor and one outdoor), as well as two hot mineral pools ideal for soaking (one indoor and one outdoor). For kids, there is an enclosed waterslide. Overnight guests will find an assortment of accommodations from cabins to motel-style rooms. If you are primarily interested in soaking, be sure to get a room in the main lodge so you can easily walk indoors to all the pools. There are two restaurants on-site, the casual Springwater Café and more formal fine dining in the Mile High Dining Room. The lounge also offers food and is a nice place to unwind after a day exploring the area. (See also Fairmont Hot Springs Resort Golf Course under *Golf.*)

✹ **Jackson Hot Springs Lodge** (406-834-3151; www.jacksonhotsprings.com), 43 miles northwest of Dillon on MT 278. A long way from anything that could be considered urban in Montana, this elegant country lodge is ideal for a little romantic getaway or a nice break from the daily grind. Located in the Big Hole River Valley between the Pioneer Mountains and the Beaverhead Mountains, guests here enjoy lovely accommodations and a clean hot mineral pool. There is a cabin, lodge rooms, and even RV hook-ups. Dining at the lodge is well known in the area, and they strive to use the best local produce and meats.

Norris Hot Springs (406-685-3303), MT 84 just east of Norris. Open Tuesday through Sunday only, this small springs is a fun place for a few hours of soaking. There is no overnight lodging, but it is clean and well kept and most nights you can have the place to yourself.

PADDLING/FLOATING **The Madison River in the Bear Trap Canyon Wilderness** is managed by the Dillon office of the Bureau of Land Management (see *To Do–Camping* and *To Do–Hiking* for contact information). The river cuts through Bear Trap Canyon and provides some of the most exhilarating whitewater in all of Montana. However, be aware that the canyon is remote, so only very experienced whitewater paddlers should attempt to run this section of river. Everyone else interested in floating this beautiful canyon should do so with a licensed professional guide. The **Yellowstone Raft Company** (1-800-858-7781; www.yellow stoneraft.com) offers all-day trips down the canyon. Please inquire for rates.

See also any of the rivers listed under *To Do–Fishing;* any of the lakes listed under *To Do–Boating;* Gates of the Mountains under *To Do–Unique Adventures;* and Red Rock Lakes National Wildlife Refuge under *Wilder Places–Wildlife Refuges and Wildlife Management Areas.*

SOUTHWEST MONTANA: GOLD WEST COUNTRY

Ice Fishing

Opportunities to ice fish in this region are plentiful, and the popularity of this pastime continues to grow. It requires patience, local knowledge, and the ability to stay warm for long periods of time. (For more information, see the listings under *To Do–Boating.*)

Ice Skating

Anywhere you can find a frozen lake or pond, you can ice skate. Exercise extreme caution on frozen waters that are not managed. For rinks that provide scheduled skating hours and maintained ice, visit **Butte Community Ice Center** (406-490-2111) at 1700 Wall Street, Butte; the **United High Altitude Sports Center** (406-494-7570) at Continental Drive and I-90, Butte; the **Queen City Ice Palace,** 400 Lola Street on the east side of Helena; and **Winninghoff Park** (406-859-3821) on West Stockton Street in Philipsburg. (See also Hauser Lake under *To Do–Boating* and Spring Meadow Lake State Park under *Wilder Places–Parks.*)

Skiing

There are many places to enjoy a downhill or cross-county ski in this region. In addition to the listings below, there are public trails throughout the Beaverhead-Deerlodge and Helena National Forests for cross-country skiers.

 **Discovery Basin Ski Area** (406-563-2184; www.skidiscovery.com), 23 miles west of Anaconda on MT 1 (along the Anaconda-Pintler Scenic Highway). This

DISCOVERY BASIN SKI AREA

THE VIEW FROM THE SUMMIT OF THE GREAT DIVIDE SKI AREA

used to be a relatively well-kept secret, but now the cat is out of the bag. And with the recent addition of more terrain, this is a legitimate destination mountain. There are still no overnight lodging accommodations here, but Anaconda and Philipsburg are within 20 minutes of the mountain. *Lifts:* 3 triples, 3 doubles. *Terrain:* 20 percent beginner, 30 percent intermediate, 50 percent expert; 1,670 feet of vertical drop; snowmaking on four runs. *Facilities:* full-service cafeteria and bar on mountain. *Ski school:* ski and snowboard lessons for all ages and several first-timer and kids and teen programs. *Rates:* $32 adults, $16 children 6–12, $16 seniors over 65, $8 easy chair only, children 5 and under free with paying adult; half- and multi-day rates available.

✈ **Great Divide Snowsports and Ski Area** (406-449-3746; www.skigd.com), Exit 200 off I-15 north of Helena, then west on MT 279 about 11 miles, then west of Marysville Road about 7 miles; follow the signs. Open Wednesday through Sunday during the season. Packed with lots of trails and great tree skiing, this small ski area is a great value. They also have one of the largest and most varied terrain parks in all of Montana. There is no overnight lodging on the mountain, but Helena is only 30 minutes away. *Lifts:* 5 doubles, 2 handle tows. *Terrain:* 140 trails—10 percent beginner, 40 percent intermediate, 50 percent expert; 1,500 feet of vertical drop; snowmaking on 10 percent of the mountain. *Facilities:* full-service cafeteria, bar, and dining room on the mountain. *Ski school:* ski and snowboard lessons and several kids' programs. *Rates:* $30 adults, $25 students and seniors, $20 adult nonholiday weekday, $15 children grades 1–5, preschoolers free with parent, beginners' tow free; half- and multi-day rates available. They also offer night skiing on Friday nights for $9.

✧ **Maverick Mountain** (406-834-3454; www.skimaverick.com), on the Pioneer Mountains Scenic Byway (FR 484; see *To See–Scenic Drives*) north of MT 278 in the Beaverhead-Deerlodge National Forest. Open Thursday through Sunday during ski season. This is a small area with only one chairlift, but there are over 200 acres of skiable terrain. It is a great option for the entire family to get away and ski together. For cross-country skiers, there are quality groomed trails and plentiful solitude. You can also access the trails that originate from **Elkhorn Hot Springs.** Lodging is available in nearby Jackson, Polaris, or Dillon. *Lifts:* one double chairlift, one handle tow. *Terrain:* 24 trails—20 percent beginner, 40 percent intermediate, 40 percent expert; 2,020 feet of vertical drop. *Facilities:* good and hearty food in the cafeteria and a friendly bar. *Ski school:* catered more to children's instruction, offering ski and snowboard lessons. *Rates:* $25 adults, $17 children 6–12, children 5 and under free; half- and multi-day rates available.

MacDonald Pass Trail System. This is a single trail, but divided up into various segments. Managed by the Helena National Forest, there are four various loops or segments, three of which are groomed by the **Last Chance Nordic Ski Club.** The trail includes 4.5 kilometers rated easiest, 17 kilometers rated more difficult, and 5.6 kilometers rated most difficult. Dogs are not allowed on any of the trails.

Mount Haggin Nordic Ski Area is 15 miles south of Anaconda. Managed by Montana Fish, Wildlife & Parks and the **Mile Hi Nordic Ski Club** (406-782-4994), this area has 25 kilometers of groomed cross-country ski trails—5 kilometers easiest, 10 kilometers more difficult, and 10 kilometers most difficult. About half of the trails are also groomed for skate skiing.

Wade Lake Ski Trails at Wade Lake Cabins (406-682-7560; www.wadelake .com), south of Cliff Lake Road; just west of the junction of US 287 and MT 87, then 6 miles to cabins and trails. Wade Lake offers 35 kilometers of groomed trails—15 kilometers easiest and 20 kilometers more difficult. You must ski in to your accommodations if you are spending the night, which might be fun for some but cumbersome for others. The cabins are cozy. In summertime this is a great place for paddling around the lake.

Snowmobiling

Snowmobiling is very popular in this region, and there are plenty of trails for your enjoyment. The 50-mile **Pioneer Mountains Scenic Byway** is closed to auto traffic in winter, creating a National Recreation Snowmobile Trail. This is a great trail for venturing into the Beaverhead-Deerlodge National Forest. Snowmobiles can be rented in Dillon, Butte, or **Elkhorn Hot Springs.** The town of **Lincoln** is also a snowmobiler destination during the winter months. The Helena National Forest manages 250 miles of trails, most notably Huckleberry Pass and Alice Creek. There are also many other dedicated snowmobile trails on national forest lands throughout the region.

UNIQUE ADVENTURES ✧ **Alder Gulch Short-Line Railroad** (406-843-5247; www.virginiacity.com/steam.htm), Virginia City. Open Memorial Day through August; $10 round-trip, $6 one-way, children 6 and under free, $35 per family.

The Alder Gulch Short-Line is a 30-inch narrow-gauge railroad owned by the state. It connects Virginia City and Nevada City. Montana's only operating steam locomotive, No. 12, is a fully restored 1910 Baldwin. It was built by the Baldwin Locomotive Works in Philadelphia as part of an order for four 30-inch gauge engines for the Mexican Railroad. The 28-foot beast is a fun way to travel between two Old West towns and offers a real taste of the past. However, try to make the trip on a weekend, as during the week you will travel on a small gas-powered locomotive.

&. ✍ **Gates of the Mountains** (406-458-5214; www.gatesofthemountains.com), Exit 209 off I-15; 20 miles north of Helena, then 3 miles east to the marina. Open Memorial Day through late September; $11 adults, $10 seniors 60 and over, $7 children 4–17, under four free, dinner cruise $35 per person. This is one of the most scenic areas of Gold West Country—and it is only accessible by boat via the Gates of the Mountains Marina. In 1805 Lewis & Clark traveled up what was then the Missouri River. It is now **Holter Lake,** due to Holter Dam. There is a geologic formation on the boat tour that Lewis & Clark named the Gates of the Mountains. Tour highlights include scenery, lots of wildlife, Indian pictographs, and lots of Lewis & Clark history. You can also stay for a picnic, enjoy a hike, fish, or camp.

Fishing Vacations with Montana Fishing Outfitters (406-439-4545; www .dragfreedrift.com), Helena area. This region of Montana is home to some of the state's most well-known fishing areas. If you are serious about exploring here with rod and reel, then enjoy one of these custom-tailored fishing vacations. From lodges to guides to just which rivers to fish on a given day, these folks will steer you in the right direction.

Old No. 1 Trolley Tours (406-723-3177; www.butteinfo.org), 1000 George Street, Butte. Seasons vary, so please inquire. This historic trolley tour takes you on a visual treat of Butte's storied past. The trolley itself is a replica of the electric trolleys once used in Butte's heyday. The drivers are also the tour guides and are very knowledgeable and enjoy answering the oddest of questions.

Ranch Vacations. A ranch vacation in Gold West Country is about as genuinely western as they come. A typical ranch vacation—but not a typical vacation by any means—may include herding cattle, sheep, or other livestock, branding livestock, cutting hay, breaking horses, and more. The time spent working versus relaxing is up to the ranch owners or hands, but also you—remember this is your vacation. All of the ranches listed below offer horseback riding, lodging, meals, and more as part of an all-inclusive package. This is only a small sample of the many ranch vacations available: **Upper Canyon Ranch and Outfitting** (406-842-5884; www.ucmontana.com), Alder; **Centennial Guest Ranch** (406-682-7292; www.beardsleyfishhuntmt.com), Ennis; **Blacktail Ranch** (see also *To Do–Horseback Riding*); Wolf Creek; **Rocking Z Guest Ranch** (see also *To Do–Horseback Riding*), Helena; **Wirth Ranch** (406-235-4243), Wolf Creek; **Alice Creek Ranch** (406-362-4810), Lincoln; **Bannack Pass Ranch** (406-681-3229), Dillon; **1880s Ranch** (406-491-2336), Anaconda; **Hidden Valley Guest Ranch** (406-683-2929), Dillon; **Hidden Hollow Hideaway Guest Ranch**

(406-266-3322), Townsend. For a complete listing of vacation ranches, visit the Gold West Country Web site (www.goldwest.visitmt.com/listings/1518.htm).

✄ **Sapphire mining** is a fun way to connect with Montana's mining past while enjoying being outdoors and taking a chance at a small fortune. Several places in this region offer hands-on mining for precious gems. These establishments all charge, typically by the bucket or pound. Give it a whirl at **Gem Mountain** (406-859-4367; www.gemmtn.com), 3835 Skalkaho Road, Philipsburg. Open daily mid-May through September. Here you can look for your own sapphire gemstone in one of the world's largest sapphire deposits. Another option is **Sapphire Gallery** (406-227-8989; www.sapphire-gallery.com), 115 E. Broadway, Philipsburg. Open daily June through August. Look through a bag of stones for your precious gem. Another option is **Spokane Bar Sapphire Mine and Gold Fever Rock Shop** (406-227-8989; www.sapphiremine.com), 5360 Castles Road, Helena. Open April through October. For a reasonable price (around $5) you can get a bag of goodies that might contain a Montana sapphire.

Wagon-Ride Dinners at the Moose Meadow Tipi (406-442-2884; www .lastchanceranch.biz), west of Helena up Colorado Gulch. Open June through September; $69 per person includes a very comfortable bus transfer from Helena, a wagon ride behind Belgian and Percheron draft horses, a full-course gourmet meal complete with Montana huckleberry cheesecake, a campfire, and live music by well-known singer and songwriter Bruce Anfinson. You will dine in a traditional tipi and enjoy a taste of Montana—both culinary and cultural.

✳ Wilder Places

PARKS ✿ ✄ **Crystal Park** is located in the Beaverhead-Deerlodge National Forest along the **Pioneer Mountains Scenic Byway,** FR 484, 17 miles north of the road's junction with MT 278. Open mid-May through mid-October (depending on weather) for day use only; $5 per vehicle. This is a unique state park in that it sits at 7,800 feet above sea level. Facilities include three picnic sites with tables and grills, information signs, toilets, and a paved trail with benches and an overlook. For kids, or anyone for that matter, the main feature of the park is to dig in the dirt for crystals. You can collect any crystals that you find, but not if you intend to resell them.

✿ **Lost Creek State Park** (406-542-5500; http://fwp.mt.gov/lands/site_280851 .aspx). Go east from Anaconda on MT 1 for 1.5 miles, then north on MT 273 for 2 miles, and then northeast 6 miles on FR 635. Open for day use and camping May 1–November 30; free. Granite and limestone are the main features here— rising high above the trails and picnic areas. For a short hike you can walk to the **Lost Creek Falls** on a well-maintained trail. Fishing and wildlife viewing are popular here as well. Look for bighorn sheep and mountain goats in late summer.

✿ **Spring Meadow Lake State Park** (406-495-3270; http://fwp.state.mt.us/ parks/parksreport.asp?mapnum=19), Spring Meadow Drive, Helena. Open year-round for day use only; free. Actually in the city of Helena, this park features a 55-acre urban respite from the daily grind. There are walking trails, swimming platforms, and fishing. In winter the lake freezes and ice skating becomes popular.

See also Lewis & Clark Caverns State Park under *To See–Natural Wonders;* Beaverhead Rock State Park and Clark's Lookout under *To See–Historic Landmarks, Places, and Sites;* Hauser Lake and Black Sandy State Park under *To Do–Boating;* and Mount Helena City Park and Sheepshead Mountain Recreation Area under *To Do–Hiking.*

FORESTS **Beaverhead-Deerlodge National Forest** (406-683-3900; www.fs.fed.us/r1/b-d), 420 Barrett Street, Dillon. South of Helena, east of Missoula, and west of Bozeman, this is Montana's largest forest, encompassing more than 3.2 million acres (larger than Yellowstone National Park) and covering lands in more than eight counties. Notable areas in the forest include the **Anaconda-Pintler Wilderness Area,** part of the **Lee Metcalf Wilderness Area,** portions of the **Continental Divide National Scenic Trail,** and part of the **Nez Perce Historic Trail.** Natural resources are abundant, including timber, mining, and grazing. In fact, one could argue that the lands within the Beaverhead National Forest (before it was designated a national forest) produced most of the world's mining wealth at one point. Recreational pursuits include biking, boating, camping, fishing, cross-country skiing, downhill skiing, snowmobiling, horseback riding, wildlife viewing, and much more. There are many campsite and cabin rentals throughout the forest, and a visitor to Gold West Country would be hard-pressed to enjoy the region without stepping foot into this forest.

Helena National Forest (406-449-5201; www.fs.fed.us/r1/Helena), 2880 Skyway Drive, Helena. Surrounding the capital city of Helena, this national forest is just under a million acres. Compared to other forests in Montana, this one is small, yet it plays host to some of the state's more interesting features: the **Gates of the Mountains** geologic formation, **Gates of the Mountains Wilderness, Scapegoat Wilderness, Big Belt Mountains, Elkhorn Mountains** (including the **Elkhorn Mountains Wildlife Management Area**), and parts of the **Continental Divide National Scenic Trail.** Recreational pursuits include biking, boating, camping, fishing, cross-country skiing, downhill skiing, snowmobiling, horseback riding, wildlife viewing, and much more. There are many campsite and cabin rentals throughout the forest. A few of my favorite sites include Refrigerator Canyon, the Mount Helena Ridge Trail, and Gates of the Mountains.

Lincoln State Forest adjoins the Scapegoat Wilderness and Helena National Forest near Lincoln. This is one of seven state forests managed by the Montana Department of Natural Resources (406-542-4300; www.dnrc.state.mt.us). These forests are managed for two purposes: to produce timber and provide watershed protection. Recreational opportunities include boating, camping, fishing, hiking, cross-country skiing, wildlife viewing, and hunting.

WILDERNESS AREAS **Bear Trap Canyon Wilderness** (406-683-2337; www.blm.gov/mt/st/en/fo/dillon_field_office/recreation/bear_trap.html), Dillon office of the Bureau of Land Management. This was the first BLM-administered land to enter into the wilderness preservation system. The 6,000-acre area offers beautiful wilderness scenery plus exciting whitewater rafting on the **Madison River** (see *To Do–Paddling/Floating*). The 1,500-foot cliffs that border the canyon provide a dramatic backdrop for nature study, hiking, rafting, and fishing along the 9-mile Bear Trap Canyon National Recreation Trail. The trail follows the river the length of the canyon but can only be accessed from the north end (no through-hiking).

Gates of the Mountains Wilderness (406-449-5490) lies northeast of Helena along the eastern edge of Holter Lake. This wilderness area covers 28,562 acres (a 38-mile stretch of river) and is an administrated unit of the Helena National Forest, located within or adjacent to it. Along the length of the corridor, look for bald eagles, red-tailed hawks, turkey vultures, great horned owls, river otters, peregrine falcons, and American white pelicans. Osprey are also common along the Missouri, as are surefooted mountain goats on sheer cliffs above the river. Bighorn sheep were successfully transplanted onto the adjacent Beartooth Wildlife Management Area. Numerous trails along the corridor offer additional wildlife-viewing opportunities—three trails lead from the Meriwether Picnic Area and one runs along the river from Hauser Dam to Beaver Creek Road. Tour boats leave from **Holter Lake** (see *To Do–Unique Adventures*) and go north through the Gates of the Mountains.

Scapegoat Wilderness (406-791-7700) lies approximately 10 miles north of Lincoln. It is administered by both the Lolo and Helena National Forests. Created in 1972 and covering 239,936 acres, the Scapegoat Wilderness straddles the Continental Divide and is located south of and adjacent to the Bob Marshall Wilderness. The Bob Marshall (see chapters 1 and 3) and Scapegoat Wilderness Complex is one of the few places outside Glacier and Yellowstone National Parks

THE OLD BLUE HOUSE STANDS BENEATH THE LAST CHANCE GULCH FIRE TOWER

in the Lower 48 that supports a population of grizzly bears. Most of the 14 lakes and about 89 miles of streams in the Scapegoat provide fishing opportunities. Primitive camping is allowed with no public facilities. Call the Lewis & Clark National Forest for camping information.

WILDLIFE REFUGES AND WILDLIFE MANAGEMENT AREAS Mount Haggin Wildlife Management Area (406-542-5500; www.fwp.state.mt.us/habitat/wma/ haggin.asp) is about 10 miles south of Anaconda along MT 569. With more than 56,000 acres of land set aside for wildlife, this area provides ample recreation opportunities. Popular pursuits are snowmobiling, cross-country skiing, and snowshoeing in winter. In summer camping, fishing, hiking, wildlife viewing, and hunting can all be enjoyed.

& **Red Rock Lakes National Wildlife Refuge** (406-276-3536; www.r6.fws .gov/redrocks) is a very remote refuge set in some of the most beautiful country in this region. To get here, take Exit 0 on I-15 (at the Montana-Idaho border), then follow MT 509 east for 28 miles. The visitor center is open year-round, daily. Set aside in 1935 mainly to provide habitat for trumpeter swans, this 45,000-acre wildlife refuge is home to deer, elk, a plethora of birdlife, and more. There are two primitive campgrounds—**Upper Lake Campground** and **Lower Lake Campground.** Recreational opportunities are many and varied here. Fish species include arctic grayling, brook trout, mountain whitefish, rainbow trout, and Yellowstone cutthroat trout. Floaters and paddlers will find solitude and plenty of water to explore on Lower and Upper Red Rock Lakes. To round things out, there is hiking, biking (mountain and road), snowmobiling, cross-country skiing, and hunting.

See also Humbug Spires Wilderness Study Area under *To See–Natural Wonders* and Sheepshead Mountain Recreation Area under *To Do–Hiking.*

✳ Lodging
BED & BREAKFASTS

Anaconda
& **Hickory House Inn Bed & Breakfast** (406-563-5481; www .hickoryhouseinn.com), 608 Hickory Street. This romantic place is in historic downtown Anaconda. The three-story brick Victorian home was once a parish for the nearby St. Paul's Church. Today, the rooms are decorated in Victorian style and this is a great jumping-off point for exploring the area around Anaconda. They all offer package deals for skiers and anglers. Rates run from $80 to $100 a night.

Mill Creek Lodging (406-560-7666; www.millcreekldoging.com). This is a nice spot away from town, yet just close enough. Please contact them for specific directions. Guests stay in the White House, which has a large living area with a wood-burning stove. The upstairs offers a bedroom that sleeps two to four guests, with a private bath. There are front and back porches where guests can sit and enjoy the wildlife. The 20-acre property has several aspen groves and a small spring. Mill Creek is nearby, and the Mount Haggin Wildlife Management Area is

0.25 mile away. The White House also can be used as a rest stop or trail-riding opportunity for people traveling with horses. Well-mannered dogs are welcome here as well. There are five indoor stalls, two 5-acre pastures, and four 48-foot pipe corrals for housing horses. Rates start at $70 per night.

Boulder

See Boulder Hot Springs Inn and Conference Center under *To Do–Hot Springs*.

Butte

&. **Toad Hall Manor Bed & Breakfast** (406-494-2625; www.toadhall manor.com), 1 Green Lane. Toad Hall Manor is a wonderful place for a relaxing change of pace, celebrating a special occasion, or a romantic getaway. So what's with the name? It is from the classic, *Wind in the Willows*. There are many rooms in this lovely restored B&B. The manor is 11,000 square feet on five levels. Marble and granite richly accent each floor, even that of the high-speed hydraulic elevator. The manor is ideally appointed for the vacationer and business traveler. There are two large wood-burning fireplaces, four TVs, VCRs, DVD player, a library of movies, in-room massages, and free off-site gym facilities. Rates $99 a night and up.

See also Copper King Mansion under *To See–Historic Landmarks, Places, and Sites*.

Dillon

&. **The Centennial Inn** (406-683-4454), 122 S. Washington in downtown Dillon. This 1905 Queen Anne–style Victorian house has four bedrooms, each with private bathroom. Period furnishings are in each room, including claw-foot bathtubs

and pedestal sinks. A full breakfast is offered each morning and you can book afternoon tea if you wish. Dinner is available, but this place is within walking distance of several places to eat in Dillon. Rates $80 a night.

&. **River's Edge Bed & Breakfast** (406-683-6214; www.riversedgelodge bandb.com), 765 Henneberry. Located outside of Dillon along the Beaverhead River. This intimate B&B offers riverside lodging on a scenic stretch of the river, yet close to town. They also can board horses for anyone traveling with their own equines. There is a small pond on the property available for fishing as well. Rates $125 and up.

Ennis

&. **The 9T9 Guest Ranch and B&B** (406-682-7659; www.9t9ranch.com), 99 Gravelly Range Road. Located 10 miles south of Ennis, overlooking the Madison River, this place's setting is stunning—peaks of the Gravelly, Tobacco Root, and Madison Ranges and the Madison River are the backdrop for this comfy ranch and B&B. The hosts here are a great resource for exploring the area. Rates $75 a night.

Helena

Barrister Bed & Breakfast (406-443-7330; www.thebarristermt.tripod .com), 416 N. Ewing in downtown Helena. The Barrister offers intimate elegance in a 1874 Victorian three-story mansion, listed on the National Register of Historic Places. The five guest bedrooms are spacious and carefully decorated to provide an intimate atmosphere, as well as warmth and comfort. All rooms have private baths, color TV, and queen-size beds. A full breakfast for two is included, which may be served in the dining room or on the sunporch. The backyard now has a spacious patio and waterfall. Rates $115 a night.

Sanders Bed & Breakfast (406-442-3309; www.sandersbb.com 328 N. Ewing, downtown Helena. This elegant B&B is filled with the rich history of Montana's territorial days and community life in the state's capital city in the late 1800s. From flyfishers to senators to teachers to anyone looking to enjoy Montana, the Sander's enjoys a great reputation around Helena and the surrounding community. The Queen Ann–style home, built in 1875, is listed on the National Register of Historic Places. Each guest room has a private bath, telephone, television, and DSL, along with charming views of the surrounding mountains and valley. Guests enjoy afternoon refreshments and a full gourmet breakfast. Rates $130 and up.

Philipsburg

♿ **Big Horn Bed & Breakfast** (406-859-3109; www.bighornmontana .com), 31 Lower Rock Creek Road. Nestled in a mountain setting on Rock Creek 15 miles west of Philipsburg, the log home features a large living and dining area with a fireplace and decks. There are two beautiful guest rooms with a shared bath. The breakfasts in the morning are a great way to start your day. You may choose to dine in the dining room or enjoy the brisk morning air on the sundeck. At day's end, when a delightful evening meal is desired, Philipsburg is only minutes away. Rates $75 and up. They also have a few private cabins.

Quigley Cottage (406-859-3812; www.philipsburgbb.com), 418 W. Broadway Street. Open April through December. This place is right in the heart of Philipsburg, but very close to everything outdoors. There are four guest rooms and a large gathering room with fireplace, antiques, plants, and collectibles. The surrounding property includes gardens and patios to enjoy in the summer months. Hearty, sumptuous breakfasts are served every morning. Rates $65 and up.

Polaris

See Elkhorn Hot Springs under *To Do–Hot Springs.*

Twin Bridges

⦿ **The Old Hotel** (406-684-5959; www.theoldhotel.com), 101 E. Main St., Twin Bridges. The Old Hotel, once the Twin Bridges Hotel, built in 1879, sits on the corner of Fifth and Main in downtown Twin Bridges. This historic three-story brick building was beautifully renovated in 1996 and still retains much of its original charm, as seen in the hardwood floors, staircases, doors, and architecture. The hotel is now a restaurant as well as a B&B catering to anyone desiring a quiet, clean, and friendly place to stay. The hosts are wonderfully friendly and will assist in any way they can. Rates $125 a night.

Virginia City

☯ **Bennet House Country Inn** (406-843-5220; www.bennetthouse inn.com), 115 E. Idaho. In an area steeped in history, you should stay in a historic building, and this one is perfect: built in 1879, yet fully restored. There are six rooms and a log cabin. Located within walking distance of all that is Virginia City, this is an ideal place for a large family or a romantic couple wanting a taste of Montana history. Rates $80 and up.

♿ **Just an Experience** (406-843-5402; www.justanexperience.com),

1570 MT 287. If the name is not intriguing enough, this is both a fun place to spend the night and a great place to delight your palate. Originally built in 1864, this log house has three rooms with queen beds. Or you can choose to stay in some newer cabins, all with private baths. A full breakfast is included with fresh fruits. A favorite is their stuffed French toast with raspberry compote. Rates $75 a night.

& **Stonehouse Inn** (406-843-5504; www.stonehouseinnbb.com), 306 E. Idaho. This 1884 Victorian is listed on the National Register of Historic Places. Originally the home of a blacksmith who settled in the area, it now includes five bedrooms with a shared bath. Each room is decorated with lots of antiques and brass beds. A full, made-to-order breakfast is included with each room. Rates $75 a night.

Wolf Creek

The Bungalow Bed & Breakfast (406-235-4276; www.bungalowbandb .com), 900 Bungalow Drive. This B&B, tucked into a very scenic draw, is minutes from the Missouri River. Built by Charles Power in 1913, the lodge is on the National Register and deserves a night or two. They also have a cabin on the property that is ideal for larger groups. The breakfasts are filling and in the evening you can literally watch the deer and antelope play while sitting on the front porch—that is, if you're not casting to rising trout on the Missouri. Rates $80 and up.

LODGES, GUEST RANCHES, AND HOTELS/MOTELS

Alder

See Broken Arrow Lodge and Outfitters under *To Do–Horseback Riding* and Upper Canyon Lodge and Outfitters and Rocking Z Guest Ranch under *To Do–Unique Adventures.*

Anaconda

Georgetown Lake Lodge (406-563-7020; www.georgetownlakelodge .com), 2015 Georgetown Lake Road. If you are planning to ski at Discovery Basin Ski Area, fish the area's lakes, or hike in the Beaverhead-Deerlodge National Forest, this is a great place to stay. There are 11 rooms, all with two double beds and satellite television. The rates here are very reasonable (around $85/night), and there is a full-service lodge on-site. In fact, they even offer weekly specials like prime rib on the weekends or taco Tuesday, where you can get tacos for two dollars.

Ennis

⌐ **Madison Valley Ranch** (1-800-891-6158; www.madisonvalleyranch .com), 307 Jeffers Road, 3 miles north of Ennis off US 287. The husband and wife team of Scott and Elizabeth Warren run this lodge, set alongside the Madison River. The views from the guest rooms are fantastic, the food is some of the best in the valley, and they even have a trout pond on the property. All rooms have their own private entrance, porch, and private baths. With complimentary beer and wine included with your stay, it is no mystery why this place books up early. They can offer all-inclusive packages or cater to one-night folks. Inquire about rates, as they vary based on season and options.

& **El Western Inn and Cabins** (406-682-4217; www.elwestern.com), located just across the river from downtown Ennis on US 287. The El

Western captures the spirit of Old West hospitality and style, but they rub off the rough edges with fluffy pillows and beautifully appointed log cabins. They have inexpensive cabins that work well for folks on a budget and larger lodges/cabins for bigger groups. There are even a few creek-side cabins for travelers who like to fall asleep to the sound of a bubbling brook. Its location near Ennis makes the El Western a great choice for families who want to feel closer to town—which would be especially nice during the Ennis Rodeo or the Madison River Fly-Fishing Festival.

Fairmont (between Butte and Anaconda)
See Fairmont Hot Springs Resort under *To Do–Hot Springs.*

Jackson
See Jackson Hot Springs Lodge under *To Do–Hot Springs.*

Helena
Lodgepole Inn (406-492-7743; www .lodgepoleinn.com). The Lodgepole Inn is nestled along the Little Blackfoot River only a mile from the Continental Divide. You can enjoy fishing, hiking, cross-country skiing, and more, all without ever having to leave the lodge. A short drive over the Divide puts you in Helena, with all its history and amenities. This is a great place to kick back and relax in the Montana wilds. Rates $95 per night.

Ovando
The Blackfoot Inn (406-793-5555; www.blackfoot-inn.com), 722 Pine St. This place is a true Montana secret that is slowly being discovered. The hosts are some of the nicest people in the entire state. There are five rooms, each with a private bath, and great views of the valley. A full breakfast comes with each room and the price is hard to beat. The inn sits in the heart of the Blackfoot Valley and is a great place to enjoy the various recreational opportunities in the valley, from hiking, fishing, and horseback riding in summer to snowmobiling and cross-country skiing in winter. The only complaint most folks have about the Blackfoot Inn: They wished they would have found out about it sooner.

Philipsburg
&. ✍ **The Inn at Philipsburg** (406-859-3959; www.theinn-philipsburg .com), 915 W. Broadway. This inn is family owned and operated. They also offer tent camping and RV hook-ups. This is a clean and very reasonably priced place to stay when skiing at Discovery or stopping along the Anaconda-Pintler Scenic Highway. The inn is within walking distance of Philipsburg's historic district. The hosts are very friendly and enjoy sharing their special piece of Montana with their guests. Pets are always welcome, as the owners have friendly dogs. Rates $75 and up.

Red Rock Lakes
Elk Lake Resort (406-276-3282; www.elklakeresortmontana.com). Take Exit 0 off I-15 at the Montana-Idaho border and go 37 miles on Red Rock Pass Road to Elk Lake Road, then north 6 miles to Elk Lake Resort on a rough road. This lodge lies on the shores of Elk Lake and borders the **Red Rock Lakes National Wildlife Refuge.** This is a full-service resort located a long way off the beaten path. There are seven cabins, each with its own style and amenities, but all with private baths, at least one queen-size bed, down comforters, and propane heaters.

There is a good restaurant on-site that serves large, tasty meals. If you are going just for food be sure to make reservations. Recreational options in and around the resort include paddling, fishing, hiking, birding, and wildlife watching. Rates $80 and up.

Three Forks

& **Sacajawea Hotel** (406-285-6515; www.sacajaweahotel.com), 5 North Main Street. The Sacajawea Hotel offers gracious accommodations in 31 guest rooms, each with TV, private bath, and telephone. The hotel was named after the famous Shoshone guide woman who led the Lewis & Clark Expedition through the area in 1805. It was founded in 1910 by John Q. Adams (no relation to the former president) to serve passengers and the crew of the Milwaukee Railroad. When rail service to Three Forks was discontinued, the Sacajawea Inn found itself in the unenviable position of being a railroad hotel without a railroad, yet it has survived nicely. The Sac, as locals call it, is an ideal place to base for exploring most, if not all, of Gold West Country. Rates $90 a night.

Twin Bridges

& **Kings Motel** (406-684-5639; www.kingsflatline.com), 307 S. Main St. Owner Matt Greemore and his family have ranched and worked in Twin Bridges for generations. Their motel, at the confluence of the Big Hole and Beaverhead Rivers, provides very reasonably priced rooms in the heart of the region's best outdoor recreation. With 12 rooms, all creatively unique in décor and layout, this place is ideal for couples, families, and larger groups. Each room has a kitchen, high-speed Internet, satellite TV, and

coffee. This place was built to be a friendly, accommodating home-away-from-home. Rates $60 and up.

OTHER OPTIONS ✿ **National Forest Cabins** (1-877-444-6777; www.reserveusa.com). A unique recreation experience within the Beaverhead-Deerlodge and Helena National Forests is the opportunity to rent a historic fire lookout or backcountry cabin. These rustic cabins and lookouts are in remote, yet spectacular settings. They are rented on a first-come, first-served basis and may be reserved through the National Recreation Reservation System. To check availability and reserve a facility, visit the central reservations office listed above.

Where to Eat

DINING OUT

Butte

✿ **After Five** (406-723-5031), 1815 Harrison Ave. The owner, Mark Sanderson, is a very talented restaurateur. He makes one of the best martinis in the state and will keep any bar patron entertained with his lively personality. You will be treated like family here—from the friendly and efficient service to the jokes Mark is known to tell at the bar. His Twenty Under Twenty wine list offers a great selection to complement an even better menu. Their specialty is steak and they do it right, an art slowly dying as more chain restaurants move into Montana. For dessert, try the deep-fried Oreo cookies.

✐ **Derby Steak House** (406-723-9086) 2016 Harrison Avenue. This award-winning restaurant serves some of the best surf and turf around.

Everything on the menu is guaranteed fresh and it's all prepared on the premises. If you want seafood this is the best place in Butte for salmon and lobster tail. This is also a good place for children as the kids' menu is varied enough that even the pickiest of eaters will find something.

Uptown Café (406-723-4735; www.uptowncafe.com), 47 E. Broadway. This is more than just a café—it is a legitimate fine-dining experience where creativity and passion for interesting and gourmet meals reign over steaks and chops. Lunches are great, but it is the dinners that often draw people from as far away as Missoula and Helena. A nice thing about the Uptown is the early bird specials. If you dine before 6:30 you get lower prices. As with a lot of great places, be sure to leave plenty of room for dessert. You will also find that the Uptown Café has been featured in many national and regional culinary magazines and newspapers—it's that good.

Ennis

&. **Continental Divide** (406-682-7600), 315 East Main Street. Since its opening in 1982, the Continental Divide has become one of the most widely acclaimed restaurants in the Northwest. Long a favorite of anglers who fish the Madison River, the restaurant has been the subject of numerous articles and reviews in major newspapers and magazines. Essentially a country bistro, the food and ambiance are unpretentious, with an emphasis on fresh ingredients and creative concepts. From veal chops to fresh seafood, the menu draws upon French, Italian, and regional influences to offer the diner a wide choice

of options. Blue jeans, tuxedos, and waders are the common attire—leave your ties at home.

Dillon

Blacktail Station (406-683-6611), 26 S. Montana Street. This place is down a flight of stairs, underneath Mac's Last Cast bar—a place worth stopping in itself. But the Blacktail is anything but a dark and seedy basement. It has been discovered and provides great food in a unique atmosphere. Jerry and Shelly will make you feel at home, and the paintings on the walls will give you something to talk about while you're waiting for your steak or chicken. The sides that come with your meal are plentiful, especially the twice-baked potato. There are lots of dessert options as well.

Fairmont

See Fairmont Hot Springs Resort under *To Do–Hot Springs*.

Helena

Benny's Bistro (406-443-0105), 108 E. 6th Avenue. This is the best place in Helena if you want tantalizing food made fresh from mostly local, organic ingredients. They serve light breakfasts, varied and hearty lunches, and creatively prepared and designed dinners in historic downtown Helena. Benny's specializes in regional American bistro cuisine, meticulously handmade food featuring all-natural ingredients and locally grown meats, poultry, and produce whenever possible. Save room for their desserts, too.

Lucca's at the Carriage House (406-457-8311), 234½ Lyndale Avenue. This small place (be sure to make reservations) creates filling, yet gourmet dishes. Their specialty is pasta, but their steaks and lamb chops are local favorites. They also have nightly specials that delight the taste buds. They serve dinner only and are only open Wednesday through Sunday, so be sure to plan ahead and call for a table. They also offer a Price Fixe menu for those who may have a hard time deciding exactly what is best.

On Broadway (406-443-1929), 106 Broadway. This upscale dining establishment prides itself on its service and atmosphere, as well as its food quality. It has been in Helena longer than most other restaurants, and for good reason—great dining and very reasonable prices. The same meal in New York or San Francisco would cost $100. The menu is a nice combination of seafood, steaks, and pasta dishes. There are also a number of vegetarian entrees and a weekly vegetarian special. The wine list is broad and prices for bottled wines are reasonable. The restaurant is smoke free.

Lakeside

Lakeside on Hauser (406-227-6076), 5295 York Road; 11 miles east of Helena on York Road in the small marina community of Lakeside. This fine-dining experience is well worth the drive and the extra time to find. The setting along the shores of Hauser Lake, especially in summer, is hard to beat. Enjoy menu items such as seared ahi, capped mushrooms, and more, as you enjoy the sunset on the Lake.

See also Wagon-Ride Dinners at the Moose Meadow Tipi under *To Do–Unique Adventures*.

Jackson

See Jackson Hot Springs Lodge under *To Do–Hot Springs*.

Three Forks

& **Sacajawea Hotel** (406-285-6515; www.sacajaweahotel.com), 5 North Main Street. The Sac offers fine dining and pub fare in a historic setting. The dining room here is a fun place to enjoy a well-cooked steak, perhaps topped off with a lobster tail.

EATING OUT

Anaconda

& ✐ **Donivans Family Dining** (406-563-6241), 211 East Park. Enjoy good old-fashioned home cooking in a unique rustic atmosphere. They also feature homemade pies, cinnamon rolls, and delicious soups every day. This is a good place for the entire family; the kids can fill up on chicken strips and adults can choose from a wide menu with everything from prime rib to burgers to massive salads.

Rose's Tea Room and Parlor (406-563-5060), 303 E. Park. This is a fun place to sit down for a snack, light breakfast, or lunch. It is decorated in Victorian fashion, and you can choose from a wide selection of teas to enjoy with your meal. The breads are made fresh. Before or after your meal, be sure to take a gander at the antiques.

See also Georgetown Lake Lodge under *Lodging–Lodges*.

Butte

& ✐ **MacKenzie River Pizza Company** (406-782-0020), 1925 Elizabeth Warren Avenue. This is part of the chain of Montana pizza companies. They offer gourmet pizzas (plus many traditional varieties) in a very casual environment. The menu includes sandwiches and salads as well—a great combo is the Taos Salad along with any of their fresh pizzas.

Paul Bunyan's Sandwich Shop (406-723-7817), 605 W. Park. This is a good place to get a filling lunch to go if you are heading out for a day of walking the historic streets of Butte or driving the Anaconda-Pintler Scenic Highway. The bread comes from a local bakery, and they use plenty of quality meats.

See also Uptown Café under *Dining Out.*

Dillon

Ġ **Longhorn Saloon** (406-683-6839), 8 N. Montana Street. This family-run steakhouse in downtown Dillon is surprisingly good. The staff is very friendly and genuinely interested in meeting new people. There are some fun things about this place, mainly the interesting mix of folks who dine here. You will see ranchers, business folks, college students, travelers, ranchers, anglers—the whole shooting match. Plus (and for some this is a hit, others a turnoff), the walls are adorned with trophy mounts of elk, deer, and even longhorn cattle.

Deer Lodge

Ġ ♪ **Scharf's Family Restaurant** (406-846-3300), 819 Main Street. Scharf's caters to all kinds of appetites and is a good spot to refuel if you have been visiting Deer Lodge area historical sites. Family dining is accompanied by a view of the Montana Territorial Prison museum across the street and beautiful Mount Powell to the west. Western ambiance for comfortable dining and the area's "come as you are" attitude make for a nice dining experience in which you feel like you are among friends.

Fairmont

See Fairmont Hot Springs Resort under *To Do–Hot Springs.*

Helena

Bert and Ernie's (406-443-5680), 361 North Last Chance Gulch. Located on historic Last Chance Gulch, they offer a friendly and casual atmosphere for residents and visitors to Montana's capital city. The menu ranges from a tasty Cajun Fowl Burger, an Ensalada Taquito, and hormone-free Montana beef to pasta, pizzas, subs, burgers, and salads. Bert and Ernie's is a family-friendly restaurant, offering a reasonably priced children's menu. All of this is offered in a smoke-free environment. **Bleachers,** their pizza parlor, is upstairs and serves some of the best pizza in town.

Ġ ♪ **Brewhouse Pub and Grill** (406-457-9390), 939½ Getchell Street. With a great mix of pub food and fine dining, they have something for everyone—burgers, pizza, salads, pastas, steak, seafood, and more. Try the beer-battered onion rings as a starter, or top off a meal with a slice of cheesecake. Relaxed and informal, they are known for the consistent quality of food, friendly and attentive service, and fresh beer. And don't let the "brewhouse" nature of the place fool you; this is a great place for kids as the bar area is separate from the main dining room and the entire establishment is smoke free.

Karmadillos Southwestern Café (406-442-2595), 139 Reeders Alley. Located with a great view of historic Last Chance Gulch, this hip and trendy place is small in winter but large in summer, when you will most likely dine outside to enjoy the view. Their slow-cooked pork is fabulous, their tortilla soup is unique to Montana, and they offer plentiful salads. Hours vary seasonally.

& **No Sweat Café** (406-442-6954), 427 North Last Chance Gulch. They describe themselves as "fine bohemian dining" and they are right and wrong, as the food is great, the company stimulating, and the coffee hot and plentiful. This is a great place for breakfast or lunch if you have time to relax and have plenty of conversation ideas—patrons must check their cell phones at the door.

✎ **Taco Del Sol** (406-443-3978), 101 North Last Chance Gulch. This is a colorful place and great for kids—the atmosphere is fun and festive and the prices very reasonable. They serve Mission-style burritos, tacos, fish burritos, and fish tacos. Mexican sodas, fruit nectars, and horchata are also available. In summer, they have an outdoor patio.

Lincoln

& **Lambkins Restaurant** (406-362-4271), 460 Main Street. The food here is served fast and with friendly service. The menu is classic small-town Montana fare—biscuits and gravy, burgers, steaks. However, this place is worth a stop, especially for the pies. Situated on the main drag in Lincoln, they are usually busy with hungry customers, but the well-trained staff keeps the tables turning and the guests happy. And you won't leave hungry.

Marysville

✎ **The Marysville House** (406-443-6677), 153 Main Street. It is too bad this place isn't closer to a larger town, but then it would be packed with people all the time. Instead, this cozy and

rustic place is a hidden gem among true-grit Montana places. Enjoy a unique, one-of-a-kind dining experience in a historic ghost town while eating dinner on picnic tables next to a cozy fire. Afterwards, play a game of horseshoes and roast marshmallows around the bonfire. The menu is simple and usually written on a chalkboard in the dining room. It consists mainly of T-bone, other steaks, pork loin, chicken, crab legs, lobster, various seafood skillets, and a vegetarian option.

Ovando

✪ **Trixi's Antler Saloon** (406-793-5611; www.ovando.net/businesses/trix-is.php), MT 200; you can't miss it. Trixi's is the Blackfoot Valley's best-known landmark, a diner and bar named after the former trick rider, roper, and showgirl who bought it in the 1950s. This place has a far-reaching reputation as a real Montana establishment. The atmosphere is always warm, friendly, and inviting. The menu is varied, from the 32-ounce T-bones to veggie burgers and everything in between. At this unique place you can listen to a local rancher visit with a couple from Germany bicycling to Alaska. You can see the dance floor sway and bend with the crowd at the 3rd of July dance. The bar comes with tractor-seat stools, and sits alongside the newly refurbished dining room. When you enter, you suspect you've stepped back into the early 20th century.

Philipsburg

& ✎ **The Sweet Palace** (406-793-3896; www.sweetpalace.com), 109 E. Broadway. This restored 1890 building just might house the largest candy store in Montana. Families bring kids from as far away as Bozeman for a stop here—regretting the sugar crash on the ride home. For nearly half a century the owners have been creating cavities in the form of sweets in all shapes and sizes. There are more than 750 varieties of homemade confections, including 72 flavors of saltwater taffy, more than 30 varieties of fudge, Moose Drool truffles, and plenty of sugar-free selections as well.

Townsend

♿ **Cowboy Coffee and Steakhouse** (406-266-3348), 316 North Front Street. The Cowboy Coffee and Steakhouse began as a small coffee shop and quickly outgrew the old location. Requests for breakfast, lunch, and dinner were noted, and for the past two years the current owner has fed happy customers. The menu features homemade soups, pies, and a variety of desserts. Daily lunch specials are complemented by the steak and seafood specials every Friday and Saturday nights. Stop in and you'll see that they are more than just coffee.

Virginia City

♿ ☏ **Roadmaster Grille** (406-843-5234; www.roadmastergrille.com), 124 W. Wallace Street. This place used to be an automobile service station (a little departure from the rootin'-tootin' days of the Old West normally celebrated in this former capital of the Montana Territory), and you will find vintage automobiles like a 1950s Buick Roadmaster. As far as the food goes, there is a self-service salad bar with all the fixings—but it is located in the back of a 1948 Chevrolet Thriftmaster pickup truck. The owners here are creative and they have put as much emphasis on the food as they have on the atmosphere—it is

good, there is plenty of it, and adults and kids will all enjoy it.

Star Bakery Restaurant (406-843-5525), 1585 US 287; located 1.35 miles west of Virginia City. This place has been a bakery since the 1860s (give or take a few years). Back then, they were known for serving bread, beer, and "vittles." Today you can enjoy full breakfasts, lunch fare, and dinners in this historic setting. This is also probably the best place for barbecue in Beaverhead County.

Wisdom

♿ **Fetty's Bar and Café** (406-689-3260), MT 43. Fetty's is known for large portions, home cooking, and friendly service. Bring your appetite and your smile because no one is a stranger here. If you are heading out for a day of exploring the Nez Perce National Trail or the Big Hole Battlefield, Fetty's should be in your plans. For dinner, try the country-fried steak with mashed potatoes and gravy. If you are hiking or cross-country skiing, try a club sandwich or a bowl of their homemade hot soup.

✳ Special Events

January: **Cool Dog Ball and Microbrew Review** (406-538-8841), Helena. Come support the Race to the Sky (see below) and sample some of the region's best microbrews. Live music and plenty of tasty adult beverages make for a fun way to kick off Montana's largest sled-dog race.

February: ☏ ☏ **Race to the Sky** (www.race2sky.com), Helena and Lincoln. Annual 350-mile sled-dog race from outside Helena to Seeley Lake.

Chocolate Festival, Anaconda. Local stores must give away chocolates to all customers or face a fine from the local constable: held in conjunction with the **Antique Quilt Exhibit and Bake Sale.**

March: ✍ **St. Patrick's Day,** Butte. Everyone should experience this at least once. There really is nothing like it in the country, except for Mardi Gras—and that is exactly what this is, Mardi Gras, Montana style.

April: ⛸ ✍ **Madison River Music Festival** (www.madisonrivermusic festival.com), Ennis. A two-day musical celebration with a different theme each year.

Walk Away from Winter, Deer Lodge. Come to the Grant-Kohrs Ranch and shake off those winter blues and take part in the bird walk or nature walk or a 4-mile run to celebrate the onset of spring.

May: ✍ **Race for the Cure,** Helena. This benefit footrace for the Komen Foundation raises funds to provide positive awareness, education, and early detection of breast cancer for women throughout Montana, as well as helping to fund the National Grants program for the Komen Foundation.

June: ✍ **Gold Rush Fever Days,** Virginia City. A celebration of the area's mining past with a parade, gold panning, and more.

✍ **Governor's Cup Road Race,** Helena. This premier road-racing event brings serious and casual runners from all corners of the country. Races range from a 5K up to a full marathon.

✍ **Montana Mule Days,** Drummond. A donkey and mule exhibit featuring events pitting animals against (no physical contact) each other in a variety of skills, a parade, food, and more.

July: ✍ **Last Chance Stampede and Fair,** Helena. One of the largest rodeos in the state, along with a carnival, livestock shows, dances, and more.

✍ **Bannack Days,** Bannack. Return to the early days in Montana's history with a celebration of mining and life in Montana's first territorial capital.

August: ✍ **Anaconda Crazy Days,** Anaconda. An annual day of wacky and crazy things in Anaconda, including a tour of historic bars, a watermelon-eating contest, food vendors, car show, live music, and more.

Heritage Days and Victorian Ball, Virginia City. Celebrate the elegant past of this mining town with a costume ball and more.

✍ **Beaverhead County Lewis & Clark Festival,** Dillon. Weeklong celebrations commemorate the passage of Lewis & Clark through this area, with reenactments, food, crafts, educational tours, music, and more.

Western Rendezvous of Art, Helena. A massive art show and celebration of western art and artists.

September: ✍ **Beaverhead County Fair,** Dillon. An annual Labor Day event that includes a large rodeo, art festival, parade, pancake breakfast, and more.

Ennis Fly-Fishing Festival, Ennis. A three-day event celebrating the fly-fishing industry and lifestyle on the Madison River.

October: **Ghost Walks Bannack,** Bannack. Join specially trained paranormal investigators on a journey to find and photograph ghosts in this ghost town.

𝄢 **Townsend Fall Fest,** Townsend. A little bit of everything with lots of old-fashioned fun for the entire family. They block off Main Street and have a good ole block party.

December: 𝄢 **Victorian Christmas at Grant-Kohrs Ranch,** Deer Lodge. A family-oriented holiday festival with children's activities, music, and decorations.

Original Governor's Mansion Holiday Home Tour, Helena. Tour Montana's original Governor's mansion, as well as other historic homes in Helena decked out in holiday attire. This is an annual fundraiser for the Original Governor's Mansion restoration projects.

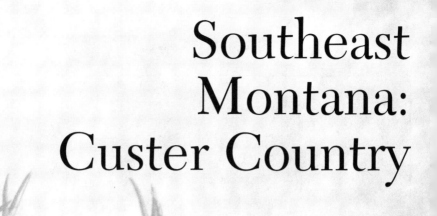

Southeast Montana: Custer Country

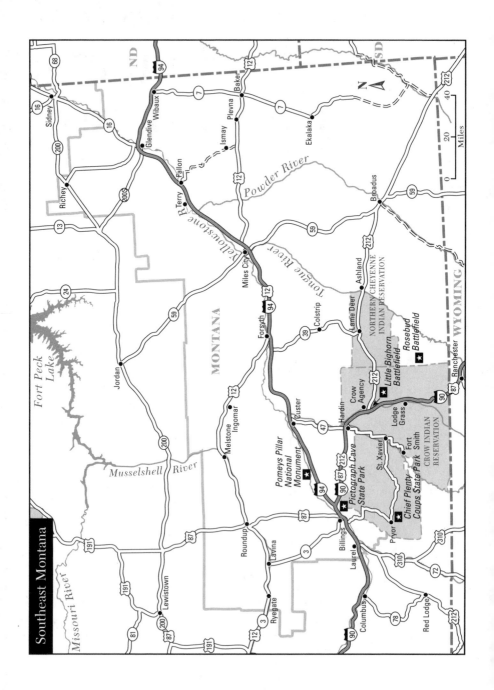

Southeast Montana

SOUTHEAST MONTANA: CUSTER COUNTRY

This region of Montana takes its namesake from Lieutenant Colonel George Armstrong Custer. In the summer of 1876 Custer and his troops and members of the Lakota Sioux, Cheyenne, and Arapaho Indian tribes all shed blood at the Battle of the Little Bighorn—commemorated today at the Little Bighorn Battlefield National Monument.

This is a huge area: with 36,500 square miles, 360 miles of interstate, 950 miles of paved state roads, and countless scenic county roads. Wide-open spaces mark this region as the High Plains, and the wide, cottonwood-lined river bottoms and vast rangeland reveal the subtle roughness of Custer Country. This region is full of pioneer and Native American history, wildlife, arts and culture, and more.

In addition to the Little Bighorn Battlefield National Monument, there are numerous other historic pioneer and Native American sites in this region. And Native Americans continue to play a prominent role here today. The Chief Joseph and Nez Perce Trails passed through this region, which is also home to the Crow Indian Reservation and the Northern Cheyenne Indian Reservation. On these reservations visitors can enjoy powwows, fishing, camping, and hiking and can partake in various cultural activities. Always inquire locally for any necessary permits before venturing onto tribal lands.

Other historical features include several U.S. military–Native American battlefields, Chief Plenty Coups State Park, Pictograph State Park, the 1806 return route of William Clark and Pompeys Pillar, the Bozeman Trail (more than 3,000 gold seekers passed through from 1864 to 1866), and many local museums.

History and museums could take up nearly all of your vacation time in this region (and is that a bad thing?). These museums are abundant and varied. Most have Native American artifacts and exhibits featuring frontier life. Some of the more obscure exhibits include the Steer Montana, where the world's largest steer is enshrined at the O'Fallon County Museum, the 22,000 seashells at Mac's Museum, the Montana Dinosaur Trail (not that obscure, but unique), and more. What will surprise you are the two art museums in the region—the Custer

County Art & Heritage Center in Miles City and the Yellowstone Art Museum and Western Heritage Center in Billings. Both house world-class art collections.

Billings is the state's largest city. Founded in 1877 as a stage stop, the area was traditionally home to the Crow Indian Tribe. The setting on the banks of the Yellowstone River, and near the Pryor, Bighorn, and Beartooth Mountains, made it an ideal place for water, game, and wild fruit. Soon the railroad came to Billings and the town boomed as the Chicago, Quincy, and Burlington lines joined the Northern Pacific. Today the city is still Montana's leader in shipping cattle and other agricultural products. It is also a hub for transportation, energy, medicine, education, cultural resources, and outdoor recreation.

Fishing on the Yellowstone and Bighorn Rivers is very accessible, and enjoyed by many who live in or visit this region. On the Yellowstone near Glendive you might even try your hand at catching a paddlefish—a massive prehistoric fish present in only a few rivers in the world. Ranch vacations are also prevalent in this region. The Custer National Forest offers hiking, camping, wildlife viewing, and more. Miles of shoreline and breathtaking scenery can be enjoyed at Bighorn Canyon National Recreation Area. And the badlands at Makoshika State Park provide a striking contrast to the High Plains.

Getting around in Custer Country's wide-open spaces is easy, but leaving is not, as the history, recreation, amenities, and more will keep you plenty busy.

GUIDANCE Baker Chamber of Commerce (406-778-2266; www.bakermt .com), P.O. Box 849, Baker 59313.

Billings Chamber of Commerce and Visitor Center (406-245-4111; www .itsinbillings.com), 815 27th Street, Billings 59107.

Carter County Chamber of Commerce (406-755-8724; www.midrivers .com~commerce), P.O. Box 108, Ekalaka 59324.

Colstrip Chamber of Commerce (406-748-8724; www.colstrip.com), 400 Woodrose Street, P.O. Box 430, Colstrip 59323.

Crow Tribe of Indians (406-638-3700; www.crownations.net), Bacheeitche Avenue, P.O. Box 159, Crow Agency 59022.

Custer Country (406-778-3336; www.custervisitmt.com), P.O. Box 1151, Baker 59313.

Forsyth Chamber of Commerce (406-347-5656; www.forsythmontana.org), P.O. Box 448, Forsyth 59327.

Glendive Chamber of Commerce (406-377-5601; www.glendivechamber .com), 313 S. Merrill, Glendive 59330.

Hardin Chamber of Commerce and Agriculture (406-665-1672; www .hardinmtchamber.com), 10 East Railway, Hardin 59034.

Hysham Chamber of Commerce (406-342-5457; www.hysham.org), P.O. Box 63, Hysham 59038.

Laurel Chamber of Commerce (406-628-8105; www.laurelmontana.org), 108 East Main Street, Laurel 59044.

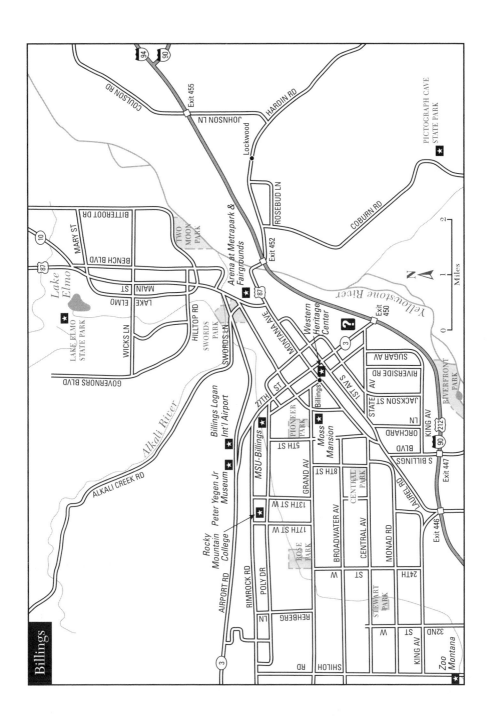

Billings

Miles City Chamber of Commerce (406-234-2890; www.mcchamber.com), 511 Pleasant Street, Miles City 59301.

Northern Cheyenne Chamber of Commerce (406-477-8844; www .ncheyenne.net), P.O. Box 991 Lame Deer 59043.

Powder River Chamber of Commerce (406-436-2778), 119 E. Wilson Street, P.O. Box 484, Broadus 59317.

Prairie County Chamber of Commerce (406-635-4770), P.O. Box 667, Terry 59349.

Roundup and Musselshell Valley Chamber of Commerce (406-323-1966; www.roundupchamber.net), P.O. Box 751, Roundup 59072.

Wibaux County of Commerce (406-796-2414), P.O. Box 159, Wibaux 59353.

GETTING THERE As you can see, Billings is the hub of this region, but the smaller towns are quite easy to find. Billings lies at the junction of I-90, I-94, and US 87. Laurel is west of Billing on I-90 and US 212. Hardin and Crow Agency lie on I-90 east of Billings. Roundup is north of Billings on US 87. Hysham is east of Billings on I-94. Miles City lies on I-94 east of Billings, where MT 59 and US 12 meet I-94. Terry, Glendive, and Wibaux are all east of Miles City on I-94. Baker is at the junction of MT 7 and US 12. Forsyth is west of Miles City on I-90 or US 12.

See also *Airports* and *Bus Service* in "What's Where in Montana."

DOWNTOWN BILLINGS

MEDICAL EMERGENCIES Big Horn County Memorial Hospital (406-665-2310), 17 N. Mile Avenue, Hardin.

Colstrip Medical Center (406-748-3600), 6230 Main Street, Colstrip.

Dahl Memorial Healthcare Association (406-775-8730), 225 Sandy Street, Ekalaka.

Deaconess Hospital (406-657-4000), 2800 10th Avenue N., Billings.

Fallon Medical Complex (406-778-3331), 202 S. 4th Street W., Baker.

Glendive Medical Center (406-365-3306), 202 Prospect Drive, Glendive.

Holy Rosary Healthcare (406-233-2600), 260 Wilson Street, Miles City.

Powder River Medical Clinic (406-436-2333), 102 E. Morris, Broadus.

Prairie Community Medical Assistance Facility (406-635-5511), 12 MT 253, Terry.

Rosebud Health Care Hospital (406-356-2161), 383 N. 17th Avenue, Forsyth.

Roundup Memorial Hospital (406-323-2301), 1202 3rd Street W., Roundup.

St. Vincent Healthcare (406-657-7000), 1233 N. 30th Street, Billings.

✳ To See

TOWNS Baker lies at the intersection of US 12 and MT 7. This tiny crossroads of a town is big on outdoor recreation. Boating, free camping, fishing, ice fishing, hunting, scenic vistas, and snowmobiling (when there is enough snow) can all be had at **Baker Lake.**

Colstrip, south of Forsyth on MT 39, is known more as the energy capital of Montana than anything else. Tours of the various energy plants and locales can be had by contacting the Colstrip Chamber of Commerce (see *Guidance*).

Crow Agency is located south of Hardin on I-90 and is the center of administration for the Crow Indian Reservation. The Crow tribe, also known as the **Absaalooke Nation,** lives mostly on the 2.3-million-acre reservation. Visitors can enjoy hiking, camping, fishing, hunting, and more, but please inquire locally for access and permits. (See Crow Country Tours under *To Do–Unique Adventures* and Crow Fair under *Special Events.*)

Ekalaka is south of Baker on MT 7. Named after the daughter of a well-respected Oglala Sioux chief, this small town is the closest town to the **Powder River Breaks.** This area also boasts the moniker, the **Bucking Horse Capital of the World.**

Hardin lies on I-90 sixty miles southeast of Billings. This slightly larger town, relatively speaking, is the closest town to the Little Bighorn Battlefield National Monument. Here you will find a small selection of lodging and dining options and the **Big Horn County Museum.** Hardin is also a good jumping-off point for venturing to the **Bighorn River** and the **Bighorn Canyon National Recreation Area.**

Hysham is located about 75 miles east of Billings on I-90. As the county seat of Treasure County, this rural farm and ranch community is a nice place to enjoy some solitude on the Yellowstone River. Camping, fishing, and boating can all be had in and around Hysham.

Laurel is about 10 miles west of Billings on I-90. It's home to the historic **Canyon Creek Battlefield;** a monument and exhibit are found in downtown Fireman's Park. Laurel also sits at the junction of I-90 and US 212—the highway to Red Lodge, the Beartooth Scenic Highway, and Yellowstone National Park.

MUSEUMS & **Big Horn County Historical Museum** (406-665-1671; www .museumonthebighorn.org), Route 1 Box 1206A (Exit 497 off I-90), Hardin. Open year-round, although the historic outbuildings are closed October to May. The center is open May through September, 8 A.M.–6 P.M., and October through April, 9 A.M.–5 P.M. Free admission. The museum complex consists of 20 historic structures, two exhibit buildings, and a main exhibit building, which features a rotating exhibit, offices, visitor center, and gift shop. This 22-acre site, once a flourishing vegetable farm, was donated in 1979 to the Big Horn County Historical Society for a museum. The farmhouse and barn are part of the original farm site. The other historic buildings have been moved to the museum from various locations in Big Horn County. As you walk on the boardwalk that leads to the museum buildings you will see items that belonged to the first hunters who roamed the High Plains in search of the buffalo, the traders and settlers who came in search of adventure, and the early-day homesteaders who toiled for a living by farming and raising livestock. They all played an important role in this area's development.

& ✑ **Carter County Museum** (406-775-6886), at the junction of MT 7 and CR 323, Ekalaka. Open year-round, Tuesday through Friday, 9 A.M.–12 P.M. and 1 P.M.–5 P.M.; Saturday and Sunday, 1 P.M.–5 P.M. Free admission. Founded in 1936, this gem of a museum has the distinct honor of being the first county museum founded in Montana. This little-known museum houses some of the finest paleontological discoveries in the United States, as well as numerous artifacts depicting the lives of Native Americans and the early settlers of Carter County. Seventy-five million years ago Carter County was home to many species of dinosaurs and their contemporaries, all living in and along the marshes that bordered the retreating Pierre Sea, which once covered much of eastern Montana. Today their remains are being retrieved from the shale and sands where they were entombed. Among the paleontological finds housed in the museum, are the mounted skeleton of a hadrosaur and the complete skulls of a triceratops and a tiny tyrannosaur. All of these were collected in local exposures of the Hell Creek cretaceous formation.

& **Custer Battlefield Museum** (406-638-1876; www.custermuseum.org), Exit 514 off I-90, Garryowen. Open year-round, daily Memorial Day through Labor Day, 9 A.M.–8 P.M., and September through May, 9 A.M.–5 P.M. Adults $4, seniors $3, and children under 12 free. The museum is located on the former site of Sitting Bull's camp, on the famous Garryowen bend of the Little Bighorn River, a traditional summer hunting campsite for many Plains Indian tribes. As the Seventh Cavalry approached in late June 1876, one of the largest Indian gatherings ever recorded in North America was taking place here. Several famous locations

associated with the Battle of the Little Bighorn are visible from Garryowen.
These include Reno's hilltop defense site, Weir Point, Last Stand Hill, Medicine Tail Coulee, the Crow's Nest, the Wolf Mountains, as well as the Little Bighorn Battlefield National Monument and Custer National Cemetery. Cavalry and Indian artifacts excavated on the site of the Battle of the Little Bighorn join large dioramas showing step-by-step battle action. Items include Little Wolf's golden eagle tail feathered war bonnet, which was worn during many battles, including the Battle of the Little Bighorn. The contract for Sitting Bull's appearance in the famous Buffalo Bill Wild West Show is on display, as is the only known and attested signature of Sitting Bull, and more.

& ✏ ♘ **Custer County Art & Heritage Center** (406-232-0635; www.ccac .milescity.org) Waterplant Road, 0.5 mile west of Miles City on US 12. Open May through September, Tuesday–Sunday, 9 A.M.–5 P.M.; open September through May, Tuesday–Sunday, 1 P.M.–5 P.M.; closed January. Free admission. This is one of the more interesting art museums in Montana. The setting is lovely, as it is housed in a restored water treatment plant (ca. 1910) and overlooks the Yellowstone River. The art center fills nearly 10,000 square feet of exhibit and work space. The building is listed on the National Register of Historic Places and earned a Montana Governor's Historic Preservation Award. The center also received a 2003 Governor's Award for the Arts. There are two large, elegant galleries, featuring national exhibitions and works from its permanent collection. Seven exhibits change annually, including regional and national collections of contemporary, traditional, and historical artworks. Permanent collection items include historical photographs from Miles City's 1800s beginning by L. A. Huffman, Evelyn Cameron, E. S. Curtis, and others. Contact the center for a current list of events and exhibits.

& **Frontier Gateway Museum** (406-365-4123), Belle Prairie Frontage Road (1 mile east of Exit 215 off I-90), Glendive. Open mid-May through mid-September, Monday–Friday, 9 A.M.–5 P.M., and Sundays and holidays, 1 P.M.–5 P.M. Free admission. The museum is historical and chronological in content. Displays range from prehistoric times to the 20th century. You will find fossils, wildlife displays, Indian artifacts, cowboy and pioneer information and history, and more.

Musselshell Valley Historical Museum (406-323-14031; www.mvhm.us), 524 1st Street, Roundup. Open daily May through September, 1 P.M.–5 P.M.; free admission. Exhibits here include fossils, a coal tunnel, Native American art and artifacts, a restored one-room schoolhouse, an old-fashioned general store, an early hospital room, and more. This museum also features a unique gift and quilt shop worth exploring. The building is listed on the National Register of Historic Places.

& ✏ **O'Fallon Historical Museum** (406-778-3265; www.bakermt.com/tourism/ museum.html), 723 S. Main, Baker. Open year-round June through September, 9 A.M.–5 P.M.; October through May, Friday–Sunday, 9 A.M.–5 P.M. Besides housing the world's largest preserved steer (5 feet, 11 inches tall, 10 feet, 4 inches long, and 9 feet, 2 inches in girth, with a certified weight of 3,980 pounds), this museum has several unique exhibits showcasing pioneer and rural life. The enormous steer, known as Steer Montana, lived 15 years, 4 months. During his life he traveled to more than 60 different state fairs, stock shows, and carnivals. Steer Montana had two brothers, Brother Spot, weighing 3,230 pounds, and Brother Bulgy, weighing 3,580 pounds—neither of which could top Steer Montana.

& **Peter Yegen Jr. Yellowstone County Museum** (406-256-6811; www .pyjrycm.org), 1950 Terminal Circle, Billings. Open Monday through Friday, 10:30 A.M.–5 P.M.; free. Located just south of, and across the parking lot from, the Billings airport, this unique history museum is worth a visit while in Billings. Housed in a restored pioneer cabin, the museum seems small at first, but the downstairs is full of exhibits ranging from historical artifacts to dinosaur fossils and more.

Powder River Historical Museum and Mac's Museum (406-436-2977; www.mcdd.net/museum), 102 W. Wilson, Broadus. Open Memorial Day through September, Monday–Saturday, 9 A.M.–5 P.M.; free. The museum was opened in June 1988 at the location of the Midland Lumber Company (formerly the Yellowstone Lumber Company). It contains many valuable historical collections, including photos and books, Indian artifacts, old guns and ammunition, pre-1900 buggies, vintage autos, rebuilt engines, threshing machines, tractors, and farm implements. A prized acquisition are battlefield artifacts from the Reynolds Campaign in 1876—a forerunner of Custer's Last Stand. In the museum's relatively few years of operation, the half-block complex has been rapidly filling up with these objects.

🖋 **Prairie County Museum and Cameron Gallery** (406-635-5575), 101 S. Logan, Terry. Open Memorial Day through Labor Day, Monday and Wednesday–Friday, 9 A.M.–5 P.M., and Saturday and Sunday, 1 P.M.–4 P.M.; free. The fun thing about this place is all the restored buildings. There is a steam-heated outhouse—the only one of its kind west of the Mississippi River. The museum complex is the essence of the old pioneer life—the way it was lived and how it was endured in eastern Montana. The Prairie County Museum houses historical files for research of events and families, including obituaries. The museum has an extensive collection of photographs, which can be reprinted for a nominal fee. An old red wooden caboose is the home of the well-known Cameron Gallery.

Range Riders Museum (406-232-4483), 0.5 mile west of Miles City on US 12, near the Art and Heritage Center (see above). Open April through October, 8 A.M.–6 P.M. Inquire for admission prices. The hub of the complex is the original log building completed in 1941. It has a wealth of displays, including pictures of early settlers, the famed Coggshall saddle, ladies' side saddles, antiquated cameras, patchwork quilts, and household utensils. Immediately adjacent is the Pioneer Memorial Hall, with over seven hundred plaques commemorating the region's pioneers. The Bert Clark gun collection includes over four hundred firearms.

Rosebud County Pioneer Museum (406-356-7547), 335 Main Street, Forsyth. Open May 15 through September 15, Monday–Saturday, 9 A.M.–6 P.M. and Sunday, 1 P.M.–6 P.M. Free admission. Located across the street from the historic **Rosebud County Courthouse,** this museum features what life was like for pioneers at the turn of the 20th century.

&. ♂ **Western Heritage Center** (406-256-6809; www.ywhc.org), 2822 Montana Avenue, Billings. Open Tuesday through Saturday, 10 A.M.–5 P.M.; closed on Mondays and legal holidays. Free admission. The Western Heritage Center building is a historic Billings destination, listed on the National Register of Historic Places. Originally, it was the Parmly Billings Library, built in 1901 by Billings's founder as a memorial to his son, Parmly. Within the beautiful main floor, old oak galleries are changing exhibits where the stories of peoples of the Yellowstone River Valley unfold. This fantastic destination museum features more than 16,000 artifacts, among them some 1,000 photographs of pioneer life in Montana. Via the American Indian Tribal Histories Project, the museum collaborates with the Crow and Northern Cheyenne Indian Tribes to create extensive exhibits featuring Native American history and culture. If you're in Billings or planning to pass through, save time for a visit.

♂ **Wibaux Museum** (406-796-9969), 112 E. Orgain Avenue, Wibaux (pronounced *Wee-bow*). Open May through September, Monday–Saturday, 9 A.M.– 5 P.M.; free. The museum is located in an older office building that was built in 1892. Several antiques that belonged to Pierre Wibaux and his wife, Mary Ellen, are housed in the museum, along with items from early settlers in this area. Pierre was the world's largest cattle rancher in the late 1800s. The story of Pierre and his life is told during the museum tour. Additional exhibits include a Montana Centennial Train Car, which went to the World's Fair in New York in 1964, an antique barber shop, and a livery stable. You can also enjoy a historic walking tour of the Wibaux Business District, Old St. Peter's Catholic Church built in 1895, and the Pierre Wibaux statue.

Yellowstone Art Museum (406-256-6804; www.yellowstone.artmuseum.org), 401 North 27th Street, Billings. Open Tuesday through Saturday, 10 A.M.–5 P.M., and Thursday, 10 A.M.–8 P.M.; free. Founded in 1964, this museum has grown and grown since its creation nearly 50 years ago. The art collection here includes contemporary art from Montana and the Rocky Mountain region. With over four thousand works, including pieces by Will James, Charles M. Russell, J. H. Sharp, and more, this museum is a must for art and history lovers.

HISTORIC LANDMARKS, PLACES, AND SITES **Bell Street Bridge** (406-377-5601; www.glendivechamber.com/bridge.htm), 200 N. Merrill Avenue, Glendive. Walk or bike across this large bridge spanning the Yellowstone River. The bridge—first built in 1894, destroyed by an 1899 ice jam, and rebuilt between 1924 and 1926—is one of the longest of its kind in Montana. It's resurrection in the 1920s occurred by an act of Congress. This bridge is over 1,300 feet long, with six steel and concrete spans. In 1992 it was closed to motor vehicles and today is part of a walking and cycling trail. (See also Bell Street Bridge Day under *Special Events.*)

&. ♂ **Chief Plenty Coups State Park** (406-252-1289; http://fwp.mt.gov/lands/site_283264.aspx), 1 mile west of Pryor (40 miles south of Billings on the Crow Indian Reservation. Open May through September, 8 A.M.–8 P.M.; the museum is open 10 A.M.–5 P.M. Situated on the Crow Reservation, this was the original home country of Chief Plenty Coups, last chief of the Crow. Today his log home and store remain as evidence of the chief's efforts to lead his people in adopting the lifestyle of the white settlers. The park is 4,033 feet in elevation and encompasses 195 acres. It has vault toilets, grills/fire rings, picnic tables, trash cans, and drinking water. No overnight camping is allowed, and for nonresident visitors the day-use fee is $2 per adult and $1 per child. On the first Saturday of each September the park holds a Day of Honor to remember Chief Plenty Coups. On this day, people partake in speeches, a craft fair, cultural activities, and a buffalo feast.

&. **Little Bighorn Battlefield National Monument** (406-638-3204; www.nps .gov/libi), on US 212 near Crow Agency. Open Memorial Day through Labor Day, 8 A.M.–9 P.M.; spring and fall, 8 A.M.–6 P.M.; winter, 8 A.M.–4:30 P.M. Admission is $10 per vehicle, $5 for pedestrians or motorcycles. This area memorializes one of the last armed efforts members of the Lakota, Cheyenne, and Arapaho tribes undertook to preserve their way of life. At this site on June 25 and 26, 1876, 263 soldiers and Lt. Col. George A. Custer met their deaths in a bloody battle along the banks of the Little Bighorn River, along with hundreds of Indians. Artifacts from the fields of battle are on display at the visitor center and museum. Visitors can enjoy interpretive programs or enjoy the self-guided walking tours available for the battle-related sites and the national cemetery. A self-guided, 5-mile tour road enables visitors to follow and observe the sites related to the battle.

Moss Mansion Historic House Museum (406-256-5100; www.mossmansion .com), 914 Division Street, Billings. Open seven days a week with hourly tours (frequency varies by season, so please call). Admission is $7 adults, $5 seniors 62 and older, $5 students with ID, $3 children ages 6–12. Constructed of red sandstone in 1903, this mansion was designed by renowned New York architect Henry Janeway Hardenberge and housed the Preston Boyd Moss family in the early 20th century. The house has been fully restored and features period furnishings, including everything from draperies to Persian carpets. The mansion is listed on the National Register of Historic Places. (See also Christmas at the Moss Mansion under *Special Events.*)

&. **Pictograph Cave State Park** (406-247-2940; www.pictographcave.org), 2300 Lake Elmo Drive, Billings. Open May through September, 8 A.M.–8 P.M.; free for residents, nonresidents $5 per vehicle. Pictograph Cave State Park is located southeast of Billings. Despite being so close to a major city, this state park has a rural and remote feel. It is located along the continuation of a sandstone cliff line that forms an impressive natural boundary and characterizes the valley. Two of the three caves that define the site complex contain evidence of habitation dating back over 4,500 years. The pictographs that give the park its name date from over 2,200 years ago. Nearly 30,000 artifacts have been collected from the site. The cave also served as the burial grounds for at least nine individuals. A 0.5-mile paved trail leads you through the park's three caves. The largest cave, Pictograph Cave, is a National Historic Landmark. Camping in the park is prohibited, but you can picnic here. Park personnel advise you to bring binoculars to view many of the pictographs.

& **Pompeys Pillar National Monument** (406-875-2233; www.blm.gov/mt/st/ en/fo/billings_field_office/Pompeys_Pillar.html or www.pompeyspillar.org), Exit 23 off I-94 about 30 miles east of Billings. Open Memorial Day through Labor Day, 8 A.M.–8 P.M., after Labor Day in September, 9 A.M.–5 P.M.; inquire about any other time periods. Admission $7 per vehicle. Made famous by William Clark of Lewis & Clark, this rock outcropping rises 200 feet above the Yellowstone River and has evidence of many more humans than just Clark. In fact, it is a sandstone history book that reads like a who's who of western frontier history. Look on the rock face for the remains of animal drawings created by people who used the area for rendezvous, campsites, and hunting. In 1806 Captain Clark carved his signature and the date into this rock. It is the only site where visible evidence of the Lewis & Clark Expedition may be viewed by the public.

Rosebud County Courthouse (406-356-7318), Main Street, Forsyth. This historic 1912 building, built primarily of sandstone, is worth venturing into before or after you check out the **Rosebud County Pioneer Museum** across the street. The courthouse is a neoclassical structure with a copper dome, stained glass, and murals inside. It is also listed on the National Historic Register of Historic Places.

FOR FAMILIES ♂ **Folf/Disc Golf Course** at Makoshika State Park (see the listing under *Wilder Places–Parks*). Perhaps one of the more scenic folf (Frisbee golf) courses in the United States, it winds its way around the badlands of the state park. You can also camp at the adjacent campground. Score cards can be picked up at the visitor center and there is no fee, but bring your own flying discs.

♂ **Waterparks in Billings.** There are two waterparks in Billings: the **Big Splash Waterpark** (406-256-5543; 5720 S. Frontage Road, Exit 446 off I-90), and **Geyser Park** (406-254-2510; 4910 Southgate Drive, Exit 447 off I-90). Big Splash Waterpark has seven slides and a kiddie pool and is a legitimate waterpark. Geyser Park has go-karts, 18-hole miniature golf, laser tag, and more. Either place is great for letting the kids run off a little road weariness.

♂ **Zoo Montana** (406-652-8100; www.zoomontana.org), 2100 S. Shiloh Road, Billings. Open year-round, 10 A.M. to a seasonally adjusted closing hour; $6 adults, $4 seniors, $3 children 3–15. The folks here have done a nice job creating habitats that enable you to view the animals without disturbing them. They also focus a lot on educational programs for schools and visitors. Featured animals include the bald eagle, Sitka deer, eastern gray wolf, river otter, wolverine, red panda, various waterfowl species, Siberian tiger, and great horned owl. The botanical garden is worth exploring as well. They also feature a children's interactive center with more than 11 domestic animals. Zoo Montana is the only zoo to be honored by a grant from the Humane Society of the United States, which reflects the zoo's level of concern for wildlife.

See also Two Moon Park under *To Do–Bicycling*, Riverside Park under *To Do–Camping*, and Montana Fun Adventures under *To Do–Unique Adventures*.

SCENIC DRIVES **US 87 from Billings to Roundup** is a 50-mile, one-way trip. As you leave the rimrock formations near Billings, you travel through rolling hills and ranch country interspersed with small stands of pine trees and vistas that go on for hundreds of miles. Less than 5 miles out of Billings you will encounter few people and few houses—a stark contrast to the urban area of Billings. This drive also takes you through the **Bull Mountains.**

Crow Agency to Alzada on US 212. This drive is a great way to leave or enter Custer Country. Winding through the Northern Cheyenne Indian Reservation and **Custer National Forest,** this two-lane highway takes you past a wide range of scenery. In Broadus, you can choose to head north to Miles City on MT 59 or stay on US 212.

Miles City to Baker US 12 is a study in contrasts—red-hued hills from eroding sandstone against the open and broad plains of eastern Montana.

St. Xavier to Pryor. This winding two-lane paved country road is for more adventuresome travelers. Views of the Pryor and Bighorn Mountains can be had, along with wide-open vistas.

Terry Badlands (406-232-7000; www.blm.gov/mt/st/en/fo/miles_city_field _office.html), MT 253 to Calypso Trail northwest of Terry. Often overlooked, these visually stunning badlands offer spires, hills, bridges, buttes, arcs, and more. They are managed by the BLM, so please contact the Miles City field office for visitation information.

NATURAL WONDERS **Capitol Rock National Natural Landmark** (605-797-4432; www.fs.fed.us/r1/custer). Located in the Long Pines Unit of the **Custer National Forest,** Capitol Rock is a massive white limestone uplift that resembles the nation's Capitol building. It's a remnant of the once continuous blanket of tertiary deposits that covered much of the Great Plains. The area is also rich in archaeology and paleontology sites, produces some oil, and supports a sizable livestock population, as well as one of the largest populations of merlins (a small falcon) in North America.

& **Medicine Rocks State Park** (406-234-0900; http://fwp.mt.gov/lands/site _283951.aspx), 25 miles south of Baker or 14 miles north of Ekalaka via MT 7, then 1 mile west on a county road. Open year-round; free. The park features marvelously sculpted sandstone formations formed by wind and rain over millions of years. Native Americans in the region believed the rocks held medicinal powers, hence the name. For travelers who want to get away from the crowds, this is a nice spot for picnicking, camping, wildlife viewing, and hiking.

✳ To Do

BICYCLING **Alkali Creek Trail,** Alkali Creek Road, Billings. This 3-mile loop trail begins at Alkali Creek School and is a beginner-friendly ride on some easygoing singletrack.

BikeNet (www.bikenet.org) is a Billings-based organization created to find, maintain, and establish new trails in the Billings area. For riding information and trails, please visit their Web site.

Custer National Forest, Long Pines Unit (605-797-4423; www.fs.fed.us/r1
.custer), 30 miles southeast of Ekalaka via MT 323. In this unit of the Custer
National Forest you will find numerous Forest Service roads, along with solitude, well-maintained trails, plenty of wildlife-viewing opportunities, and stands
of large ponderosa pines. Because of the region's remoteness, it is a good idea to
travel in pairs or be sure you are very experienced and understand the risks (and
rewards) of biking solo in a remote area. This is also a great place for hiking,
horseback riding, and in winter (with enough snow) snowmobiling and cross-
country skiing.

Rimrock Trails, near Airport Road and MT 3, Billings. Including **Black Otter
Trail** and **Zimmerman Trail East,** this network of trails takes you across varied
terrain, all suitable for beginners. Some interesting rock formations include slick-
rock, sandstone, and breathtaking views of five mountain ranges (Bull, Pryor,
Bighorn, Beartooth, and Crazy) and the city below. These trails are very close to
the Billings, but once you're out on one of them the views quickly make you for-
get you're in a city of 100,000 people.

Two Moon Park, Yellowstone River Road, Billings. This is a good place for a
family who is interested in riding and hiking. The longer **Dutcher Trail** connects you to **Coulson Park.** These trails are just a few of the many opportunities in the Billings area. For more information, visit www.bikenet.org.

See also Bell Street Bridge under *To See–Historic Landmarks, Places, and Sites;*
Riverfront Park under *To Do–Snow Sports;* and Makoshika State Park under
Wilder Places–Parks.

THE RIMROCKS PROVIDE A GOOD VIEW OF BILLINGS, MONTANA'S LARGEST CITY

BOATING **Bighorn Canyon National Recreation Area** (406-666-2412; www
.nps.gov/bica). The Yellowtail Dam Visitor Center in Fort Smith is open Memorial Day through Labor Day, 9 A.M.–5 P.M. Call for off-season hours. The recreation area is open year-round; $5 per vehicle per day or $30 annual pass. On
60-mile-long Bighorn Lake, boaters will enjoy a beautiful canyon with boating
access to camping, fishing, wildlife viewing, picnicking, and more. Boating provides the best access as few roads lead into the recreation area.

& **Baker Lake** (406-778-2266; www.bakermt.com), off US 12 in Baker. Open
year-round; free. This is a small lake near a small town, but it provides boating,
fishing (crappie, perch, and walleye), swimming, and picnicking. In winter, ice
fishing is also popular.

Deadman's Basin Reservoir (406-444-2535; http://fwp.mt.gov/fishing/guide/
q_Deadmans_Basin_Reservoir__1094258463457_0_1.aspx), west of Ryegate on
US 12, then 1 mile north at mile marker 120. Open year-round; free. A state
managed area offering boating, fishing, and swimming.

Tongue River Recreation Reservoir State Park (406-234-0900; http://fwp
.mt.gov/fishing/guide/q_Tongue_River_Reservoir__1068000450836.aspx), 6 miles
north of Decker on MT 314, and then 1 mile east on a county road. Open year-
round for day use and camping. Fees apply for nonresidents and overnight
camping. This place is remote and offers solitude, but it's slowly gaining in popularity. There are 106 RV-accessible camping sites and excellent fishing for crappie, smallmouth bass, walleye, and perch.

See also Riverside Park under *To Do–Camping* and Lake Elmo State Park under
Wilder Places–Parks.

CAMPING There are many private campground and RV parks in this region. And
if you want to rough it, there are probably a hundred possible places to pitch a
tent, as most fishing access sites, state parks, and BLM lands allow overnight
camping. You can rest assured that at any public site there will be signs stating
whether or not overnight camping is allowed. If in doubt read all posted signs,
especially if you are unclear about the need to pay a fee.

Crazy Head Springs Recreational Area (406-477-6503), 1.5 miles south of
US 212 between Lame Deer and Ashland. This area is located on the Northern
Cheyenne Indian Reservation and a permit is required. There are several natural
springs flowing into ponds where you can fish or swim. Camping and picnicking
can also be enjoyed here, but please call the Northern Cheyenne Natural
Resources Department before venturing to this unique area.

Custer National Forest (605-797-4434; www.fs.fed.us/r1/custer), 1310 Main
Street, Billings. The **Sioux Ranger District** near Ekalaka has four free, pack-
in/pack-out campgrounds in Montana: **Ekalaka Park, Lantis Springs,
Wikham Gulch,** and **McNab Pond,** which also has fishing for crappie, smallmouth bass, and rainbow trout in a stocked pond. The **Ashland Ranger District** has three free, pack-in/pack-out campgrounds: **Cow Creek, Holiday
Spring,** and **Red Shale.** It also has the **Whitetail Cabin,** which can be
reserved through the National Reservation System (1-877-444-6777; www
.recreation.gov).

Riverside Park (406-628-4796), Exit 434 off I-90, then south on US 212 for 0.8 mile in Laurel. Open for camping mid-May through September, with a small self-service fee. This is a Laurel city park, but it still feels quite natural; sitting on the banks of the Yellowstone River among the cottonwoods is very appealing. The campground features hot showers, RV hook-ups, a fishing access, a boat ramp, and a playground. The park used to be a POW camp for German and Japanese prisoners during WWII.

Steve McClain Memorial Park (406-778-2266; www.bakermt.com), US 12, then south of 3rd Street W., Baker. Free overnight camping facilities, including barbecue grills, picnic tables, bathrooms, and RV dump stations.

See also Medicine Rocks State Park under *To See–Natural Wonders;* Deadman's Basin Reservoir and Tongue River Recreation Reservoir State Park under *To Do–Boating;* Makoshika State Park under *Wilder Places–Parks;* Pryor Mountains Wild Horse Range under *Wilder Places–Wildlife Refuges and Wildlife Management Areas;* and Bighorn Canyon National Recreation Area under *Wilder Places–Other Wild Places.*

FISHING **The Bighorn River** (406-247-2940; http://fwp.mt.gov/fishing/guide/q _Bighorn_River__1074636461629_0_112.482002258301.aspx) is accessible via MT 313 and MT 47. Best known for its remarkable trout fishing, the Bighorn River runs for 47 miles from Yellowtail Dam to the Yellowstone River by way of Fort Smith and Hardin. Because its flows in Montana generate from a dam, the water is clear and consistent, creating a trout haven in the water below the dam.

A LUCKY ANGLER ON THE BIGHORN RIVER NEAR FORT SMITH

Photo Courtesy of Bighorn Kingfisher Lodge

Other than brown and rainbow trout, species include mountain whitefish, channel catfish, northern pike, sauger, smallmouth bass, and walleye. There are many access points along the river and most allow overnight camping.

The Musselshell River (406-234-0900; http://fwp.mt.gov/fishing/guide/q _Musselshell_River__1078992474520.aspx), along US 12 between Ryegate and Melstone. More a muddy prairie river than a mountain stream, this river is home to channel catfish, northern pike, sauger, smallmouth bass, and walleye.

The Powder River (406-234-0900; http://fwp.mt.gov/fishing/guide/q_Powder _River__1054362467419.aspx) runs south of Broadus on MT 59 and is home to channel catfish, sauger, and shovel-nosed sturgeon. This river provides some solitude, and anglers seeking to catch something unique can try for a shovel-nosed sturgeon.

The Tongue River (406-234-0900; http://fwp.mt.gov) is about as far from Busby as you can go on MT 314 and still be in Montana. The first few miles of the river below the dam offer a few trout, but once you get more than a mile or two the catch includes channel catfish, sauger, shovel-nosed sturgeon, smallmouth bass, and walleye. Overnight camping is permitted at the access site below the dam.

The Yellowstone River (406-247-2940; http://fwp.mt.gov/fishing/guide/q _Yellowstone_River__1039825479787.aspx) is accessible for most of its length in this region via I-90, I-94, or MT 200. Most of the trout fishing occurs on the river upstream of Laurel; however, many species reside in the river from Laurel all the way down to its confluence with the Missouri near Sidney. The Yellowstone is the nation's longest free-flowing river—670 miles of undammed water. Fish species in this region include brown trout, burbot, channel catfish, mountain whitefish, paddlefish, sauger, smallmouth bass, and walleye. An occasional rainbow trout or Yellowstone cutthroat trout may be caught. There are plenty of access sites along the river and most offer camping for a nominal fee. (See also Paddlefishing at Intake Dame Fishing Access Site under *To Do–Unique Adventures*.)

GOLF Briarwood Country Club (406-245-2966), 3429 Briarwood Boulevard, Billings; 18 holes.

Circle Inn Golf Links (406-248-4202), 1029 Main Street, Billings; nine holes.

Cottonwood Country Club (406-377-8797), Country Club Road, Glendive; nine holes.

Eagle Rock Golf Course (406-655-4445), 5624 Larimer Lane, Billings; 18 holes.

Exchange City Golf Club (406-652-2553), 19 S. 19th Street, Billings; 18 holes.

Forsyth Country Club (406-356-7710), 3 miles west of Forsyth on Frontage Road; nine holes.

Fort Custer Golf Club (406-665-2597), 3.5 miles north of Hardin on MT 47; nine holes.

Lake Hills Golf Club (406-252-9244), 1930 Clubhouse Way, Billings; 18 holes.

Laurel Golf Club (406-628-4504), 1020 Golfcourse Road, Laurel; 18 holes.

Miles City Town & Country Club (406-232-1500), 4th Street, Miles City; nine holes.

Peter Yegen Jr. Golf Club (406-656-8099), 3400 Grand Avenue, Billings; 18 holes.

Pine Ridge Country Club (406-323-2880), 72 Golfcourse Road, Roundup; nine holes.

Ponderosa Butte Golf Course (406-748-2700), 1 Long Drive, Colstrip; nine holes.

Pryor Creek Golf Club (406-256-0626), 1292 Pryor Creek Road, Huntley; 27 holes.

Rolling Hills Golf Course (406-436-2608), 3 miles west of Broadus at the Y intersection; nine holes.

HIKING **Camps Pass Trail,** located in the Custer National Forest. The trailhead is located 18 miles east of Ashland on US 212. There are two loop hikes here, and they offer views of ponderosa forests and the rolling hills of the Northern Cheyenne Indian Reservation.

Diane Gabriel Trail in Makoshika State Park (406-377-6256; www.makoshika .org), Snyder Avenue through the town of Glendive. This 1.5-mile loop runs through badlands, passes a fossilized dinosaur, and then finishes through some grasslands. For some exciting views of the badlands, take the short, steep side trail to an overlook.

Howery Island Nature Trail (406-232-7000), just off MT 311, 6 miles south of Hysham. This scenic trail is located in the Howery Island Wildlife Management Area along the Yellowstone River. There are several interpretive signs on the 1.3-mile trail. Keep your eyes peeled for deer, foxes, hawks, bald eagles, and numerous waterfowl. In spring wildflowers also blanket the area.

Om-Ne-A-Trail in the Bighorn Canyon National Recreation Area (406-666-2412; www.nps.gov/bica), Fort Smith. This trail begins at the Yellowtail Dam in the lower portion of Bighorn Canyon. There are 6 miles of trails here, but only the first few hundred yards are steep. This is a good trail for learning about the Bighorn Canyon.

& **William L. Matthews Wildlife Recreation Area** (406-233-2800; www.mt .blm.mcfo), 7 miles east of Miles City. Open year-round for day use only; free. Covering 80 acres and designed with the handicapped in mind, this concrete trail provides hiking along the Yellowstone River, picnic tables, and fishing.

HORSEBACK RIDING In addition to the many ranches that offer riding in Custer Country (see *To Do–Unique Adventures*), there are plenty of other riding opportunities. A good place to start would be to contact Custer National Forest (406-657-6200; www.fs.fed.us/r1/custer) and inquire about trails in the **Ashland Ranger District** or the **Sioux Ranger District.**

PADDLING/FLOATING **Pirogue Island State Park** (406-234-0900; http://wp.mt
.gov/lands/site_283962.aspx). Floaters find this isolated and undeveloped
cottonwood-covered **Yellowstone River** island an excellent spot to view wildlife,
envision the Corps of Discovery's travel along the river, and hunt for moss
agates. The island is a haven for waterfowl, bald eagles, and whitetail and mule
deer. During low water, a small channel provides foot access to the island from
the mainland, and it is always available by floating the river. Other activities
include hiking, biking, horseback riding, fishing, and picnicking.

See also the Riverside Park under *To Do–Camping;* the Bighorn River, Musselshell River, Powder River, Tongue River, and Yellowstone River under *To
Do–Fishing;* Deadman's Basin Reservoir, Tongue River Recreation Reservoir,
and Bighorn Canyon National Recreation Area under *To Do–Boating.*

SNOW SPORTS

Ice Fishing
Opportunities to ice fish are plentiful in this region, especially as the popularity
of the pastime grows. It requires patience, local knowledge, and the ability to
stay warm for long periods of time. (For more information, see the listings under
To Do–Boating.)

Ice Skating
Anywhere you can find a frozen lake or pond, you can ice skate. But exercise
extreme caution on frozen waters that are not managed. For a rink that provides
scheduled skating hours and maintained ice, visit the **Centennial Ice Area**
(406-256-1192; 427 Bench Boulevard, Billings). See also Baker Lake and Deadman's Basin under *To Do–Boating.*

Snowmobiling
In Custer Country the ability to snowmobile depends entirely on snowpack and
winter storms. It is best to contact the **Custer National Forest** (406-657-6200;
www.fs.fed.us/r1/custer) for current snow and trail conditions.

Cross-Country Skiing
Arapooish Pond and Recreation Park (406-247-2940; http://fwp.mt.gov), 1
mile north of Hardin off MT 47. Open year-round for day use only; free. The
park has a nice trail that is available for cross-country skiing in winter, snow conditions permitting. There is also an aerated 29-acre pond offering all-season fishing for smallmouth and largemouth bass and rainbow trout.

Camps Pass Ski Trail (406-842-5432; www.fs.fed.us/r1/custer). There are two
ungroomed cross-country ski trails, snow conditions permitting: 2 kilometers
easy, 2 kilometers more difficult, and 6 kilometers most difficult.

Riverfront Park (406-657-8371), S. Billings Boulevard, Billings. Open year-
round for day use only; free. An urban park on the banks of the Yellowstone
River in the town of Billings. Snow conditions permitting, cross-country skiers
can find a small network of trails.

UNIQUE ADVENTURES **Crow Country/Reservation Tours with Westfork**
(406-666-2462; www.forevermontana.com/tours.htm), located in St. Xavier. Cre-

ate your own Crow Country getaway. All tours are designed specifically for you, whether historic and archaeological sites, deserts, high foothills, mountains, and pristine wild areas. The He Does It and Half families have created this unique tour company to help people better understand the history of life on the Crow Indian Reservation.

Crow Scouting Party Camps (406-639-2280), based out of Lodge Grass. They use tepees, tepee tents, and bed rolls while exploring the Crow Reservation and surrounding areas, including the Wolf and Big Horn Mountains. On their tours you will travel in comfort in Suburbans and 4-wheelers to different locations and points-of-interest. They offer fire-cooked meals and will take you to various historical and cultural sites based on what you would like to experience.

Frontier Adventures (406-461-6894; www.exploremontana.com/fa1/), 6360 Big Belt Drive, Helena. Trips run during specific dates in the summer months in various locations throughout Custer Country. You will explore the Yellowstone River with a guide in a safe and comfortable raft. On their unique trips you will learn about Lewis & Clark, Native American culture and history, ethnobotany, geology, fossils, and more. You will camp and enjoy meals prepared for you. You can even choose to camp in a tepee if you wish. Advance reservations are highly recommended.

Montana Fun Adventures (406-254-7180; www.montanafunadventures.com), P.O. Box 21905, Billings 59104. These folks are able to organize and run tours throughout Custer Country and other regions of Montana. They offer everything from a two-hour microbrew tour to the Old West Ghost Town Tour. In Billings they offer trolley tours, hayrides, and more. Contact them for a seasonal schedule, rates, and reservation information.

Paddlefishing at Intake Dame Fishing Access Site (406-232-0900; http://fwp.mt.gov/lands/site_283784.aspx or www.glendivechamber.com/pfish.htm). Modern paddlefish (*Polyodon spathula*) have been around for millions of years and have adapted to their environment since being introduced into the Yellowstone River in 1963. It is possible that they are the oldest remaining big-game species, land or water, in North America. Near Intake, the town of Glendive is considered the Paddlefish Capital of the World and draws over three thousand anglers annually to this short stretch of the Yellowstone River. The roe is particularly cherished, and the Glendive Chamber of Commerce will ship it overseas as caviar. Paddlefish steaks also make great table fare. Paddlefish season runs from May 15 through June 30 every year. You will need a Montana fishing license and a special paddlefish tag. Overnight camping is allowed at the Intake Fishing Access Site.

Ranch Vacations. A ranch vacation in Custer Country is about as genuinely western as they come. A typical ranch vacation (but not a typical vacation by any means) may include herding cattle, sheep, or other livestock, branding livestock, cutting hay, breaking horses, and more. The time spent working versus relaxing is up to the ranch owners or hands, but also you—remember, this is your vacation. All of the ranches listed below include horseback riding, lodging, meals, and more as part of an all-inclusive package. This is only a small sample of the many ranch vacations available: **Cross M Working Guest Ranch** (406-557-

2667), Miles City; **Double Spear Ranch** (406-259-8291), Pryor; **Hougen Ranch** (406-358-2204), Melstone; **The Lodge at Diamond Cross Ranch** (406-757-2220), Birney; **Runamuk Guest Ranch** (406-323-3614), Roundup. For a complete listing, visit the Custer Country Web site's ranch vacation page (custer.visitmt.com/lodging_06.html).

Roundup Cattle Drive, Inc., Annual Cattle Roundup (1-800-257-9775; www.roundupcattledrive.com), P.O. Box 205, Roundup 59072. Reservations are required and transportation from Billings and back is included. The roundup is held every year, usually in late August. You can be one of 50 guests from around the world who spend six days rounding up hundreds of cattle. The cattle are sorted, checked by a vet, and then moved to a large ranch near Roundup. During the downtime (when not on horseback and herding cattle), you can enjoy dancing, scavenger hunts, or just relax and enjoy life under the Big Sky. Meals are served via a chuckwagon and include everything from steaks to chicken to even a vegetarian option. Please inquire for rates and reservations.

7th Ranch Historical Tours (406-638-2438; www.historicwest.com), Exit 514 at Garryowen. Based near the Battle of the Little Bighorn site, these friendly folks offer historical tours throughout Custer Country. They specialize in custom, individually planned tours on horseback or via four-wheel drive. They offer day trips and overnight trips. A few of their more popular tours are: Little Bighorn and Rosebud Battlefield areas, Lewis & Clark trail at Pompeys Pillar, St. Labre Indian Mission, various known and unknown pictograph caves, Deer Medicine Rocks where Sitting Bull had his visions, and more. Please inquire for rates and availability.

✳ Wilder Places

PARKS &. **Lake Elmo State Park** (406-247-2940; http://fwp.state.mt.us/parks/parksreport.asp?mapnum=8), US 87 north of Pemberton Lane and then west for 0.5 mile, Billings. Open year-round for day use; free for residents, $5 nonresidents. Close to Billings, this is more of a city park than a wild place. In summer it is a popular spot for swimming. There are also some interesting interpretive exhibits at the regional state park headquarters, located on the lake's south shore.

&. **Makoshika State Park** (406-377-6256; www.makoshika.org), through the town of Glendive on Snyder Avenue. Open Memorial Day through Labor Day, 10 A.M.–6 P.M., and Labor Day through Memorial Day, 9 A.M.–5 P.M.; free for residents, $5 per vehicle for nonresidents. *Makoshika* means "bad earth, land, or spirits" in Sioux. This name is appropriate for the state's largest state park. With jagged badlands and vistas that extend for hundreds of miles, this place feels desolate and isolated. At the park are dinosaur fossils, including a *Tyrannosaurus rex*. There is a substantial visitor center with interpretive exhibits on the park's geology, fossils, terrain, and human inhabitants. You can also enjoy picnicking, hiking, a scenic drive, camping, biking, wildlife viewing, two shooting ranges, snowmobiling (snow permitting), and a folf (Frisbee golf) course.

Rosebud Battlefield State Park (406-234-0900; http://fwp.mt.gov/lands/site_283981.aspx), 25 miles east of Crow Agency on US 212, then south on

MT 314 for 20 miles, and then 3 miles west; follow the signs. Open for day use; free. Remote yet beautiful, this 3,000-acre rolling prairie state park preserves the site of the June 17, 1876, battle between the Sioux and Cheyenne Indians and General Crook's soldiers. Quiet and undeveloped, the park includes prehistoric sites and the homestead and ranch of the Kobold family. Take your own food and your camera and plan for plenty of time to appreciate a slice of history.

See also Chief Plenty Coups State Park and Pictograph Cave State Park under *To See–Historic Landmarks, Places, and Sites;* Medicine Rocks State Park under *To See–Natural Wonders;* Two Moon Park under *To Do–Bicycling;* Tongue River Recreation Reservoir State Park under *To Do–Boating;* Riverside Park under *To Do–Camping;* Pirogue Island State Park under *To Do–Paddling/Floating;* and Arapooish Pond and Recreation Park and Riverfront Park under *To Do–Snow Sports.*

FORESTS **Custer National Forest** (406-797-4432; www.fs.fed.us/r1/custer), 1310 Main Street, Billings. The entire lands administered by Custer National Forest include 1.2 million acres. These lands are split into three ranger districts, including the Beartooth Ranger District, which borders Yellowstone National Park. In Custer Country, the **Sioux Ranger District** has eight tracts of land in the vicinity of Ekalaka, while the **Ashland Ranger District** administers the lands near Ashland and Otter along MT 484. The Ashland district has three distinct areas set aside for hiking and horseback riding: Cook Mountain, King Mountain, and Tongue River Breaks. Recreational pursuits include biking, boating, camping, fishing, cross-country skiing, horseback riding, wildlife viewing, and much more. There are many campsite locations throughout the forest and a visitor to Custer Country would be hard-pressed to enjoy the region without stepping foot into this forest.

WILDLIFE REFUGES AND WILDLIFE MANAGEMENT AREAS **Lake Mason National Wildlife Refuge** (406-538-8706; www.fws.gov/refuges/profiles/index.cfm?id=61523), 8 miles northwest of Roundup. Part of the larger **Charles M. Russell National Wildlife Refuge** system (see chapter 6), this 18,000-acre refuge is a combination of prairie and wetlands. It is home to migrating waterfowl, raptors, and small population of prairie dogs.

Pryor Mountains National Wild Horse Range (406-896-5013; www.blm.gov/mt/st/en/fo/billings_field_office.html), accessible from various routes south of Billings. Created in 1968, this was the first national wild horse range in the United States. Wild horses from the Pryor Range are popular among wild horse enthusiasts because the horses share many characteristics with Spanish mustangs, which may number among their ancestors. There are said to be approximately 180 wild horses on the range. Primitive camping is available, but be sure to check rules and regulations. The Penn's Cabin is available on a first-come, first-served basis. Proper planning with the Billings field office is the best way to enjoy a visit to the range.

See also Howery Island Nature Trail and William L. Matthews Wildlife Recreation Area under *To Do–Hiking.*

OTHER WILD PLACES ⅋ *✎* **Bighorn Canyon National Recreation Area** (406-666-2412; www.nps.gov/bica). The Yellowtail Dam Visitor Center in Fort Smith is open Memorial Day through Labor Day, 9 A.M.–5 P.M.; hours for the rest of the year vary, so please inquire. Cost: $5 per vehicle or $30 for an annual pass. With more than 70,000 acres of land in Wyoming and Montana, this area includes the 60-mile-long Bighorn Lake. Boating in the canyon is remarkably scenic (see *To Do–Boating*). There are two distinct sections of the area, and the only way to go from one to the other is by boat. There is a popular kids' program, the Bighorn Canyon's Junior Ranger Program, where kids partake in several fun and educational activities. Upon completion, kids receive a unique Junior Ranger badge.

Four Dances Natural Area (406-896-5013; www.blm.gov/mt/st/en/fo/billings _field_office/four_dances.html), 2 miles east of downtown Billings, east of Coburn Road and west of the Yellowstone River. Open year-round for day use only; free. This 765-acre tract of land is a unique riparian area very close to a major metropolitan area. For that, it is listed as an Area of Critical Environment Concern. You can enjoy birding, hiking, and wildlife viewing.

Sundance Lodge Recreation Area (406-896-5013; www.blm.gov/mt/st/en/fo/ billings_field_office/sundance_lodge.html), Thiel Road, Laurel. Open year-round for day use only; free. This 400-acre park is near the confluence of the Clarks Fork of the Yellowstone River and the main stem of the Yellowstone River. It used to be a working livestock ranch, but since 1997 it has been a public park with trails for biking, hiking, horseback riding, and wildlife viewing.

✳ Lodging
BED & BREAKFASTS

Billings
The Josephine Bed & Breakfast (406-248-5898; www.thejosephine .com), 514 N. 29th Street. This place is close to everything in downtown Billings—within walking distance, in fact. The beautiful B&B was built in 1912, but over the years the owners have continually renovated to keep up with 21st-century convenience. There are five rooms, all with private baths, wireless Internet, and a delicious made-to-order breakfast. Rates $90 and up.

Pine Hills Bed & Breakfast (406-252-2288), 4424 Pine Hills Drive. This place is a nice spot away from town, yet just close enough so that you can be in Billings in less than 15 minutes. Please contact them for spe-

cific directions. The B&B is a five-bedroom cabin located in Pine Hills. It is very quiet and peaceful. Rates $70 and up.

Sanderson Inn (406-656-3388), 2038 S. 56th Street W. This home was built in 1905 and features three rooms. The rooms are fondly named after the early residents of the home, who were related to the present proprietor. All rooms are light and airy with softly flowered wallpaper, handmade quilts, sheepskin throw rugs on hardwood floors, and fluffy curtains on windows that look over adjacent pasture lands. In all of the guest rooms you will find many of the original restored antiques. Rates $60 and up.

V Lazy B Bed & Breakfast and Horse Motel (406-669-3885; www.cruising-america.com/vlazyb), 12960 Medicine Man Trail, Molt (about 13 miles west of Billings). Please call for directions. Located in horse country just west of Billings, it offers western hospitality—you don't have to have horses to stay here—and scenic views of sunrises and sunsets from the large wraparound deck. Hike or ride your mount along the canyon nature trails on this 45-acre property. Four guest rooms are offered for your stay. The Bunkhouse in the barn features a kitchenette, TV/VCR, private bath, and queen bed. The Sundowner Room, located on the main floor in the house, is spacious and offers a queen bed, private bath, and deck. The lower level provides a separate entry and two bedrooms; one queen/one double, shared bath, and large family room. Breakfast time is flexible and overnight horse boarding is available. Rates $70 and up.

Broadus

Oakwood Lodge (406-427-5474), S. Pumpkin Creek Road, 25 miles west of Broadus on US 212. This 1991 lodge offers peace and quiet and is wheelchair accessible. The log lodge is on a 1,000-acre ranch, and it's a great location for walking or fossil hunting. There are three guest rooms with private baths, a great room, library, gazebo, deck, and limited handicapped access to the main lodge. A hearty ranch breakfast is included with the room. The lodge is open in all seasons and is adjacent to the Custer National Forest. Enjoy excellent hunting, wildlife viewing, hiking, rockhounding, and photography opportunities. Rates $60 and up.

Colstrip

Lakeview Bed & Breakfast (406-748-3653; www.lakeviewbnb.com), 7437 Castle Rock Lake Drive. This 9-bedroom B&B (three rooms face the lake) is built on a gentle slope overlooking picturesque Castle Rock Lake, one of southeastern Montana's best-kept secrets. Hostess Debby Haas welcomes you to this scenic lake and the relaxing atmosphere of rolling hills covered with ponderosa pines. This handsome B&B certainly shares company with some of the best B&Bs in Montana, but this one has lots of privacy and is on the shores of a lake teeming with fish. They even have pedal boats for exploration and exercise. Rates $90 and up.

Forsyth

Lasting Impressions Bed & Breakfast (406-346-7067; lastingimpressions montana.com), 214 N. 13th Street. Built in 1914, this lovely home is a gem in the small town of Forsyth. Each room has a queen-size bed, TV with VCR, and cable. The four comfortable air-conditioned guest rooms share two large bathrooms on the second floor. There is a screened-in front porch with a swing, evening refreshments, numerous movies on hand, fax machine available, and wireless high-speed Internet. Rates $70 and up.

Glendive

Charley Manley Bed & Breakfast (406-365-3207; www.charley-montana .com), 103 N. Douglas Street. History buffs will enjoy a night or two in this 1907 mansion. The grand 8,000-square-foot, 25-room home was built for millionaire stockman Charles Krug and is listed on the National Register of Historic Places. Guests enjoy more than 2,000 square feet of public space, including 10-foot ceilings with

9-foot quartersawn oak pocket doors, abundant carved original wood in quartersawn oak and mahogany, beveled and leaded glass windows, butler's pantry, antique bank vault door on the family wine cellar, columned fireplaces, mahogany conversation area, Krug family antique furnishings, books, art, and linens. Rates $90 and up.

Hostetler House Bed & Breakfast (406-377-4505), 113 N. Douglas Street. Located one block from the historic Bell Street Bridge across the Yellowstone River and two blocks from downtown shopping and restaurants, this charming 1912 historic home has three comfortable guest rooms done in casual country décor with twin, double, and queen beds. They even have a hot tub and an enclosed sunporch. Rates $70 and up.

Hardin

Kendrick House Inn Bed & Breakfast (406-665-3035), 206 N. Custer. Built in 1915 and decorated in vintage English and French style, this is a good spot for exploring the area's historical and cultural highlights while staying in relative sophistication. All rooms have a pedestal sink, antique framed beds, and period dressers, as well as several yesteryear memorabilia collections of crazy quilts, half-doll pincushions, vintage teacups, and vintage books. Bathrooms are equipped with claw-foot tubs, showers, pedestal sinks, and pull-chain toilets. Guest areas include a library with television and a parlor/living room and porches. In the formal dining room, and true to the boardinghouse style, a large Montana breakfast is served for all guests. Enjoy evenings spent in conversation or reading in the large fenced-in flower garden. Rates $90 and up.

Hysham

Cat Coulee Beds 'n' Birds (406-342-5692), 48 Cat Coulee Lane. Please call for specific directions. These are remote cabins on a private pheasant hunting preserve. They are intended for folks willing to rough it a little bit. The tradeoff is a great rural setting overlooking a beautiful creek bottom and pine-covered hills. Rates $110 per cabin.

Lodge Grass

✍ **Wald Ranch** (406-639-2457; www .waldranch.net), HC 45 Box 809, located on MT 463 southwest of Lodge Grass. Although not a normal B&B, this is a great place for a base while in the area. They are an authentic working ranch, so you may see them irrigating, putting up hay, feeding the livestock, doctoring animals, branding, and doing all sorts of ranch activities. You will be sleeping and eating in the new log ranch house. The lower level has guest rooms with king-size beds, plenty of closet space, a large family room, and a large bathroom. Laundry facilities and an ironing board and iron are available. Outside is a lower and upper deck to watch wildlife and birds, just read, relax, or gaze at the beautiful sunset or sunrise, star-filled sky at night, or beautiful scenery during the day. Rates $110 and up.

Miles City

Helm River Bed & Breakfast (406-421-5420; www.huntmontanafree .com), HC 32 Box 4161, south of Miles City on MT 332. In a beautiful setting, with the Yellowstone River in view, this place has nearly 7,500 acres to explore. They cater to hunters during the season, and they're usually booked up well in advance. But the remainder of the year the hosts have plenty of room for nonhunting guests. Rates $90 and up.

Wibaux

Nunberg's N Heart Ranch Bed & Breakfast Inn (406-795-2345), HC 71, Box 7315, 7 miles south of Wibaux on MT 7. Enjoy true country living in one of three guest rooms in a 1913 restored farmhouse. They make a great breakfast, and this is an ideal place to stay if you need a break from city life. Rates $70 and up.

LODGES, GUEST RANCHES, AND HOTELS/MOTELS

Baker

Ringneck Rendezvous (406-778-2988), 4740 MT 7. This is a vacation rental, but very close to town. Located in an original 1908 farmhouse, the Ringneck Rendezvous features a full kitchen, laundry facilities, and television. Adjacent to 640 acres of open land, this is ideal for anyone who wants to hunt ringneck pheasants or who wants a little more space to explore.

Fort Smith

Kingfisher Lodge (406-666-2326; www.bighornkingfisher.com), P.O. Box 7828, located on MT 313 in Fort Smith. With views of the Bighorn Mountains and a wide array of lodging options, the folks here have the best home base if you plan to explore the Bighorn River or Bighorn Canyon National Recreation Area. Guests can choose to stay in one of the lodge's rooms—with two double beds, private bathroom, small refrigerator, and air-conditioning—or opt for a restored farmhouse. They can arrange fishing guides for the river and bird hunts as well. Rates $100 and up.

Fort Smith Cabins (406-666-2550; www.flyfishingthebighorn.com), P.O.

Box 7827, located on MT 313 in Fort Smith. These clean, comfortable, and economical cabins overlook the Bighorn River. The cabins are equipped with satellite television, air-conditioning, heat, a mini fridge, and very comfortable beds. There are private decks on each cabin where anglers can enjoy the sunset.

Miles City

R Lazy 4 Ranch Cabin (1-800-685-7206), Powderville Stage, located 20 miles east of Miles City of US 212. This private cabin was built from hand-harvested timber off the R Lazy 4 Ranch. Located on a working ranch, guests here will get a real taste of Montana living—or enjoy peace and quiet. On premises there is great wildlife viewing, biking, birding, and hiking. In winter cross-country skiing can also be had if the snow permits.

✳ Where to Eat
DINING OUT

Billings

Enzo Bistro (406-651-0999), 1502 Roseburg Lane. This fun place serves contemporary bistro food with a Mediterranean feel in a relaxed comfortable farmhouse. The freshest fish from both coasts are a specialty, as well as aged meat cooked on a wood-fire grill. Traditional and modern specials are featured every day. Authentic pizzas and flatbread are cooked in an Italian wood-fired oven. An extensive selection of wines and beers complement the eclectic menu.

George Henry's Restaurant (406-245-4570), 404 N. 30th. Perhaps one of the more elegant choices in Billings, this is a beautiful restaurant housed in an old historic home. The home was built in 1882 and is nestled in the financial district in downtown Billings. They feature the finest of gourmet dinners and lunches, along with homemade desserts. The seafood specialties include walleye, pike, salmon, halibut, shrimp, scallops, and scampi. The steaks and meat specialties are of the finest quality and are prepared to your discriminating taste. Be sure to save room for dessert.

&. **The Granary** (406-259-3488), 1500 Poly Drive. After a massive redesign, this Billing establishment is chic and trendy, but it still retains a real Montana feel. For over 25 years, the Granary has taken pride in serving the finest naturally aged hand-cut beef, prime rib, fresh seafood, and chicken. There is a full-service bar and a great outdoor patio/deck. They also serve Misty Isle Farms aged Northwest Black Angus Beef certified choice, naturally raised and pasture-fed and free from antibiotics, hormones, or growth stimulants.

&. ✪ **Walkers American Grill and Tapas Bar** (406-245-9291; www .walkersgrill.com), 2700 1st Avenue N. This is a full-service restaurant with a full bar. Walkers is a well-established local favorite and a destination for travelers, theatergoers, and museum patrons alike. Menu selections offer freshness and simplicity, while the professional waitstaff contribute friendly service in a casual, city-dining setting. They have been a recipient of the Award of Excellence by *Wine Spectator* for several years and have received writeups in the *Wall Street Journal, Billings Gazette,* and *Montana Magazine.* They have also garnered regional and national recognition for serving such famous guests as Mel Gibson, Lou Gosset Jr.,

Jon Voight, Garrison Keillor, Joan Baez, poet Alan Ginsberg, and most notably, President Bill Clinton.

Broadus
&. **Judges Chambers Restaurant** (406-436-2002), 101 S. Wilbur (US 212). The 1929 home of Honorable Judge Ashton Jones has been restored and now hosts this great little place in the heart of a culinary desert. The owners describe their menu as "prairie food," and that means offerings are made from the freshest ingredients, many of which come from the chef's personal garden. This new and exciting cuisine combines the best ingredients and recipes from Montana with the fine subtleties of European tastes. If you are passing through you must plan time to dine here—it is just that unique.

Ingomar
Historic Jersey Lilly Bar and Café (406-358-2278), Main Street (US 12). Located in a building that once housed a bank (ca. 1914), this tiny place serves breakfast, lunch, and dinner. You probably won't find anyone other than a local here, but occasionally travelers stop in and everyone makes them feel immediately like locals. Their bean soup is homemade and known throughout the region. The building is also listed on the National Register of Historic Places, so you will be dining with a bit of history.

Miles City
&. **Club 519** (406-232-5133), 519 Main Street. Located on the second floor of the Professional Building in downtown Miles City, this place is surprisingly hip for being in the heart of one of the largest ranching towns in Montana. They feature steaks (no

surprise there), but the chef is always thinking up new tastes and the atmosphere is enjoyable and relaxing.

EATING OUT

Baker
Corner Bar (406-778-3278), 1 Main Street. There is nothing luxurious or fancy about this place—except for the steaks. They can cook up one of the best steaks in the region. They also offer tasty lunch specials. Most everything comes with fries or onion rings. They have a small casino area and occasionally offer some entertainment.

Billings
Artspace (406-245-1100), 2919 2nd Avenue N. A place for the alternative crowd, but not a place for your taste buds to suffer. They offer tasty café fare and some of the better coffee in the downtown area.

Montana Brewing Company (406-252-9200), 113 N. Broadway. For good service, fresh beer, and a wide array of pub food, this is one of the best places in Billings. Even if you are not a beer drinker, you will find the homemade soups and varied menu to your liking. Their wood-fired pizzas are very good, and they even have a pretty good selection of vegetarian options.

Colstrip
♿ ♨ **The Coal Bowl** (406-748-2695), 6111 Homestead Boulevard. This is a good place for kids and adults. If the kids get too bored there is a bowling alley on the premises. And if that doesn't keep them entertained there are plenty of historic photographs on the walls to peruse. Oh yeah, the food is good and plentiful as well.

Ekalaka
Deb's Coffee Shop (406-775-8718), Main Street. A great place for lunch while exploring the open country around Ekalaka. They have pizza by the slice, homemade soups, big sandwiches, ice cream, and homemade pies.

Forsyth
Buff's Bar, Casino, and Restaurant (406-346-7386), 845 Main Street. People love the deer and antelope mounts all over the walls here. The food is good, but it is the down-home Montana ranch atmosphere that is worth the visit.

Top That! Eatery (406-346-7825), 983 Front Street. A fun place for adults and kids as you get to order from a wide menu but then choose many toppings to add to whatever you ordered. From tacos to pizzas to salads, you will not go hungry here. Save room for dessert, too.

Fort Smith
Polly's Place on the Bighorn (1-866-6-POLLYS) on MT 313 in Fort Smith. Polly's is an institution on the Bighorn. Open from late March into November, Polly's is the only game in town for consistently good food year in and year out. Fort Smith is a tiny place and catering to diners might be difficult, but the folks at Polly's have it down. Great food served with quality, caring customer service, and hours that accommodate boaters and anglers.

Glendive
Beer Jug, Inc. (406-377-9986), 313 N. Merrill Avenue. Unofficially known as the Paddlefish Headquarters for years, they have a full menu. Try their nachos if you are hungry for

lots of food and something spicy. The atmosphere is warm and cozy and the prices very reasonable. In summer or fall their patio is a great spot to enjoy a Montana evening while eating good food.

Coffee Den at the Book N Bear Nook (406-377-4938), 104 S. Merrill Avenue. Located in a quaint bookstore in downtown Glendive, this small café serves fresh sandwiches, homemade soups, and great coffee drinks. They offer fresh-baked goods for breakfast, including a daily quiche. For lunch their large baked potatoes topped "how you like them" are popular with the locals, but their cheesecakes often steal the show.

Hardin

✔ **Lariat Country Kitchen** (406-665-1139), 721 N. Center Avenue. The setting is very country, with decorations that make you feel like you stepped into a farmhouse. The service will make you feel at home and the food is filling and tasty. This is a good place for families and kids.

✔ **Shawna's Grill/Sweet-N-Such** (406-665-1453), 1426 N. Crawford. The menu at this small restaurant is varied, with burgers, steaks, seafood, pasta, and daily specials. Their specials change daily. However, what sets Shawna's apart are the six homemade desserts made daily.

Laurel

Owl Junction Diner (406-628-4966), 1203 E. Main Street. A favorite among locals, this small diner serves breakfast, lunch, and dinner. For nearly a century, this diner has fed generations of Laurelens from the same location. The menu is quite diverse, but most folks who eat here choose the side of pork. Slow-roasted,

there are few things like it in this region of Montana.

Miles City

Airport Inn (406-232-9977), MT 59 north of town. Located at the very small Miles City airport, the atmosphere here takes flight—literally—as the décor is loaded with model airplanes and the like. The food is good, but all the models and the seasonal deck overlooking the Yellowstone River really make this worth the trip.

Golden Spur Sports Bar–Milestown Brewing Company (406-232-3544), 1014 S. Haynes Avenue. Despite the moniker of sports bar, this establishment has such a wide menu and friendly service that kids will feel welcome here. Adults will enjoy fresh beers made on the premises.

Roundup

♿ ✔ **Busy Bee Family Dining and Gift Shop** (406-323-2204), 317 1st Avenue W. The salad bar here is massive and a must-have when ordering anything off their menu—which includes steaks, burgers, chicken, seafood, and pastas. One or two nights a week they also offer a prime rib special—get there early if you don't want to risk their running out. They are also open for breakfast and feature homemade breads and goodies.

Pioneer Café (406-323-2622), 229 Main Street. For some serious country cooking like biscuits and gravy, country-fried steak, or homemade cinnamon rolls, they know how to do it here. The atmosphere is very "come as you are" and you are likely to dine with someone who in a hour or so will be tending cattle or running a tractor.

✳ Special Events

January: **Annual Southeastern Montana Juried Exhibit** (406-234-0635), Miles City. The Southeastern Montana Juried Exhibit features some of the best works being produced by professional and amateur artists throughout Montana and adjoining states. Works include paintings, drawings, photographs, sculptures, and more.

February: 🐾 🐾 **Artwalk Downtown** (www.artwalkbillings.com), Billings. Artwalk Downtown was established in 1994 as a venue to promote fine art and fine-art crafts in Billings. The 32 participating galleries offer a wide variety of works for your visual enjoyment.

March: 🐾 **Eastern Montana Celtic Festival,** Glendive. A weekend of Irish culture, food, and fun that features a corned beef and cabbage lunch, Irish dancing, and more.

April: **Professional Bull Riders NILE (Northern International Livestock Exposition) Invitational Weekend** (www.thenile.org), Billings. Forty-five of the toughest men in the world, elite members of the Professional Bull Riders, Inc. (PBR), take on some of the most ferocious bulls in America. It's man against beast in the greatest show on dirt.

May: 🐾 **Buzzard Day,** Makoshika State Park. An annual event to celebrate the return of the turkey vultures.

Living History Weekend, Glendive. History is alive at this event centered around explorers and Native Americans and the Lewis & Clark Expedition; unique foods, living history exhibits, music, and more round out the festivities.

⊙ **World Famous Miles City Bucking Horse Sale** (406-234-2890; www.buckinghorsesale.com), Miles City. For days, the town of Miles City celebrates everything about bucking horses with a rodeo, a parade, trade shows, craft shows, races, food, and the trying debuts of future rodeo stars—both horse and cowboy.

June: 🐾 **Strawberry Festival** (406-259-5454), Billings. An unofficial kickoff to the summer season that honors the unofficial fruit of summer. Vendors sell food, crafts, and more.

Custer's Last Stand Reenactment and Little Big Horn Days (1-888-450-3577; www.custerslandstand.org), Hardin. An annual reenactment of the battle between the U.S. Calvary and the Native American tribes of the area. Also included is a weeklong celebration of western heritage, including a quilt show, grand ball, concerts, parades, food, and more.

Colstrip Days Celebration, Colstrip. A community party featuring fireworks, children's activities, parades, a golf tourney, an art show, and more.

Annual Ghost Tour of Miles City, Miles City. This annual tour is open to the public and provides great family entertainment. The tour covers approximately nine blocks in one of Miles City's three historic districts. Ghosts in costume tell of their past, including information about Miles City's history during their lives.

July: 🐾 **Northern Cheyenne Fourth of July Celebration,** Lame Deer. This is the largest powwow held on this reservation. Timed for Independence Day, this event lasts several days and includes dancing, fun runs, parades, vendors, and feasts of traditional Native American foods.

August: ✍ **Crow Fair Powwow and Rodeo,** Crow Agency. Annual celebrations including powwows, a rodeo, drumming circles, a parade, dance contests, and more.

✍ **Montana Fair** (406-256-2400; www.metrapark.com), Billings. The largest statewide fair in Montana, the event features concerts, a rodeo, a carnival, a parade, vendors, and lots more.

September: **Bell Street Bridge Day,** Glendive. An annual event to commemorate this historic landmark.

✍ **Medicine Rocks Black Powder Shoot,** Ekalaka. A shooting festival for smokeless or black powder loads (participants are typically in period costumes); participants aim for various targets and vendors and food are abundant.

Oktoberfest, Laurel. This celebration of the harvest includes a variety of artisans and vendors, kindergarten and inflatables, great food, silent auction, beergarten, polka music, large dance floor, and a wide variety of entertainment.

October: ✍ **Northern International Livestock Exposition (NILE) Stock Show, Pro Rodeo, and Horse Extravaganza** (406-256-2495; www.thenile.org), Billings. A pro rodeo gala event featuring cowboys and cowgirls from all over the country; livestock exhibits, seminars, trade shows, and horse sales.

November through early January: **Christmas at the Moss Mansion,** Billings. They decorate the home in Christmas fashion, trim out a tree in every room in the mansion, and offer tours. (See also *To See–Historic Landmarks, Places, and Sites.*)

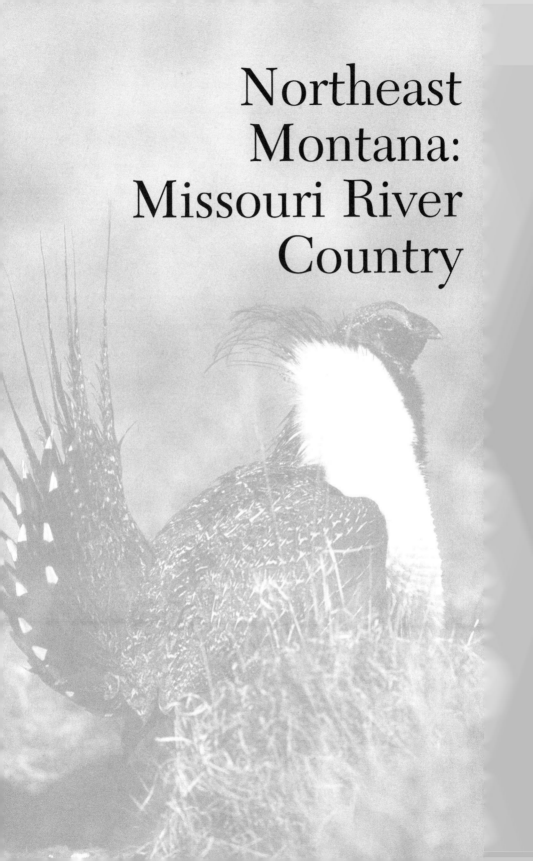

Northeast Montana: Missouri River Country

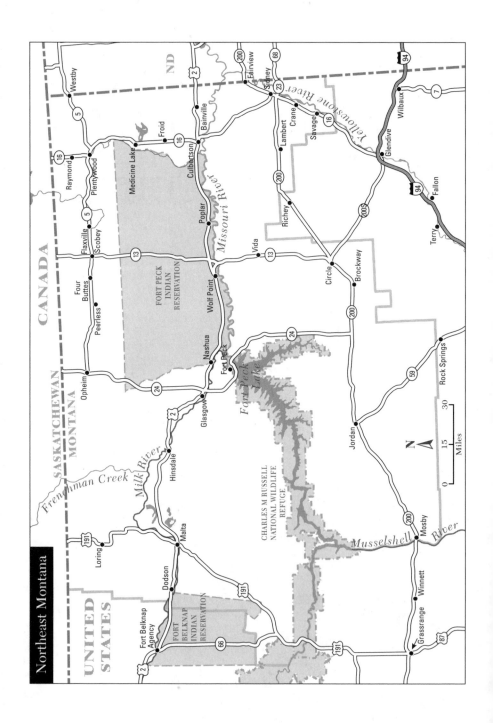

Northeast Montana

NORTHEAST MONTANA: MISSOURI RIVER COUNTRY

A s the name suggests, the centerpiece of this region is the mighty Missouri River. After Lewis & Clark passed through here over two hundred years ago, fur traders, cattle barons, gold seekers, outlaws, cowboys, vigilantes, rustlers, and horse thieves used the river as a roadway to explore and settle this remote area. But before them all, Assiniboine and Sioux Native American tribes hunted and traveled this massive area of what is now Montana's northeast corner—in fact, on any given day a herd of thousands of buffalo could be seen across the wide horizon.

Those days are long gone, but the vastness of the land and its amazing geography still remain. This landscape of island mountain ranges, buttes, river breaks, canyons, badlands, and relatively untouched rolling hills and prairie has a grand openness that is unmatched in all of Montana, and perhaps across the country. This area has fewer people than any other region in the state, and the small towns are separated by giant swaths of open space. But like the Native Americans and explorers who came before them, it is the people and towns that help make this such an interesting area.

In 1805, when Lewis & Clark fought the currents of the Missouri and ventured into what would become Montana, they decided that the present-day border of Montana and North Dakota would be a fine location for a fort. Eventually, that place would become the Fort Union Trading Post. The fort is now a National Historic Landmark and is a great first stop for visitors heading into Montana from North Dakota. Lewis & Clark were in this region for nearly six months. Today US 2 parallels a good portion of their route along the Missouri.

The towns of Wolf Point and Glasgow lie very close to the expedition's path and the Charles M. Russell National Wildlife Refuge borders both shores of the Missouri River and offers many, albeit very remote, opportunities to engage in the Corps of Discovery's journey—as well as to enjoy a wealth of deer, elk, antelope, numerous waterfowl, and upland birds and large tracts of public land.

If the path of Lewis & Clark and Native American life are still too recent history for you, be sure to visit the Hell Creek Fossil Area, where interpretive exhibits abound and prehistoric dinosaur remains depict the lives of the "original" residents of this region. Along the way you will encounter quaint ranching towns, many of which are home to museums and historic sites.

This region includes massive Fort Peck Lake, a 134-mile-long reservoir with over 1,500 miles of shoreline in the Charles M. Russell National Wildlife Refuge. The lake and surrounding area provide endless recreational opportunities, including boating, fishing, hiking, paddling, floating, horseback riding, camping, wildlife viewing, bicycling, cross-country skiing (when snow conditions permit), and much more. Angling enthusiasts may want to plan a tour of the Fort Peck State Fish Hatchery and then perhaps spend a day fishing on the lake.

There are two Indian reservations in this region: the Fort Belknap Indian Reservation and the Fort Peck Indian Reservation. As with most reservations, please be sure to inquire locally before venturing onto tribal lands.

The towns that dot the landscape are small in population but most offer the basic services: food, phone, gas, lodging, Internet, and more. However, before venturing from a town be sure to fuel up and stock up on essentials (water, a few snacks, etc.) as it is not uncommon to travel 100 miles or more before finding the next general store.

Nearly all of the highways listed in this section are paved and well maintained, although there is no interstate here. If venturing off the main roads onto a gravel road, always be aware of incoming weather; a heavy rain or large snowstorm could make exploring dangerous.

If you want to get away from things and experience a special part of the state that is often overlooked by the mobs of tourists and thrill-seekers that descend on western Montana, Missouri River Country is a hidden gem. The landscape hasn't changed much here in the last few hundred years, but for visitors much has changed, as numerous friendly small towns now provide services, with accessibility to great wildlife viewing, historical sites, museums, and much more.

GUIDANCE **Daniels County Chamber of Commerce** (406-487-2061; www .scobey.org), 120 Main Street, Scobey 59263.

Fort Peck Indian Reservation (406-768-5155; www.fortpecktribes.org), Fort Peck Tribal Museum (see *To See–Museums*), P.O. Box 1027, Poplar 59255.

Garfield County and the Town of Jordan Chamber of Commerce (406-557-6158; www.garfieldcounty.com), 434 Main Street, P.O. Box 370, Jordan 59337.

Glasgow Chamber of Commerce (406-228-2222; www.glasgowmt.net), 23 US 2, P.O. Box 832, Glasgow 59230.

Malta Chamber of Commerce (406-654-1776; www.maltachamber.com); Phillips County Museums (see *To See–Museums*), P.O. Box 1420, Malta 59538.

Medicine Lake Chamber of Commerce (406-789-2242).

Missouri River Country (1-800-653-1319; www.missouririver.visitmt.com), P.O. Box 387, Wolf Point 59201.

Forsyth Chamber of Commerce (406-347-5656; www.forsythmontana.org), P.O. Box 448, Forsyth 59327.

A DOWNTOWN PARK NEAR THE TRAIN DEPOT IN MALTA

Richey Chamber of Commerce (406-773-5634), 205 Antelope Avenue, P.O. Box 205, Richey 59259.

Saco Chamber of Commerce (406-527-3218).

Sheridan County Chamber of Commerce and Agriculture (406-765-1733; www.plentywood.com), 501 1st Avenue W., P.O. Box 104, Plentywood 59254.

Sidney Area Chamber of Commerce and Agriculture (406-433-1916; www.sidneymt.com), 909 S. Central Avenue, Sidney 59270.

Town of Culbertson (406-787-5821; www.culbertsonmt.com), 11 Broadway Avenue, P.O. Box 351, Culbertson 59218.

Wolf Point Chamber of Commerce (406-653-2012; www.wolfpoint.com), 218 3rd Avenue S., Wolf Point 59201.

GETTING THERE US 2 is the main route through this region, with a few other highways providing access to small towns. Culbertson, Wolf Point, Glasgow, and Malta all lie along US 2. Plentywood and Scobey are along MT 5. Sidney, Circle, and Jordan lie along MT 200. MT 24 runs north-south through the region, inter-secting US 2 at Glasgow. The Fort Peck Indian Reservation lies north of US 2, south of MT 5, east of MT 24, and west of MT 16.

See also *Airports* and *Bus Service* in "What's Where in Montana."

MEDICAL EMERGENCIES **Daniels Memorial Hospital** (406-487-2296), 105 5th Avenue E., Scobey.

Frances Mahon Deaconess Hospital (406-228-3500), 621 3rd Street S., Glasgow.

Roosevelt Memorial Medical Center (406-787-6281), 818 2nd Avenue E., Culbertson.

Sheridan Memorial Hospital (406-765-1420), 440 W. Laurel Avenue, Plentywood.

Sidney Health Center (406-488-2100), 216 14th Avenue S.W., Sidney.

Trinity Hospital (406-653-2100), 315 Knapp Street, Wolf Point.

✳ To See

TOWNS **Culbertson** is on US 2 near where the Big Muddy River meets the Missouri River, near the junction of MT 16 and US 2. A friendly place with approximately a thousand residents, Culbertson is most happening during the annual **Roosevelt County Fair**. The town has a nice city park with a public swimming pool, perfect for those hot summer days.

Fort Peck sits near **Fort Peck Dam.** The town was created in 1933 for the sole purpose of supporting the building of the massive dam. Today the tiny town is home to a museum, the **Fort Peck Theatre's** summer programs, and the **Fort Peck Dam Museum and Interpretive Center.** Around Fort Peck you will find an abundance of recreational opportunities, including boating, fishing, hiking, bicycling, hunting, and more.

Jordan lies along MT 200 and is the seat of Garfield County. The **Garfield County Museum** features highlights of local and regional history, but the main draw for this town is its proximity to remote lands and the **Charles M. Russell National Wildlife Area.** Fossil enthusiasts will enjoy this area, as a *Tyrannosaurus rex* was found here in 1904. Historic Main Street is also worth a drive.

Landusky and **Zortman** are south of Malta on US 191. These are the best jumping-off places for venturing into the lone mountain range in this region, the

AN ABANDONED GRAIN ELEVATOR

Little Rocky Mountains. These two towns are also near the **UL Bend National Wildlife Refuge** and the **Charles M. Russell National Wildlife Refuge.** Both of these refuges are unique because they are the only places left in Montana where elk range on their native prairie habitat all year long. These towns offer mining history as well, dating back to 1880.

Sidney lies at the junction of MT 16 and MT 200 and is home to the region's only 18-hole golf course. But more importantly it is the closest town to the confluence of the Missouri and Yellowstone Rivers (which actually happens in North Dakota). The **Lewis & Clark Information Center** offers interpretive exhibits. Just over the border, the **Missouri-Yellowstone Confluence Interpretive Center** at Fort Union is a great side trip while you're in Sidney.

Westby is in the extreme northeastern corner of Montana on MT 5. It is close to Montana's border with Canada and North Dakota. With less than three hundred people, this town was originally in North Dakota, but when the Great Northern Railroad was built they moved it to Montana.

Wolf Point is on the Missouri River and US 2 below Fort Peck Dam. The town offers a museum and historical society. The town's name dates back to the 1860s and 1870s, when fur trappers would stack their wolf hides along the river and wait for the steamboat engineers to transport their cargo downriver.

MUSEUMS ♿ **Culbertson Montana Museum and Visitor Center** (406-787-6320; www.culbertsonmt.com), 1 mile east of Culbertson on US 2. Open daily May through September, 9 A.M.–6 P.M., and Sunday 8 A.M.–8 P.M.; free. As you walk through the rooms of this local museum, it is clear that some thought when into its planning. Most exhibits take you back 50 to 100 years. There are the following restored buildings: a little country church, a one-room school, a general store/post office, doctor's office, barber shop, and of course the country kitchen and living quarters. Just as Grandma's kitchen always had the coffee pot on, after the tour you will find complimentary coffee and a homemade cookie to go with it. Outdoor exhibits include a blacksmith shop, wagon barn, 1923 Great Northern caboose, an authentic Sioux tepee, and dozens of antique tractors (courtesy of the Northeast Montana Threshers Association).

♿ ✍ ✪ **Great Plains Dinosaur Museum and Field Station** (406-654-5300; www.montanadinosaurdigs.com) is at the junction of US 2 and US 191 in Malta. Open May through September, Monday through Saturday, 10 A.M.–5 P.M. and Sunday, noon–5 P.M.; $5 adults, $3 children 12 and under. A true working science center but great fun for all ages, as you can see and participate in actual paleontological activities. Watch scientists as they work on incredibly well-preserved dinosaurs, such as Leonardo, a rare dinosaur mummy listed in the *Guinness Book of World Records* as the best-preserved dinosaur. The center offers lectures, educational programs, and a unique gift store with a variety of special gifts and souvenirs for all ages.

♿ ✍ **Fort Peck Tribal Museum** (406-768-5155; www.fortpecktribes.org), 605 Indian Avenue, Poplar. Open daily 8 A.M.–4:30 P.M.; free. Exhibits cover the history and culture of the Assiniboine and Sioux tribes. They also have a nice collection of Native American arts and crafts.

&. **MonDak Heritage Center Museum and Gallery** (406-433-3500), 120 3rd Avenue S.W., Sidney. Open year-round (except January), Tuesday through Friday, 10 A.M.–4 P.M. and Saturday, 1 P.M.–4 P.M.; $3 adults, $1 children. This art gallery and historic museum features a restored "frontier town" with a wooden sidewalk, a doctor, dentist, sheriff, and more. They also have a wide selection of quilts for sale and the **Annual Quilt Show** is a local hit during the month of February.

&. **Phillips County Museum** (406-654-1037; www.maltachamber.com/museum), 431 US 2, just east of Malta. Open year-round, Monday through Saturday, 10 A.M.–5 P.M. and Sunday, 12:30 P.M.–5 P.M.; free. This museum lies on the Lewis & Clark Trail. The purpose of the museum is to preserve the natural, historic, and cultural heritage of the Phillips County region for others to enjoy. Historical exhibits include mining, Native Americans, dinosaurs, outlaws, and farm/ranch/homestead items. There are photographs, books, and notebooks pertaining to the area, plus newspapers from the 1890s through 1980 containing local historical information.

&. **Poplar Museum** (406-768-5223), US 2 across the highway from Fort Peck Community College. Open daily June through Labor Day, 11 A.M.–5 P.M.; free. Housed in the old tribal jail, this small museum has a collection of intricate beadwork and Sioux-Assiniboine quilts. Some of the artwork is for sale.

&. **Sheridan County Museum** (406-765-1733), 1 mile east of Plentywood on MT 16. Open daily Memorial Day through Labor Day, 1 P.M.–5 P.M.; free. Completed in 1968, the exhibits feature Sheridan County's early days. In conjunction with the Sheridan County Agriculture Museum and Civic Center, visitors to the museum will see Montana's longest interior mural, by local artist Bob Southland. If interested, you can take a nice walk to a monument featuring Sitting Bull's surrender site.

TINY NASHUA, MONTANA

&. **Valley County Pioneer Museum** (406-228-8692; www.valleycountymuseum
.com), 816 US 2, on the western edge of Glasgow. Open Memorial Day through
Labor Day, Monday through Saturday, 8 A.M.–5 P.M. and Sunday, 1 P.M.–4 P.M.;
$3 adults, $2 students, children under 6 free. The museum is supported by Valley County, the Historical Society, and Friends of the Museum. Their unique
theme is "From Dinosaur Bones to Moonwalk." Displays include the Chief First
to Fly Indian collection, dioramas, murals, pictures of pioneers, and the Stan
Kalinski room with an ornate cherrywood bar and collection of 220 animal and
bird mounts. They are also in the process of restoring a 1920s homestead.

HISTORIC LANDMARKS, PLACES, AND SITES &. **Daniels County Museum &
Pioneer Town** (406-487-5965; www.scobey.org), seven blocks west of Main
Street on 2nd Avenue. Open Memorial Day through Labor Day, 12:30 P.M.–
4:30 P.M. and Labor Day through Memorial Day, 10 A.M.–2 P.M.; free. Sitting on
20 acres and boasting 35 buildings that have been restored or built for the museum, they have created a fun place to explore this area's past. They have an extensive collection of antique cars, tractors, and machinery. If you really want to get a
taste of life in the past visit during **Pioneer Days** (see *Special Events*).

✪ **Fort Peck Dam,** MT 24 seventeen miles south of Glasgow; follow the signs.
Two establishments provide interpretive exhibits near the Fort Peck Dam. The
dam is one of the largest hydraulically filled earth dams in the world, measuring
21,026 feet long, with a height of 250.5 feet. The five turbines can generate
185,250 kilowatts of power. Its original purpose was not only to control floods
but to create jobs in a depression-saddled economy. In 1933, the undertaking
was the nation's largest public works project. The building of the dam, at its peak
in 1936, provided 10,456 jobs; it was completed in 1940. **The Fort Peck Interpretive Center and Museum** (406-526-3493; www.nwo.usace.army.mil/html/
Lake_Proj/fortpeck/museum.html) is 1.5 miles east of Fort Peck on Lower Yellowstone Road. Open daily May through September, 9 A.M.–5 P.M.; and October
through April, Monday through Friday, 10 A.M.–4 P.M. Free admission. To put it
bluntly, this is a cool place. The Interpretive Center is the result of a unique
partnership between Fort Peck Paleontology, Inc., the U.S. Fish & Wildlife Service, and the U.S. Army Corps of Engineers. They feature two of Montana's
largest aquariums, showcasing native and game species of Fort Peck Lake and
the Missouri River. In the main lobby is a life-sized, fleshed-out model of Peck's
Rex, the *Tyrannosaurus rex* discovered 20 miles southeast of Fort Peck. A skeleton cast of the dinosaur is on display in the exhibit hall. More dinosaur fossils are
also on exhibit. Other displays include present-day and historical animals of the
Charles M. Russell National Wildlife Refuge and the construction history of Fort
Peck Dam. **The Fort Peck Dam and Power Plant Museum** (406-526-3431;
www.corpslakes.us/fortpeck) is located on Lower Yellowstone Road. Open daily
Memorial Day through Labor Day, 9 A.M.–5 P.M.; free. The museum recalls the
history of the construction of the dam and power plants. There is a display of
fossils collected from the area, including a triceratops skull.

✐ &. **Fort Union Trading Post National Historic Site** (701-572-9083; www
.nps.com/fous), 24 miles northeast of Sidney on ND 1804. Open Memorial Day

THE VAST EXPANSE OF FORT PECK LAKE

through Labor Day, 8 A.M.–8 P.M. Central time; Labor Day through Memorial Day, 9 A.M.–5:30 P.M. Free admission. This historic trading post was built in 1828 by the American Fur Trading Company. The grounds of the fort straddle the Montana–North Dakota border just north of Fairview. In 1805 on these grounds, Lewis & Clark entered into what is now Montana. The fort remained an important and active site for trappers, traders, and Native Americans until 1867. Today a fully restored **Bourgeois House** is a main attraction of the grounds, and there is a visitor center, tepees, an Indian trade house, and more.

FOR FAMILIES & ✐ **Children's Museum of Northeastern Montana** (406-228-4FUN; www.kidslove2learn.com), US 2, downtown Glasgow. Open year-round, Saturday and Tuesday only, 10 A.M.–3 P.M.; $2 adults, $1 children. With 10 exhibits, adults and children will find plenty of things to entertain and educate. You can learn about the entire ranching process in From Seed to Market, view an exhibit featuring musical instruments from around the world, try a hands-on paleontological exhibit in which kids can uncover fossils, and much more.

SCENIC DRIVES **Bainville to Fort Union Trading Post National Historic Site on MT 327.** This route winds through farm and ranchlands for a dozen miles along the Missouri River. The road is gravel but well maintained as you make your way to **Fort Union**. The badlands along the drive are a stark contrast to the rolling plains dotted with small ranches and farms.

Bitter Creek Wilderness Study Area. To make this drive safely, please obtain a map from the Bureau of Land Management (406-228-3750). The drive is

accessible via US 2 west of Glasgow. Take Bristch Road north for 15 miles. It is
strongly suggested that you drive a high-clearance, four-wheel-drive on this
route. And don't try this route in windy, snowy, or rainy conditions, as the road
may become impassable if wet. With all that being said, this route traverses
some of the more scenic terrain in this region. Wildlife abounds, so look for
antelope, mule and whitetail deer, grouse, coyotes, foxes, and more. If you have
time try the full loop; you will have some great views of barren badlands that you
can even venture into. Among these badlands are stands of aspen and cottonwoods (in the fall the changing colors are beautiful). If you know where to look
and what to look for you may even find a few remnant tepee rings from a long
time ago. There are three other Wilderness Study Areas nearby: **Burnt Lodge
WSA, Cow Creek WSA,** and **Antelope Creek WSA.** You can get information
on these at the local BLM office in Glasgow at the number above.

Bowdoin National Wildlife Refuge Auto Tour Route (406-654-2863; http://
bowdoin.fws.gov), 7 miles east of Malta off US 2; turn at the sign for the refuge.
This is a 15-mile loop drive around Lake Bowdoin. You might see deer, antelope,
birds, and more as you drive near and then slightly farther away from the shore
of the placid lake. If you want to get out, there are several pullouts along the
route where you can take a closer look or stretch your legs. (See also *To
Do–Bicycling* and *Wilder Places–Wildlife Refuges.*)

Charles M. Russell National Wildlife Refuge Auto Tour Route, NWR 101,
located 55 miles south of Malta off US 191. This is a 20-mile, self-guided auto
tour. Much of the land here is truly the same as when Lewis & Clark saw it over
two hundred years ago. On the drive you will have great views of the Missouri
River Breaks and the opportunity to see abundant wildlife, birds, and perhaps an
elk or two.

NATURAL WONDERS **Hell Creek State Park and Fossil Area** (406-444-3750;
http://fwp.mt.gov/lands/site_283992aspx) is located north of Jordan on MT 543.
This is one of the more remote, yet scenic areas in the whole region. In the early
1900s a *Tyrannosaurus rex* was unearthed at this National Historic Landmark.
This site also produced a triceratops, an ancient alligator, and more. This trip is
really worth experiencing. (See also Hell Creek State Park under *Wilder
Places–Parks.*)

Medicine Lake Site is located in the Medicine Lake National Wildlife Refuge,
20 miles north of Culbertson (south of Plentywood) on MT 16. This is a National
Natural Landmark because over 15,000 years ago heavy glaciers scraped this
landscape into what is it today, along with centuries of wind and rain. Even to
the untrained eye, most glacial evidence is easily viewed—things like glacial tills,
terrace deposits, outwash plains, twisting ridges known as eskers, and kames
(stratified hills with steep sides). See also *Wilder Places–Wildlife Refuges.*

WINERIES **Rolling Hills Winery** (406-787-5787), 220 6th Street N., Culbertson; follow the signs outside town. They've been around long enough now to be
an important part of Culbertson. But, still, a winery in northeastern Montana?
Yep. And they make some great wine from local fruits such as chokecherries,
blueberries, raspberries, and more.

✳ To Do

BICYCLING Bowdoin National Wildlife Refuge Auto Tour Route (406-654-2863; http://bowdoin.fws.gov), 7 miles east of Malta off US 2, turn at the sign for the refuge. There are 15 miles of road here, but be aware of auto traffic. The ride will expose you to lots of wildlife (more than 250 bird species), some great vistas, and more. If you are feeling more adventuresome you can begin your ride in Malta, but be very cautious while riding on US 2. (See also *To Do–Scenic Drives* and *Wilder Places–Wildlife Refuges.*)

BOATING Fort Peck Lake (406-526-3411; http://fwp.mt.gov/fishing/guide/q_Fort_Peck_Lake__1068985477252_0_1.aspx), south of Glasgow via MT 24. This lake is massive—134 miles long, with 1,500 miles of shoreline. The entire lake lies within the **Charles M. Russell Wildlife Refuge.** The most used boat ramp is the one at the dam at Fort Peck Marina. However, there are numerous boat ramps along the shoreline where you could launch your boat.

CAMPING There are many private campgrounds and RV parks in this region. If you want to rough it, there are probably a hundred possible places to pitch a tent, as most fishing access sites, wildlife refuges, state parks, and BLM lands allow overnight camping. You can rest assured that at any public site there will be signs stating whether or not overnight camping is allowed. If in doubt read all posted signs, especially if you are unclear about the need to pay a fee.

Camp Creek Campground, 1 mile northeast of Zortman on Dry Fork Road. Open year-round; small fee. This campground is located on BLM lands near the Little Rocky Mountains, and a small grocery store and food are within a mile. There is plenty of solitude here, but also fresh and good-tasting water.

♿ ✿ **Camping at Fort Peck Lake** (406-526-3224; www.nwo.usace.army.mil/html/Lake_Proj/fortpeck/welcome.html), south of Glasgow via MT 24. There are

A RURAL CHURCH IN MISSOURI RIVER COUNTRY

dozens of campsites around Fort Peck Lake. Contact the U.S. Army Corps of Engineers at the above number to get more information. Some of the more popular sites are the Downstream Campground, the Pines, Flat Lake, and Rock Creek Marina.

✓ **Trafton Park,** north of the rest stop at the intersection of US 191 and US 2 in Malta. Open May through November; admission $5. In summer this campground is shaded by large cottonwood trees. Plus, its location in Malta is nice because you are always close to something for the kids to do. There are restrooms, water, a playground, picnic tables, horseshoe pits, barbecue grills, and easy access to fishing, floating, and paddling. You are also within walking distance of the **Phillips County Museum.**

See also Nelson Reservoir under *To Do–Fishing* and *Wilder Places–Parks.*

FISHING **Fort Peck Lake** (406-526-3411; http://fwp.mt.gov/fishing/guide/ q_Fort_Peck_Lake__1068985477252_0_1.aspx), south of Glasgow via MT 24. Anglers on Fort Peck Lake will enjoy action on a variety of stocked species—walleye, northern pike, sauger, lake trout, chinook salmon, and smallmouth bass, as well as the prehistoric paddlefish. Paddlefish have existed for nearly 70 million years and are found only in the Missouri and Yellowstone Rivers and the Yangtze River in China.

The Lower Missouri River (406-454-5840; www.fwp.state.mt.us) offers anglers lots of water and a variety of species to target. The river begins in southwestern Montana, although the water there is much different from what you'll find in this region. Next, the river flows for nearly 150 miles from Fort Benton to the Fred Robinson Bridge (US 191) in the Charles M. Russell National Wildlife Refuge. The Lower Missouri River is the water below Fort Peck Dam. There are brown and rainbow trout in the first few miles, and after 5 or 6 miles the species shift to walleye, catfish, and smallmouth bass. (See also Fort Peck Lake and the Lower Missouri River under *To Do–Paddling/Floating.*)

Medicine Lake National Wildlife Refuge (406-789-2305; www.fws.gov/ medicinelake/), 20 miles north of Culbertson on MT 16. The northern section of the lake is part of the Medicine Lake Wilderness, including Medicine Lake and five smaller lakes. Species include crappie, perch, walleye, and pike. No motorized boats are allowed, so this is a nice place for paddling as well. Just be sure to check all regulations, as they may change to protect wildlife.

Nelson Reservoir (406-454-5840; http://fwp.mt.gov/fishing/guide/q_Nelson_ Reservoir__1075485484911_0_1.aspx) lies east of Malta off US 2. On this 4,000-acre reservoir you will find boaters, swimmers, and anglers. Fish species include black crappie, burbot, channel catfish, lake whitefish, northern pike, smallmouth bass, walleye, and yellow perch. Access is available via the shoreline, but if you can paddle or float you stand a much better chance of catching something. Overnight, free camping is permitted here; amenities include toilets, water, and picnic tables.

See also the Milk River under *To Do–Paddling/Floating.*

GOLF Airport Golf Club (406-653-2161), 3 miles east of Wolf Point on MT 25, Wolf Point; nine holes.

Marian Hills Golf Club (406-654-5527), 100 Doral, Malta; nine holes.

Plentywood Golf Club (406-765-2532), 709 N. Sheridan Street, Plentywood; nine holes.

Scobey Golf Course (406-487-5322), Golf Course Road, Scobey; nine holes.

Sidney Country Club or **Forsyth Country Club** (406-433-1894), MT 16 north of Sidney; 18 holes.

Sunnyside Golf Club (406-228-9519), 95 Skylark Road, Glasgow; 18 holes.

HIKING Beaver Creek Nature Trail, near Fort Peck Dam, departs from the Downstream Recreation Area. This is a moderate trail and the distances can vary depending on how far you want to hike. (The trails are paved so be on the look-out for cyclists.) While hiking, you will see various bird species and have great views of the Missouri River. Wildlife-viewing opportunities include mule deer, antelope, and more. If you're camping in the area, this is a nice morning hike to get the blood pumping and some fresh air in the nose.

&. **Bowdoin National Wildlife Refuge** (406-654-2863; www.fws.gov/bowdoin), 7 miles east of Malta off US 2; follow the signs. This short, easy loop trail leaves from near the refuge headquarters. The stroll takes you to a small wetland and then a wildlife blind where you can view birds at the Pearce Waterfowl Production Area. If you are interested in longer expeditions, be sure to check with the local office for closures and to ensure that you aren't hiking in a well-used hunting area.

HORSEBACK RIDING There are many opportunities for horseback riding in Missouri River Country. In addition to the many ranches that offer riding (see *To Do–Unique Adventures*), the **Charles M. Russell National Wildlife Refuge** offers plenty of open space for riding.

HOT SPRINGS Sleeping Buffalo Hot Springs (406-527-3370), 17 miles east of Malta and 10 miles west of Saco on US 2. This hot springs was discovered in 1922, when a man exploring for oil encountered a tremendous flow of hot mineral water. Today there are three pools open for your pleasure: one indoor pool at 106 degrees and one at about 90 degrees, and an outside slide pool at about 100 degrees. Each pool has an individual inlet and outlet of constantly flowing water. The indoor pools are open year-round. The water comes from an artesian well that is about 3,200 feet deep.

PADDLING/FLOATING Fort Peck Lake (406-406-526-3411; http://fwp.mt.gov/ fishing/guide/q_Fort_Peck_Lake__1068985477252_0_1.aspx), south of Glasgow. This lake is 134 miles long and has 1,500 miles of shoreline. Canoers and kayak-ers should be experienced and be constantly aware of the dangers of strong winds and motorized craft—both certainties on this lake. Stay close to shore and exercise caution. You can still venture out and have a blast. Canoes can be rented

from the **Missouri River Outpost** (406-439-8438), located 1 mile south of Fort
Peck Dam on MT 117. (See also Fort Peck Dam under *To See–Historic Land-marks, Places, and Sites* and Charles M. Russell National Wildlife Refuge under *Wilder Places–Wildlife Refuges.*)

The Lower Missouri River (406-454-5840; www.fwp.state.mt.us) stretches from US 191 south of Zortman to the North Dakota border. For paddlers, the river offers Lewis & Clark history and beautiful cottonwoods, but always watch the weather forecast for strong winds and thunderstorms. (See also under *To Do–Fishing.*)

The Milk River (406-454-5840; www.fwp.state.mt.us), accessible via US 2, just watch for access signs. This long river starts in Montana, heads up into Canada, and then wanders back down into Montana. For paddlers, the river offers an easygoing trip before it joins the mighty Missouri River. Anglers may find some fishing for smallmouth bass, channel catfish, sturgeon, whitefish, and pike. This is a nice float, but watch the weather forecast for strong winds and powerful thunderstorms.

See also Nelson Reservoir under *To Do–Fishing* and Bowdoin National Wildlife Refuge and Medicine Lake National Wildlife Refuge under *Wildlife Places–Wildlife Refuges.*

SNOW SPORTS

Ice Fishing
Opportunities to ice fish are plentiful in this region, especially as the popularity of the pastime grows. It requires patience, local knowledge, and the ability to stay warm for long periods of time. (For more information, see the listings under *To Do–Boating.*)

Ice Skating
Anywhere you can find a frozen lake or pond, you can ice skate. But exercise extreme caution on frozen waters that are not managed. For skating information, please contact the local chambers of commerce (see *Guidance*).

Snowmobiling
In Custer Country the ability to snowmobile depends entirely on snowpack and winter storms. It is best to inquire locally before heading out with plans to snow-mobile. For more information, contact any of the local chambers of commerce (see *Guidance*).

UNIQUE ADVENTURES ✿ **Big Sky Trails** (406-654-1989), P.O. Box 1568, Malta. They are located 4 miles north of US 2; please call for specific directions. These folks can serve up just about any cool adventure in the region. Trips are typically five days long, with camping, fishing, and sightseeing. There are also plenty of opportunities to view wildlife. You can also partake in horseback riding, cattle drives, or hunting with both bow and rifle. Being located near the Charles M. Russell National Wildlife Refuge, they also offer birding tours. The best months are June through December.

⌀ **Judith River Dinosaur Institute** (406-696-5842; www.montanadinosaur digs.com), Box 51177, Billings. Headquartered in Billings, these folks offer hands-on "real digs" for serious folks interested in getting down and dirty digging for dinosaurs. This is not for casual visitors. Space each week is limited to 16 people, so plan ahead. The work is hard, intense, tedious, and hot and dusty, but it can be very rewarding. The minimum age for dig participants is 14 years.

Ranch Vacations. A ranch vacation in Missouri Country is about as genuinely western as they come. A typical ranch vacation (but not a typical vacation by any means) will include anything from herding cattle, sheep, or other livestock, branding livestock, cutting hay, breaking horses, and more. The time spent working versus relaxing is up to the ranch owners or hands, but also you—remember, this is your vacation. All of the ranches listed below include horseback riding, lodging, meals, and more as part of an all-inclusive package. This is only a small sampling of the many ranch vacations available: **Montana River Ranch** (406-769-2200), Bainville; **Burke Ranch** (406-228-2295), Glasgow; **Beaver Creek Trail Rides and Guest Ranch** (406-658-2111), Malta; **IOU Ranch** (406-557-2544), Sand Springs; **Old West Wagon Trains, Inc.** (406-648-5536), Hinsdale; and **Sand Creek Clydesdales Ranch Vacations & Wagon Trains** (406-557-2865), Jordan; among others. For a complete listing, visit the Missouri River Country Web site's "ranch vacation" page (http://missouririver.visitmt.com/cities.html).

Sharp-Tailed Grouse Courtship Dancing Ritual (406-789-2305; http://medicinelake.fws.gov), at the Medicine Lake National Wildlife Refuge, 20 miles north of Culbertson on MT 16. This is quite an experience if you can find the time to fit it in—and it is worth it. Between mid-April and the end of May, you can watch male grouse try to woo and impress potential mates. The number of people allowed to view is limited, so plan ahead, preferably for early in the mating season. You are also encouraged to arrive an hour before sunrise and watch until the dance is done; don't leave too early because just when you think the dance is done, they may surprise you.

✴ Wilder Places

PARKS ♿ ⌀ **Hell Creek State Park** (406-232-0900; http://fwp.mt.gov/lands/site_283992.aspx), 25 miles north of Jordan via MT 543; follow the signs. Open year-round; free for residents, $5 for nonresidents, camping $13–$15 per night depending on season. This 172-acre park is located on Fort Peck Lake's Hell Creek Bay and offers four boat ramps, swimming, fishing, hiking, wildlife viewing, and picnicking. Plus, the drive from Jordan is very scenic. This is a good place for families, as the site has many amenities such as water, flush toilets, barbeque grills, and more.

WILDLIFE REFUGES ♿ **Bowdoin National Wildlife Refuge** (406-654-2863; http://bowdoin.fws.gov), 7 miles east of Malta off US 2; follow the signs. Open year-round, no overnight camping. Please inquire for an entrance permit. Created in 1936, this place was set aside for migratory waterfowl, but it now

BOWDOIN RESERVOIR

serves as important habitat for many species. Covering more than 15,000 acres, with saline (because of evaporation) and freshwater wetlands, native prairie, shrubs, and grasses, this is a prime location for wildlife and numerous bird species. At any given time you could see more than 250 bird species—including pelicans, cormorants, great blue herons, and more. Plus, over 30 mammals call this area home at any given time. Spring is the best time to visit here because the birdlife is astounding. Other recreational opportunities include hiking, bicycling, paddling, cross-country skiing (when snow permits), an auto tour, and bird hunting. Nearby national wildlife refuges—they are unstaffed but all part of the Bowdoin system—include **Black Coulee, Creedman Coulee, Hewitt Lake, and Lake Thibadeau.**

& ♪ **Charles M. Russell National Wildlife Refuge** (406-538-8706; http:// cmr.fws.gov) is accessible in many ways, as it covers most of the shoreline of Fort Peck Lake and surrounding areas. The scenery in and around the refuge is stunning, yet a bit more subtle than many of the lands in western and southwestern Montana. However, what you often will find here is abundant solitude. Much of this area was explored by Lewis & Clark, and it still looks similar to what they saw. Dinosaur fossils are plentiful in the refuge, and a visit here is likely to include a sighting of a dinosaur dig or two. The refuge covers 1.1 million acres (half the size of Yellowstone National Park and bigger than Glacier National Park), so there is a lot to explore. Topography includes prairies, badlands, forests, and riparian areas. Recreational opportunities include bicycling, boating, fishing, hiking, horseback riding, camping (primitive camping only in most areas, but there are several developed areas as well), swimming, children's playgrounds, many historic sites (including a National Homestead), and more. The Missouri

River in the refuge is designated a National Wild and Scenic River, and it offers historical significance, great paddling/floating opportunities, fishing, and more. This refuge is truly an overlooked highlight of Montana.

Medicine Lake National Wildlife Refuge (406-789-2305; www.fws.gov/medicinelake/), 20 miles north of Culbertson on MT 16. This is a prime area for birding, wildlife viewing, and photography. In 1937 the U.S. government set aside 23,700 acres for wildlife conservation in later years. Subsequent acquisition increased the refuge to its present size of 31,457 acres, which includes the adjacent **Medicine Lake Wilderness Area.** Geologists and paleontologists will enjoy a visit to this refuge, as it is located above the ancestral Missouri River channel, which originally flowed north to Hudson Bay. A blanket of glacial till was left here long ago after a massive sheet of ice receded, resulting in rocky rolling hills with numerous wetlands and marshes. In the more recent past, Indians frequently used this area as a campsite while pursuing migratory buffalo herds and waterfowl flocks. Many of the surrounding hills contain rings of stones that mark ceremonial sites or campsites.

UL Bend National Wildlife Refuge (406-538-8706; www.fws.gov/refuges/profiles/index.cfm?id=61529), south of Malta and west of Jordan. This 20,000-acre wildlife area is surrounded by the Charles M. Russell National Wildlife Refuge. The remote area is really a refuge within a refuge. In fact, it's actually designated as wilderness. You will find plenty of native prairie, forested coulees, river bottoms, and badlands. Wildlife-viewing opportunities include elk, mule deer, antelope, bighorn sheep, sage and sharp-tailed grouse, bald eagles, and more. This area is also home to the endangered black-footed ferret, which lives in the burrows created by the black-tailed prairie dogs. The ferrets feed almost exclusively on the prairie dogs, making a unique balance of nature. Charles M. Russell famously portrayed the rich diversity of native wildlife and habitats of the area in many of his paintings. Due to the size and remoteness of this place, little has changed since the days of the Lewis & Clark Expedition and the era of outlaws and homesteaders.

See also Bitter Creek Wilderness Study Area under *To See–Scenic Drives*.

❋ Lodging

BED & BREAKFASTS

Froid
Sparks' Bed & Breakfast and Guest House (406-963-2247), HC 61 Box 31; located 13.5 miles east of Froid on MT 405. They offer a variety of lodging options. The rooms are large, and they have a guest house for larger families or groups. In the guest house there is a fully equipped kitchen, and on the grounds there is an outdoor pool, RV hook-ups, laundry facilities, and more. For dog owners, they also offer a kennel service. A deluxe continental breakfast is served. Keep your eyes peeled for wildlife on the property. Rates $60 and up.

Mosby
♿ ✿ **Hill Ranch Oasis** (406-429-6801), P.O. Box 5234, MT 200, Milepost 161. Primarily catering to hunters, this place is also good for anyone who enjoys viewing wildlife. They offer a large continental break-

fast, and if you desire, a full evening meal. The ranch grounds are a fun place to just sit back and enjoy the vast expanse of this area. They offer guests satellite TV, a pool table, a Ping-Pong table, and more. Rates $70 and up.

Malta

🖋 **Tillmans Bed & Breakfast** (406-658-2514; www.tillmansofmontana .com), 17 miles south of Malta off US 2 on US 191. This is a beautifully restored roadhouse with rooms accommodating up to 10 guests. Originally built in the early 1900s, Tillmans served as a stopover point for people traveling to and from Malta in the Missouri River area. They offer home-cooked meals and can arrange any sort of activity in the area. Being close to Fort Peck Lake and the Charles M. Russell National Wildlife Refuge, this is a good place to base for fishing, hiking, boating, cross-country skiing, and more. They can even create an all-inclusive package, with lodging and meals combined with various activities such as horseback riding or hunting. Rates $50 and up.

Westby

Hilltop House Bed & Breakfast (406-385-2533), 301 E. 2nd Street. This is a restored 1930s house. It lies in the extreme corner of northeastern Montana (almost at the border with North Dakota and Canada). The views here are great, and this is a good place for hikers and anglers. There are few amenities in the area, but the folks here will help you in any way possible. Rates $50 and up.

Wolf Point

The Meadowlark (406-525-3289), 872 Nickwall Road. This is a fine place to stay—a little out of place in this remote region, but certainly not pretentious by any means. Wolf Point is ideally situated for exploring the best of this region. A stay here includes a farm-style breakfast in the host's nearby home. Meals are prepared on a full-sized cast iron AGA Cooker. They offer the climate-controlled Rose and Badlands Suites. The Rose has one bedroom, bath w/shower, laundry, kitchen, and dining and living room with a queen sofa bed. An upright grand piano and TV are in this suite. The Badlands has one bedroom, bath w/shower, sitting room with TV, and organ. It is decorated in beautiful knotty pine with handcrafted quilts. Rates $90 and up.

LODGES, GUEST RANCHES, AND HOTELS/MOTELS

Circle

Wolf Farms Vacation Home (406-485-2736; www.midrivers.com/~ajw1), located 10.5 miles north of Circle, then 4 miles west on MT 13. This is a very nice place if you want to get away from it all and enjoy peace and quiet and solitude, but still have the option to explore as much as you want. The guest house features private rooms, each furnished with period antiques. They only allow same-party guests, so you will not have to worry about sharing anything with unknown guests. They also offer horseback riding as part of the lodging. Rates $125 and up.

Fort Peck

Fort Peck Hotel (406-526-3266), 175 S. Missouri Street. Open April through December. Built in the 1930s, this place is filled with history and friendly faces. They offer lodging, fine dining, and a very nice lounge. The building is listed on the National

Register of Historical Places. The rooms each have a double and single bed. Most rooms have a shower, and some have a large claw-foot tub. Walking down the wooden floor of the hallway and into the lobby is like walking back in time—that sounds silly, but the sound of a wood floor really does serve up nostalgia. Internet access and Direct TV are available in the lobby. Breakfast, lunch, and dinner are served in the beautiful Fort Peck Dining Room. As you sit on a wooden rocking chair on the large front porch, you will savor the small-town Montana lifestyle.

Glasgow

Burke Ranch (406-228-2295; www .burkeranch.com), 628 3rd Avenue North (mailing address). They are located 60 miles south of Glasgow in the Charles M. Russell National Wildlife Refuge. There are private cabins with all the amenities. They also offer a bunkhouse with accommodations for up to eight people. For folks on a tight budget, they offer a restored schoolhouse that offers hostel-style sleeping arrangements. This is an ideal place if you want to explore the refuge or boat on Fort Peck Lake. Please inquire about rates, as they have so many options.

Hinsdale

Rock Creek Outfitters and Lodge (406-648-5524; www.milkrivermontana .com), 1291 Rock Creek Road. This is a modern lodge, and each room has a private bathroom. Amenities include three meals a day, horseback riding, guided tours, entertainment, and airport transportation. You can also "a la carte" things if you like, but this place is great for enjoying a relaxing vacation and not having to worry about any details. Rates start at $400 per person per day and include pretty much everything (room, meals, and an assortment of activities.

Jordan

&. ✒ **Hell Creek Marina** (406-557-2345; www.hellcreekmarina.com), P.O. Box 486; located 35 miles north of Jordan on MT 543. They offer cabin rentals with little beyond the basics. However, this is a very interesting part of Montana and worth a visit. Be sure to book early, as these fill up fast.

Lambert

✒ **Gray's Coulee Guest Ranch** (406-774-3778), CR 120, P.O. Box 252; located 6 miles south of Lambert (about 20 miles west of Sidney). There are 6,000 acres to explore here. They can serve up an entire ranch vacation with everything included or you can piece together your trip and do some on your own. Either way, you will enjoy the relaxation and scenery of this ranch. For children, inquire about their Learning Vacations. Rates vary according to package and length of stay, so please inquire.

Saco

Beaver Creek Lodge (406-527-3204), 210 Montana Avenue; located south of US 2, just across the railroad tracks. This truly is a home away from home. They offer a quaint lodge with six bedrooms, three bathrooms, and laundry facilities. Hunting, fishing, hiking, and more are very close by. The property is available to rent nightly, weekly, or monthly. Singles, couples, or groups will find this place pleasant, clean, and convenient. Please inquire, as rates vary according to length of stay and size of group.

Zortman

&. ✒ **Buckhorn Store, Cabins & RV Park** (406-673-3162), 1st and Main

Street; located 7 miles off US 191. They offer cabins with kitchenettes. RVers will find hook-ups, and there are a few tent sites. The general store sells the basics. Rates vary according to accommodations.

Whispering Pines Vacation Homes (406-673-3304), 1100 Thompson Avenue. This is a two-bedroom, one-bath fully furnished home. They also allow pets and there is plenty of room for them to roam. Located near the Little Rocky Mountains, you can partake in hiking, hunting, biking, fishing, and cross-country skiing (when snow permits). Rates $60 and up.

See also Ranch Vacations under *To Do–Unique Adventures.*

✳ Where to Eat

DINING OUT
Glasgow
Sam's Supper Club (406-228-4614), 307 Klein Avenue. Locally owned and operated for nearly 40 years, this is a fine-dining establishment. Steaks are their specialty, but they also offer seafood and pasta selections. Surprisingly, they even have a few tasty vegetarian options. The children's and seniors' menus are varied and reasonably priced.

Malta
& **Roger's Saloon and Chuckwagon** (406-654-9987), 147 S. 1st E. Daily specials complement a full menu of steaks, barbeque, seafood, burgers, and more. The décor here is worth a visit as they have many old photographs and a few animal mounts on the walls. They provide a fun taste of life in Missouri River Country.

& **Tin Cup Bar and Grill** (406-654-5527) overlooks the scenic Marian Hills Golf Club and offers a full menu

with consistently good service. This is a good place for a romantic date away from the kids or just a nice meal in a beautiful setting. The best time to dine here is near sunset during the summer or fall months.

Plentywood
& **Dr. DeBelles** (406-765-2830), 1 mile east of Plentywood on MT 16. The name might be a little confusing, but it is supposed to be pronounced as "doctor the belly." And that is just what you will get—some good fortune for your stomach and palate. The menu is varied and fun, but the owners always suggest beef because this is the heart of some of Montana's best beef country. If you aren't up for steak, try any of their chicken dishes; they won't disappoint.

Ingomar
Historic Jersey Lilly Bar and Café (406-358-2278), Main Street (US 12). Located in a building that once housed a bank (ca. 1914), this tiny place serves breakfast, lunch, and dinner. You will mostly find locals here, but occasionally a traveler stops in and everyone makes them feel at home. Their bean soup is homemade and known throughout the region. The building is also listed on the National Register of Historic Places, so you will be dining with a bit of history.

Sidney
& **Cattle-Ac Niteclub, Casino, and Steakhouse** (406-443-7174l), 119 N. Central Avenue. If the name doesn't entice you to visit this place, then the food will. The décor is classic small-town Montana, with a twist. On most nights you will be dining with locals because not a lot of tourists travel through Sidney (which is too bad, but

it's changing). But the locals will be here because they want great food.

&. **South 40** (406-433-4999), 209 2nd Avenue N.W. This restaurant offers fine dining in a casual atmosphere. They are known for miles around as a premier spot to feast on slow-roasted prime rib. Their steaks are always cooked right, and the rustic atmosphere is the perfect blend of casual and comfortable. They also have an extensive salad bar. A children's menu is available, along with a selection of meals for senior citizens. The lounge and full casino are located away from the dining room, so this place works well for kids. If you want to keep the party rolling, the lounge offers karaoke, electronic darts, and signature fishbowl drinks for a fun time.

See also Fort Peck Hotel under *Lodging–Lodges, Guest Ranches, and Hotels/Motels.*

EATING OUT

Culbertson
Wild West Diner (406-787-5374), near the junction of US 2 and MT 16. If you can start with a pie and not spoil your dinner, do it. If you must have dessert last, their homestyle menu will surely have something you can enjoy.

Fort Peck
Gateway Supper Club (406-526-9988), located 3 miles west of Fort Peck on MT 24. You will enjoy their deck overlooking Fort Peck Lake. The fresh-caught walleye (in season) is the best thing on the menu, but if fish is not your thing they offer plenty of other choices.

✪ **Missouri River Outpost** (406-526-3231), 1 mile below Fort Peck Dam on MT 117. They are known

throughout eastern Montana for providing quality service for folks fishing and paddling the Missouri River. However, they are also known for their ability to create good food a long way from any major town. Their menu is mostly steak and seafood, but their true claim to fame is that they serve the largest steak dinner in Montana. The best part: If you can eat the entire thing in less than one hour the dinner is free. They also have burgers, salads, and more.

Glasgow
&. ✍ **Eugene's Pizza** (406-228-8552), 193 Klein Avenue in the Big G shopping center. Pizza is in their name, but they have a little of everything—steak, chicken, burgers, seafood, etc. They are also known for their pizza (of course) and their specialty ribs, aptly called "Eugene's ribs."

✍ **Flicks** (406-228-2377), 531 2nd Avenue. This is the place for a morning treat and the freshly baked caramel rolls are the best.

✍ **Johnnies Café** (406-228-4222), 433 1st Avenue S. They have been in Glasgow since 1914, but over the years this local favorite has had several owners. Currently a couple originally from Kalispell owns and operates it, and they have made it the best it has ever been. They serve breakfast, lunch, and dinner, and you're sure to find something to enjoy.

Jordan
✍ **Soda Fountain at the Jordan Drug Company** (406-557-6180), 437 Main Street. Located in downtown Jordan (what there is of it), this nostalgic place will take you back many years. This is a true soda fountain, and it has changed little since its 1937

opening. Try a double malted shake in any flavor and your taste buds will thank you.

Malta

&. **Cattleman's Steakhouse** (406-654-2654), 174 S. 1st Avenue E. Located in downtown Malta, they serve up a full menu of great steaks, seafood, sandwiches, and burgers. Beer and wine are available, with live music most weekends.

&. ♪ **Stretch's Pizza** (406-654-1229), 140 S. 1st E. They have a massive game room where the little ones can run off some energy. This place has consistently good pizza, with some burger and chicken options on the menu as well. And their homemade pies are quite a treat.

Westside Restaurant (406-654-1555), US 2, on the west side of town. They are known more for their massive salad bar than for anything else. They do have a full menu, but the salad bar is very extensive and chock-full of a wide variety of items.

Plentywood

Randy's Restaurant (406-765-1661), 323 W. 1st Avenue. For breakfast, lunch, or dinner, the home cooking in this casual family-owned place will fill you up and delight those taste buds. The service can be fast or slow depending on whether you want to get back to exploring or enjoy a leisurely meal. Their chili special is always worth having.

Poplar

Buckhorn Bar (406-768-5221), 203 2nd Avenue W. More than just a bar, this is often the social center of Poplar. They have a full menu, so don't let the name fool you. Try their weekly Indian taco special.

Scobey

The Shirt Stop & Coffee Break (406-487-5902), 103 Main Street. Perhaps the only coffeehouse/silk screen business in Montana, these friendly folks will design a shirt for you while you enjoy a cup of coffee, roll, or sandwich. They also offer espresso drinks and smoothies while you wait.

Sidney

&. **The Bean Bag** (406-433-8388), 110 N. Central Avenue. A full-service coffeehouse with great espresso, lattes, and more. They often have a few fresh-baked goods as well, but get there early because the locals know the cat's out of the bag.

&. **M & M Café** (406-433-1714), south of Sidney on MT 16. They have the best breakfasts in town and their homemade lunches and dinners will delight. No matter what you have for breakfast, be sure to enjoy one of their caramel or cinnamon rolls. The dinner menu includes steaks, burgers, chicken, salads, and a nightly special. If the food doesn't keep you coming back, the pleasant service will.

♪ **Pizza House** (406-433-1971), 710 South Central in downtown Sidney. In addition to pizza, this small and friendly place has good pastas, tacos, and an enormous taco salad. There are a few games for kids, and even some for adults as they have one of the few Pac-Man video games left in Montana.

Westby

Prairie Kitchen (406-385-2404), 211 Main. This place is hard to find, not because Westby is large, but because Westby is really a long way from anywhere with a lot of people. The town itself is a great place to get away from it all. If you like birds, the town lies on a major migratory bird route. The Prairie Kitchen serves up some of the best mashed potatoes and gravy this side of Chicago.

Wolf Point

& **M/Ds** (406-653-2401), US 2 in downtown Wolf Point. The owners, Dee and Marlene, take great pride in serving a small menu that is big on taste. They offer homemade cinnamon rolls for breakfast (or any time of day), burgers, homemade soups, and fresh-baked pies that are the perfect close to a meal here. In fact, some locals even eat a slice of pie for breakfast. On Sunday, try their buffet from 11 A.M.–3 P.M.

& **Old Town Grill** (406-653-1031), US 2 in downtown Wolf Point. They offer a nice mix of American, Mexican, and Asian fare. The window-side booths will keep you entertained while you're eating. They also feature daily soups and specials. A remodel in recent years has kept things nice and new.

✳ Special Events

February: �@ 🐟 **Ice Fishing Tournament,** Glasgow. More than just a serious fishing tournament, there are events for kids and more. Top prize is $2,000.

March: ✐ **Milk River Wagon Train Feed and Dance,** Malta. Tall tales, dances, and a feast of Rocky Mountain oysters (if you have to ask, don't), and more.

April: & **Northeast Montana Farm Expo,** Plentywood. Agricultural and household exhibits from Montana, North Dakota, and Canada. Educational seminars daily. Friday night's banquet includes a featured guest speaker.

May: ✐ **Mother's Day Style Show & Luncheon,** Malta. Treat yourself, friends, and family to the Spring Style Show, presented by Family Matters and complemented by a salad buffet luncheon.

Annual McCone County Wagon Train, Wolf Point. Camp out under the stars while enjoying a real Old West wagon train.

May and June: **Rock Creek Walleye Tournament on Fort Peck,** Fort Peck. One of America's best walleye waters sets the stage for an exciting event where walleye over 10 pounds are often caught.

June: ✐ **Montana Dinosaur Festival,** Malta. The best of Montana dinosaurs are featured throughout this festival. A dig pit, vendors in the park, Dino Camp (fossil mold making), and educational programs.

Frontier Days, Culbertson. For over 40 years this community festival has featured parades, rodeo, community follies, and other entertainment.

Glasgow Feather Fest, Glasgow. A two-day event celebrating local and migratory bird species during an important part of the migration.

Badlands Celebration, Brockton. A powwow that celebrates native culture and traditions through dancing, food crafts, and fellowship with one another. All members of the general public are welcome to participate.

June and July: ✐ **Prairie Fest,** Plentywood. Prairie Fest is a gathering of young and old, residents and visitors, families and friends, to celebrate Sheridan County and its way of life.

Fort Kipp Celebration, Poplar. This powwow celebrates native culture and traditions through dancing, food, crafts, and more.

Wolf Point Horse Stampede, Wolf Point. A rodeo featuring a parade, carnival, "Human Stampede," and more.

Sunrise Festival of the Arts, Sidney. One of eastern Montana's premier events, with attendance in the thousands. The finest artists and crafters in a three-state area display and sell their creations in scenic Central Park beneath colorful canopies. Food, crafts, and more.

July and August: ✍ **Richland County Fair and Rodeo,** Sidney. An annual event known as the show window of agricultural achievement in eastern Montana and western North Dakota. Rodeo, parade, livestock exhibits, big-name entertainment, and more.

August: **Daniels County Fair,** Scobey. A family fair featuring rodeo action, demolition derby, music, a night show, 4-H events, open class exhibits, carnival, petting zoo, commercial exhibits, and parade.

Northeast Montana Fair, Glasgow. A large fair featuring a PRCA rodeo and wild horse race, plus a bike rodeo, food booths, commercial and machinery displays, and games. An admission fee is charged for the rodeo, demolition derby, and talent show.

Indian Arts Showcase, Sidney. Assiniboine and Sioux from the Fort Peck Indian Reservation, along with the Three Affiliated Tribes (Mandan, Hidatsa, and Arikara) from the Fort Berthold Indian Reservation in North Dakota, demonstrate the arts and crafts of the Indian people with speakers and demonstrations both days, along with a drum and dance group. Some crafts are for sale, others are demo only.

August and September: **Fall Wagon Train,** Jordan. Enjoy the remnants of the homestead era, the wondrous landscape, numerous rock formations, and abundant wildlife.

September: **Town and Country Day,** Circle. A fun run, followed by free breakfast and a kid/community parade. Other activities include an auction, with free lunch served by the local phone company, farmer's market, kids' games, football, volleyball games, free barbecue, and more.

Labor Day Wagon Train, Culbertson. An ideal opportunity to see just what our ancestors went through as they ventured into the unknown. Either on horseback or in a wagon, this event will provide an experience long to be remembered and to share with your children.

Northeast Montana Threshing Bee and Antique Show, Culbertson. Threshing bundles, sawing logs, parade of old tractors and machinery, small engine display, shingle saw, lumber planer, flea market space, car show, free barbecue, and more.

INDEX

A

A. B. Guthrie Memorial Trail, 202

Absaalooke Nation. *See* Crow Indians

Absaroka Dogsled Treks, 154

Absaroka Lodge, 167

Absaroka-Beartooth Wilderness Area, 122, 143, 145–47, 157

Absarokee: lodging, 159

accommodations: overview, 29. *See also specific accommodations and destinations*

Ackley Lake State Park, 208

Adventure Whitewater (Red Lodge), 149

After Five, 266

agriculture: overview, 21

air (helicopter) tours, 80, 117

Airport Golf Club (Wolf Point), 320

Airport Inn (Miles City), 304

airports, 21–22. *See also specific airports*

Alameda's Hot Springs Retreat, 71–72

Alberton: lodging, 86

Alberton Gorge, 65, 73

Alder Gulch Short-Line Railroad, 256–57

Alice Creek Ranch, 257

Alkali Creek Trail, 288

Alt, David, 27

Alta Campground, 61–62

Alta Meadow Ranch, 79

Alzada, 288

American Computer Museum, 129

American Indians. *See* Native Americans; *and specific tribes*

AMTRAK, 22, 33–34, 188

Anaconda, 226, 232, 241–42; eating, 268; emergencies, 231; information, 228; lodging, 261–62, 264; sights/activities, 235–37, 241–45, 249, 254–59; special events, 271–72

Anaconda Chamber of Commerce, 228

Anaconda Community Hospital, 231

Anaconda Country Club, 249

Anaconda Crazy Days, 272

Anaconda Hills Golf Course, 201

Anaconda Smelter Stack State Park, 236–37

Anaconda-Pintler Scenic Highway, 226, 232, 234, 241–42

Anaconda-Pintler Wilderness Area, 82, 242, 259

animals. *See* birdwatching; wildlife; wildlife refuges; zoos

Antelope Creek Wilderness Study Area, 317

antiques, 22

Antiques USA, 22

Apgar Campground, 112

Apgar Village Lodge, 117

Apgar Visitor Center, 108–9

Arapaho Indians, 48, 277, 286

Arapooish Pond and Recreation Park, 294

Archie Bray Foundation, 237

area code, 22

Arrowhead Meadows Golf Course, 201

Arts Chateau (Butte), 234–35

Arts in the Park (Kalispell), 102

Artspace (Billings), 303

Artwalk Downtown (Billings), 305

Ashland Ranger District, 290, 293, 297

Assiniboine Indians, 29, 48, 186, 313, 314, 331

Augusta, 185–86

auto travel. *See* car travel

Avalanche Campground, 112

Avalanche Gorge, 114–15

B

Babb, 110

Bad Rock Bed & Breakfast Inn, 87

Badlands Celebration, 330

Bailiwick Farm Bed & Breakfast, 86

Bainville, 316, 322

Baker, 281; eating, 303; emergencies, 281; information, 278; lodging, 301;

sights/activities, 283–84, 288, 290, 291
Baker Chamber of Commerce, 278
Baker Lake, 281, 290
Bangtail Bicycle Shop, 139
Bangtail Ridge Trail, 139
Bannack Days, 237, 272
Bannack Ghost Walks, 272
Bannack Pass Ranch, 257
Bannack State Park, 237
Bar S Supper Club, 216
Baring Falls, 114
Barrel Mountaineering, 156
Barrett Hospital and Health Care, 231
Barrister Bed & Breakfast, 262–63
Bar-3 BBQ, 172
Basin Lakes National Recreation Trail, 144–45
Basin Medical Center, 185
Bayview Inn (Polson), 93
Bean Bag, 329
Bear Creek Guest Ranch (East Glacier Park), 79
Bear Creek Lodge (Thompson Falls), 90
Bear Creek Saloon (Red Lodge), 175
Bear Creek Trail, 74
Bear Gulch Pictographs, 190
Bear Paw Battlefield, 190–91, 251
Bear Paw Ski Bowl, 205
Bear Trap Canyon Wilderness, 249, 253, 259–60
Bear Trap National Recreation Trail, 249
Beardance Inn and Cabins, 86–87
Beargrass Grill, 216
bears, 34, 85, 111; Grizzly Wolf & Discover Center, 136; hunting, 29; safety tips, 22–23
Beartooth Café, 170–71
Beartooth Hospital and Health Center, 127
Beartooth Mountain Guides, 156
Beartooth Mountains, 137, 138, 154, 156, 157

Beartooth Nature Center, 158, 177
Beartooth Plateau, 136–37
Beartooth Ranger District, 141–42, 157
Beartooth Scenic Byway, 24, 124, 136–37
Beartooth Whitewater, 149
Beartooths, Museum of the, 131–32
Beaver Creek County Park, 208–9
Beaver Creek Golf Course, 201
Beaver Creek Lodge, 326
Beaver Creek Nature Trail, 320
Beaver Creek Trail Rides and Guest Ranch, 322
Beaverhead Chamber of Commerce, 228
Beaverhead Country Club, 249
Beaverhead County Fair, 272
Beaverhead County Lewis & Clark Festival, 272
Beaverhead County Museum, 232–33
Beaverhead River, 237; fishing, 246
Beaverhead Rock State Park, 237
Beaverhead-Deerlodge National Forest, 30, 242, 259; biking, 243; boating, 244–45; cabin rentals, 266; campgrounds, 245; cross-country skiing, 254; Crystal Park, 242, 258; hiking, 251
Beavertail Hill State Park, 80–81
Beer Jug, Inc., 303–4
Belgrade: eating, 172–73; information, 125; lodging, 165–66; special events, 177, 178
Belgrade Chamber of Commerce, 125
Belgrade Fall Festival, 177
Bell Street Bridge, 285
Bell Street Bridge Day, 306
Belt: eating, 217
Belt Creek, 203, 209

Belton Chalet & Lodge, 109–10, 118–19
Benefis Healthcare, 185
Bennet House Country Inn, 263
Benny's Bistro, 267
Benton Lake National Wildlife Refuge, 210
Berkeley Pit, 237–38
Bernice's Bakery, 100
Bert and Ernie's (Great Falls), 216; (Helena), 269
bicycling. See biking
Big Arm State Park, 56
Big Belt Mountains, 187, 259
Big Creek Campground, 62
Big EZ Lodge, 160
Big Hole National Battlefield, 238, 251
Big Hole River, 232; fishing, 246–47
Big Horn Bed & Breakfast, 263
Big Horn County Historical Museum, 282
Big Horn County Memorial Hospital, 281
Big Lake Wildlife Management Area, 159
Big Moose Resort, 166
Big Mountain Golf Club, 67
Big Sandy: activities, 206–7; emergencies, 185; information, 182; lodging, 211
Big Sandy Chamber of Commerce, 182
Big Sandy Medical Center, 185
Big Sheep Creek Backcountry Byway, 242
Big Sky, 127–28; eating, 170, 173; information, 125; lodging, 160, 164–65; sights/activities, 133, 137, 139–40, 144–58; special events, 176
Big Sky Bed & Breakfast, 87–88
Big Sky Chamber of Commerce, 125
Big Sky Golf Course, 144
Big Sky Resort, 139, 150–51
Big Sky Trails (Malta), 321

Big Sky Waterpark (Columbia Falls), 52
Big Sky Winterfest, 176
Big Splash Waterpark, 287
Big Spring Creek, 200
Big Timber: eating, 170; emergencies, 127; information, 125; lodging, 160; sights/activities, 135, 138, 142–45, 148
Big Timber Inn Bed & Breakfast, 160
Big Timber Ranger District, 142
Big Timber Waterslide, 135
Big Timber/Sweet Grass Chamber of Commerce, 125
Bigfork, 44; eating, 94–95, 98; information, 41, 42; lodging, 86–87; sights/activities, 67, 79; special events, 103
Bigfork Area Chamber of Commerce, 41
Bigfork Summer Playhouse, 44
Bighorn Canyon National Recreation Area, 31, 298; boating, 290; hiking, 293
Bighorn Lodge Bed & Breakfast, 89
Bighorn River, 291–92
bighorn sheep, 29, 34, 53, 79, 196, 242, 260, 324
BikeNet (Billings), 288
biking, 23; Custer Country, 288–89; Glacier Country, 57–59, 111; Gold West Country, 243; Missouri River Country, 318; Russell Country, 182, 196–97; Yellowstone Country, 139–40, 177
Bill Roberts Golf Course, 249
Billings, 25, 278, 287–88; eating, 301–3; emergencies, 281; information, 278; lodging, 298–99; map, 279; sights/activities, 284–98; special events, 305–6; transportation, 280
Billings Chamber of

Commerce and Visitor Center, 278
Billings Logan International Airport, 21
birdwatching, 23–24; Custer Country, 293, 294, 297; Glacier Country, 53–54, 72–73, 85, 111; Gold West Country, 260–61; Missouri River Country, 317, 320–23, 330; Russell Country, 210–11
Bison Creek Ranch (East Glacier), 116
Bison Range, National, 45, 54, 84–85
Bite of Bozeman, 177
Bitter Creek Wilderness Study Area, 316–17
Bitterroot Bistro & Catering Company, 95
Bitterroot National Forest, 30, 81–82, 242; biking, 58–59; boating, 60; campgrounds, 61–62; cross-country skiing, 74; Darby Historical Visitor Center, 50; hiking, 68–69; Skalkaho Wildlife Preserve, 85; skiing, 75
Bitterroot River, 44; fishing, 63
Bitterroot River Inn and Conference Center, 92
Bitterroot Valley, 44, 55
Bitterroot Valley Bluegrass Festival, 102
Bitterroot Valley Chamber of Commerce, 41
Black Eagle Falls, 196
Black Otter Trail, 289
Black Powder Shoot, 102, 220
Black Sandy State Park, 245
Blackfeet Community Hospital, 44
Blackfeet Indian Reservation, 29, 39–40, 45; information, 41; lodging, 91; special events, 102; transportation, 43
Blackfeet Indians, 45–48, 48, 105, 116
Blackfoot Inn (Ovando), 265

Blackfoot River, 233; fishing, 63–64; rafting, 73
Blacktail Mountain, 74
Blacktail Ranch (Wolf Creek), 252, 257
Blacktail Station (Dillon), 267
Blaine County Museum, 182, 191
Blodgett Overlook Trail, 68
Blue Creek Trail, 242
Blue Damsel Lodge, 91
Blue Lake Trail, 145
Blue Mountain Bed & Breakfast, 88
Blue Mountain Recreation Area, 57
Blue Winged Olive Bed & Breakfast, 162
boat cruises: Flathead Lake, 78–79; Holter Lake, 257, 260; Upper Missouri River, 208
boating, 24; Custer Country, 290; Glacier Country, 59–61, 111–12; Gold West Country, 244–45; Missouri River Country, 318; Russell Country, 197–98; Yellowstone Country, 140–41. *See also* paddling
Bob Marshall Wilderness, 54, 80, 82, 209–10; campgrounds, 62, 200
Bob's Riverfront Restaurant, 218
Bogart's Restaurant, 175
Bohart Ranch Cross-Country Ski Center, 151
Bonanza Creek Country Guest Ranch, 207
Book, Festival of the (Missoula), 103
Book N Bear Nook, 304
Boulder Batholith, 242–43
Boulder Hot Springs Inn and Conference Center, 252
Boulder River, 138, 143, 148
Bowdoin National Wildlife Refuge, 317, 318, 320, 322–23
Bowman Lake, 111–12; campground, 112

Bozeman, 124, 133; eating, 170, 173–74; emergencies, 127; information, 125; lodging, 160–61, 165–66, 169; map, 134; sights/activities, 129–59; special events, 176, 177; transportation, 126
Bozeman Area Chamber of Commerce, 125
Bozeman Children's Museum, 135
Bozeman Deaconess Hospital, 127
Bozeman Hot Springs, 147
Bozeman Ranger District, 142
Bozeman Recreation Department's Ice Skating Rinks, 150
Bozeman Trail, 28, 133
Bozeman/Gallatin Field, 21
Bray (Archie) Foundation, 237
Breaks Ale House and Grill, 218
Brewery Follies, 234
Brewhouse Pub and Grill, 269
Briarwood Country Club, 292
Bridge Creek Backcountry Kitchen and Wine Bar, 171–72
Bridger: activities, 144, 146, 156; information, 125; special events, 176–77
Bridger Bowl Ski and Snowboard Resort, 151–52
Bridger Chamber of Commerce, 125
Bridger Creek Golf Course, 144
Briggs Creek Trail, 203
Broadus: eating, 302; emergencies, 281; information, 280; lodging, 299; sights/activities, 284, 288, 292, 293
Broadwater Health Center, 231
Broken Arrow Lodge and Outfitters, 252
Broken Hart Ranch, 146

Brookies Cookies, 98
Brookside Bed & Breakfast, 159
Brothel Museum, 235
Browning, 45, 110; emergencies, 44; information, 41; lodging, 91; sights/activities, 48, 49
Buckaroo Eatery and Coffeehouse, 217–18
Buckhorn Bar (Poplar), 329
Buckhorn Store, Cabins & RV Park (Zortman), 326–27
Buck's T4 Lodge, 164; Dining Room, 170
Buffalo Café, 101
Buffalo Hill Golf Club, 67
Buffalo Jump State Parks, 133, 135, 193
Buff's Bar, Casino, and Restaurant, 303
Bull Mountains, 287–88
Bull River Campground, 62
Bull Run Guest Ranch, 203, 207
Bulldog Pub and Steakhouse, 99
Bullwinkle's Saloon and Restaurant, 172
Bungalow Bed & Breakfast, 264
Bunkhouse Bed & Breakfast, 163
Buns 'N' Beds Deli and Cabins, 174
Bureau of Land Management (BLM), 24, 32
Burke Ranch, 322, 326
Burnt Lodge Wilderness Study Area, 317
bus service, 24
Busy Bee Family Dining and Gift Shop, 304
Butte, 225–26, 240; eating, 266–69; emergencies, 231; information, 228; lodging, 262; map, 232; sights/activities, 234–61; special events, 272; transportation, 231
Butte Community Ice Center, 254
Butte Country Club, 249
Butte Field Office, 246

Butte/Bert Mooney Airport, 21–22
Butte-Silver Bow Art Center, 235
Butte-Silver Bow Chamber of Commerce, 228
Buzzard Day, 305
Buzz's Brew, 119–20
Bynum Reservoir, 204
byways: overview, 24. See also specific byways

C

C. M. Russell Museum, 189, 220
Cabin Fever Quilters Show, 103
Cabinet Mountains Wilderness, 45, 82–83
Cabinet Ranger District, 62
Cabinet View Country Club, 67
Cabins at Glacier Raft Company, 119
Café Max, 95–96
Cajun Mary's Café, 120
Calvert Hotel, 214–15
Calypso Trail, 288
Cameron Gallery, 284
Camp Creek Campground, 318
Camp Disappointment, 39, 49
Campground Owners Association of Montana, 33
camping (campgrounds), 24–25; RV parks, 32; Custer Country, 290–91; Glacier Country, 61–63, 112–13; Gold West Country, 245–46; Missouri River Country, 318–19; Russell Country, 198–200; Yellowstone Country, 141–42
Camps Pass Ski Trail, 294
Camps Pass Trail, 293
canoeing. See paddling
Canyon Ferry Reservoir, 244, 248
Canyon Street Grill (West Yellowstone), 175–76
Capitol Building (Helena), 240

Capitol Rock National Natural Landmark, 288
car travel: byways, 24; highways, 28; mileage, 30; to Montana, 23; road reports, 32; speed limits and seat belts, 33
Carbella Recreation Site, 141
Carbon County Historical Society & Museum, 129
Careless Creek Ranch Getaway, 207–8
Carousel for Missoula, 52
Carter County Chamber of Commerce, 278
Carter County Museum, 282
Carter Ferry, 192
Cascade: activities, 203, 207; eating, 216
Cascade County Courthouse, 191
Cascade Falls, 68
Cascade National Recreation Trail, 68
casinos, 27; Baker, 303; Forsyth, 303; Havre, 219; Lolo, 72; Polson, 97; Sidney, 327–28
Castle Museum (White Sulphur Springs), 188–89
Cat Coulee Beds 'n' Birds, 300
Cat Eye Café, 173
Cattail Marsh Nature Trail, 244
Cattail Marsh Recreation Area, 244
Cattle-Ac Niteclub, Casino, and Steakhouse, 327–28
Cattleman's Steakhouse, 329
caverns, 243, 286
Cedar Creek Golf Course, 67
cell phones, 25
Celtic Festival, 305
Centennial Guest Ranch (Ennis), 257
Centennial Ice Area, 294
Centennial Inn (Dillon), 262
Central Montana Medical Center, 185
Central Montana Museum (Lewistown), 188

Chalet Sports (Bozeman), 139
Charles M. Russell National Wildlife Refuge, 195, 297, 313, 323–24; boating, 318; campgrounds, 199
Charles Water Nature Trails, 68–69
Charles Waters Campground, 61
Charley Manley Bed & Breakfast, 299–300
Charlie Russell Chew-Choo, 206, 221
Charlie Russell Manor, 212
cherries, 21, 44, 87
Cherry Creek Trail, 249
Chester: emergencies, 185, 231; information, 182; lodging, 211; special events, 220–21
Chester/Liberty County Chamber of Commerce, 182
Chico Hot Springs, 140, 147, 166; Dining Room, 171
Chief Joseph, 190–91
Chief Joseph Cross-Country Ski Trails, 74
Chief Joseph Park (Harlowton), 187
Chief Joseph Ranch (Darby), 79
Chief Mountain International Highway, 110
Chief Plenty Coups State Park, 285–86
Children's Museum of Bozeman, 135
Children's Museum of Montana (Great Falls), 194
Children's Museum of Northeastern Montana (Glasgow), 316
Chinook: information, 182; sights/activities, 191, 201; special events, 221
Chinook Chamber of Commerce, 182
Chinook Golf Course, 201
Chippewa Cree Business Committee, 183
Chippewa Cree Recreation Area, 205

Chippewa Indians, 29, 48, 220
Chocolate Festival, 271–72
Choteau, 186; eating, 217–18; emergencies, 185; information, 183; lodging, 211, 213; sights/activities, 190, 198–208
Choteau Chamber of Commerce, 183
Choteau City Park, 199
Choteau Country Club, 201
Choteau Ranger Station, 186
Christmas for the Critters, 177
Chuckwagon BBQ, Hay, and Dinner Horse Rides at the 320 Guest Ranch, 154
cigarette smoking, 33
Circle: lodging, 325; special events, 331
Circle Inn Golf Links, 292
City Brew, 24
City Club Lanes & Steak House, 170
Clack (H. Earl) Memorial Museum, 189
Clark, Charles, 234–35
Clark, William. *See* Lewis & Clark
Clark, William A., 234; Copper King Mansion, 238–39
Clark and Lewie's, 216–17
Clark Canyon Reservoir, 242, 244
Clark Fork River, 54, 57, 69; campgrounds, 63; fishing, 64–65; rafting, 73
Clark Fork River Trail, 57
Clark Fork Riverfront Trail System, 40, 57, 69
Clark Fork Valley Hospital, 44
Clarke, John, 48
Clarks Fork of the Yellowstone River, 122, 298; fishing, 143
Clarks Fork Valley Museum, 129
Clark's Lookout State Park, 237
Clary Coulee Trail, 202
Clearwater River Canoe

Trail, 54, 72–73
Clearwater State Forest, 83–84
Cliff Swallow Fishing Access Site, 143
climate, 25
Clinic at West Yellowstone, 127
Clinton: lodging, 91
Club 519, 302–3
Coal Banks Landing Recreation Site, 199
Coal Bowl, 303
Coal Creek State Forest, 84
coffee: overview, 24. *See also specific cafés and coffeehouses*
Coffee Den at the Book N Bear Nook, 304
Coffee Hound, 219
Collins Mansion Bed & Breakfast, 212
Colstrip, 281; activities, 293; eating, 303; emergencies, 281; information, 278; lodging, 299; special events, 305
Colstrip Chamber of Commerce, 278
Colstrip Days Celebration, 305
Colstrip Medical Center, 281
Columbia Falls, 40; eating, 98; information, 41; lodging, 87; sights/activities, 52, 59, 62, 68
Columbia Falls Chamber of Commerce, 41
Columbus, 137; emergencies, 127; information, 125; sights/activities, 131, 137, 138, 142, 144
Columbus Stillwater Golf Course, 144
Como, Lake, 60; campgrounds, 61
Computer Museum, 129
Confluence Trail, 145, 157
Conrad: emergencies, 185; golf, 202; information, 183; special events, 220
Conrad Area Chamber of Commerce, 183

Conrad Mansion Museum, 46, 49
Continental Divide, 27, 105, 117; National Scenic Trail, 259
Continental Divide (restaurant; Ennis), 267
Cooke City, 128; eating, 170–71, 174; information, 125; lodging, 166; sights/activities, 136–38, 142, 154
Cooke City Chamber of Commerce, 125
Cool Dog Ball and Microbrew Review, 271
Cooney Reservoir State Park, 140–41
Copper King Mansion, 238–39
Copper Village Museum and Arts Center, 235
Corner Bar (Baker), 303
Corral Steakhouse, 173; Motel at, 164
Cottonwood City, 236
Cottonwood Country Club, 292
Cottonwood Hills Golf Course, 144
Coulson Park, 289
Council Grove State Park, 50
counties: overview, 25
Courtney Hotel, 229, 234
Cow Creek Campground, 290
Cow Creek Wilderness Study Area, 317
Cowboy Coffee and Steakhouse, 271
Coyote Roadhouse Restaurant, 94–95
Crail Ranch, 133
Crazy Head Springs Recreational Area, 290
Crazy Mountain Cattle Company, 156
Crazy Mountain Inn, 215
Crazy Mountain Museum, 129–30
Cree Indians, 29, 48, 220
Cromwell Dixon Campground, 246

Crooked Falls, 196
Cross M Working Guest Ranch, 295–96
cross-country skiing, 33; Custer Country, 294; Glacier Country, 74–77, 115; Gold West Country, 254–56; Russell Country, 205; Yellowstone Country, 150–54
Crow Agency, 281, 285–86, 288; information, 278; special events, 306
Crow Country/Reservation Tours, 294–95
Crow Fair Powwow and Rodeo, 306
Crow Indian Reservation, 29, 277, 278, 281, 306; tours, 294–95
Crow Indians, 285–86
Crow Scouting Party Camps, 295
cruises. *See* boat cruises
Crystal Lake Campground, 202
Crystal Lake Forest Service Cabin, 202
Crystal Lake Shoreline Loop Trail, 202
Crystal Park, 242, 258
Culbertson, 312; eating, 328; emergencies, 311; information, 311; sights/activities, 313, 317; special events, 330–31
Culbertson Montana Museum and Visitor Center, 313
Custer, George Armstrong, 277, 286, 305
Custer Battlefield Museum, 282–83
Custer Country, 277–306; map, 276.
Custer County Art & Heritage Center, 283
Custer National Forest, 30, 157, 297; biking, 289; campgrounds, 141–42, 143, 290; Capitol Rock, 288; hiking, 293; horseback riding, 293; snowmobiling, 154, 294

Custer's Last Stand Reenactment, 305
Customs, U.S., 106
Cut Bank: campgrounds, 112; emergencies, 44; information, 41; sights/activities, 46–47, 67; special events, 102–3
Cut Bank Area Chamber of Commerce, 41
Cut Bank Golf and Country Club, 67
Cutter, Kirtland: Conrad Mansion Museum, 46, 49
cycling. See biking

D

Dahl Memorial Healthcare Association, 281
Dailey Lake, 141
Daly, Marcus, 50, 225, 226, 235
Daly Mansion, 50
Daniels County Chamber of Commerce, 310
Daniels County Fair, 331
Daniels County Museum & Pioneer Town, 315
Daniels Memorial Hospital, 311
Dante's Creative Cuisine (Great Falls), 217
Dante's Inferno (Big Sky), 173
Darby: eating, 98–99; lodging, 87, 91–92; sights/activities, 50, 79
Darby Historical Visitor Center, 50
Darby Ranger District, 61
Deaconess Hospital, 281
Deadman's Basin Reservoir, 187, 290
Deb's Coffee Shop, 303
Decision Point Overlook, 202
Deer Crossing Bed & Breakfast, 88
Deer Lodge, 233; eating, 269; emergencies, 231; information, 229; sights/activities, 236, 239, 249; special events, 272, 273

Deer Lodge Golf Club, 249
Deerlodge National Forest. See Beaverhead-Deerlodge National Forest
Departure Point, 245
Derby Steak House, 266–67
Desert John's Saloon Museum, 236
Devil's Kitchen, 186
Devils Slide, 138
Diamond Cross Ranch, 296
Diamond R Guest Ranch, 79
Diane Gabriel Trail, 293
Dillon, 232–33; campgrounds, 246; eating, 267, 269; emergencies, 231; information, 228; lodging, 262; sights/activities, 237, 243, 244, 246, 249, 253, 257, 259–60; special events, 272; transportation, 231
Dillon Field Office, 246
Dillon Visitor Information Center, 228
dining. See specific establishments and destinations
dinosaurs, 25–26; Carter County Museum, 282; Clack Memorial Museum, 189; Fort Peck Interpretive Center and Museum, 315; Great Plains Dinosaur Museum and Field Station, 313; Hell Creek Fossil Area, 317; Judith River Dinosaur Institute, 322; Montana Dinosaur Festival, 330; Montana Dinosaur Trail, 25–26, 132, 186, 190; Museum of the Rockies, 132; Old Trail Museum (Choteau), 190; Timescale Adventures, 208
Discovery Basin Ski Area, 254–55
Divide Bridge Campground, 246
Dr. DeBelles, 327
Dog Sled Adventures (Whitefish), 79
dogsledding, 33, 79, 102, 154, 271
Dome Mountain Wildlife

Management Area, 158
Donivans Family Dining, 268
Dori's Café, 219
Dotson's Saloon, 98–99
Double Arrow Resort, 79, 94; eating, 97; golf, 67; horseback riding, 69–70
Double Spear Ranch, 296
Dragon Hollow Play Area, 52–53
Drummond: special events, 272
Dry Wolf Trail, 202–3
Duck Inn's Mediterranean Room and Vineyard, 217
dude ranches, 26; Custer Country, 295–96, 298, 301; Glacier Country, 79, 91–92; Gold West Country, 257–58, 264–65; Missouri River Country, 322, 325–26; Russell Country, 207–8, 213–16; Yellowstone Country, 155–56, 164–66. See also specific ranches
Dumas Brothel Museum, 235
Dupuyer: activities, 203, 207; information, 183; lodging, 211
Dupuyer Community Club, 183
Dutcher Trail, 289
Duvall Inn, 214

E

Eagle Bend Golf Club (Bigfork), 67
Eagle Falls Golf Club (Great Falls), 201
Eagle Rock Golf Course (Billings), 292
Earthquake Area and Visitor Center, 138–39
East Glacier, 110; eating, 119–20; golf, 113; information, 107; lodging, 116–17
East Glacier Chamber of Commerce, 107
East Glacier Motel & Cabins, 116
Eastern Montana Celtic Festival, 305

Eastlick Pond-Big Lake Wildlife Management Area, 159

1880s Ranch (Anaconda), 257

Ekalaka, 281; campgrounds, 290; eating, 303; emergencies, 281; information, 278; sights/activities, 282, 288–90, 297; special events, 306

Ekalaka Park Campground, 290

El Western Inn and Cabins, 264–65

Electric City Waterpark (Great Falls), 194

Elk Country Grill, 218

Elk Foundation Wildlife Visitor Center, 85–86

Elk Lake Resort, 265–66

Elkhorn Ghost Town and State Park, 239

Elkhorn Hot Springs, 252–53, 256

Elmo: lodging, 87

Elmo, Lake, 296

Elwell, Lake, 197–98, 200

Emerald Greens Gold Club, 201

Emerald Sunrise Bed & Breakfast, 88

emergency services, 26

Emigrant: eating, 171, 174; lodging, 161, 166–67

Empire Builder, 22, 33–34, 188

Ennis, 233; activities, 249, 257; eating, 267; emergencies, 231; information, 229; lodging, 262, 264–65; special events, 272

Ennis Chamber of Commerce, 229

Ennis Fly-Fishing Festival, 272

Ennis National Fish Hatchery, 233

Enzo Bistro, 301

Ernie's Bakery and Deli, 176

Essex: eating, 120; lodging, 117; special events, 102

Eugene's Pizza, 328

Eureka: information, 41; sights/activities, 52, 53; special events, 103

Eureka Chamber of Commerce, 41

Eureka Montana Quilt Show, 103

Eureka Reservoir, 204

events, 26, 30, 32. *See also specific events*

Evergreen Motel, 93

Exchange City Golf Club, 292

Expedition Pizza Company, 218

F

Fairfield: information, 183; lodging, 211–12, 213

Fairfield Area Chamber of Commerce, 183

Fairmont Hot Springs Resort, 253; Golf Course, 249

Faithful Street Inn, 168

Fallon Medical Complex, 281

Farm Expo, Northeast Montana, 330

farmer's markets, 26; Circle, 331; Cut Bank, 102–3

farms: overview, 21

Fat Tire Frenzy, 177

Feasts for the Beasts, 177

Federation of Fly Fishers' Fly-Fishing Discovery Center, 130–31

Festival of Lights (Belgrade), 178

Festival of the Book (Missoula), 103

festivals, 26, 30. *See also specific festivals*

Fetty's Bar and Café, 271

5th Street Diner (Great Falls), 218

Finley Point State Park, 56, 81

Finn & Porter Missoula, 96

Firebrand Food & Ale, 119

First Night Missoula, 103

First Peoples Buffalo Jump State Park, 193

Fish Creek Campground, 112

fish hatcheries, 195–96, 233, 310

fishing, 27; Custer Country, 291–92, 295; Federation of Fly Fishers' Fly-Fishing Discovery Center, 130–31; Glacier Country, 63–67, 73, 113; Gold West Country, 246–49, 257; Missouri River Country, 319; Russell Country, 200–201; Yellowstone Country, 142–44. *See also* ice fishing; paddlefishing

Fishing Outfitters Association of Montana, 27, 28

Flathead Convention and Visitor Bureau, 41

Flathead Indian Reservation, 29, 39–40, 45, 48, 50, 55–56, 66; campgrounds, 62; The People's Center, 45, 48, 77

Flathead Lake, 44, 45, 55–56; boat tours, 73, 79; boating, 59; ice fishing, 73; Wild Horse Island, 56, 78–79

Flathead Lake Raft Company, 73

Flathead Lake State Park, 56

Flathead National Forest, 30, 82; campgrounds, 62

Flathead River, 32, 65–66; campgrounds, 62; fishing, 65–66; paddling, 73, 115

Flathead Valley, 40; map, 65

flea markets: Culbertson, 331; Lewistown, 219

Flicks, 328

floating. *See* paddling

Flying R Guest Cabins, 91–92

Folf/Disc Golf Course, 287

Forsyth: eating, 303; emergencies, 281; information, 278; lodging, 299; sights/activities, 284, 287, 292

Forsyth Chamber of Commerce, 278, 310

Forsyth Country Club, 292, 320

Fort Assiniboine Historic Site, 191–92

Fort Belknap Indian Reservation, 29, 186, 310

Fort Belknap Tourism Office, 183

Fort Benton, 186–87; eating, 218; emergencies, 185; information, 183; lodging, 213–14; sights/activities, 189, 193, 196, 202; transportation, 185

Fort Benton, Montana's Heritage Complex, 189

Fort Benton Chamber of Commerce, 183

Fort Berthold Indian Reservation, 331

Fort Custer Golf Club, 292

Fort Kipp Celebration, 330

Fort Missoula, 40, 47, 49–51

Fort Missoula Historical Museum, 47

Fort Owen State Park, 50

Fort Peck, 312; eating, 328; lodging, 325–26; special events, 330

Fort Peck Dam, 312, 315

Fort Peck Dam and Power Plant Museum, 315

Fort Peck Dam Museum and Interpretive Center, 312, 315

Fort Peck Hotel, 325–26

Fort Peck Indian Reservation, 29, 310, 313, 331; Tribal Museum, 313

Fort Peck Lake, 318; campgrounds, 318–19; fishing, 319; paddling, 320–21

Fort Peck Theatre, 312

Fort Peck Tribal Museum, 313

Fort Smith: eating, 303; lodging, 301

Fort Smith Cabins, 301

Fort Union Trading Post National Historic Site, 315–16

Fortine: activities, 68, 79

Fortune Ranger District, 62

Four Dances Natural Area, 298

419 Wine Bar & Restaurant, 97

Fox Cottage, 211–12

Fox Hollow Bed & Breakfast, 160

Fox Ridge Golf Course, 249

Foxglove Bed & Breakfast, 89

Foxwood Inn Bed & Breakfast, 213

Frances, Lake, 198; Ice Derby, 219

Frances Mahon Deaconess Hospital, 311

Frank Church-River of No Return Wilderness, 82

Franklin Street Guest House, 213

Freeheel and Wheel, 140, 176

Freezeout Lake Wildlife Management Area, 210

Frenchtown Pond State Park, 81

Fresno Reservoir, 197

Froid: lodging, 324

Frontier Adventures (Helena), 295

Frontier Gateway Museum (Glendive), 283

Frontier Museum (Deer Lodge), 236

G

G Bar M Ranch, 156

Gallagher's Irish Rose Bed & Breakfast, 163

Gallatin Field, 21

Gallatin Gateway, 137; lodging, 167; special events, 176

Gallatin Gateway Inn, 167

Gallatin Historical Society Pioneer Museum, 131, 133

Gallatin National Forest, 30, 157; biking, 139; cabin rentals, 169; campgrounds, 142; snowmobiling, 154

Gallatin Petrified Forest, 145

Gallatin River, 137, 148, 176; fishing, 143

Gallatin River Lodge, 165–66

Gallatin Whitewater Festival, 176

gambling, 27. *See also* casinos

Gannon Ranch Golf Course, 201

Garden Wall Inn Bed & Breakfast, 90

Gardiner, 124, 128, 140; campgrounds, 141–42; eating, 174–75; emergencies, 127; information, 125; lodging, 161–62, 167; sights/activities, 138, 146, 147, 149; transportation, 126

Gardiner Chamber of Commerce, 125

Gardiner Guest House, 161–62

Gardiner Ranger District, 142

Gardiner-Mammoth Road, 140

Garfield County Chamber of Commerce, 310

Garfield County Museum, 312

Garnet Backcountry Byway, 53

Garnet Ghost Town, 53

Garnet Mountain Range, 53

Garnet National Winter Recreation Trail System, 53

Garryowen, 282–83

Gasthaus Wendlingen Bed & Breakfast, 90–91

Gates of the Mountains, 242, 257, 259

Gates of the Mountains Wilderness, 243, 259, 260

Gateway Supper Club, 328

Gelandespring Lodge, 75–76

General Wm. Ashley, 208

geography of Montana, 27

geology of Montana, 27

George Henry's Restaurant, 301–2

Georgetown Lake, 232, 244–45

Georgetown Lake Lodge, 264

Geyser Park, 287
Ghost Rails Inn (Alberton), 86
ghost tours, 236, 272, 305
ghost towns, 53, 192–93, 234, 237, 239
Giant Springs State Park, 187, 195–96, 196
Gibson Park, 194
Gilt Edge, 193
Glacier Country, 39–120; map, 38. *See also specific destinations*
Glacier Country Regional Tourism Commission, 42
Glacier County Historical Museum, 46–47
Glacier Ice Rink, 74
Glacier National Park, 30–31, 39–41, 105–20; campgrounds, 112–13; eating, 119–20; emergencies, 108; information, 107; lodging, 116–19; map, 106; sights/activities, 108–15; tours, 115; transportation, 108; visitor centers, 108–9; wildlife, 111
Glacier Park Boat Company, 112
Glacier Park Lodge & Resort, 116
Glacier Park Lodge and Golf Resort, 113
Glacier Park Red Bus Tours, 115
Glacier Raft Company Cabins, 119
Glacier St. Mary Lodge Resort, 118
Glacier View Golf Course, 67, 113
Glacier View Ranger District, 62
Glacier Village Restaurant, 119–20
Glasgow: eating, 327, 328; emergencies, 311; information, 310; lodging, 326; sights/activities, 315–22; special events, 330–31; transportation, 311
Glasgow Chamber of Commerce, 310
Glasgow Feather Fest, 330
Glendive: eating, 303–4; emergencies, 281; information, 278; lodging, 299–300; sights/activities, 283, 285, 292, 293, 295–96; special events, 305–6
Glendive Chamber of Commerce, 278
Glendive Medical Center, 281
Going-to-the-Sun Road, 111, 114, 115
Gold Fever Rock Shop (Helena), 258
Gold Rush Fever Days, 272
Gold West Country, 225–73; map, 224. *See also specific destinations*
Golden Spur Sports Bar, 304
Goldsmith's Bed & Breakfast, 89
golf, 27–28; Custer Country, 292–93; Glacier Country, 67–68, 113; Gold West Country, 249; Missouri River Country, 320; Russell Country, 201–2; Yellowstone Country, 144
Governor's Cup Road Race, 272
Governors Mansion, Original, 240, 273
Granary, The (Billings), 302
Grand Hotel and Bed & Breakfast (Big Timber), 160
Grand Union Hotel (Fort Benton), 213–14
Granite County Medical Center, 231
Granite County Museum and Cultural Center, 234
Granite Ghost Town State Park, 239, 241–42
Granite Park Chalet, 109–10, 117, 118
Granite Peak, 138, 156
Grant-Kohrs Ranch National Historic Site, 233, 239, 272, 273
Grasshopper Glacier, 138
Grassy Mountain Lodge, 215
Gray's Coulee Guest Ranch, 326
Great Bear Wilderness, 82, 209–10
Great Divide Snowsports and Ski Area, 255
Great Falls, 181, 187; campgrounds, 199–200; eating, 216–17, 218; emergencies, 185; information, 183, 185; lodging, 212, 214; map, 184; sights/activities, 189–210; special events, 220; transportation, 185
Great Falls Chamber of Commerce, 183
Great Falls International Airport, 21
Great Northern Bar & Grill (Whitefish), 101
Great Northern Bed & Breakfast (Chester), 211
Great Northern Railway, 49, 109, 117–18, 188
Great Northern Steak and Rib House (East Glacier), 119
Great Plains Dinosaur Museum and Field Station, 313
Greater Ruby Valley Chamber of Commerce and Agriculture, 229
Green Meadow Country Club, 249
Green Mountain Trail, 138
Greycliff Prairie Dog Town State Park, 156–57
Greyhound Bus, 24
Grinnell Glacier, 113
Grizzly Outfitters, 139
Grizzly Trails Ranch, 203, 207
Grizzly Wolf & Discover Center, 136
guest ranches. *See* dude ranches
guides and outfitters: overview, 28. *See also specific guides and outfitters*
Guthrie, A. B., Jr., 190
Guthrie (A. B.) Memorial Trail, 202

H

H. Earl Clack Memorial Museum, 189
Hailstone National Wildlife Refuge, 158–59
Halfbreed Lake National Wildlife Refuge, 158–59
Hamilton: campgrounds, 61; eating, 95, 99; emergencies, 44; information, 41; lodging, 87–88, 92; sights/activities, 48–50, 60, 67, 68; special events, 102; transportation, 42–43
Hamilton Golf Club, 67
Hanging Valley National Recreation Trail, 250
Happy Days Café, 219
Hardin, 281; eating, 304; emergencies, 281; information, 278; lodging, 300; sights/activities, 282, 291, 292, 294; special events, 305
Hardin Chamber of Commerce and Agriculture, 278
Harlem Golf Course, 201
Harlowton, 187; eating, 218; emergencies, 185; golf, 201; information, 183
Harlowton Chamber of Commerce and Agriculture, 183
Harvest Hills Golf Course, 201
Harvest Moon Brewery, 217
Hauser Lake, 245, 248; eating, 268
Havre, 187–88, 192; eating, 217, 219; emergencies, 185; information, 183; lodging, 212; sights/activities, 189–97, 201, 205; special events, 220; transportation, 185
Havre Area Chamber of Commerce, 183
Havre Badlands, 194–95
Havre Beneath the Streets, 192
Havre Railroad Museum, 192
Havre Residential Historic District, 192
Hawley Mountain Guest Ranch, 156
Hawthorne House, 89
Headwaters Golf Course, 144
Headwaters Heritage Museum, 131
Headwaters of the Yellowstone Bed & Breakfast, 162
Hebgen Lake, 141
Hebgen Lake Ranger District, 142
Heidi's Convenience Store, 117
Helena, 25, 33, 227–28; eating, 267–70; emergencies, 231; information, 229; lodging, 262–63, 265; map, 230; sights/activities, 234–61; special events, 271–73; transportation, 231
Helena Chamber of Commerce, 229
Helena National Forest, 30, 259, 260; biking, 243; cabin rentals, 266; campgrounds, 246; cross-country skiing, 254, 256; hiking, 250; Refrigerator Canyon, 243
Helena Regional Airport, 21
Helen's Corral Drive Inn, 174–75
helicopter tours, 80, 117
Hell Creek Fossil Area, 317
Hell Creek Marina, 326
Hell Creek State Park, 317, 322
Hells-A-Roarin' Outfitters, 146
Helm River Bed & Breakfast, 300–301
Hewitt Lake, 323
Hickory House Inn Bed & Breakfast, 261
Hidden Hollow Hideaway Guest Ranch, 257–58
Hidden Lake Nature Trail, 113
Hidden Moose Lodge Bed & Breakfast, 91
Hidden Valley Guest Ranch, 257
High Country Trails, 70
Highland View Golf Course (Butte), 249
Highlands Golf Club (Missoula), 67
hiking, 28; Custer Country, 293; Glacier Country, 68–69, 78–84, 113–15; Gold West Country, 249–52; Missouri River Country, 320; Russell Country, 202–3; Yellowstone Country, 144–45. See also specific trails
Hill, Walter, 167–68
Hill Ranch Oasis (Mosby), 324–25
Hilltop House Bed & Breakfast (Westby), 325
Hinsdale: activities, 322; lodging, 326
Historic Crail Ranch, 133
Historic Downtown Bozeman, 133
Historic Hotel Calvert, 214–15
Historic Jersey Lilly Bar and Café, 302, 327
Historic Uptown Butte, 240
historical markers and trails: overview, 28
history: overview, 28
Hitch'n Rail Ranch, 203
Hobson, 207, 208
Hockaday Museum of Art, 47, 102
Hole in the Wall Ranch, 70
Holiday Spring Campground, 290
Holland Falls National Recreation Trail, 69
Holland Lake Lodge, 74
Holland Lake Lodge Trail, 57
Holter Dam, 245
Holter Lake Recreation Area, 242, 245; boat cruise, 257, 260; boating, 245; fishing, 248
Holy Rosary Healthcare, 281
Homestead Ranch (Hobson), 207
Hoover City, 192–93

Hornet Peak Look, 57
horseback riding: Custer Country, 293; Glacier Country, 69–71, 79, 115; Gold West Country, 252; Missouri River Country, 320; Russell Country, 203–4; Yellowstone Country, 146–47, 155–56. *See also* dude ranches
horses: Miles City Bucking Horse Sale, 305; Wolf Point Horse Stampede, 331; World Famous Miles City Bucking Horse Sale, 305
Hostetler House Bed & Breakfast, 300
Hot Spot Thai, 96–97
hot springs, 29; Glacier Country, 71–72; Gold West Country, 252–53; Missouri River Country, 320; Russell Country, 204; Yellowstone Country, 147. *See also* specific hot springs
Hot Springs (town), 45, 71–72; information, 42
Hot Springs Chamber of Commerce, 42
hotels. *See* specific hotels
Hougen Ranch, 296
Howery Island Nature Trail, 293
Huckleberry Festival, 103
Huckleberry House, 88
Huckleberry Mountain Nature Trail, 114
HuHot Mongolian Grill, 100
Humbug Spires Wilderness Study Area, 242–43
Hungry Horse Ranger District, 62
Hungry Horse Reservoir, 59–60
hunting, 29, 321
Hyalite Canyon, 142, 156
Hyalite Reservoir, 141
Hyndman, Donald, 27
Hysham, 281–82; information, 278; lodging, 300
Hysham Chamber of Commerce, 278

ice climbing, 156
ice fishing, 33; Custer Country, 294; Glacier Country, 73; Gold West Country, 254; Missouri River Country, 321, 330; Russell Country, 204
ice skating, 33; Custer Country, 294; Glacier Country, 73–74; Gold West Country, 254; Missouri River Country, 321; Russell Country, 204; Yellowstone Country, 150
IMAX Theater (Yellowstone), 136
Indians. *See* Native Americans; *and specific tribes*
Ingomar: eating, 302, 327
Inn at Philipsburg, 265
Inn Dupuyer Bed & Breakfast, 211
Inn on Broadway, 93
Intake Dame Fishing Access Site, 295
International Choral Festival, 102
International Wildlife Film Festival, 102
Internet access, 29
IOU Ranch, 322
Irish Fair, 102
Island Lake, 145
Itch-Kep-Pe Park, 142
Izaak Walton Inn, 74–75, 117; Dining Room, 120

Jack Milburn Trail, 202
Jackson Hot Springs Lodge, 253
James Kipp Recreation Area, 195, 199
Jammer Joe's Grill and Pizzeria, 118
Jawbone Creek Golf Course, 201
Jefferson District, 200
Jefferson Division, 209
Jefferson River, 247
Jersey Lilly Bar and Café, 302, 327

Jewel Basin Hiking Area, 82
Jim Bridger Day, 176–77
John Bozeman's Bistro, 170
Johnnies Café, 328
Johnson's of St. Mary, 118
Johnstad's Bed & Breakfast, 161
Joliet: special events, 178
Jordan, 312; eating, 328–29; information, 310; lodging, 326; sights/activities, 317, 322–24; special events, 331
Jordan Drug Company Soda Fountain, 328–29
Josephine, Lake, 113
Josephine Bed & Breakfast, 298
Judges Chambers Restaurant, 302
Judith Basin Area Chamber of Commerce, 183
Judith Landing Recreation Area, 199
Judith River Dinosaur Institute, 322
Judith River Wildlife Management Area, 210–11
Judith Shadwows Golf Course, 202
Just an Experience, 263–64

K
Kalispell, 40; eating, 95–96, 99; emergencies, 44; information, 41, 42; lodging, 88, 92–93; sights/activities, 47, 62, 67–70, 73, 81; special events, 102; transportation, 42–43
Kalispell Chamber of Commerce, 42
Kalispell Grand Hotel, 92–93, 96
Kalispell Regional Medical Center, 44
Kalispell/Glacier Park International Airport, 21
Kaniksu National Forest, 30
Karmadillos Southwestern Café, 269–70
kayaking. *See* paddling
K-Bar Café and Pizza, 174
Kendall, 193

Kendrick House Inn Bed & Breakfast, 300
Kim Williams Nature Area Trail, 69
Kingfisher Lodge, 301
Kings Hill National Scenic Byway, 24, 195, 203
Kings Hill Recreation Area, 205, 206
Kings Motel, 266
Kings Ranch Golf Course, 67
Kintla Lake Campground, 112
Kipp (James) Recreation Area, 195, 199
Koocanusa, Lake, 45, 53, 58, 66–67; campgrounds, 62–63
Kootenai Falls, 56
Kootenai Indians. *See* Salish-Kootenai Indians
Kootenai National Forest, 30, 45, 55, 82–83; campgrounds, 62; hiking, 69
Kootenai River, 45, 53; fishing, 66–67
Kootenay National Park, 66–67
Kreis Pond Mountain Bike Trails, 58
Kries Pond Campground, 63
Kwa Taq Nuk Marina, 79

L

La Parilla, 173
La Provence, 95
Labor Day Wagon Train (Culbertson), 331
Lake Como Recreation Area, 60, 61
Lake Elmo State Park, 296
Lake Frances Ice Derby, 219
Lake Hills Golf Club, 292
Lake House Bar, Grill, and Casino (Polson), 97
Lake Koocanusa Scenic Byway, 53
Lake Louise National Recreation Trail, 250
Lake Mary Ronan State Park, 81
Lake Mary Ronan Wilderness Golf Course, 67

Lake Mason National Wildlife Refuge, 297
Lake McDonald Lodge, 118
Lake Shel-oole Campground, 199
Lakeshore Rentals (Whitefish), 94
Lakeside: eating, 268; information, 42
Lakeview Bed & Breakfast (Colstrip), 299
Lambert: lodging, 326
Lambkins Restaurant, 270
Lame Deer: information, 280; special events, 305–6
Land of Magic Steakhouse, 171
Landusky, 312–13
Lantis Springs Campground, 290
Larchmont Municipal Golf Course, 67
Lariat Country Kitchen, 304
Last Chance Nordic Ski Club, 256
Last Chance Stampede and Fair, 272
Lasting Impressions Bed & Breakfast, 299
Laughing Water Ranch, 79
Laurel, 282; eating, 304; information, 278; sights/activities, 291–93, 298; special events, 306
Laurel Chamber of Commerce, 278
Laurel Golf Club, 293
Lazy E-L Working Guest Ranch, 156
Leave No Trace principle, 34
Lee Metcalf Wilderness Area, 157–58, 259
Lehrkind Mansion Bed & Breakfast, 160–61
Leigh Lake Trail, 69
Leininger Ranch Log Cabins, 215
Lewis & Clark, 79–80, 181, 242, 309, 316, 323; Camp Disappointment, 39, 49; Confluence Trail, 145, 157; Fish Exhibit (Livingston), 130–31; Gallatin Historical

Society Pioneer Museum, 131, 133; Judith Landing Recreation Area, 199; Memorial (Fort Benton), 193; Mormon Creek, 52; Museum of the Rockies, 132; Native Plant Garden, 130; Pompeys Pillar National Monument, 287; Tower Rock State Park, 193–94; Trail, 28, 296, 314
Lewis & Clark Caverns State Park, 243
Lewis & Clark Festival (Cut Bank), 102–3; (Dillon), 272; (Great Falls), 220
Lewis & Clark National Forest, 30, 195, 209; cabins rentals, 216; campgrounds, 199–200; hiking, 202; snowmobiling, 206
Lewis & Clark National Trail Interpretive Center (Great Falls), 189–90, 194, 220
Lewis & Clark Native Plant Garden, 130
Lewis & Clark Trail, 28, 296, 314
Lewistown, 182, 188, 192–93; eating, 217, 219; emergencies, 185; information, 183; lodging, 212, 214–15; sights/activities, 192–93, 200, 202, 206; special events, 219, 221; transportation, 185
Lewistown Area Chamber of Commerce, 183
Lewistown Art Center, 188
Libby, 45; eating, 99–100; emergencies, 44; information, 42; lodging, 88, 93; sights/activities, 53–53, 55, 67, 74; special events, 102–3
Libby Area Chamber of Commerce, 42
Libby Café, 100
Libby Nordicfest, 103
Libby Ranger District, 62
Liberty County Chamber of Commerce, 182
Liberty County Harvest Festival, 220–21

Liberty County Hospital, 185, 231
Lime Creek Cabin, 142
Lincoln, 233; activities, 256, 257; eating, 270; information, 229; special events, 271
Lincoln State Forest, 259
Lincoln Valley Chamber of Commerce, 229
Linda Vista Golf Course, 67
Linehan Outfitting Company, 94
Little Belt Mountains, 188, 195, 197
Little Big Horn Days, 305
Little Bighorn, Battle of the, 277, 282–83, 286
Little Bighorn Battlefield National Monument, 277, 286
Little Rocky Mountains, 312–13
Living History Weekend (Glendive), 305
Livingston, 124, 128; eating, 171, 175; emergencies, 127; information, 125; lodging, 162, 167–68; sights/activities, 130–32, 142, 144–47, 154, 156; special events, 177; transportation, 126
Livingston Area Chamber of Commerce, 125
Livingston Country Club, 144
Livingston Depot Center, 131
Livingston Memorial Hospital, 127
Livingston Ranger District, 142
Livingston Roundup and Rodeo, 177
Lodge Grass: lodging, 300
Lodge on Butler Creek, 93
Lodgepole Campground (Beaverhead-Deerlodge), 245
Lodgepole Inn (Helena), 265
Lodgepole Tipi Village (Browning), 91
lodging: overview, 29. See

also specific lodgings and destinations
Log Cabin Cafe and Bed & Breakfast, 163–64
Log Gulch, 245
Logan: eating, 171
Logan Pass Visitor Information Center, 109
Logging Creek Campground, 112–13
Logging Lake, 115
Lolo Hot Springs Resort, 72
Lolo National Forest, 30, 53–54, 83; biking, 57, 58, 59; campgrounds, 63; hiking, 68, 69; paddling, 72–73
Lone Mountain Ranch, 165
Lone Peak Tram, 154–55
Lonesome Spur Ranch, 156
Long Pines Unit, 288, 289
Longhorn Saloon, 269
Lookout Pass Ski Area, 75
Loon and Fish Festival, 102
Loon Lake, 53, 55
Lost Creek Falls, 258
Lost Creek State Park, 258
Lost Johnny Campground, 62
Lost Lake Cabin Trail, 250
Lost Trail National Wildlife Refuge, 85
Lost Trail Powder Mountain, 75
Lower Missouri River: fishing, 319; paddling, 321
Lucca's at the Carriage House, 267–68

M
M & M Café, 329
McClain (Steve) Memorial Park, 291
McClelland Ferry, 192
McCone County Wagon Train, 330
McDonald, Lake, 111–12, 118
MacDonald Pass Trail System, 256
McGinnis Meadows Cattle Ranch & Guest Ranch, 70, 79

McGregor Lake Campground, 62
Mackenzie River Pizza Company, 173–74; (Bozeman), 173–74; (Butte), 268–69
Maclean, Norman, 137
McNab Pond Campground, 290
Mac's Museum, 284
Madison Buffalo Jump State Park, 133, 135
Madison Canyon Earthquake Area and Visitor Center, 138–39
Madison Meadows Golf Course, 249
Madison River, 233, 260; campgrounds, 246; fishing, 247–48; floating, 253
Madison River Music Festival, 272
Madison Valley Hospital, 231
Madison Valley Ranch, 264
Maggie's, 99
Maiden, 193
Makoshika State Park, 287, 296; Buzzard Day, 305; hiking, 293
Malta: eating, 327, 329; information, 310; lodging, 325; sights/activities, 313, 314, 317–24; special events, 330; transportation, 311
Malta Chamber of Commerce, 310
Mambo Italiano, 101
Manhattan Chamber of Commerce, 125
Many Glacier Campground, 113
Many Glacier Hotel, 109, 117
Many Glacier Ranger Station, 109
maps: overview, 30. See also specific destinations
Marcus Daly Historical Society Museum and Archives, 235
Marcus Daly Memorial Hospital, 44
Marian Hills Golf Club, 320
Marias Medical Center, 185

Marias Museum of History and Art, 188

Marias Pass, 117

Marias River: fishing, 200

Marias Valley Golf and Country Club, 202

markets. *See* farmer's markets; flea markets

Mark's In & Out, 175

Martinsdale: lodging, 215

Marysville, 240; eating, 270

Marysville House, 270

Master Suite B&B (Kalispell), 88

Matthews (William L.) Wildlife Recreation Area, 293

Maverick Mountain, 256

M/Ds (Wolf Point), 330

Meadow Creek Golf Course (Fortine), 68

Meadow Lake Golf and Ski Resort (Columbia Falls), 68

Meadow Lark Country Club (Great Falls), 202

Meadowlark, The (Wolf Point), 325

Meagher County Chamber of Commerce, 183

Meagher County Museum, 188–89

Medicine Lake Chamber of Commerce, 310

Medicine Lake National Wildlife Refuge, 317, 319, 322, 324

Medicine Lake Outfitters, 146

Medicine Lake Site, 317

Medicine Lake Wilderness Area, 319, 324

Medicine Rocks Black Powder Shoot, 306

Medicine Rocks State Park, 288

Meeteetse Trail, 140

Memorial Falls Trail, 203

Meriwether Lewis Two Medicine Fight Site, 49

Meriwether Picnic Area, 260

microbreweries: overview, 30. *See also specific microbreweries*

Mile Hi Nordic Ski Club, 256

mileage, 30

Miles City: eating, 302–4; emergencies, 281; information, 280; lodging, 300–301; sights/activities, 283–84, 288, 293–96; special events, 305; transportation, 280

Miles City Annual Ghost Tour, 305

Miles City Bucking Horse Sale, 305

Miles City Chamber of Commerce, 280

Miles City Town & Country Club, 293

Milestown Brewing Company, 304

Milk River, 187–88; paddling, 321

Milk River Wagon Train Feed and Dance, 330

Mill Creek Lodging, 261–62

Mineral Community Hospital, 44

Mineral County Chamber of Commerce, 42

Mineral County Fair, 103

Mineral Museum (Butte), 235

Mining, World Museum of (Butte), 236

Mint Bar and Café (Belgrade), 172–73

Mint Bar and Grill (Lewistown), 217

Miracle of American Museum, Inc., 45

Mission Creek Bed & Breakfast, 162

Mission Mountain Country Club, 68

Mission Mountain County Visitor's Center, 42

Mission Mountain Wilderness, 82

Mission Mountain Winery, 35, 55

Missoula, 40; campgrounds, 61–63; eating, 96, 100–101; emergencies, 44; information, 42; lodging, 88–89, 93; map, 43; sights/activities, 47–86; special events, 102, 103; transportation, 42–43

Missoula Art Museum, 47

Missoula Carousel, 52

Missoula Chamber of Commerce, 42

Missoula Community Medical Center, 44

Missoula Convention and Visitors Bureau, 42

Missoula County Courthouse, 50

Missoula International Airport, 21

Missoula Ranger District, 63

Missouri Breaks National Backcountry Byway, 195, 199

Missouri Headwaters State Park, 145, 157

Missouri Inn (Cascade), 216

Missouri River, 32, 181, 187, 309, 313; ferries, 192; fishing, 200, 248, 319. *See also* Lower Missouri River; Upper Missouri River

Missouri River Breaks National Monument, 181, 196, 204

Missouri River Breaks Tours (Big Sandy), 206–7

Missouri River Canoe Company (Virgelle Ferry), 207

Missouri River Country, 309–31; map, 308. *See also specific destinations*

Missouri River Headwaters Heritage Museum, 131

Missouri River Medical Center (Fort Benton), 185

Missouri River Outpost (Fort Peck), 321, 328

Missouri-Yellowstone Confluence Interpretive Center, 313

M-K Campground, 142

Monarch Area Community Association, 185

MonDak Heritage Center Museum and Gallery, 314

Montana, Fish, Wildlife & Parks, 27, 29, 33, 34

Montana: The Magazine of Western History, 28, 236

Montana Area Office of the Bureau of Reclamation, 24

Montana Atlas & Gazetteer, 30

Montana Audubon, 23–24

Montana Auto Museum, 233, 236

Montana Backcountry Adventures, 155

Montana Brewing Company, 303

Montana Bunkhouse and Paradise Cabin, 215

Montana Coffee Traders, 24, 98

Montana Department of Transportation Traveler Information, 32

Montana Dinosaur Festival, 330

Montana Dinosaur Trail, 25–26, 132, 186, 190

Montana Dude Ranchers' Association, 26

Montana Fair, 306

Montana Fishing Outfitters, 257

Montana Fun Adventures, 295

Montana Historical Society (Helena), 28, 235–36

Montana Horses (Three Forks), 146–47

Montana Law Enforcement Museum, 236

Montana Mule Days (Drummond), 272; (Hamilton), 102

Montana Natural History Center (Missoula), 47

Montana Outfitters and Guides Association, 28

Montana Plant Life, 34

Montana River Action, 32

Montana River Ranch, 322

Montana Snowbowl Ski Area, 75–76

Montana Snowmobile Adventures, 206

Montana State Brewers' Association, 30

Montana State Capitol Building, 240

Montana State Fair, 220

Montana State Golf Association, 28

Montana State University: Museum of the Rockies, 132

Montana Storytelling Roundup, 102

Montana Sunrise Lodge, 215–16

Montana Tech: Mineral Museum, 235

Montana Vacation Homes, 169

Montana Visitor Center (Shelby), 188

Montana Watercolor Watermedia National Exhibition, 103

Montana Whitewater, 148

Montana Winter Fair, 219

Montana Winter Planning Kit, 33

Montana Zoo (Billings), 287

Montana's Historical Highway Markers, 28

Montana's Lewis & Clark Memorial, 193

"Montana's Museum" (Helena), 28, 235–36

Montana's Rib and Chop House, 171

Moonlight Basin Ski Resort, 152

Moonlight Dinners (Sky Mountain), 155

Moose Meadow Tipi: Wagon-Ride Dinners, 258

Mormon Creek, 52

Morning Light Coffee Roasters, 24

Morrell Falls National Recreation Trail, 69

Mosby: lodging, 324–25

Moss Mansion Historic House Museum, 286, 306

Mother's Day Style Show & Luncheon, 330

Mount Haggin Nordic Ski Area, 256

Mount Haggin Wildlife

Management Area, 261

Mount Helena City Park, 250

Mount Helena Ridge-National Recreation Trail, 243

Mount Sentinel Trail, 69

Mountain Bike and Fine Arts Festival (Rapelje), 177

mountain goats, 29, 34, 85, 111, 258, 260

Mountain Home-Montana Vacation Rentals, 169

mountain lions, 22, 29, 34, 111, 158

Mountainview Medical Center (White Sulphur Springs), 185

Mule Days (Drummond), 272; (Hamilton), 102

mule deer, 22, 29, 79, 85, 294, 320, 324

Murray Hotel, 167–68

Museum of the Beartooths, 131–32

Museum of the Northern Great Plains, 189

Museum of the Plains Indian (Browning), 45, 48

Museum of the Rockies (Bozeman), 132

Museum of the Upper Missouri (Fort Benton), 189

Museum Sunday Sampler (Great Falls), 220

music festivals, 30. *See also specific festivals*

Musselshell River: fishing, 292

Musselshell Valley Chamber of Commerce, 280

Musselshell Valley Historical Museum, 283

Mystic Lake, 145

N

Nap's Grill, 99

National Americans: buffalo jumps, 133, 135, 193

National Bison Range, 45, 54, 84–85

national forests: overview, 30. *See also specific forests*

national monuments, 30–31; Little Bighorn Battlefield, 277, 286; Missouri River Breaks, 181, 196, 204; Pompeys Pillar, 287; Upper Missouri River Breaks, 181, 196, 204
national parks: overview, 30–31. *See also* Glacier National Park; Kootenay National Park; Yellowstone National Park
national recreation areas, 31. *See also specific recreation areas*
National Weather Service, 34
National Wild Horse Range, 297
national wildlife refuges. *See* wildlife refuges
Native Americans, 29, 39–40, 228, 277; Bear Paw Battlefield, 190–91, 251; Carter County Museum, 282; Chief Plenty Coups State Park, 285–86; Custer Battlefield Museum, 282–83; Fort Peck Tribal Museum, 313; Little Bighorn Battlefield National Monument, 277, 286; Madison Buffalo Jump State Park, 133, 135; Museum of the Plains Indian, 45, 48; Native Ed-Ventures (Pablo), 77–78; Ninepipes Museum of Early Montana, 48; The People's Center, 45, 48, 77; pictographs, 190, 257, 286; powwows, 220, 305–6, 330; Rosebud Battlefield State Park, 296–97. *See also specific tribes*
Native Ed-Ventures (Pablo), 77–78
Natural Bridge Falls, 138
Nee-Mo-Poo Trail, 28, 228, 250–51, 259
Nelson Reservoir, 319
Nevada City, 234
Nez Perce Indians, 48, 191, 228, 238; Big Hole National Battlefield, 238, 251;

Nee-Mo-Poo Trail, 28, 228, 250–51, 259
Nez Perce National Historic Park, 238
9T9 Guest Ranch and B&B (Ennis), 262
Ninemile Historic Remount Depot, 83
Ninemile Ranger District, 63
Ninepipe National Wildlife Refuge, 85
Ninepipe Ranger Station, 58
Ninepipes Museum of Early Montana, 48
1906 Trail, 250
No Sweat Café, 270
Norris Hot Springs, 253
North American Indian Days, 45, 102
North Dickey Lake Campground, 62
North Valley Hospital, 44
North-Central Montana, 181–221; map, 180. *See also specific destinations*
Northeast Montana, 309–31; map, 308. *See also specific destinations*
Northeast Montana Fair, 331
Northeast Montana Farm Expo, 330
Northeast Montana Threshing Bee and Antique Show, 331
Northern Agricultural Research Center, 48, 191–92
Northern Cheyenne Chamber of Commerce, 280
Northern Cheyenne Fourth of July Celebration, 305–6
Northern Cheyenne Indians, 29, 277, 285, 288, 290
Northern International Livestock Exposition Stock Show, Pro Rodeo, and Horse Extravaganza, 306
Northern Montana Hospital, 185
Northern Pacific Beanery, 171
Northern Rockies Heritage Center, 50–51

Northern Rockies Medical Center, 44
Northern Rodeo Association, 32
Northwest Connections, 78
Northwest Montana, 39–120; map, 38. *See also specific destinations*
Northwest Montana Wetland Management District, 85
Northwest Peaks Scenic Area, 83
Noxon: lodging, 89
Nunberg's N Heart Ranch Bed & Breakfast Inn, 301

O
Oakwood Lodge, 299
O'Brien Creek Farm, 71
O'Fallon Historical Museum, 283–84
Oktoberfest, 306
Old Baldy Golf Course, 249
Old Faithful Fall Cycle Tour, 177
Old Fort Benton, 186–87, 189
Old Hotel (Twin Bridges), 263
Old Montana Prison (Deer Lodge), 233, 236
Old No. 1 Trolley Tours (Butte), 257
Old Post (Missoula), 100
Old Saint Nick Day, 178
Old Saloon and Livery Stable (Emigrant), 174
Old Town Grill (Wolf Point), 330
Old Trail Museum (Choteau), 190
Old West Wagon Trains, Inc. (Hinsdale), 322
Old Works Golf Course (Anaconda), 27–28, 249
Om-Ne-A-Trail, 293
On Broadway, 268
Oregon Short-Line 1903 Train Car, 135
Original Governors Mansion, 240, 273
Our Home Bed & Breakfast, 212

outfitters: overview, 28. *See also specific outfitters*
Outlook Inn Bed & Breakfast, 89
Ovando: eating, 270; lodging, 265
Overland Golf Course, 144
Owl Junction Diner, 304
Oxford Bar & Café, 100

P
Pablo, 45; sights/activities, 48, 77–78
Pablo National Wildlife Refuge, 85
paddlefishing, 144, 278, 292, 295, 319
paddling (floating, canoeing, rafting), 31–32; Custer Country, 294; Glacier Country, 72–73, 115; Gold West Country, 253; Missouri River Country, 320–21; Russell Country, 204; Yellowstone Country, 148–49, 176
Paintbrush Adventures, 147
Painted Horse Grille, 96
Painted Rocks State Park, 60
Painted Rocks Winery, 55
Palisade Falls National Recreation Trail, 145
Pangea Expeditions, 73
Paola Creek Bed & Breakfast, 116
Parade Rest Ranch, 156
Paradise Chamber of Commerce, 42
Paradise Gateway Bed & Breakfast, 161
Paradise National Forest Scenic Byway, 53–54
Paris Gibson Square Museum of Art, 187, 190
Park & Ponder Coffeehouse, 194
Parker Homestead State Park, 135
passports, 106
Paul Bunyan's Sandwich Shop, 269
Paul's Pancake Parlor, 100
Paxson, Edgar S., 47, 50

Peace Park. *See* Glacier National Park
Pear Lake Trail, 243
Pend d'Oreille Indians, 48, 50, 77–78
Penny's Gourmet To Go, 218
People's Center, 45, 48, 77
Pepperbox Ranch, 79
Peter Yegen Jr. Golf Club, 293
Peter Yegen Jr. Yellowstone County Museum, 284
Phantom Links Golf Club, 68
Pheasant Tales Bed and Bistro, 212
Philipsburg, 234, 241–42; campgrounds, 245; eating, 270–71; emergencies, 231; information, 229; lodging, 263, 265; transportation, 231
Philipsburg Chamber of Commerce, 229
Phillips County Museum, 314, 319
Pickle Barrel, 175
Pictograph Cave State Park, 286
pictographs, 190, 257, 286
Pine Butte Guest Ranch, 202, 207
Pine Butte Swamp Preserve, 202
Pine Creek Falls, 145
Pine Creek Lake, 145
Pine Hills Bed & Breakfast, 298
Pine Meadows Golf Course, 202
Pine Ridge Country Club, 293
Pintler Ranger District, 245
Pioneer Café (Roundup), 304
Pioneer Lodge (Fort Benton), 213
Pioneer Medical Center (Big Timber), 127
Pioneer Mountains Scenic Byway, 24, 242, 252–53, 256, 258
Pirogue Island State Park, 294

Pishkun Reservoir, 198
Pizza House (Sidney), 329
PJs Restaurant and Casino, 219
Place to Ponder-Bakery & Café, 99
Placid Lake State Park, 61
Plains, 68; information, 42
Plains Indian, Museum of the (Browning), 45, 48
Plains-Paradise Chamber of Commerce, 42
Plains-Thompson Falls Ranger District, 63
Planetarium, Taylor, 132
Plants of the Rocky Mountains, 34
Plentywood: eating, 327, 329; emergencies, 312; information, 311; sights/activities, 314, 320; special events, 330; transportation, 311
Plentywood Golf Club, 320
Pointer Scenic Cruises, 79
Pollard, The, 168
Pollo Grille, 97
Polly's Place on the Bighorn, 303
Polson, 45; eating, 96–97, 101; emergencies, 44; information, 42; lodging, 89, 93; sights/activities, 45, 68, 73, 79
Polson Chamber of Commerce, 42
Polson Country Club, 45, 68
Polson-Flathead Historical Museum, 45
Pompeys Pillar National Monument, 287
Pondera Golf Club, 202
Pondera Medical Center, 185
Ponderosa Butte Golf Course, 293
Poplar: eating, 329; information, 310; sights/activities, 313–14; special events, 330
Poplar Museum, 314
Powder River: fishing, 292
Powder River Chamber of Commerce, 280
Powder River Historical Museum, 284

Powder River Medical Clinic, 281
Powell County Chamber of Commerce, 229
Powell County Medical Center, 231
Powell County Museum, 236
powwows, 220, 305–6, 330
Prairie Community Medical Assistance Facility, 281
Prairie County Chamber of Commerce, 280
Prairie County Museum, 284
Prairie Fest (Plentywood), 330
Prairie Kitchen (Westby), 329–30
Prairie Marsh Wildlife Drive, 210
Professional Bull Riders NILE Invitational Weekend, 305
Pryor, 288
Pryor Creek Golf Club, 293
Pryor Mountains National Wild Horse Range, 297
Ptarmigan Dining Room, 117
public lands: overview, 32

Q
Quake Lake, 138–39
Quartz Creek Campground, 113
Quartz-Loon Scenic Drive, 53, 55
Queen City Ice Palace, 254
Quickee's, 101
Quigley Cottage, 263
quilts (shows), 103, 176, 220, 272, 305, 314
Quinn's Hot Springs Resort, 72

R
R Lazy 4 Ranch Cabin, 301
Race for the Cure, 272
Race to the Sky, 271
rafting. *See* paddling
Railroad-Daly Loop, 58–59
Rainbow Falls, 196
Rainbow Ranch Lodge, 164–65, 170

ranches. *See* dude ranches; *and specific ranches*
Rancho Deluxe Steak House and Rio Café, 101
Randy's Restaurant, 329
Range Riders Museum, 284
Rankin, Jeanette, 35
Rare Earth Unlimited, Inc., 136
Rattlesnake National Recreation Area, 31, 83
Rattlesnake Trail, Upper, 251
Ravalli, Anthony, 51–52
Ravalli County Museum, 48–49
Raven Crest Bed & Breakfast, 211
Raynolds Pass, 137–38
Red Bird, 96
Red Dog Saloon & Pizza, 99
Red Lodge, 128, 137; campgrounds, 141–42; eating, 171–72, 175; emergencies, 127; information, 125; lodging, 163, 168; sights/activities, 129, 136–37, 140–41, 144–45, 152–53, 156–58; special events, 176–77; transportation, 126
Red Lodge Area Chamber of Commerce, 125
Red Lodge Mountain Golf Course, 144
Red Lodge Mountain Man Rendezvous, 176
Red Lodge Mountain Resort, 152–53
Red Lodge Nordic Center, 153
Red Lodge Reservations, 168
Red Rock Lakes: lodging, 265–66
Red Rock Lakes National Wildlife Refuge, 261
Red Shale Campground, 290
Redford, Robert, 137
Reed Point: lodging, 163; special events, 177
Refrigerator Canyon, 243
Rendezvous Ski Trails, 140, 153–54, 177
resorts. *See specific resorts*

restaurants. *See specific restaurants and destinations*
Rexford Ranger District, 62
Reynolds Campaign, 284
Rhubarb Festival, 220
Rich Ranch, 79
Richey Chamber of Commerce, 311
Richland County Fair and Rodeo, 331
Ricketts Museum, 48–49
Rimrock Trails (Billings), 289
Rimrock Trailways, 24
Ringneck Rendezvous, 301
Rising Sun Bistro, 98
rivers: overview, 32. *See also specific rivers*
River Bend Bed & Breakfast (Yaak), 91
river rafting. *See* paddling
River Rock Lodge (Big Sky), 165
River Runs Through It, A (movie), 137
River Wild, A (movie), 56
Riverbend Bed & Breakfast (Fairfield), 211
Riverfront Park (Billings), 294
River's Bend Golf Course (Thompson Falls), 68
River's Edge Bed & Breakfast (Dillon), 262
River's Edge Trail (Missouri River), 196–97
Riverside Country Club (Bozeman), 144
Riverside Park (Laurel), 291
road reports, 32
Roadmaster Grille (Virginia City), 271
Roadside Geology of Montana (Alt and Hyndman), 27
Robideau, Frank, 131
rock climbing, 156, 242
Rock Creek, 143; campgrounds, 142
Rock Creek Outfitters and Lodge, 326
Rock Creek Walleye Tournament, 330

rockhounding, 32, 71, 136, 192–93, 258

Rockhounding Montana, 32

Rockies, Museum of the (Bozeman), 132

Rocking Tree Ranch, 156

Rocking Z Guest Ranch, 252, 257

Rocky Boy's Indian Reservation, 29, 183, 205; Powwow, 220

Rocky Mountain Discovery Tours (Missoula), 79–80

Rocky Mountain Division, 209; campgrounds, 199–200

Rocky Mountain Elk Foundation Wildlife Visitor Center, 85–86

Rocky Mountain Front, 27, 181–82, 185–87, 209

Rocky Mountain Museum of Military History, 49

Rocky Mountain oysters, 330

rodeos, 32, 176, 177, 220, 306, 331

Roger's Saloon and Chuckwagon, 327

Rolling Hills Golf Course, 293

Rolling Hills Winery, 317

Ronan: emergencies, 44; information, 42; sights/activities, 68, 81

Ronan Chamber of Commerce, 42

Roosevelt Arch, 128

Roosevelt Memorial Medical Center, 311

Roscoe, 137, 156

Rosebud Battlefield State Park, 296–97

Rosebud County Courthouse, 284, 287

Rosebud County Pioneer Museum, 284, 287

Rosebud Health Care Hospital, 281

Rose's Tea Room and Parlor, 268

Ross Creek Cedar Grove Scenic Area, 56

Roundup: eating, 304; emergencies, 281; information, 280; sights/activities, 283, 287–88, 293, 296

Roundup and Musselshell Valley Chamber of Commerce, 280

Roundup Cattle Drive, Inc., Annual Cattle Roundup, 296

Roundup Memorial Hospital, 281

Ruby Reservoir, 248–49

Ruby Reservoir Site, 246

Ruby River: fishing, 248–49

Ruby Valley Hospital, 231

Ruby's 100 Percent Montana Burgers, 219

Ruhl, Donald J., 131

Runamuk Guest Ranch, 296

Running Eagle Falls Nature, 114

Running of the Sheep, 177

Russell, Charles M., 235–36, 240, 285, 317, 320, 323; Auction and Exhibitors Show, 220; Museum, 189

Russell Country, 181–221; map, 180. *See also specific destinations*

Russell Country, Inc., 185

Russell Country Inn (Great Falls), 214

Russell (Charles M.) National Wildlife Refuge, 195, 297, 313, 323–24; boating, 318; campgrounds, 199

Russell's Fireside Dining Room, 118

Rusty Spur Guest House and Gallery, 213

RV parks, 32–33. *See also* camping

Rye Creek Guest Ranch, 92

S

Sacagawea, 124, 128, 193, 237, 244

Sacajawea Hotel, 168, 266; dining, 172, 268

Sacajawea Park, 128

Saco: information, 311; lodging, 326

Saco Chamber of Commerce, 311

safaris. *See* wildlife safaris

St. Helena Cathedral, 240–41

St. Ignatius, 45, 51; information, 42

St. Ignatius Chamber Visitor Center, 42

St. Ignatius Mission, 51

St. James Hospital, 231

St. John's Lutheran Hospital, 44

St. Joseph Medical Center, 44

St. Luke Community Hospital, 44

St. Mary: eating, 118

St. Mary Lake, 111–12; campground, 113

St. Mary Visitor Center, 109

St. Mary's Mission, 39, 51–52

St. Nick's Nordic Festival, 176

St. Patrick Hospital, 44

St. Patrick's Day, 272

St. Peter's Hospital, 231

St. Regis, 53–54

St. Vincent Healthcare, 281

St. Xavier, 288; activities, 294–95

Salish-Kootenai Indians, 29, 39, 41, 45, 48, 50, 56, 77–78

Salmon Lake State Park, 61

Sam's Supper Club, 327

Sand Creek Clydesdales Ranch Vacations & Wagon Trains, 322

Sanders Bed & Breakfast, 263

Sanderson Inn, 298

Sapphire Gallery (Philipsburg), 258

sapphire mining, 192–93, 258

Sawtooth Deli, 174

S-Bar Shepherd Ranch, 156

Scapegoat Wilderness Area, 209–10, 233, 259, 260–61

Scharf's Family Restaurant, 269

Scobey: eating, 329; emergencies, 311; information,

310; sights/activities, 315, 320; special events, 331; transportation, 311
Scobey Golf Course, 320
Scotty's Table, 96
Scriver, Bob, 193
Sean Kelly's, 100–101
Seasons Restaurant, 97
Seeley Creek Mountain Bike-Nordic Ski Trails, 59
Seeley Lake, 46; campgrounds, 63; eating, 97; information, 42; lodging, 94; sights/activities, 54, 55, 59, 61, 67, 69–70, 72–73, 79; special events, 102
Seeley Lake Area Chamber of Commerce, 42
Seeley Lake Campground, 63
Seeley Lake Ranger District, 63
Seeley-Swan Valley, 54
Selway-Bitterroot Wilderness Area, 82, 92
Seven Lazy P Ranch, 207
7th Ranch Historical Tours, 296
sharp-tailed grouse at Medicine Lake National Wildlife Refuge, 317, 319, 322, 324
Shawna's Grill/Sweet-N-Such, 304
Sheepshead Mountain Recreation Area, 251
Shelby, 188; campgrounds, 199; emergencies, 185; information, 185
Shelby Area Chamber of Commerce, 185
Sheridan County Chamber of Commerce, 311
Sheridan County Museum, 314
Sheridan Memorial Hospital, 312
Shirt Stop & Coffee Break, 329
Showdown Montana Ski Area, 205, 206; bike trails, 197
Showthyme, 98
Sidney, 313; eating, 327–29;

emergencies, 312; information, 311; sights/activities, 314–16, 320; special events, 331
Sidney Area Chamber of Commerce, 311
Sidney Country Club, 320
Sidney Health Center, 312
Signal Point Golf Club, 202
Silk Stocking District, 188
Silver Bow Chamber of Commerce, 228
Silver Crest Ski Trail, 205
Silver Gate, 128; lodging, 163–64
Silver Moon Kayak Company, 73
Sioux Indians, 29, 191–92, 296–97, 313, 314, 331
Sioux Ranger District, 290, 293, 297
Sitting Bull, 192, 277, 282–83, 286, 296, 314
Skalkaho Falls, 242
Skalkaho Highway, 242
Skalkaho Pass, 242
Skalkaho Wildlife Preserve, 85
ski festivals, 102, 177
Skidway Campground, 246
skiing, 33; Glacier Country, 74–77; Gold West Country, 254–56; Russell Country, 205; Yellowstone Country, 150–54
Sky View Ranch, 207
Skyline National Recreation Trail, 53
Sleeping Buffalo Hot Springs, 320
Sleeping Giant Wilderness Study Area, 245
Slow Rise Bakery, 218
Sluice Boxes State Park, 203, 209
Smith River, 201
Smokejumper Visitor Center, 49
smoking, 33
snow sports. See cross-country skiing; ice fishing; ice skating; skiing; snowmobiling; snowshoeing

snowmobiling, 33; Custer Country, 294; Gold West Country, 256; Missouri River Country, 321; Russell Country, 206; Yellowstone Country, 154
snowshoeing, 33; Glacier Country, 71, 115; Gold West Country, 261; Yellowstone Country, 150–51
Snowy Mountain Coffee, 218
Snowy Mountains, 181, 188
Snowy View Bed & Breakfast, 212
Soda Butte Lodge, 166
Soda Fountain at the Jordan Drug Company, 328–29
Somers: lodging, 89
Sommers Chamber of Commerce, 42
Sourdough Ranch Adventures, 203–4
South 40 (Sidney), 328
South-Central Montana, 122–78; map, 123. See also specific destinations
Southeast Montana, 277–306; map, 276. See also specific destinations
Southeastern Montana Juried Exhibit, 305
Southland, Bob, 314
Southwest Montana, 225–73; map, 224. See also specific destinations
Spa Hot Springs Motel (White Sulphur Springs), 204
Sparks' Bed & Breakfast and Guest House, 324
special events, 26, 30, 32. See also specific events
Sperry Chalet, 109–10, 117–18
Spice of Life Café, 95
Spokane Bar Sapphire Mine, 258
Spotted Bear Campground, 62
Spotted Bear Ranger District, 62
Sprague Creek Campground, 113

Spring Gulch Campground, 61

Spring Hill Campground, 245

Spring Meadow Lake State Park, 258–59

Square Butte, 196

Stanford: emergencies, 185

Star Bakery Restaurant, 271

State Capitol Building (Helena), 240

State of Montana's Lewis & Clark Memorial, 193

state parks, 33; Ackley Lake, 208; Anaconda Smelter Stack, 236–37; Bannack, 237; Beaverhead Rock, 237; Beavertail Hill, 80–81; Big Arm, 56; Black Sandy, 245; Chief Plenty Coups, 285–86; Clark's Lookout, 237; Cooney Reservoir, 140–41; Council Grove, 50; Elkhorn Ghost Town and, 239; Finley Point, 56, 81; First Peoples Buffalo Jump, 193; Flathead Lake, 56; Fort Owen, 50; Frenchtown Pond, 81; Giant Springs, 187, 195–96, 196; Granite Ghost Town, 239, 241–42; Greycliff Prairie Dog Town, 156–57; Hell Creek, 317, 322; Lake Elmo, 296; Lake Mary Ronan, 81; Lewis & Clark Caverns, 243; Lost Creek, 258; Madison Buffalo Jump, 133, 135; Makoshika, 287, 296, 305; Medicine Rocks, 288; Missouri Headwaters, 145, 157; Painted Rocks, 60; Parker Homestead, 135; Pictograph Cave, 286; Pirogue Island, 294; Placid Lake, 61; Rosebud Battlefield, 296–97; Salmon Lake, 61; Sluice Boxes, 203, 209; Spring Meadow Lake, 258–59; Thompson Falls, 81; Tongue River Recreation Reservoir, 290; Tower Rock, 193–94; Travelers Rest, 39, 52; Wayfarers, 56; West Shore, 56; Whitefish Lake, 59, 61; Wild Horse Island, 56, 78–79; Yellow Bay, 56

Steer Montana, 283–84

Stemple Pass, 233

Steve McClain Memorial Park, 291

Stevensville, 39; campgrounds, 61; lodging, 90; sights/activities, 50, 51–52, 68–69

Stevensville Hotel, 90

Stevensville Ranger District, 61

Stillwater Community Hospital, 127

Stillwater County and Area Chamber of Commerce, 125

Stillwater Lodge, 159

Stillwater River, 137; fishing, 143, 147; paddling, 147, 149

Stockade Lounge, 118

Stone School Inn Bed & Breakfast (Valier), 212–13

Stonehouse Inn (Virginia City), 264

Strawberry Festival, 305

Stretch's Pizza, 329

Styren Ranch Guest House, 213

Sugar Beet Festival, 221

Sula Ranger District, 61

Summit Station Lodge (East Glacier), 117

Sun Point Nature Trail, 114

Sundance Lodge Recreation Area, 298

Sunnyside Golf Club, 320

Sunrise Festival of the Arts, 331

Superior: emergencies, 44; golf, 67; information, 42; special events, 103

Superior Ranger District, 63

Swan Lake Campground, 62

Swan Lake Chamber of Commerce, 42

Swan Lake Ranger District, 62

Swan River, 44

Swan River National Wildlife Refuge, 85

Swan River State Forest, 84

Sweet Grass Chamber of Commerce, 125

Sweet Grass Ranch, 156

Sweet Palace, 270–71

Swiftcurrent Lake, 112

Sydney's Mountain Bistro, 172

Symes Hot Springs Hotel, 72

Symes-Wicks House Bed & Breakfast (Lewistown), 212

T

Taco Del Sol, 270

Tally Lake, 57; campground, 62

Tally Lake Ranger District, 62

Tamarack Time!, 103

Taylor Planetarium, 132

Ten Lakes Scenic Area, 83

Ten Spoon Vineyard and Winery, 55

10,000 Waves Raft and Kayak Adventures, 73

Terry: emergencies, 281; information, 280; sights/activities, 284, 288

Terry Badlands, 288

Teton Medical Center, 185

Teton Pass Ski Area, 205

Thain Creek Campground, 203

Thibadeau, Lake, 323

Thompson Falls: information, 42; lodging, 90

Thompson Falls Bed & Breakfast, 90

Thompson Falls Chamber of Commerce, 42

Thompson Falls Ranger District, 63

Thompson Falls State Park, 81

Thompson River, 84

Three Forks, 124, 128; eating, 172, 268; information, 125; lodging, 168, 266; sights/activities, 131, 135, 144, 148; special events, 178

Three Forks Chamber of Commerce, 125
Three Forks Winter Stroll, 178
Three Rivers Ranger District, 62
3D International Restaurant and Lounge, 217
320 Guest Ranch, 147, 165; Chuckwagon BBQ, Hay, and Dinner Horse Rides, 154
Tiber Dam State Recreation Area, 197–98
Tillmans Bed & Breakfast, 325
Timberline Trail, 145
Timescale Adventures, 208
Tin Cup Bar and Grill (Malta), 327
Tin Cup Lodge B&B (Darby), 87
Tipu's Tiger Indian Cuisine, 101
Toad Hall Manor Bed & Breakfast, 262
Tobacco Valley Historical Village, 52, 103
Tongue River: fishing, 292
Tongue River Recreation Reservoir State Park, 290
Top That! Eatery, 303
Tower Rock State Park, 193–94
Town and Country Day (Circle), 331
Townsend: activities, 244, 246, 249, 257–58; eating, 271; emergencies, 231; information, 229; special events, 273
Townsend Chamber of Commerce, 229
Townsend Fall Fest, 273
Trafton Park, 319
Trail Creek Winery, 55
Trail of the Cedars Nature Trail, 114–15
Trailsend Tours (Coram), 80
Travel Montana, 24, 25, 26, 33, 34
Travelers Rest State Park, 39, 52

Trestle Creek Golf Course, 68
Trinity Hospital, 312
Triple Creek Ranch, 92
Triple Divide Ranch, 79
Trixi's Antler Saloon, 270
Trout House and Guest Cabin, 166–67
Trout Lake, 115
Troy: information, 42; lodging, 94; sights/activities, 56, 62–63, 66, 71
Troy Chamber of Commerce, 42
Tupelo Grille, 98
Turner Mountain Ski Area, 53, 76
Twin Bridges: information, 229; lodging, 263, 266
Two Medicine: campgrounds, 113
Two Medicine Creek, 114
Two Medicine Dinosaur Center, 208
Two Medicine Formation, 208
Two Medicine Lake, 111–12
Two Medicine Ranger Station/Camp Store, 109
Two Moon Park, 289
Two Rivers Rendezvous, 103

U

Uhlorn Trail, 202
UL Bend National Wildlife Refuge, 313, 324
Ulm Pishkum/First Peoples Buffalo Jump State Park, 193
United High Altitude Sports Center, 254
University of Montana, 40
University of Montana Golf Course, 68
Upper Canyon Ranch and Outfitting, 257
Upper Missouri River, 181, 182, 195, 196; campgrounds, 199; canoeing, 207; keelboat cruises, 208; Museum of the Upper Missouri (Fort Benton), 189
Upper Missouri River Breaks

Interpretive Center (Fort Benton), 189
Upper Missouri River Breaks National Monument, 181, 196, 204
Upper Missouri River Keelboat Company, 208
Upper Musselshell Museum, 187
Upper Rattlesnake Trail, 251
Uptown Café (Butte), 267

V

V Lazy B Bed & Breakfast and Horse Motel, 299
Valier: information, 185; lodging, 212–13; special events, 219
Valier Area Development Corporation, 185
Valley County Pioneer Museum, 315
Valley View Golf Club (Bozeman), 144
Victor: lodging, 90
Virgelle Ferry, 192
Virginia City, 234; eating, 271; information, 229; lodging, 263–64; sights/activities, 252, 256–57; special events, 272
Virginia City Chamber of Commerce, 229
Virginia City Depot Information Center, 229
Virginia City Overland Stagecoach & Horseback, 252
Virginia City Players, 234
Virginia Falls, 114
Vivienne's Fifth Street Café, 99
Vixen Lane Guest House, 211–12
Voss Inn, 161

W

Wade Lake Cabins, 256
Wade Lake Ski Trails, 256
Wagon-Ride Dinners at the Moose Meadow Tipi, 258
Wahkpa Chu'gn Archaeological Site, 194

Wald Ranch, 300

Walk Away from Winter, 272

Walkers American Grill and Tapas Bar, 302

Walton Goat Lick Overlook, 111

waterparks, 52, 135, 194, 287

Waterton Lakes National Park of Canada: information, 107. *See also* Glacier National Park

Wayfarers State Park, 56

WD Ranch, 156

weather, 25; updates, 34

Weatherson Inn Bed & Breakfast, 163

Welcome Creek Wilderness Area, 83

West Fork Ranger District, 61

West Glacier: eating, 120; lodging, 116, 118–19

West Glacier Restaurant, 120

West Rosebud Lake, 145

West Shore State Park, 56

West Yellowstone, 128–29, 137, 140; campgrounds, 142; eating, 172, 175–76; emergencies, 127; information, 125; lodging, 164, 168; sights/activities, 132–42, 153–56; special events, 177; transportation, 126

West Yellowstone Bed & Breakfast, 164

West Yellowstone Chamber of Commerce, 125

West Yellowstone Clinic, 127

Westby, 313; eating, 329–30; lodging, 325

Western Café (Bozeman), 174

Western Heritage Center (Billings), 285

Western Rendezvous of Art, 272

Westfork, 294–95

Westside Restaurant (Malta), 329

Wheatland Memorial Hospital, 185

Whispering Pines Vacation Homes, 327

White Sulphur Springs: eating, 219; emergencies, 185; information, 183; lodging, 213, 215–16; sights/activities, 188–89, 201, 203, 204

Whitefish: campgrounds, 62; eating, 97–98, 101; emergencies, 44; information, 42; lodging, 90–91, 94; sights/activities, 59, 79; special events, 102, 103

Whitefish Chamber of Commerce, 42

Whitefish Christmas Stroll, 103

Whitefish Ice Rink, 74

Whitefish Lake Golf Club, 68

Whitefish Lake State Park, 59, 61

Whitefish Mountain Resort, 59, 76–77

Whitefish Winter Carnival, 102

Whitehall Chamber of Commerce, 229

Whitetail Cabin (Custer National Forest), 290

Whitetail Golf Course (Stevensville), 68

Whole Famdamily, 219

Whoop-Up Days, 220

Why Lazy Tree Ranch, 207

Wibaux: information, 280; lodging, 301; sights, 285

Wibaux County of Commerce, 280

Wibaux Museum, 285

Wikham Gulch Campground, 290

Wild Horse Hideaway Bed & Breakfast (Elmo), 87

Wild Horse Island State Park, 56, 78–79

Wild Horse Plains Golf Course (Plains), 68

Wild Rose Bed & Breakfast, 116

Wild West Diner (Culbertson), 328

Wild West Winterfest (Bozeman), 176

wilderness areas, 34; Absaroka-Beartooth, 122, 143, 145–47, 157; Anaconda-Pintler, 82, 242, 259; Antelope Creek, 317; Bear Trap Canyon, 249, 253, 259–60; Bitter Creek, 316–17; Bob Marshall, 54, 62, 80, 82, 200, 209–10; Burnt Lodge, 317; Cabinet Mountains, 45, 82–83; Cow Creek, 317; Frank Church-River of No Return, 82; Gates of the Mountains, 243, 259, 260; Great Bear, 82, 209–10; Humbug Spires, 242–43; Lee Metcalf, 157–58, 259; Medicine Lake, 319, 324; Mission Mountain, 82; Rattlesnake, 31, 83; Scapegoat, 209–10, 233, 259, 260–61; Selway-Bitterroot, 82, 92; Sleeping Giant, 245; Welcome Creek, 83

wildflowers: overview, 34

wildlife: overview, 34; safety tips, 22–23. *See also* birdwatching; wildlife refuges; *and specific wildlife*

Wildlife Adventures, Inc. (Victor), 71

Wildlife Film Festival (Missoula), 102

Wildlife Museum of the West (Ennis), 233

wildlife refuges (management areas), 34–35; Beartooth Nature Center, 158, 177; Benton Lake National Wildlife Refuge, 210; Bowdoin National Wildlife Refuge, 317, 318, 320, 322–23; Charles M. Russell National Wildlife Refuge, 195, 297, 313, 323–24; Dome Mountain Wildlife Management Area, 158; Eastlick Pond-Big Lake Wildlife Management Area, 159; Freezeout Lake Wildlife Management Area, 210; Hailstone National Wildlife Refuge, 158–59;

Halfbreed Lake National Wildlife Refuge, 158–59; Judith River Wildlife Management Area, 210–11; Lake Mason National Wildlife Refuge, 297; Lost Trail National Wildlife Refuge, 85; Medicine Lake National Wildlife Refuge, 317, 319, 322, 324; Mount Haggin Wildlife Management Area, 261; National Bison Range, 45, 54, 84–85; Ninepipe National Wildlife Refuge, 85; Pablo National Wildlife Refuge, 85; Pryor Mountains National Wild Horse Range, 297; Red Rock Lakes National Wildlife Refuge, 261; Rocky Mountain Elk Foundation Wildlife Visitor Center, 85–86; Skalkaho Wildlife Preserve, 85; Swan River National Wildlife Refuge, 85; UL Bend National Wildlife Refuge, 313, 324; William L. Matthews Wildlife Recreation Area, 293; Wolf Keep Wildlife Sanctuary, 86

wildlife safaris: Russell Country, 206; Yellowstone National Park, 156

William L. Matthews Wildlife Recreation Area, 293

Williamson Park Campground, 199

Willow Creek Reservoir, 201, 204

Windy Mountain Trail, 203

wineries, 35, 55, 317

Winifred, 195; activities, 203–4

Winninghoff Park, 254

Winter Carnivals (Red Lodge), 176; (Whitefish), 102

winter sports. *See* cross-country skiing; ice fishing; ice skating; skiing; snowmobiling; snowshoeing

Wirth Ranch, 257

Wisdom: eating, 271

Wise River, 24, 242

Wolf Creek: lodging, 264

Wolf Farms Vacation Home, 325

Wolf Keep Wildlife Sanctuary, 86

Wolf Point, 313; eating, 330; emergencies, 312; golf, 320; information, 310, 311; lodging, 325; special events, 330–31; transportation, 311

Wolf Point Chamber of Commerce, 311

Wolf Point Horse Stampede, 331

Wolfer's Diner, 219

Woodland Park, 81

World Famous Miles City Bucking Horse Sale, 305

World Museum of Mining (Butte), 236

Y

Yaak: lodging, 91

Yaak Falls, 55

Yaak Loop Scenic Tour, 54–55

Yaak River, 54–55; campground, 62–63

Yaak Valley, 54–55

Yegen Jr. (Peter) Yellowstone County Museum, 284

Yellow Bay State Park, 56

Yellowstone Art Museum, 285

Yellowstone Country, 122–78; information, 125; map, 123. *See also specific destinations*

Yellowstone Gateway Museum, 132

Yellowstone Historic Center Museum, 132

Yellowstone IMAX Theater, 136

Yellowstone National Park, 31, 123–25, 159; campgrounds, 141–42; emergencies, 127; entry points, 127–29; information, 125; lodging, 169–70; map, 126; sights/activities, 129–56; transportation, 126

Yellowstone Raft Company, 149, 253

Yellowstone River, 122, 128, 313; Bell Street Bridge, 285; fishing, 143–44, 292, 295; paddling, 149, 253, 294, 295

Yellowstone Safari, 156

Yellowstone Ski Festival, 177

Yellowstone Suites B&B, 162

Yellowtail Dam, 291, 293; Visitor Center, 290, 298

Yesterday's Playthings, 236

Yogo City, 192–93

Z

Zimmerman Trail East, 289

zoos, 35; Grizzly Wolf & Discover Center, 136; Zoo Montana, 287

Zortman, 312–13; campgrounds, 318; lodging, 326–27